The rural war

MANCHEStER
1824

Manchester University Press

The rural war

Captain Swing and the politics of protest

Carl J. Griffin

MANCHESTER UNIVERSITY PRESS
Manchester and New York

*distributed in the United States exclusively
by Palgrave Macmillan*

Published by Manchester University Press
Oxford Road, Manchester M13 9NR, UK
and Room 400, 175 Fifth Avenue, New York, NY 10010, USA
www.manchesteruniversitypress.co.uk

Distributed in the United States exclusively by
Palgrave Macmillan, 175 Fifth Avenue, New York,
NY 10010, USA

Distributed in Canada exclusively by
UBC Press, University of British Columbia, 2029 West Mall,
Vancouver, BC, Canada V6T 1Z2

British Library Cataloguing-in-Publication Data
A catalogue record for this book is available from the British Library

Library of Congress Cataloging-in-Publication Data applied for

ISBN   978 0 7190 8626 7 hardback

First published 2012

Typeset
by Action Publishing Technology Ltd, Gloucester
Printed in Great Britain
by CPI Antony Rowe Ltd, Chippenham, Wiltshire

For Mum and Dad

Contents

List of figures

Acknowledgements

The ideas on which this book is based have been in gestation for a long time, during which time many debts have been incurred and, thanks to a shared interest in rural protest, many friends made. My initial interest in Swing started when I was an undergraduate student at the University of Bristol, further developed as a doctoral student and then as post-doctoral research fellow at Bristol – both funded by the Economic and Social Research Council. The book has been written since my appointment at Queen's University, Belfast, something made possible owing to a policy of allowing staff generous amounts of time for research. To paraphrase one time Queen's sub-librarian Philip Larkin, being in Belfast gives one a useful perspective on England. My thanks are due to both institutions, and to the universities of Southampton and Oxford for their support before my arrival in Belfast.

More immediately, this book would not exist without the many institutions whose archives I have consulted and whose staff have so diligently assisted my research. In addition to the British Library at St Pancras and the British Library Newspaper Library at Colindale, the National Archives at Kew has been at times a second home and always a wonderful place to work. I should also like to thank them for permission to reproduce figures 7.1 and 10.1. I should also like to thank the archivists in the following records offices: in Kent, the Centre for Kentish Studies at Maidstone, Canterbury Cathedral Archives, and Medway Studies Centre at Strood; in Hampshire, the wonderful Hampshire County Record Office at Winchester, Southampton Archives, and University of Southampton Special Collections; in Dorset, the Dorset History Centre in Dorchester; in Sussex, the East Sussex County Record Office at Lewes and the West Sussex County Record Office at Chichester; and in Surrey, the Surrey

History Centre at Woking. May such institutions long be the pride of regional civic life. Staff at the following local studies libraries have also been most patient and kind: Ashford, Bath, Brighton, Bristol, Canterbury, Chichester, Dorchester, Dover, Eastbourne, Folkestone, Gravesend, Lewes, Maidstone, Portsmouth, Reading, Slough, Southampton, Taunton, and Winchester.

Parts of some chapters, as well as some of the ideas that run through the book, have been presented at countless seminars and conferences. The audiences and fellow contributors have helped shape my ideas and have made this book what it is. Any remaining misapprehensions are, of course, entirely my own. I would like to make particular mention of fellow delegates at the 2008 European Social Science History Conference, the Captain Swing Reconsidered Conference, Spring 2010 Agricultural History Society Conference, and Rural History 2010. Seminars at the universities of Bristol, Gloucestershire, Oxford, Queen's University Belfast, and Trinity College Dublin also proved particularly helpful and enjoyable.

Special thanks must be made to those whose company, commentary, discussion and feedback have massively shaped my understanding of the early nineteenth-century countryside and made my task so pleasurable. For some the wounds are probably still raw, for others they have healed and perhaps been forgotten, but all have proved pivotal: Malcolm Chase, David Fletcher, Alun Howkins, Peter Jones, Briony Mcdonagh, Katrina Navickas, Steve Poole, Adrian Randall, Barry Reay, Iain Robertson, Samantha Shave, Keith Snell, Rose Wallis, Roger Wells and especially Andrew Charlesworth. My colleagues at Bristol, Southampton, Oxford and Queen's all deserve thanks, especially Bruce Campbell, Adrian Evans, the late Les Hepple, Keith Lilley, Steve Royle, Ian Shuttleworth and Sarah Whatmore. Special thanks go to Paul Glennie, my doctoral supervisor at Bristol, a wonderful guide and an inspirational historical geographer.

Debts of a more personal (and pecuniary) nature are legion. In particular, without the support of my sister Katie and her family, and my aunt Ann Francesconi and Martin Blandy most of the research in East Sussex, Surrey and London would not have been possible. To friends and family who have lived with this book, my eternal thanks for allowing me to sometimes spend more of my time with Captain Swing than them. To Suzanne especially, without your constant encouragement and toleration of my locking myself away there would be no book. Finally, the biggest thanks must be reserved for my parents, Mary and Roy Griffin. It is they who generated and have sustained my abiding love for the English countryside and have in every way made this book possible. It is to them that it is dedicated.

Belfast, Epiphany 2011

Abbreviations

BC	*Berkshire Chronicle*
BG	*Brighton Gazette*
BGu	*Brighton Guardian*
BH	*Brighton Herald*
CC	*County Chronicle*
CKS	Centre for Kentish Studies
CWPR	*Cobbett's Weekly Political Register*
DCC	*Dorset County Chronicle*
DHC	Dorset History Centre
ESCRO	East Sussex County Record Office
HA	*Hampshire Advertiser*
HC	*Hampshire Chronicle*
HCRO	Hampshire County Record Office
HIris	Hastings and Cinque Ports Iris
HT	*Hampshire Telegraph*
KC	*Kentish Chronicle*
KG	*Kentish Gazette*
KH	*Kent Herald*
MG	*Maidstone Gazette*
MJ	*Maidstone Journal*
PHer	*Portsmouth, Portsea and Gosport Herald*
RG	*Rochester Gazette*
RM	*Reading Mercury*
SA	*Sussex Advertiser*
SHC	Surrey History Centre
SM	*Southampton Mercury*
SWA	Sussex Weekly Advertiser
TNA	The National Archives
TT	*The Times*
WSCRO	West Sussex County Record Office

Introduction

The dawn of the current millennium was heralded by a defiant turn to nostalgia. Despite government attempts to stamp the event with an undeniably 'modern' touch, whatever they felt that might mean, many local communities did not toe the line. In towns and villages throughout Britain there was a tangible sense of *fin de siècle* in the new millennial histories that were written – histories usually offering a rosy past in contrast to an uncertain future. While some proposed schemes were fantastical, most were more modest, attempting to render the past digestible by reducing local, or even national, histories into small revue-sized chunks. One such production was staged at Petham, a small village just outside Canterbury. The cast and crew, a 'talented bunch' of 'a few professionals and many local amateurs', according to the *Kentish Gazette* reporter, set to music the story of 'life in the district from about AD 90 to the present day'. One scene in particular was singled out for praise: the stage was dominated by a mock-up threshing machine, which was subsequently destroyed in a startling recreation of the 'Luddite riots' of 1830, made even more dramatic by the 'lively orchestration [which] was truly complimentary'. The 'fact' that the riots started in the neighbouring parish of Lower Hardres was presented almost as a matter of local pride.[1]

The Petham performance was better publicised than the actual start of the protests of 1830. Indeed, as the beginnings of, to quote William Cobbett, 'rural wars' go, the destruction of a threshing machine at Wingmore, a small hamlet in the Elham Valley of East Kent, on 24 August 1830 was inauspicious. On 25 August 1830, while reaping at Ottinge in the parish of Elham, Ingram Swaine was approached by fellow labourer Selden Bayley. The previous evening, so Bayley related, a threshing machine had been broken at Wingmore by a group of 'three or four and twenty' men.[2] This event was not reported in the Kentish or national press. Nor was the occurrence related to the local magistrates or the Home Office. Against the backdrop of the recent revolution in France, the death of George IV and the ensuing general election, and the unfurling parliamentary reform crisis, this was small beer. Alluded to only in a subsequent farmers' information and a machine-breakers' deposition, news that Kentish labourers – a group with an impressive pedigree of starting rebellions – were protesting again hardly raised an eyebrow.

The first report of events in the Elham Valley appeared in the Canterbury press on 3 September, by which time five threshing machines had been destroyed, the first national report appearing in the *Standard* and *The Times* on 27 September.[3] From such a low-key beginning, by the end of December, machine-breaking, and wages and poor relief demonstrations, accompanied by the sending of threatening letters and a huge wave of incendiarism, had overwhelmed a vast swathe of rural England. In some places, protests also took the form of attacks on migrant workers and political demonstrations.

Initially, protests were confined to the vicinity of the Elham Valley, the machine-breakers effectively unhindered by the local magistracy until the arrest of the 'ringleaders' on 27 September. While the intensity of protests declined immediately thereafter, the trial of these first machine-breakers and their subsequent sentence of only four days' imprisonment – against the maximum sentence of seven years' transportation – acted to encourage others to 'rise'. Literally overnight, protests spread rapidly, both in East Kent and into the area between Sittingbourne and Maidstone, where the focus shifted to wages rather than machinery. From the latter place, protests physically diffused via mobile groups throughout West Kent and, by 3 November, into the Weald. Concurrently, an indigenous set of protests started at Battle and Brede, focusing on wages and poor relief, setting the form for another wave of protest that spread through the Weald and into East Sussex in early November.

From 13 November, protests, apparently with no direct connection to those in East Sussex, started in north-west Sussex, with other geographically non-contiguous waves of protest starting in more southerly parts of West Sussex over the ensuing days. At this point, what had already started to take the form of a protest movement lost its geographical coherence. Instead of diffusing in an essentially linear way, the protests from 14 and 15 November now had multiple foci: machine-breaking on the West Sussex-Hampshire borders; wages assemblages in north Hampshire; and a multifaceted set of protests around Thatcham in Berkshire, spreading into Wiltshire on 19 November. In Berkshire, Hampshire and Wiltshire, the protests spread rapidly, burned brightly and soon faded, a stiffened governmental response acting to change the pattern and intensity of subsequent protests. Indeed, elsewhere in the south the movement was only manifest in an intensive form in isolated pockets, most notably on Cranborne Chase and in the Blackmore Vale in Dorset, and in the vicinity of High Wycombe, Buckinghamshire, where highly mechanised paper mills were targeted.

Beyond apparently isolated protests in the Midlands and the North, intensive protests in East Anglia in December in many ways represented a separate movement, informed as much by the cultural memory of the 1816 Bread of Blood riots and the 1822 wave of protests as by the southern protests. Few further overt protests occurred beyond 1 December, though there was a clear resort to incendiarism in response to the military-led repression in south-central England.[4] While it is unclear how many individuals were arrested, in the government-driven suppression some 644 individuals were gaoled, 505 individuals transported to New South Wales and Van Diemen's Land, and 19 individuals executed for their involvement.[5]

The name given to this rural rising is 'Swing', the pseudonym used to sign off many of the threatening letters sent to farmers and others during the autumn and winter of 1830. The name stuck remarkably quickly. On 21 October, *The Times*, reporting the sending of the first 'Swing' letters, noted the 'extraordinary alarm' generated by 'proceedings of "Swing"'. By 5 November, a placard detailing state sinecures and pensions had been entitled '"Swing", eh', and by 29 November a report of a fire at Kenchester (Herefordshire) mentioned the 'notorious Captain Swing'.[6] Such reports were soon reinforced by the blanket press coverage of the special commissions set up to try 'Swing' protestors in Berkshire, Buckinghamshire, Dorset, Hampshire and Wiltshire, and by the numerous widely publicised 'instant histories'.[7] Such histories not only attest to the power of the *nom de guerre* Swing – the grandson of Ned Ludd and an English Captain Rock as some commentators put it[8] – but also the public interest in, and appetite for analysis about, the protests of 1830. In the ensuing 170 years, arguably little has changed. The appeal might not be so immediate, but Swing has maintained a remarkable hold on the popular historical imagination: George Eliot even chose to end *Middlemarch* with an allusion to the protests of 1830.[9] It is not only posterity, as E.P. Thompson famously claimed, that places an 'enormous condescension' onto to the heads of lost peoples but also the processes of mythologisation used to construct consumable histories in the present.[10]

Despite the preoccupation of Swing's instant histories with incendiarism, popular conceptions now rest firmly on the idea that the movement was solely concerned with the iniquities of the machine. *Captain Swing*, Hobsbawm and Rudé's classic study of the movement, attempted to log the number of different disturbances throughout the country. Their figures, although now shown to seriously underestimate the level of reported disturbances, support this popular conception: 390 threshing machines were broken, with 26 cases of destruction of other agricultural machinery. And yet, in Swing's initial theatre of the south-east, incendiarism was, apparently, the most frequently resorted to, and visible, form of the disturbances.[11]

While there was no such thing as the 'typical' Swing incident, many of the 'open' protests assumed a form that was repeated from place to place. Indeed, the early actions of the Elham machine-breakers set a pattern that would become archetypal. During their second 'outing', and having arrived at a predetermined farm, four men stood in the road 'a rod and a half' away from the farmyard gate to keep watch. The rest of the party entered the yard, thirty of whom then formed a line in front of the house 'to prevent anyone coming to know any of the Company'.

> About 20 of the company went to the Barn ... and some brought out a Threshing Machine. The Party then broke it to pieces ... There was a great noise and shouting all the while they were breaking the machine – they were engaged about 20 minutes or half an hour in breaking the machine. The company then assembled at the yard Gate and gave 3 cheers.[12]

Depositions relating to their fourth outing reveal a growing confidence. Some of the gang on their way to target Hardres Court stopped off at a local public house. After a few pints of beer, the gang moved onwards, making a great noise as they marched along the green lanes. One of the labourers at Hardres Court even heard them whistling, singing and hollering. On arrival, a 'long string' of men went into the yard, with four or five others waiting in the road near the gate to watch for soldiers, having been told by a hop drier working in the farmyard that troops were on their way to the farm. The barn doors were duly forced open and the machines dragged out into the yard where they were destroyed. The destruction complete, the men reassembled by the corner of the farmyard and gave three cheers. They then arranged their next machine-breaking episode and dispersed into the night.[13] The protests combined the organised and spontaneous, the customary and the innovative, the ceremonial and the raucous.

Swing was, and remains, a hugely important historical landmark. Its telling and retelling also proving turning points in our understanding of rural protest. Hobsbawm and Rudé's treatment of Swing sought to locate the outbreak of disturbance within the context of the rural proletariats' self-determination and the cultures and communities in which they lived and worked. Indeed, *Captain Swing* was truly the first sustained application of E.P. Thompson's agenda for the study of the English working class to the countryside.[14] Along with Thompson, Hobsbawm and Rudé were especially sensitive to the variety and sophistication of the responses of the proletariat to both dramatic change and social oppression. The tables in *Captain Swing* listed not only machine-breaking and incendiarism as tactics deployed during Swing but also the sending of threatening letters; wage, tithe, enclosure, food, rent and workhouse riots; strikes; political demonstrations; assaults; demanding money by menaces; and even burglary.[15]

In fifteen chapters, four appendices and 365 pages, and having consulted every 'substantial body of source-materials', Hobsbawm and Rudé had not only 'superseded' earlier accounts of Swing but had self-avowedly written 'a comprehensive study of the disorders'.[16] But, as they admitted, theirs was not the last study of the 'social movements of British farm labourers in the first part of the 19th century'. For social historians, they continued, 'there remains plenty ... to do'. Reviewers concurred: the 'best way of repaying our debt to Hobsbawm and Rudé' was to 'follow up their work'.[17] In the forty-two years since *Captain Swing*'s publication, several historians have risen to this challenge, questioning the comprehensiveness of Hobsbawm and Rudé's study, highlighting the greater importance of radical politics, modelling the movement's diffusion, and, most notably, digging deeper into Swing's local archives to offer rich microhistories of Swing.[18] Cumulatively, the myriad local studies and revisionist essays published have challenged Hobsbawm and Rudé's agenda and analyses, paving the way for a major review of the movement. *Captain Swing* stands as a fine and highly readable account of the movement but it no longer stands archivally, analytically or conceptually. And yet, until now, their study remains the only systematic analysis of Swing.

Beyond the need for systematic analysis to piece back together the local studies into the context of a protest movement that spread from East Kent throughout rural England, there is much that we do not know. We still do not know why Swing started in the Elham Valley of East Kent, nor why it subsequently diffused in the ways it did into the rest of Kent and into the Weald of Sussex. Nor do we know anything of the involvement of women or of the gender politics of the protests. We know virtually nothing of Swing's impact on local public policy, and little of how popular politics and the 'politics of the parish' coalesced. *The Rural War* not only 'fills' these gaps but also asks new questions of Swing's archive, rendering the analysis offered in *Captain Swing* obsolete. Hobsbawm and Rudé's study remains an important touchstone in our evolving understanding of Swing and rural protest, but in all but the national focus of their study, this book supersedes *Captain Swing*.

The rural war

By focusing on the south-eastern counties of Hampshire, Kent, Sussex and Surrey – the area where Swing started, was most intensive, and lasted longest – this book attempts to explain the protests in context: locally, culturally, economically, politically and socially. It also acknowledges that Swing did not occur in a vacuum, but instead had precedence, that the individual protestors had specific motivations based on their experiences and desires, and that the protests had consequences. Utilising developments in social movement studies, it defines both the essence of a Swing incident and shows how the series of localised protests were both motivated by events elsewhere and fitted into a protest movement, albeit a movement in its political sense to which few Swing activists actually subscribed.

Any attempt now to offer a new national account of Swing that tried to answer the most salient questions about the events of 1830 would be both impossibly unwieldy and analytically unsatisfactory.

For while the local contexts that underpinned south-eastern Swing varied from the cornlands to the Weald, from the downs to the marshes, as Navickas has shown in her study of 'Swing in the North' the experience of pauperisation and impoverishment that underpinned southern Swing was very different to that of the industrialising communities of the north.[19] Even in Berkshire and Wiltshire – the counties where, according to Hobsbawm and Rudé, the most threshing machines were broken[20] – the conditions of southern Swing were different, the movement starting indigenously rather than through physical 'contagion', lasting a mere matter of days. Even in Hampshire where protests were almost as short-lived, Swing had diffused into the county – around two poles at Havant and Petersfield – as well as starting indigenously in the Dever Valley.

Hobsbawm and Rudé noted in the introduction of *Captain Swing* that their job had been made possible because the new county record offices had made accessible parts of Swing's archive that John and Barbara Hammond could not have consulted. This book has similarly been made possible by the deposition – and cataloguing – of substantial estate archives in the county depositories since 1969. In addition to the statutory quarter sessions and parish vestry minutes, much has been made of these collections of estate correspondence. More critically, though, the continued existence of archives and local reference and university libraries with their holdings of local newspapers, both in bound and microfilm form, has facilitated the consultation for the Swing period of every extant south-eastern newspaper. Home Office, Post Office and War Office correspondence files, Treasury Solicitor papers and Assize files have been consulted at the Public Record Office, Kew, while pamphlets were analysed at the British Library.

What follows is divided into four parts, the first analyses the intellectual and social context(s) of Swing, the second the protests and their diffusion, the third the politics of Swing, and the final part the reaction to the protests and their aftermath. Chapter 1 examines our changing understandings of Swing, locating the arguments of this book in terms of the historiographical evolutions in the study of rural history and popular protest. Chapter 2 examines the impact of pauperisation and the concurrent changes in employment, poor relief and protest practices. If the introduction and impact of wage subsidies dramatically altered the way in which labour and its remuneration were regulated in the 1790s and 1800s, it was the problem of rural

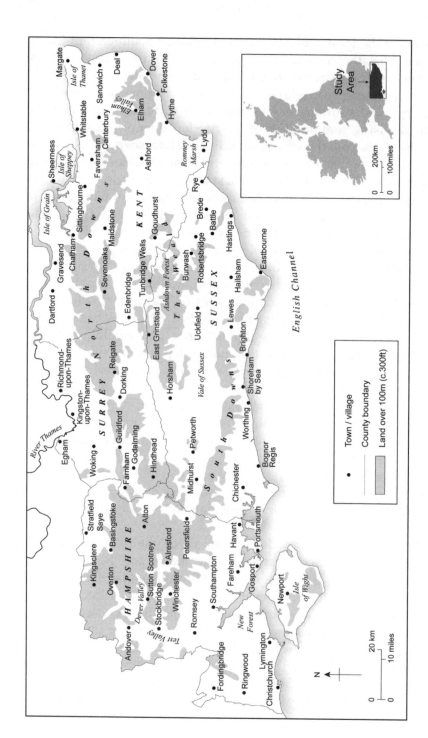

0.1 Map of south-east England

mass unemployment after the end of the Napoleonic Wars that determined the social and economic conditions that underpinned Swing. Farmers and vestries sought to reduce costs, those now out of work were left to the parish to find their (increasingly parsimonious) support. Such demoralising make-work schemes defined the period and conditioned many labourers. Against this backdrop, it is shown that collective protests persisted despite the suppression of the subsistence protests of the 1790s and 1800s, while post-1815 the resort to the weapons of rural terror – especially against the users of threshing machines and poor law officials – increased to unprecedented levels. Thus by 1815, all of Swing's grievances and forms were evident. Chapter 3 shows that in 1829 and the early months of 1830 the complaints and protests of rural workers became yet more insistent and desperate. In particular, it was a series of fires in the summer of 1830 centring on the town of Sevenoaks that first alerted the government and the wider nation to the fact that southern England was a social powder keg.

An essential definition of a protest movement is that events in one locale at one particular time influence later events elsewhere. Without such a string of influences and stimuli to action, there is no movement, rather a random series of unrelated events. As such, Part II analyses how Swing unfurled. Chapter 4 offers a systematic account of the unfurling protests, from the destruction of the first threshing machine at Wingmore on 24 August to the opening of the Hampshire Special Commission on 18 December, offering detailed microstudies of the local resort to protest but set within a regional framework. It represents a reappraisal of how – and where – Swing occurred. Part II then concludes with an examination of the mechanisms of diffusion, the organisational structures and solidarities of Swing groups, the patterning of protesting, the role of agents provocateurs, and the relation between the different protest practices deployed in late 1830. Chapter 5 ends with an analysis of the connection between collective protests and incendiarism. Arson, it is shown, was an integral tool that helped to reinforce 'open' protests.

Part III begins with Chapter 6's analysis of how the 'politics' of work and welfare were manifest in Swing. It considers the politics of the regulating of work in relation to the use of machinery, the provision of work, the condition of 'worklessness' and the ways in which parochial make-work schemes were subject to attack during Swing. Chapter 7 asks to what extent radical campaigning informed

Swing, and whether rural workers were to be found issuing radical critiques of the agrarian system, built on their parish political experiences. It is shown that even in the smaller market towns and larger villages, those motivated by radical politics were central to many Swing risings and radical political discourses invoked in Swing's claims. Part III, and Chapter 8, conclude with consideration of the ways in which Swing was informed by complex gender politics, attacking 'female' threshing machines and reasserting an embattled labouring masculinity. While most Swing groups deliberately excluded women, many women still had legitimate grievances, and thus occasionally did join wages and poor relief protests or acted as lone incendiaries and threatening letter writers.

Part IV begins with an analysis of the attempts to 'suppress' Swing. Chapter 9 demonstrates that in issuing 'lenient' sentences to the first machine-breakers, the actions of the East Kent authorities helped to shape the movement and instigated a more interventionist approach from central government. Yet even this firmer line proved ineffectual against the snowballing movement in the Weald. Here, the support of many farmers made enrolling special constables difficult, and attempts to suppress ultra-mobile assemblages became impossible without military support. Arguably more influential was central government intervention in securing evidence and organising trials through the dispatch of Treasury Solicitor Maule to Kent and Sussex, and lawyer William Tallents to Winchester. Chapter 10 then addresses the local social policy response to Swing. It is shown that not only were rapid revisions made to parochial policy but that the response to Swing was both innovative and, despite the importance of local precedents, wide-ranging. Before concluding, the book offers an examination of the resort to protest between the 1830 trials and December 1833, challenging the received understanding that Swing was crushed as too simplistic. The weapons of rural terror were frequently used to avenge prosecutors and those who had reneged on wages agreements, wages protests and attacks on migrant labourers and threshing machines also continued into the summer of 1831. As well as maintaining its momentum in some places and later reviving in others, Swing also morphed into different forms, both real and phantasmagorical.

Notes

1 *Kentish Gazette*, 6 July 2000.

2 Centre for Kentish Studies (hereafter CKS), Q/SBe 120/11, Deposition of Ingram Swaine, 6 October 1830.

3 *Kentish Gazette*, 3 September; *Standard*, 27 September; *The Times*, 27 September 1830.

4 This and the previous paragraph are based on the analysis advanced in chapters 4, 5 and 11, and E. Hobsbawm and G Rudé, *Captain Swing* (London: Lawrence & Wishart, 1969).

5 Hobsbawm and Rudé, *Captain Swing*, pp. 308–9.

6 *The Times*, 21 October, 6 and 8 November; *Morning Post*, 29 November 1830.

7 C.Z. Barnett, '*Swing!*' *A farce, in one act* (London: J. Duncombe, 1831); R. Taylor, *Swing: or, Who are the Incendiaries? A tragedy [in five acts, in prose and in verse]* (London: R. Carlisle, 1831); 'Francis Swing' (pseud.), *The History of Swing, the Noted Kent Rick Burner. Written by himself* (London: R. Carlisle, 1830); G.W. (Gibbon Wakefield: pseud.), *A short Account of the life and death of Swing, the Rick-Burner; written by one well acquainted with him* (London: E. Wilson, 1831), 19th edition, includes the supposed 'confession' of Thomas Goodman, now under sentence of death, in Horsham jail, for rick-burning; Francis Swing, *The Genuine Life of Mr Francis Swing* (London: W. Joy, 1831); Anon. ('Swing'), *A letter from Swing to the people of England* (Lichfield: T.G. Lomax, 1830); E. Wakefield, *Swing Unmasked; or, the causes of rural incendiarism* (London: E. Wilson, 1831); J. Parker, *Machine-breaking and the changes occasioned by it in the village of Turvey Down. A tale of the times* (Oxford: Parker and Rivington, November 1831).

8 For instance, see: *Taunton Courier*, 8 December; *Freeman's Journal*, 25 November 1830.

9 G. Eliot, *Middlemarch* (London: Penguin, 1991), originally published 1871–72, p. 22.

10 E.P. Thompson, *The Making of the English Working-Class* (London: Penguin, 1968), p. 13.

11 Hobsbawm and Rudé, *Captain Swing*, pp. 304–5. See: C. Griffin, '"There was no law to punish that offence" Re-assessing *Captain Swing*: Rural Luddism and Rebellion in East Kent, 1830–31', *Southern History*, 22 (2000), 131–63.

12 CKS, Q/SBe 120/34, 35 and 14b, depositions of Ingram Swaine, Isaac Croucher, Thomas Larrett, all 19 October, and John Collick, 8 October 1830.

13 CKS, Q/SBe, 120/2 f, b, c, a, d and e, and 120/8b; depositions of Richard Castle, John Fairman, Francis Castle, William Dodd, George Castle and Thomas Castle, all 19 September, and Deposition of John Whitnall, 5 October 1830.

14 The one chapter on 'The Field Labourers' took 26 of the 931 pages of text of the 1968 edition: Thompson, *The Making*, ch. 7.

15 Hobsbawm and Rudé, *Captain Swing*, pp. 304–5, 80 and chs 4 and 5.

16 *Ibid.*, p. 14; A. Randall, '*Captain Swing*: a retrospect', *International Review of Social History*, 54:3 (2009), 423.

17 Hobsbawm and Rudé, *Captain Swing*, p. 175.

18 For a useful summary of these currents see: S. Poole, 'Forty years of Rural History from below: Captain Swing and the Historians', *Southern History*, 32 (2010), 18.

19 K. Navickas, 'Captain Swing in the north: the Carlisle riots of 1830', *History Workshop Journal*, 71 (2011), 5–28.

20 Hobsbawm and Rudé, *Captain Swing*, pp. 304–5.

Part I

Swing in context

Acts of protest do not just happen. When read out of context, some protests may appear to be spontaneous, but even those events that do not have a clearly discernible pre-history are necessarily a function of past events and experiences. Those men who first came together in the Elham Valley in August 1830 to destroy threshing machines did not do so on a whim. These initial acts of machine-breaking in Kent occurred in a rich context of anti-machine antagonism in England. From late eighteenth-century 'pre'-Luddite attacks on machinery in the Western cloth industry, through the famed Luddite protests in the Midlands and North in the 1810s, the East Anglian risings of rural workers in 1816 and 1822, and the 1826 'Cotton Riots', the English machine was never entirely safe from assault.[1] The first events in 1830 may have caught the authorities off guard, but attacks on machines in early nineteenth-century England were never, as Hobsbawm and Rudé suggested of Swing, 'bolt[s] from the blue'.[2]

The first section of *Rural War* explores Swing's pre-history, placing the events of 1830 into context. Understanding context for a movement with so rich a historiography as Swing also necessitates an analysis of the changing ways in which historians have explained the events of 1830. As such, Chapter 1 explores the different currents in Swing's historiography, placing past historians' conceptions of Swing into the wider context of changing themes in rural history and popular protest. This established, Chapters 2 and 3 examine the economic, social, political and past protest contexts of Swing. This is not to say that Swing – or any other movement – can be entirely understood through a reading of its roots, rather that Swing's specific local, regional and national contexts help us to understand both the form of Swing and its demands and discourses. Chapter 2 specifically analyses the situation of the rural worker from the early 1790s to 1828, exploring the impact of pauperisation, the nature of work and worklessness, changing poor relief practices and rural workers' responses. It is shown that mass unemployment during the post-Napoleonic rural depression underpinned not only the resort to protest before Swing but also during 1830 itself. Chapter 3 then offers a detailed analysis of the clear upturn in protest in 1829 and the winter and spring of 1830. It pays particular attention to a series of fires in and around the west Kent town of Sevenoaks in the late spring and summer of 1830 that both predated and predicted many aspects of Swing and also drew attention from central government fearful of revolutionary threats in the city and countryside alike.

Notes

1 A. Randall, *Before the Luddites: Custom, Community and Machinery in the English Woollen Industry, 1776–1809* (Cambridge: Cambridge University Press, 1991); M. Thomis, *The Luddites, Machine-Breaking in Regency England* (Newton Abbott: David & Charles, 1970); A. Peacock, *Bread or Blood: A Study of the Agrarian Riots in East Anglia in 1816* (London: Victor Gollancz, 1965); A. Charlesworth, 'The spatial diffusion of rural protest: an historical and comparative perspective of rural riots in nineteenth-century Britain', *Environment and Planning D: Society and Space*, 1:3 (1983), 251–62 ; D. Walsh, 'The Lancashire "rising" of 1826', *Albion*, 26:4 (1994), 601–21.
2 E. Hobsbawm and G. Rudé, *Captain Swing* (London: Lawrence & Wishart, 1969), p. 98.

1

Rough men, pleasant histories

Beyond impressionistic, local studies of Swing in the late nineteenth century,[1] John and Barbara Hammonds' *The Village Labourer* (1911) was the first archival analysis of Swing. As the title suggests, this was not just an account of the events of 1830. Rather, it was a teleological study in the classic Fabian mould; charting the decline of field workers from enclosure, to pauperisation via 'Speenhamland' wage subsidies, ending with rebellion in the form of Swing. To them, Swing was 'the last labourers' revolt', the protests being put down by the combined forces of the British state and the labourers consigned to their fate as embittered applicators of capital. If the Hammonds' account offered a holistic analysis of Swing from the first protests in Kent to the special commissions, it was not so much a systematic national study as, in retrospect, an initial attempt to provide a framework to understand the events of 1830.[2] As subsequent critics levelled, their account variably lacked detail, underestimated the extent and intensity of protest, was too emotive and lacking in objectivity, and was ideologically predisposed towards the protestors' cause and against the defence of property – supposedly a function of their 'radical' Liberalism.[3] But however partial their analyses were, all subsequent studies are clearly in the Hammonds' debt, both analytically and methodologically, for analysing the events of 1830 not only from the perspective of the landed classes but also from that of the protestors themselves. Indeed, as Eric Hobsbawm and George Rudé, arguably Swing's most famous historians, subsequently noted, *The Village Labourer* was not only a groundbreaking study of the movement but it was also a pioneering work of history 'from below'.[4]

Between 1911 and the publication of Hobsbawm and Rudé's *Captain Swing* in 1969, interest in Swing was sustained through a series of studies that built on the Hammonds' account, adding local depth and detail.[5] E.P. Thompson too had analysed Swing in his seminal *The Making of the English Working Class*, though he acknowledged that even his extended treatment of the 'field labourers' in the revised 1968 edition was somewhat unsatisfactory.[6] Hobsbawm's first reference to Swing came in his 1952 paper analysing machine-breaking in history, a paper that was later reprinted in his 1964 book *Labouring Men*. Neither publication offered a systematic analysis of Swing but instead showcased Hobsbawm's evolving interest in popular protest and history from below.[7] Of the two authors, it was arguably Rudé who had hitherto offered the most subtle and sophisticated readings of the movement, his analyses noting that there was much more to Swing's protest canon than machine-breaking, that there were important local/regional variations in the resort to protest, and that other members of rural society than field workers were Swing activists.[8]

If many of the key aspects of *Captain Swing* were already evident in these earlier studies, nothing could have prepared readers for the scope of their study. In the introduction, there is an overwhelming sense of satisfaction with the product of their labours. Claiming the Hammonds' book suffered from 'avoidable weaknesses' in addition to a subsequent 60 years of rural historical scholarship having made their study 'inevitabl[y] obsolescen[t]', *Captain Swing*, they continued, 'supersedes the Hammonds', in every respect but [readability]', a sly dig at the earlier authors' emotive language. The new study attempted, again in Hobsbawm's words, 'to describe and analyse the most impressive episode in the English farm-labourers' long and doomed struggle against poverty and degradation' through reconstructing 'an entire epoch' in the history of rural workers.[9]

The opening chapters were critical in developing this understanding of the lifeworld and mentality of rural workers, analysing the changing agricultural systems of early nineteenth-century England, the labour and poverty of rural workers, the (as broadly-defined) culture of village life, and the impact of the post-Napoleonic Wars agrarian depression on farm labourers. Chapters 5–9 were at the core of *Captain Swing*, offering four regional surveys of 'the riots' in the south-east, Hampshire and the West Country, the Home Counties and the Midlands, and East Anglia and the north, supported by the tabulation of 1,475 Swing 'incidents' in appendix III. Part 3 analysed the 'pattern' of the revolt as well as asking in the, by now, classic Rudé style of identifying 'faces in the crowd', who Swing and his victims and allies were. The book concluded by examining Swing's 'repression', the aftermath of the movement, and, in arguably the most novel but ill-fitting chapter, analysing the new lives of Swing transportees in Australia.

Swing was, Hobsbawm and Rudé had shown, both more spatially extensive than the Hammonds had suggested and more intensive in the previously identified centres of protest. Swing activists were overwhelmingly young men, mostly employed as agricultural labourers, though rural and urban artisans were also involved, as were, in some locales, farmers who sought to exploit Swing's social force and terror to enforce rent and tithe reductions. But ultimately, according to the (Marxist) analysis advanced in *Captain Swing*, the protests highlighted the fracturing of rural society into distinct classes. At the top, the landowners and the clergy; in the middle tenant farmers; and at the bottom the landless labourers who still 'accepted the ancient symbols of ancient ideals of stable hierarchy' that had been rendered meaningless by agrarian capitalism. Possessed, though, not of a new consciousness or having connected with the urban reform movement, Swing protestors could only call on 'archaic' protest 'weapons'. Their 'improvised, archaic, spontaneous movement' might have generated sympathy from some farmers and even from some relics of the old paternalistic gentry, but was ultimately crushed by all the resources of a British state whose responsibility was to the interests of capital not labour.[10]

Perfectly politically attuned to the time – coming in the wake of the 1968 student protests, the anti-Vietnam War protests, and rising concerns about agricultural and environmental degradation – *Captain Swing* found a ready readership. Reviewers were also quick to praise the authors' efforts. To Richard Cobb, the 'two names on the cover' were 'a guarantee of sound scholarship, imaginative insight, skilful investigation and intensive, ingenious research'. He was not disappointed.[11] But criticisms there were. These essentially fell into three categories: disagreements about the Marxist framework deployed (Mingay); a concern that too much emphasis was placed on the riotous rather than the ruling (Himmelfarb); and the view that the study too often lacked detail to help substantiate the broader argument (Cobb, Hawkins, Russell, Thompson). If the first two concerns were simply reflections of debates as to the place of 'history from below' and social history approaches in the historical canon, the latter critique opened up the possibility for future studies. Thompson thought their analysis underrepresented both the radical presence in

Swing as well as brushing over how women's protests fitted (or did not fit) the movement. There was, in short, much still to do.[12] Cobb also thought that what was needed to explain the localised risings, which Hobsbawm and Rudé could only treat with the broadest of brushes, was to dig deeper into local archives. Kent in particular, Cobb noted, needed detailed study: 'now that the ground has been so carefully surveyed and so minutely mapped out' other historians 'should take up where they have left off'. 'And now', he concluded, 'to the study of Lower Hardres' – the place where Hobsbawm and Rudé mistakenly identified the first case of threshing machine-breaking.[13]

The legacy of Hobsbawm and Rudé

And yet, notwithstanding the possibilities showcased by *Captain Swing*'s reviewers and facilitated by Hobsbawm and Rudé's labours, as Iain Robertson has recently suggested, the legacy of their book has been somewhat diffuse.[14] Beyond Eric Richards' 1974 treatment of Swing in the West Midlands,[15] it was not until ten years after *Captain Swing*'s publication that new research sought to question their, by now, orthodox understanding. This came from two very different (and initial) approaches: Roger Wells's essay setting out a longer run account of the proletarianisation of rural workers and Andrew Charlesworth's mapping of Hobsbawm and Rudé's data from the famous appendix III.[16] If Charlesworth's study represented the first genuine revision of Hobsbawm and Rudé's thesis, it was Wells's paper that proved most instantly influential, sparking off a debate about the form of protest and social change in the late Georgian countryside. It was Charlesworth – again – who first challenged Wells's identification that after the bloody suppression of the national wave of food rioting in 1795 it was to 'covert' methods of protest that the rural poor subsequently turned to right their wrongs. 'Overt' protests, Charlesworth asserted, persisted both in the form of Swing – the largest episode of machine-breaking in British history – the 1816 'Bread or Blood' riots and 1822 labourers' protests in East Anglia.

If the ensuing debate floundered on definitions of overt and covert, it did usefully highlight both the depth of pre-Swing protest, the wide number of weapons in the rural protestors' toolbox and the variable geography of their deployment, as well as the centrality of the poor law in generating rural conflict. In short, if there was little analytical consensus, there was a shared belief in the need for detailed studies of the 'everyday lives' of rural workers.[17] It was this conclusion, and the continued influence of E.P. Thompson's study of the 'moral economy' of the English crowd in the eighteenth-century marketplace,[18] that set the subsequent agenda for the study of rural protest. The late 1980s through to the mid-1990s saw the publication of groundbreaking works by, among others, John Archer, Barry Reay, Andrew Charlesworth, Ian Dyck, Jeanette Neeson, Adrian Randall and Roger Wells, all of which focused on either long-run analyses of protest or isolated one-off protest episodes.[19]

The other important trend was the shift away from national and regional studies – the exception being Archer's analysis of animal maiming and incendiarism in East Anglia – towards local studies. As noted above, Cobb in his glowing review of *Captain Swing* urged the reader on to the intensive study of Lower Hardres. While his actual call has not been acted upon, the message has been emphatically received.[20]Applications have taken two different conceptual paths. One has attempted to highlight the complexities of what have otherwise appeared to be dramatic yet simplistic and reactionary responses of the rural poor to systematic oppression. Reay's study of the millenarian last pitched battle on English soil, David Eastwood's analysis of resistance to the enclosure of Otmoor, and, most recently, Steve Poole's account of the events surrounding the last scene of crime execution at Kenn in Somerset in 1830, all place protest events under the microscope to better understand the genesis, response to, and aftermath of protest events.[21]

The other approach uses the small area study not to understand the locale for its own intrinsic historical merits, but because the study area allows a lens to be directed on broader historical changes. The local provides a laboratory in which to test theories. While much of this work has been pragmatically driven to small area studies, some studies have been more theoretically driven. If the influence of the French *Annales* school on British social history has been strongly felt, that of Carlo Ginzburg and his fellow northern Italian 'microhistorians' has been less obvious but arguably more important in, as Muir puts it, 'isolat[ing] and test[ing] the many abstractions of social thought'.[22] While it is important to acknowledge the limitations of this approach – the necessary archival richness being possibly symptomatic not of a totally representative place or parish but rather somewhere that did things differently – several fine studies have shown the potential. Again, Reay's work provides the clearest application of these theoretical ideals, returning to the scene of the last pitched battle on English soil to offer a detailed cultural, economic and social view of the series of communities that provided the personnel for the 'rising'. Similarly, Wells's studies of social control and criminality in Burwash represented an attempt to place into context a seemingly peculiarly unruly Wealden parish.[23]

And yet, there is a sense in which all protests recorded in the archive were exceptional. Indeed, a critical stumbling block towards the historical study of everyday forms of rural resistance is the oxymoronic nature of the call. Whereas through various forms of ethnographic research, not least participant observation, the 'everyday' can be uncovered, the archive is forever limited to what was recorded. 'Rescuing' the beliefs, aspirations, talents, angers, worries and loves of the vast majority of the English population from not only the condescension of posterity but also from the propagandist myths of early political reformers and the early folklorists, will almost inevitably lead to new condescensions and distortions, for these voices are nearly always most audible in those situations which are not 'everyday'.

The privilege granted to protest studies within social history is a function of this problem: beyond the statutory recording of births, marriages and deaths, or from 1841 onwards the decennial Census, most late eighteenth- and early nineteenth-century rural workers were recorded only when they were caught living against the grain. Therefore, as the apparatus of state did not record the thousand little strategies of resistance, the writing of everyday forms of resistance within History, despite, as Lüdtke sees it, attempting to emphasise the agency of people and not the power of static structures, tends to replicate abstract structures of power rather than social lives.[24]

Historians must not, therefore, assume that histories of 'everyday' resistances represent anything other than exceptional crises in individual lives. Nor should we conceive that the practices of Swing were different to those 'everyday' resistances, but rather that Swing was an aggregation of these other exceptional human practices. That the shift to close local analyses and to considerations of more 'everyday' manifestations of protest came at the expense of studies exclusively devoted to Swing therefore represents something of a fallacy, substituting one form of exceptionalism for another. That it was not until Wells's 1997 study of William Cobbett's influence at Battle in 1830 that Swing was again the sole subject of a published study should be a matter of regret. This is not to say that other previous protest studies ignored Swing altogether. Rather, in longer run, studies of rural protest by Archer, Charlesworth, Randall and Newman, Richardson, and in Dyck's study of Cobbett our understandings of Swing have advanced – but only in fragmented ways. Swing has been placed into context, but in so doing much that was exceptional and unique about Swing has been inadvertently marginalised. If the study by Hobsbawm and Rudé set the initial agenda, it must be concluded that subsequent studies of Swing have tended to follow rather than lead the post-*Captain Swing* agenda.

New dawns

The early 1990s represented the high watermark of the wave of rural protest studies directly influenced by Thompson and Hobsbawm and Rudé, a series of outstanding monographs appearing that represented the culmination of several decades of endeavour. By then, that generation of scholars had assumed managerial responsibilities, met the obligations of the first UK Research Assessment Exercise or taken posts overseas and thus away from English archives, and – in the case of Charlesworth – had already started to develop radically different research programmes. Publications in the late 1990s therefore also tended to represent the long-established agenda: Rule and Wells' compendium of largely already published essays; and Randall and Charlesworth's edited proceedings of a conference held in 1991 to mark the 20th anniversary of the publication of Thompson's 'moral economy' paper.[25] An exception was another Randall and Charlesworth edited book, a collection of essays largely, if not exclusively, based on a large UK Economic and Social Research Council-funded project on market cultures in the south-west of England.[26] Drawing on the established localities orthodoxy, anthropologist James Scott's pioneering analyses of the 'hidden transcripts' of peasant resistance,[27] and emergent work in folklore studies and social history on customary ceremony,[28] the essays offered something palpably different. Betraying both different conceptual stimuli and asking new questions of the archive, the essays of the project team heralded a potential way forward that was sensitive to local 'values' – the one sociological determinant that Thompson insisted underpinned moral economies – and cultural systems.

While Randall's excellent *Riotous Assemblies* (published in 2006) offered the perfect elucidation of the clash between commercialising imperatives and custom-bound plebeian communities in the familiar contexts of food rioting and Luddism in the cloth industries, a broader conception of the importance of protest cultures has underpinned a decisive recent shift in protest studies.[29] Also influenced by Andy Wood's close readings of the politics of social conflict in the sixteenth and seventeeenth centuries and Kevin Binfield's linguistic analysis of the 'writings of the Luddites',[30] since 2006, a series of studies from a new generation of protest scholars has reinvigorated the field, uncovering 'new' archives and asking new questions of existing archives. While this 'new protest history' is still in its infancy, in the work of Peter Jones, Briony McDonagh, Katrina Navickas, and Iain Robertson – whose initial work on protest in the Scottish Highlands in the late 1990s offered perhaps the first indication of a Kuhnian shift in our readings of rural protest – some key tenets are emerging:[31] a willingness to revise the assumptions of landmark texts; a focus on signs and symbolism; an appreciation of the importance of gender and identity in shaping protest; and, a belief in the necessity of embedding protest in the interplay between the local and the central.

Perhaps most radically, such work has also been attentive to the affective dimensions of environmental and material worlds in shaping the protests of rural workers. Building on earlier foundational work by Hobsbawm and John Rule on 'social criminality', the concept that certain acquisitive property crimes contained an element of resistance,[32] work on political clothing and symbols by Navickas and on plant maiming by this author has shown the ways in which the seemingly inert could be mobilised to make complex political statements.[33] While no cases of plant maiming were identified as being connected to the Swing rising, the conclusion that we need to be alert to both the material and symbolic worlds of workers applies to Swing. This realisation also tends to reinforce the importance of customary cultural forms and practices. Indeed, as Poole has noted, the 'cultural turn' in protest studies has been most obviously manifested in the analysis of Swing in Jones's work on the role of ritual in crowd negotiations.[34]

Until recently, studies of rural protest have overwhelmingly been focused on southern England. The work of Timothy Shakesheff on Herefordshire, of Robertson on Gloucestershire, and of Navickas on Cumberland, Lancashire and Yorkshire has started to redress this imbalance.[35] However, following Charlesworth's studies of diffusion and community interaction,[36] we need also to pay closer attention to all spatialities, whether it is urban–rural interactions, spaces of organisation, or micro-level diffusion processes. David Kent and Norma Townsend's fine study examining the acts of protest committed by Wessex Swing activists and the new lives they forged in Australia,[37] and Jones's study of protestors' movements in the 'individual "moments" of protest' in and around the Berkshire market town of Hungerford offer a useful start. But in relation to the enormity of different contexts and practices in Swing, micro-studies alone cannot tell us how the events of 1830 transcended the initial local context(s) of the Elham Valley to spread throughout rural England.[38]

Beyond the slew of papers published since 2006, the most striking evidence of an upturn of interest in Swing came in the form of the Family and Community History Research Society (FACHRS) choosing Swing as their national research project and a conference dedicated to Swing at the University of Reading in March 2009. The FACHRS project mobilised the efforts of its membership throughout England to uncover Swing incidents, and in the true spirit of Rudé quantified some 3,300 cases between 1830 and 1832, double the number tabulated in *Captain Swing*. While the resulting book – a series of essays examining different facets of Swing in different locales – is fittingly a fine testament to the powers of collective action, it is neither critical nor systematic. The 'data' suffers from a lack of a definition as to what a Swing incident was – or was not, with one chapter detailing the 'cholera riots' in 1832 without offering any explanation as to connection to the events of 1830. The book also suffers from a lack of systematic analysis, the fascinating individual chapters lacking any overarching framework, the book therefore does not offer an understanding as to what the 3,300 incidents in totality mean.[39] That it adds little to our academic understanding of Swing is perhaps irrelevant, for as a collective endeavour it speaks volumes about the centrality of the movement in the telling of the history of the countryside and of modern Britain.

The Reading conference was held by the Southern History Society to mark the 40th anniversary of the publication of *Captain Swing*. Bringing together many rural and protest historians, the conference provided glowing testimony to both the depth of interest in Swing and the fact that many new questions were being asked of the events of 1830. The papers in the subsequent volume of *Southern History* range in both spatial scale and conceptual approach, all offering a useful reappraisal of Hobsbawm and Rudé's study. Together, they attest to the usefulness of both local and comparative study doing much to extend our knowledge of Swing, but most strikingly serve to highlight what we do not know. In all of the essays there is a sense of an ongoing project: Poole noting our almost complete ignorance of the role of women; Randall questioning the place of machinery in rural society; Wallis our need to think critically about local–central relationships in Swing's 'repression'; Hill reminding us of the need to locate Swing in relation to policy attempts to come to terms with the post-1815 agrarian depression.[40] The papers begin to address these lacunae in our knowledge of Swing, but the questions remain.

Post-*Captain Swing*, through focusing on the local our understanding of the events of 1830 has undeniably become far more nuanced, not least in relation to the social and protest context of Swing and about its localised forms and intensities. Yet in relying on micro-histories we are in danger of forgetting Swing's exceptional scale and transformative nature. In focusing on localised protests out of context of the wider evolution and diffusion of the movement we ignore the fact that Swing was more than the sum of its local parts. This book – the first detailed treatment of the events of 1830 in over 40 years – has this understanding at its core. It not only asks new questions of Swing's archive but also questions what it meant to protest, how Swing was possible and how the protests transformed rural social relations.

Notes

1 For instance see: T.E. Roach, 'The riots of 1830', *Hampshire Notes and Queries*, 8 (1896), 97–8.
2 J.L. Hammond and B. Hammond, *The Village Labourer* (London: Longman [1911] 1978), 4th edition, chs 10–11.
3 As Eric Hobsbawm damningly put it, accounts by 'Fabians and Liberals' were necessarily flawed because of their default ideological position of believing 'that strong-arm methods in labour action are less effective than peaceful negotiation': 'The machine-breakers', *Past & Present*, 1 (1952), 57. For excellent analyses of the limitations of, and a survey of subsequent critiques, of *The Village Labourer* see: A. Charlesworth, 'An agenda for historical studies of rural protest in Britain, 1750–1850', *Rural History*, 2:2 (1991), 231–40; S. Poole, 'Forty years of Rural History from below: Captain Swing and the Historians', *Southern History*, 32 (2010), 1–20.
4 E. Hobsbawm and G. Rudé, *Captain Swing* (London: Lawrence & Wishart, 1969), p. 13.

5 A. Colson, 'The Revolt of the Hampshire Agricultural Labourers and its Causes, 1812–1831' (MA dissertation, London University, 1937); M. Dutt, 'The Agricultural Labourers' Revolt of 1830 in Kent, Surrey and Sussex' (PhD dissertation, London University, 1966); N. Gash, 'The Rural Unrest in England in 1830 with Particular Reference to Berkshire' (BLitt dissertation, Oxford University, 1934); W.H. Parry Okedon, 'The Agricultural Riots in Dorset in 1830', Proceedings of the *Dorset Natural History and Archaeological Society*, 52 (1930), 75–95; P. Singleton, 'Captain Swing in East Anglia', *Bulletin of the Society for the Study of Labour History*, August (1964), 13–14.

6 E.P. Thompson, *The Making of the English Working Class* (London: Victor Gollancz, 1963, revised 1968), ch. 7.

7 Hobsbawm, 'The machine-breakers', 57–70; Hobsbawm, *Labouring Men: Studies in the History of Labour* (London: Weidenfeld & Nicolson, 1964).

8 G. Rudé, *The Crowd in History: A Study of Popular Disturbances in France and England, 1730–1848* (London: Lawrence & Wishart, 1964); Rudé, 'Rural and urban disturbances on the eve of the first Reform Bill, 1830–1831', *Past & Present*, 37 (1967), 87–102.

9 Hobsbawm and Rudé, *Captain Swing*, pp. 13–14, 15 and 18.

10 *Ibid.*, pp. 17–19.

11 R. Cobb, 'A very English rising', *Times Literary Supplement*, 3,524 (11 September 1969), 989.

12 *Ibid.*; R. Russell, *Agricultural History Review*, 18:2 (1970), 173–5; R. Hawkins, *Historical Journal*, 13:4 (1970), 716–17; G. Mingay, *English Historical Review*, 85:337 (1970) 810–14; G. Himmelfarb, 'The writing of social history: recent studies of 19th century England', *Journal of British Studies*, 11:1 (1971), 149–50; E.P. Thompson, 'Rural riots', *New Society* (13 February 1969), 251–2.

13 Cobb, 'A very English rising', 992.

14 I. Robertson, '"Two steps forward, three steps back": the dissipated legacy of Captain Swing' *Southern History*, 32 (2010), 85–100.

15 E. Richards, '"Captain Swing" in the West Midlands', *International Review of Social History*, 19:1 (1974), 86–99.

16 R. Wells, 'The development of the English rural proletariat and social protest, 1700–1850', *Journal of Peasant Studies*, 6 (1979), 115–39; A. Charlesworth, *Social Protest in a Rural Society: The Spatial Diffusion of the Captain Swing Disturbances of 1830–1831* (Norwich: Geobooks, 1979).

17 Wells, 'English rural proletariat'; A. Charlesworth, 'The development of the English rural proletariat and social protest, 1700–1850: a comment', *Journal of Peasant Studies*, 8:1 (1980), 101–11. The debate continued with the following papers: R. Wells, 'Social conflict and protest in the English countryside in the early nineteenth century: a rejoinder', *Journal of Peasant Studies*, 8:4 (1981), 514–30; J. Archer, 'The Wells-Charlesworth debate: a personal comment on arson in Norfolk and Suffolk', *Journal of Peasant Studies*, 9:4 (1982), 277–84; D. Mills and B. Short, 'Social change and social conflict in nineteenth-century England: the use of the open-closed village model', *Journal of Peasant Studies*, 10:4 (1983), 253–62; M. Reed, 'Social change and social conflict in nineteenth-century England: a comment', *Journal of Peasant Studies*, 12:1 (1984), 109–23; and, D. Mills, 'Peasants and conflict in nineteenth-century England: a

comment on two recent articles', *Journal of Peasant Studies*, 15:3 (1988), 395–400. These essays were collected together in an edited volume with some further reflections by the editors: see M. Reed and R. Wells (eds), *Class, Conflict and Protest in the English Countryside, 1700–1880* (London: Frank Cass, 1990).

18 E.P. Thompson, 'The moral economy of the English crowd in the eighteenth-century', *Past & Present*, 50 (1971), 76–136.

19 Most notably: J. Archer, *By a Flash and a Scare: Arson, Animal Maiming, and Poaching in East Anglia 1815–1870* (Oxford: Clarendon Press, 1990); B. Reay, *The Last Rising of the Agricultural Labourers: Rural Life and Protest in Nineteenth-Century England* (Oxford: Clarendon Press, 1990); Reay, *Microhistories: Demography, Society, and Culture in Rural England, 1800–1930* (Cambridge: Cambridge University Press, 1996); I. Dyck, *William Cobbett and Rural Popular Culture* (Cambridge: Cambridge University Press, 1993); A. Randall and A. Charlesworth (eds), *Markets, Market Culture and Popular Protest in Eighteenth-Century Britain and Ireland* (Liverpool: Liverpool University Press, 1996); Randall and Charlesworth (eds), *Moral Economy and Popular Protest: Crowds, Conflict and Authority* (London: Macmillan, 2000); J. Neeson, *Commoners, Common Right, Enclosure and Social Change in England 1700–1820* (Cambridge: Cambridge University Press, 1993); A. Randall, *Before the Luddites*; R. Wells, *Wretched Faces: Famine in Wartime England 1763–1803* (Gloucester: Alan Sutton, 1988); Wells, 'Social protest'; Wells, 'The moral economy of the English countryside', in Randall and Charlesworth, *Moral Economy and Popular Protest*, pp. 209–72; Reed and Wells, *Class, Conflict and Protest*; J. Rule and R. Wells, *Crime, Protest and Popular Politics in Southern England 1740–1850* (London: Hambledon, 1997).

20 The journal *Rural History* has been at the forefront in promoting intensive, localised studies. For two excellent examples see: B. Short, 'Conservation, class and custom: lifespace and conflict in a nineteenth-century forest environment', *Rural History*, 10:2 (1999), 127–54; S. Hipkin, 'Sitting on his penny rent: conflict and right of common in Faversham Blean, 1595–1610', *Rural History*, 11:1 (2000), 1–35.

21 Reay, *Last Rising*; D. Eastwood, 'Communities, protest and police in early nineteenth-century Oxfordshire: the enclosure of Otmoor reconsidered', *Agricultural History Review*, 44:1 (1996), 35–46; S. Poole, '"A lasting and salutary warning": incendiarism, rural order and England's last scene of crime execution', *Rural History* 19:2 (2008), 163–77.

22 J. Revel, 'Introduction', and I. Wallerstein, 'Annales as resistance', in J. Revel and Lynn Hunt (eds), *Histories: French Constructions of the Past* (New York: The New Press, 1995); E. Muir, 'Introduction: observing trifles', in E. Muir and G. Ruggiero (eds), *Microhistory and the Lost Peoples of Europe* (Baltimore: Johns Hopkins University Press, 1991), p. viii.

23 Reay, *Microhistories*; Wells, 'A rejoinder'; Wells, 'Crime and protest in a country parish: Burwash, 1790–1850', in Rule and Wells, *Crime, Protest and Popular Politics*, pp. 169–235.

24 A. Lüdtke, *The History of Everyday Life: Reconstructing Historical Experiences and Ways of Life* (Princetown, NJ: Princeton University Press, 1995).

25 Rule and Wells, *Crime, Protest and Popular Politics*; Randall and Charlesworth,

Moral Economy and Popular Protest.

26 Randall and Charlesworth, *Markets, Market Culture and Popular Protest.*

27 J. Scott, *Weapons of the Weak: Everyday Forms of Peasant Resistance* (New Haven, CN: Yale University Press, 1985); Scott, *Domination and the Arts of Resistance: Hidden Transcripts* (New Haven, CN: Yale University Press, 1990).

28 See especially: B. Bushaway, *By Rite: Custom, Ceremony and Community in England 1700–1880* (London: Junction Books, 1982).

29 A. Randall, *Riotous Assemblies: Popular Protest in Hanoverian England* (Oxford: Oxford University Press, 2006).

30 K. Binfield (ed.), *The Writings of the Luddites* (Baltimore: Johns Hopkins University Press, 2004); A. Wood, *The Politics of Social Conflict: The Peak Country, 1520–1770* (Cambridge: Cambridge University Press, 1999); Wood, *Riot, Rebellion and Popular Politics in Early Modern England* (Basingstoke: Palgrave, 2002).

31 K. Navickas, 'The search for General Ludd: the mythology of Luddism', *Social History*, 30:3 (2005), 281–95; Navickas, *Loyalism and Radicalism in Lancashire, 1798–1815* (Oxford: Oxford University Press, 2009); Navickas, 'Moors, fields, and popular protest in south Lancashire and the West Riding of Yorkshire, 1800–1848', *Northern History*, 46:1 (2009), 93–111; Navickas, 'Captain Swing in the north: the Carlisle riots of 1830', *History Workshop Journal*, 71 (2011), 5–28; B. McDonagh, 'Subverting the ground: private property and public protest in the sixteenth-century Yorkshire Wolds', *Agricultural History Review*, 57:2 (2009), 491–506; P. Jones, 'Swing, Speenhamland and rural social relations: the "moral economy" of the English crowd in the nineteenth century', *Social History*, 32:3 (2007), 272–91; Jones, 'Finding Captain Swing: protest, parish relations, and the state of the public mind in 1830', *International Review of Social History*, 54:3 (2009), 429–58; I. Robertson, 'The role of women in protests in the Scottish Highlands', *Journal of Historical Geography*, 23:2 (1997), 187–200; Robertson, 'Governing the Highlands: the place of popular protest in the Highlands of Scotland', *Rural History*, 8:1 (1997), 109–24. Some aspects of this new 'agenda' were with impressive foresight set out in an essay by Andrew Charlesworth: 'An agenda for historical studies of rural protest'.

32 E. Hobsbawm, 'Distinctions between socio-political and other forms of crime', *Bulletin of the Society for the Study of Labour History*, 25 (1972), 5–6; J. Rule, 'Social crime in the rural south in the eighteenth and nineteenth centuries', *Southern History*, 1 (1979), 135–53.

33 K. Navickas, '"That sash will hang you": political clothing and adornment in England, 1780–1840', *Journal of British Studies*, 49:3 (2009); C. Griffin, '"Cut down by some cowardly miscreants": Plant maiming, or the malicious cutting of flora, as an act of protest in eighteenth- and nineteenth-century rural England', *Rural History*, 19:1 (2008), 29–54.

34 Poole, 'History from below', 19; Jones, 'Swing, Speenhamland and rural social relations'.

35 T. Shakesheff, *Rural Conflict, Crime and Protest: Herefordshire, 1800–1860* (Woodbridge: Boydell & Brewer, 2003); Robertson, '"Two steps forward, three steps back'; Navickas, 'Moors, fields and popular protest'; Navickas, 'Swing in the north'.

36 A. Charlesworth, 'The spatial diffusion of rural protest: an historical and comparative perspective of rural riots in nineteenth-century Britain', *Environment and Planning D: Society and Space*, 1:3 (1983), 251–63; Charlesworth, 'From the moral economy of Devon to the political economy of Manchester, 1790–1812', *Social History*, 18:2 (1993), 205–17.

37 D. Kent and N. Townsend, *The Convicts of the 'Eleanor': Protest in Rural England, New Lives in Australia* (London: Merlin Press, 2001).

38 Jones, 'Finding Captain Swing', 443.

39 M. Holland (ed.), *Swing Unmasked: The Agricultural Riots of 1830 to 1832 and Their Wider Implications* (Milton Keynes: FACHRS, 2005), Appendix 1, and the accompanying CD-Rom, *Swing Unmasked* (Milton Keynes: FACHRS, 2005).

40 Poole, 'History from below', 18; A. Randall, '"The Luddism of the poor": *Captain Swing*, machine breaking and popular protest', *Southern History*, 32 (2010), 41–61; R. Wallis, "We do not come here ... to inquire into grievances we come here to decide law': prosecuting Swing in Norfolk and Suffolk', *Southern History*, 32 (2010), 159–75; J. Hill, 'The immediate reaction to the Swing Riots in Surrey, 1832–1834', *Southern History*, 32 (2010), 176–200.

2

Life and labour on and off the parish

While the directions and fortunes of studies of rural workers have varied over the years, the influence of John and Barbara Hammonds' seminal book, *The Village Labourer*, persists. Their emphasis on enclosure, protest and the centrality of the poor laws have shaped the research agenda ever since. Indeed, as Keith Snell noted in *Annals of the Labouring Poor*, 'the old poor law provides the key to a social understanding of the eighteenth century'.[1] This statement also holds for the early nineteenth century. The received understanding is as follows. At some point in the second half of the eighteenth century – Snell suggests around 1780 – poor relief in the south became relatively less generous. This shift was necessitated by structural unemployment, rising poor rates, and, post-1815, a chronic agrarian economic depression.[2] Against the supposed trend of decreasing beneficence, or rather increased stinginess, magistrates increasingly intervened in the operation of the poor laws. In times of crisis, after either having had their claims rejected or only partially met by the vestry, the needy increasingly resorted to the Bench to gain redress. This was most noticeable during the food crises of 1795–96 and 1800–1 when large groups of men were frequently to be seen descending upon rural Benches, but was also a feature of 'normal' times too. Roger Wells has even claimed that 'the successful mediation of the Bench between capital and labour in the form of systemised relief schemes' was instrumental in lessening tensions in the countryside between 1802 and 1809.[3]

As well as the day-to-day dealings with the parish poor, magistrates also took pre-emptive – and unprecedented – steps in formulating social policy. The most famous, or rather infamous, pre-emptive magisterial policy was that adopted by the Newbury

Bench meeting on 6 May 1795 at the Pelican Inn in the Berkshire hamlet of Speenhamland. While the story is now so well ingrained in English social history that it hardly bears repeating, a few details are worth noting. The purpose of the magistrates' meeting had been publicly advertised to consider labourers' wages and the price of corn.[4] The decision to adopt a sliding scale of cash payments in correlation to the price of corn funded through the poor rates and delivered through the overseer and vestry was no on-the-hoof policy decision. Indeed, a similar scale was adopted at precisely the same time at nearby Basingstoke, while a 'bread scale' had also been devised at the Dorset Quarter Sessions three years previously.[5] As James Huzel has noted, such scales were important to those families in desperate need of support, and, as the fame and notoriety of the Speenhamland scale shows, important from a policy perspective too.[6] However, notwithstanding the resolve of the justices to enforce it, even in its 'native' Berkshire, the Speenhamland scale was adopted by very few parishes.[7] Still, as recent syntheses by Lynn Hollen-Lees, Steve King and Alan Kidd attest, the 'Speenhamland story' still looms large over much poor law scholarship.[8]

Rather than talking of the Speenhamland system, it makes more sense to talk of Speenhamland-style schemes.[9] The parish chests of England are full of examples of late eighteenth and early nineteenth-century formal and de facto scales that bear only a family resemblance to that devised at the Pelican. In terms of the day-to-day experience of parochial support, semi-formalised or ad-hoc systems adopted by individual parishes were of considerable importance. Evidence abounds in extant parish records of supplementary payments made to labouring families, whether listed as 'to make up the wages' or under various subterfuges such as child allowances. A frank admission of the entrenched nature of these schemes was made by Lord Sheffield in his plea to his resident parish of Fletching in the Sussex Weald at the start of the grain crisis of 1799–1801: that those 'whose earnings will not maintain their families' must be relieved with any consumable other than bread corn.[10] Earlier attempts to improve labouring living standards in Kent took a different approach. Rather than placing the burden of below subsistence wages onto a 'much broader section of ratepayers', farmers acted multilaterally to increase wages.[11]

The relationship between the Bench, the parish and labouring families therefore needs some revision. An analysis of poor-law-related cases brought before magistrates is instructive. Grievances about workhouse conditions were rarely resolved in inmates' favour. Complaints that the master of the Winchester House of Industry was not allowing the children an adequate diet had excited 'a spirit of discontent' both in and outside the house, prompting three magistrates to make an inspection. No matter how 'disagreeable' the supper of rice and milk was to some of the children, the magistrates reported that all was well. Similarly, when an inmate of the Coulsdon poorhouse complained to a local magistrate that the house was badly managed, the magistrate made an announced visit, upon which all was found to be satisfactory. Moreover, the significant overlap in personnel between the Bench and the vestry helped to seal the fate of many complainants.[12]

Bench social policies could also be easily manipulated by parish vestries. The case of the Malling, Kent, Bench is indicative. A Speenhamland-style scale of minimum incomes for different categories of the rural poor was established in 1795 but was not made 'compulsory', and in order to become binding at the parish level it would require a claimant to make a complaint to the magistrates before the vestry was compelled. The Yalding vestry – within the Malling Petty Sessional division – clearly understood this and pronounced that no person resident outside the parish was to be relieved without the order of a magistrate.[13]

On the parish

Evidence beyond the grain crises of the 1790s offers further corroboration of this revision. Although grain prices between 1811 and 1813 occasionally exceeded even the peaks of 1800, the poor did not need to protest in the same way as during the 1794–96 and 1799–1801 crises. The massive increase in the scope of the poor laws in 1795 through the adoption of Speenhamland-style scales and systematic income subsidies was not suddenly reversed when grain prices stabilised in late 1801. Thus, while real wages for field workers across southern England as a whole declined between 1795 and 1811 – there were localities where exceptional labour demands meant that real wages actually increased – relief payments in many localities helped to maintain a minimum income. Indeed, the very practice of applying to the Bench suggests that the poor not only clearly understood the dynamic interplay between prices, wages and relief but also knew how best to remedy any perceived imbalance. Such was the crisis in agrarian parishes in the late eighteenth century, partly attributable to the decline of live-in service and apprenticeship and declining real wages,[14] that many ad-hoc initiatives were also fashioned. As John Broad has noted, in times of acute crisis, such as the early months of 1795, 'money raised from the rates was concentrated on meeting urgent need'.[15]

It is beyond reasonable doubt that Bench-sanctioned schemes betrayed a genuine paternalist ethos. Outside Berkshire – admirably treated by Mark Neuman – the exact impulses and policy-making procedures await their historian. It is worth noting though that in Hampshire, the scale produced appears to have been the product of a Quarter Sessions resolution. The 1795 Epiphany Sessions asked *all* Benches to form a sub-committee to report back on: poor rates; rents; population; manufactories; the rate of wages; the employment of women and children; the existence of poorhouses/Houses of Industry (and their effects on the poor rates and morals of the poor); Sunday and charity schools; the price of wheat, bacon, flour, meat and other necessities; the practice of calculating a family's necessary subsistence on their applying for relief; 'the mode of living' among the poor; and, the existence of friendly societies.[16]

Three outcomes from these laudable intentions have been identified. First, this 'new' system of relief became firmly entrenched in the very culture of the parish. Labourers now had a quasi-statutory base from which to claim minimum 'rights'. Claimants' mobilisation of a 'rights' discourse became integral to the day-to-day operation of the poor law system. In a sense this was nothing new but rather an intensification of existing dynamics. Notwithstanding that in the early years of the (old) poor law magistrates were astonished that the poor 'did not seek to mobilise whatever rights they might have under the Elizabethan statutes', Steve Hindle has claimed that by the mid-eighteenth century this had 'turned into resentment that the indigent were only too enthusiastic in claiming relief'. Hindle goes on to state that 'the poor had come to believe not only that they might claim public relief, but that they had every right to do so'.[17]

This emergent discourse of rights (or 'entitlements') had striking echoes with, and presumably drew inspiration from, other systems of entitlement and rights. As E.P. Thompson noted, the morals that underwrote popular intervention in the eighteenth-century English marketplace were underwritten by the Books or Orders first issued to magistrates during lean periods in the final decades of the sixteenth century. Over time, these orders became understood by the wider populace and became encoded into popular claims. They provided the words and actions for plebeian repertoires of resistance.[18] Common rights had underpinned the manorial agrarian system and provided the backbone of common law.[19] Even with regard to enclosure, some rights were only partially extinguished. The thin line between that which was 'common' and that which was 'customary' meant that upon enclosure, actions practised since time immemorial, such as using trackways or gleaning in the post-harvest field, continued.[20] Thus enclosure neither necessarily eliminated practised rights, nor dimmed the community memory of other (now) lost rights. As Jeanette Neeson has so powerfully shown, the practice of common and customary rights and the memory of once-practised rights underpinned much plebeian culture.[21]

Rural workers in some contexts also treated field labour as a right. Parish vestries often tried to prevent farmers from hiring non-parishioners, fearful that servants hired for a calendar year would become chargeable to the parish through the laws of settlement, and of increasing the parochial burden in supporting those out of work. According to the mid-eighteenth-century Sussex diarist Thomas Turner, farmer French of East Hoathly masterminded a scheme to bring 'in many poor into the parish from other parishes, some with certificates and some without, until the parish is full of poor' in order to 'pull down the price of this and some poor men's wages'.[22] By the late 1810s little had changed. At Eling, a large parish between Southampton and the New Forest, a vestry meeting was called in February 1819 to decide 'what measures to take to alleviate the very great expense incurred' by supporting the unemployed labourers. It was resolved that the 50 labourers from other parishes employed by the farmers were to be discharged.[23]

These dynamics fostered a 'culture of xenophobia' (the phase is Snell's),[24] that served to (culturally) legitimise attacks on both non-indigent and migrant workers and those who sought to employ such workers. Such attacks were most commonly targeted at Irish migrant harvest workers, increasing with frequency and ferocity in the late 1820s,[25] but could also be directed at all 'foreigners'.[26] This is not to say that all rural labouring families' lives were exclusively bound by the parish – current work on pauper letters highlights both the mobility and beyond-the-parish mutuality of the poor[27] – but that the parish was central to all claims. As Peter Jones has stated, during Swing rows with parish officers those from outside of the parish were deliberately excluded.[28]

In the context of the 1790s, these discourses coalesced around a more specifically defined popular political call to rights. While the huge demand for both volumes of Thomas Paine's *The Rights of Man* did not in itself directly correspond to a politicisation of rural workers, the conservative backlash attests to the genuine fears of rural elites.[29] But this could, and did, go wrong. Efforts to stir up anti-Paine feeling at Shipley (Sussex) backfired when the parish clerk publicly defended Paine's ideas. Similarly, it was reported in the Hampshire press that in a small village near Devizes, a fiddler refused to play 'God Save the King' at a staged burning of an effigy of Paine. In turn, both the clerk and the fiddler were also burnt in effigy.[30] Such high-profile spectacles, building on popular customary ceremonial forms, may have furthered the popular spread of Paine's conception of rights. As Glynn Williams asserted, hundreds of reports testified to the penetration of Paine's ideas into every corner of British society.[31] This language of rights became firmly ensconced in discourses of popular protest. An anonymous letter posted on the market house at Odiham, Hampshire, in March 1800 threatened to set fire to all the farmers' premises in the kingdom, having the backing of 'some Gentlemen' who wanted to see 'the poor righted'.[32] Labourer John Thatcher was even indicted at the 1794 Kent Lent Assizes for sending a threatening letter to 'the Gentleman and farmers' of Wealden Sandhurst provocatively signed Thomas Paine.[33]

Second, Speenhamland-style relief practices were easily manipulated by particular groups of ratepayers towards their own economic ends. The logical extension of the parish 'making up' the wages of labourers earning less than the minimum scale was that farmers cut wages as low as possible, thereby spreading employment costs to all ratepayers. As long as demand was more or less equal to supply in local labour markets, farmers still needed to employ a regular coterie of workers. Moreover, they might even pay a premium to employ the most efficient and productive workers, or at least seek to employ the 'best' workers in the parish before their fellow vestrymen. But when farmers cut back their workforces post-1815, wage subsidies provided no protection against pauperisation and de facto unemployment. Those labourers who remained directly employed by the farmers were invariably married and with children, because, in the words of Rev. Pratt of Sedlescombe (Sussex), at 'full wages' they would still receive child allowances from the parish.[34] Speenhamland-style systems, without close magisterial surveillance or the active vestry intervention of members of the gentry and nobility, could act to subsidise farmers. As Snell has stated, 'free labour [had] to become pauperised to find employment'.[35]

This manipulation of local labour markets incensed many ratepayers who were forced to not only subsidise the wages of farmers' men, but under allocation schemes had also to engage labourers themselves. Rev. Wake, the rector and tithe holder of Over Wallop in Hampshire, even published a stinging attack on his fellow vestry men for their 'abuse of the poor rate'. According to Wake's solicitor: 'As to the stemming of men, I always told you there was no such law. If an overseer has paupers out of employ, and he cannot find any for them, the whole parish must contribute, by a just and equal rate, to support them. Pray do not be so imposed on.' Wake duly took his case to the 1819 Hampshire Lent Quarter Sessions.[36] Vestry-generated policy had no basis in statute law. Thus, notwithstanding the potential benefits of roundsmen-type schemes, legal challenges were likely to be upheld.

Mindful of this potential pitfall, in February 1829 the Brenchley (Kent) vestry enquired of their local magistrates as to legality of 'labour rates' (or 'Oundle Plan'). This was an allocation scheme backed by a rate against which the cost of allocated labour was worked out. If the ratepayer did not employ their allotted labourers, they had to pay the rate. The 1824 Select Committee on the Employment of Agricultural Labourers had also noted the potential problems and duly offered their support for a Bill placed before Parliament that would give legal sanction to labour rates. Despite their support, the Bill never reached the statute book.[37]

Those who avowed the strictest adherence to the tenets of political economy were also stern critics of all parochial interventions in the labour market. Allowances of whatever kind, so their argument went, did not reward the utility of the labour performed. By 1827 the Berkshire magistrates had realised the effect of their earlier policy. 'The reward of industry' had been reduced to bare subsistence, wages 'should best find their own level'. Justices were to 'use powers' to correct 'this abuse'.[38] The 1828 Select Committee on the Employment of Labourers from the Poor Rates reported that it believed it should be made illegal to aid the wages of labourers from the poor rate, adding that the 'right to employment' was at odds with the law. In future, the market should determine the rate of wages. Technically, the report was correct, for in law, outside of those parishes which had adopted Gilbert's Act of 1782 which forbade the relief of the able-bodied *inside* the workhouse, there was nothing in the statute which sanctioned the payment of outrelief to anyone but the young, infirm and elderly.[39]

The stance taken by the authors of the 1828 report was at variance with the evidence presented to their committee. Henry Boyce, the overseer of Walderslade (Kent), while believing in the Smithian notion that if wages were lower more labourers would be employed, saw that in practice those currently not employing any labourers would still not be in any position to be employers, while those with the necessary capital would be 'over-burdened with labourers'. In the neighbouring parish of Ash, Boyce noted that every Thursday there was an auction for the unemployed labourers. But although a notional bid of a penny would secure the services of a labourer, often no bids were made.[40]

With this in mind, it is extremely difficult to delineate between the active intervention of the parish (that is to say, all ratepayers) in the labour market and the policies forced on to parishes by farmers acting in collusion. This confusion was compounded by the fact that in many southern parishes there was little compositional difference between the 'parish' and the 'farmers'. Despite these problems, it is still possible to study those schemes formally devised by vestries that sought to place all, or most, able-bodied labourers into work with the farmers. The most famous scheme was the 'roundsman' system, also known as the billet, the yardland, the stem (especially in Hampshire and Wiltshire), or the ticket. The system worked as follows. Those out of employment were sent to the farmers in turn, hence being sent 'round' the parish, to be engaged either wholly or partially at the expense of the parish. A far more common scheme, at least in the south-east, was the quota system whereby the farmers' rental, rateable value or acreage determined the number of parishioners employed. This scheme was made necessary by the obvious abuses engendered by the pure roundsmen scheme. Simply put, if the parish was willing to subsidise the wages of the otherwise unemployed, why not seek a subsidy on all workmen by making those previously employed independently of the parish system redundant. Occasionally, vestries attempted to legislate against such gross manipulations by stating that the 'surplus' labourers were only to be employed at work not done by their normal labourers. Such a policy was, in practice, impossible to police.[41]

Third, the Speenhamland-style relief practices, whatever the initial humane intentions, were famously described by Malthus as 'a direct, constant, and systemical encouragement to marriage', whereby the initial amelioration of poverty would over time create more poverty.[42] Malthus's contention has subsequently been subjected to analysis and re-analysis, with poor law reformers and, more latterly, social historians variously mobilising the archive to support or refute his thesis. The most notorious support for Malthus's argument came in the form of the *Poor Law Commissioners' Report* of 1834. This, in the words of Tawney, 'brilliant, influential, and wildly unhistorical document',[43] selectively mobilised evidence collected in the *Rural Queries* of 1832 to offer 'proof' of Malthus's thesis and thus provide categorical evidence of the urgent need to instigate a centrally controlled union workhouse-based system.[44] Beatrice and Sidney Webb, true to Fabian form, were deeply critical of both the quasi-social scientific methods and Benthamite views of the reports compilers. The original Elizabethan poor laws, subsequent statutory developments and local non-statutory policy innovations were, they claimed, incoherent, often manipulated beyond the original purpose, and, when Speenhamland-style schemes were systematised, 'calamitous'. But, nonetheless, they were not in themselves responsible for the demographic boom of the 1810s or creeping pauperisation. The root cause of these problems was, essentially, the intensification of agrarian capitalism.[45]

Some fifty years later, the Webbs' argument was reasserted by Mark Blaug. Based on an analysis of parliamentary returns, Blaug asserted that 'hardly any of the dire effects ascribed to the Old Poor Law stand up in the light of available empirical knowledge'. The intellectual argument came full circle when, in 1989, George Boyer suggested that 'Malthus was right after all'. Analysing census data, Boyer concluded that wage subsidies in the form of child allowances did act to encourage early marriage and, in turn, couples to have children from a younger age.[46] More recently, Samantha Williams has asserted from an examination of two Bedfordshire communities that 'it seems highly unlikely that allowances were the cause of early marriages and larger families ... allowances ... were a necessary *response* to the sharply worsened circumstances after 1790'. Instead, different parishes met needs in different and dynamic ways.[47]

Beyond dependence

Williams' work has important resonances with that of Samantha Shave, whose study of the north Dorset parish of Motcombe has shown that not only did relief regimes shift over time but also that the vestry and overseers met the needs of each individual on application. Besides pensioners, no one individual was ever constantly in receipt of parish relief, whether in the form of child allowances or wages. There was no such thing, Shave concludes, as a rural dependant poor.[48] Notwithstanding the potentially homogenising effects of shared laws and Bench-sanctioned scales, each individual parish had a huge degree of autonomy in deciding how to interpret, devise and implement policy. Parishes even devised their own bread scales independently of local Benches. For instance, the vestry of the Hampshire parish of Amport resolved in January 1816 that:

> Mr Green offers Household bread at 1 3.5*d* pr Gallon, therefore the allowance of Head is to be 1*s* 10*d* – giving an advantage of 1/2 (half) to the poor (and the sixpence above is to be taken from the Household price in future).

As bread prices declined in the late autumn of that year, so the vestry resolved to reduce allowances and take money out of the allowance to help pay the poor's house rents.[49]

A useful place to begin to think through parochial autonomy in the face of magisterial intervention is the uptake of scales as reported in parliamentary returns. According to Baugh, post-1815, most parishes gave some form of child allowance, whereas Boyer states that post-1822 scales were being abandoned in the south-east.[50] Between 1824 and 1832, the proportion of all parishes paying such allowances declining from 75 per cent to 50 per cent. While the average proportion of parishes paying allowances might be 50 per cent, this figure disguised significant local variations. Some 82 per cent of all reporting parishes from Sussex paid allowances, with figures of 74 per cent, 73 per cent and 72 per cent in Hampshire, Berkshire and Wiltshire respectively. Yet only 44 per cent of Dorset parishes and 19 per cent of Bedfordshire parishes paid any allowance.[51]

What does this show? In short, it demonstrates that statistical analyses based on small sample parochial returns made in pro-forma documents cannot possibly capture the vast range of pre-Swing parochial relief practices. Moreover, it is by no means clear that a parish answering 'yes' to a question enquiring whether they used a scale system meant that they paid child allowances or 'made up' labourers wages through systematic roundsmen schemes. Either way, both parliamentary returns and parish records show that from the early 1820s, poor law expenditure started to decline. This was not a result of improving conditions for rural capitalists or labouring families, but rather a function of changing parochial regimes and increasingly stingy poor relief entitlements. The more widespread – and now legally-sanctioned under the Sturges-BourneAct – appointment of assistant overseers appears to have been particularly significant in reducing expenditure.[52] As such, while in the years immediately prior to Swing Speenhamland-style payments were still widely implemented in many southern counties, they had become less generous. They had also mutated into a policy tool by which local labour markets could be effectively micro-managed by the parish. Wage supplements morphed into a device that enabled farmers to slash wages. In practice, Wells has asserted, this was achieved through the payment of allowances in aid-of-wages, which depended on family size. In many cases, families with more than two young children were supported by the parish as farmers tended to set wages at a level that would support a husband, wife and only two children. This system, Wells suggests, became 'embedded in the principal cornlands'.[53]

Wells' conclusion is important because it refutes the idea that all farmers sought to manipulate Speenhamland-style practices and abuse their vestry positions in forcing the majority of wages costs onto the broader community of ratepayers. If he is correct in stating that in many southern parishes the norm was for farmers to pay wages up to a level deemed adequate to the support of a man, wife and two children, then claims that farmers exploited their dual position as employers and vestry members has been overplayed. But this conclusion is necessarily totalising. For every parish subsidising wages through the payment of systematic allowances, there was another parish that was not systematic and did not have formally devised policies.

While the spatiality of allowance practices awaits its historian, it would appear from the demands of Swing groups that the area bounded by the Weald to the east, the South Downs to the south, the Dever Valley to the west and the North Downs to the north comprised the key zone of allowance-paying parishes. This is not to say that in most of Kent and Surrey and in the coastal plains of Hampshire and Sussex allowances were not important. Rather, these more capitally intensive areas relied more squarely on workhouses and the use of labour allocation schemes. Here too the demand for labour was greater – especially in construction – and the farmers more prosperous.[54]

If allowance schemes met the challenge of the Napoleonic period, the major challenge of the post-Napoleonic period was unemployment. Perhaps unsurprisingly in light of the rapidly unfurling circumstances, and the fact that seasonal and short-term unemployment had long been endemic in most southern parishes,[55] vestries were slow to react. Records for 1815 and 1816 show that few systematic employment schemes were implemented. The provincial press, save for occasional reports that reductions were about to be made in the naval bases, were also silent on unemployment. Yet, according to Rev. Gleig of Waltham, 1816 was 'one of the worst years' for unemployment. 'Multitudes of disbanded soldiers and sailors ... [were] sent back to their parishes', inverting the war years dynamic of 'a competition among the farmers to find men' to a 'a competition among the men to find masters'. Yet farmers, backed by broader vestry support, were reluctant to cut wages. Against a backdrop of declining food prices, this inevitably led to the farmers 'strik[ing] off a certain number from their employ [so that] numbers of young, healthy, and willing persons no longer knew where to apply for a day's work'.[56] At Eling, by July 1816 there were 60 labouring men out of employ. This was from a total population of 3,798 souls and 756 families, of whom 407 were primarily engaged in agriculture, meaning that at the start of the harvest, some 14.7 per cent of agricultural families were afflicted by outright unemployment.[57] This rapid increase in unemployment caught vestries off guard. In the words of Gleig:

> [Vestries] could neither understand nor manage it. They would not listen to the applications of the young and healthy, but refused them peremptorily both relief and employment. For a while the lusty paupers bore with repulse; but the demands of hunger were pressing: they ascertained that an appeal lay from the parish vestry to the bench of magistrates, and to the magistrates their complaints were carried.[58]

As the agricultural depression deepened, so did the problem of unemployment. Despite land agent Edward Wakefield's observation that the labourers living in the 'light [soil] lands' were hit hardest, it was on the heavy soils of the Weald that problems were most acute.[59] By 1821, the Battle Petty Sessional District, so reckoned the clerk to the Bench, contained about 1,000 men 'with no useful employment'.[60] Two years later, sixteen Kentish Wealden parishes with a total population of 21,719 inhabitants contained 8,263 paupers of whom 682 were unemployed men. The situation at Burwash (Sussex) was worse still. Over half of the 2,000 residents were paupers, and during the winter 80–90 men were constantly out of work.[61] Not only were labourers thrown out of employ but also many hitherto successful petty agriculturalists were forced into day labouring, further swelling the ranks of the unemployed and driving down wages. This dynamic was further compounded by the fact that, in the Weald 'a great number' of 'moderately sized farms' were available to rent, owing to the 'oppressive and ruinous poor rates'. During the summer of 1822 in Mayfield alone, nineteen farms were reported to be unoccupied.[62]

The situation elsewhere was only moderately less severe. 'Open' parishes in particular were prone to above average unemployment. Southwick, though close to the rapidly expanding Brighton with its huge demand for construction labourers, suffered from being 'surrounded by parishes which are in the hands of sole proprietors' (i.e. tightly regulated 'closed' parishes). Cottages were easily (and profitably) erected in Southwick, the parish thereby providing a ready workforce to its neighbours.[63] 'Open' Bentley in north Hampshire was dominated by Holt Forest – with all its opportunities to illicitly eke out a living – and the labour-intensive hop industry. And yet a third of the poor relief budget was expended on supporting unemployed labourers, with another third used to subsidise the wages of those in work. The depression hit even the most prosperous of parishes that did not have closely regulated populations. In many parishes on the capitally intensive West Sussex coastal plain 'a great many men' were out of employ, the result, according to a select committee respondent, of an increased resort to threshing machines.[64]

After the nadir of 1822, the fortunes of southern agrarian communities undoubtedly improved, but by the late 1820s the situation was again chronic. Wages had stabilised at early 1820s levels, but the increased uptake of select vestries and assistant overseers inevitably led to more stringent relief regimes in many parishes.[65] Furthermore, effective unemployment rates were as bad, if not worse, than during the early 1820s. By 1828 at West Grinstead (Sussex) 86 of the 300 (28.7 per cent) settled labourers were employed directly by the parish. Neighbouring Shipley was similarly beleaguered. Out of 240 agricultural labourers, 192 were supported in some form by the parish, of whom between 40 and 80 labourers were employed directly by the parish. The consequences were cultural as well as economic. At Walderslade, the 30 to 40 men 'in the prime of life' employed by the parish were, in the mind of the overseer, 'degraded in their own estimation; as well as in the estimation of their beholders, hooked onto carts and wheelbarrows, dragging stones to the highway'.[66]

The experience at Walderslade highlights not only the demoralising and potentially debasing nature of unemployment, but also the difficulty faced by parishes in employing those out of work. The problem was not only one of money and capital but also of policy and principle. That any parish managed to agree on an unemployment scheme was no mean feat. One can sense the frustration in a meeting of the Hartfield vestry called in May 1826 to consider how to employ the poor to 'prevent the impending Ruin now hanging over their Heads'.[67] While the introduction of plural weighting under the Sturges-Bourne Act made reaching an agreement easier, effectively allowing the voices of smaller ratepayers to be ignored, vestry squabbles were the rule rather than the exception. While disputes rarely made it into vestry minutes, and votes on policy decisions were rarely detailed, occasionally we get some illuminating detail. In October 1823, farmer Mund of Cholsey (Berkshire) attempted to regulate wages for all agricultural task-work. However, farmer Langford intervened and stated, for the record, that he did 'not agree to this nonsense proposed'.[68] Diaries occasionally also shed light on the difficulties of policy-making, the diary of Elham excise officer William Hall being particularly instructive:

> 25 March 1819: Parish officers chosen then ate [at] Rose [and Crown], staid late got rather croggy.
> 8 May: Parish meeting last night between Westfield and Oxley didn't break up 'till 2am.
> 28 May: Parish meeting, no quarrelling, Oxley and Westfield shook hands.
> 23 July: Oxley + Parish at variance, meeting at Cock.[69]

Vestry meetings were not only plagued by drinking and quarrelling but also by poor attendance.[70] With this in mind, it is not surprising that many parishes had difficulty with policy formation. Despite the obvious appeal of subsidised roundsmen and allocation schemes to larger farmers, road working was something that many parishes fell back on as less contentious and not as prone to abuse. But even road working was problematic. Many parishes were simply too small to be able to afford an assistant overseer or permanent surveyor to implement and supervise employment schemes. In such parishes, policy was often devised ad hoc by the overseer or by those present at vestry meetings dealing with individuals seeking work.

Besides securing (male) labour and relief from the parish, labouring households sustained themselves in many other ways. As King and Tomkins have asserted, rural workers got by balancing resources in their 'economy of makeshifts'. In rural areas, this predominantly combined waged labour, of all members of the household, both salaried and by piece, poor relief payments, charity, mutual support, the exercise of common rights, including gleaning, and theft, including poaching and smuggling. In addition, Williams has suggested that 'exemption from local taxes ... foraging on wastes, credit, loans, selling and pawning goods, barter, friendly societies, rent arrears' as well as 'begging, vagrancy, squatting, defrauding the poor law ... petty unlicensed brewing, prostitution, and receiving stolen goods' were all ways of getting by.[71] A survey of Norfolk and Suffolk labouring families in the mid- to late 1830s found that only half the income of an average household derived from the oldest male's daily earnings. A further third came from the labour of women and children, including from gleaning, while 15 per cent came from the harvest earnings of all members of the family.[72] Some forty years previously the household budgets assembled by David Davies and Frederick Eden, though showing variations depending upon family size and location, suggested a broadly similar composition.[73] But such surveys are necessarily idealised, detailing what both the interviewee and interviewer wanted to divulge and record. Clearly, such accounts would not contain information on illicit activities, nor, by virtue of the desire to quantify, could they detail mutual assistance.

Notwithstanding the problems in reconstructing meaningful household budgets, some historians have attempted to look at individual components of the 'economy of makeshifts'. For the Lancashire parish of Cowpe, King has ranked the resources available to the poorest families in the early nineteenth century. Perhaps unsurprisingly, poor relief and wages formed the most important sources, with charity, working for the parish and credit from shopkeepers also of significant importance.[74] Sara Horrell and Jane Humphries have suggested, on the basis of analysing 1,350 family budgets, that poor relief and 'self-provisioning' contributed on average 13 per cent of the household incomes of field-working families before the New Poor Law.[75] Although there were regional variations in the generosity of poor relief payments – all parishes were statutorily bound to provide relief – there was no uniformity in the availability of commons and arable fields from which to glean. For instance, from a study of eleven communities in Buckinghamshire, Cambridgeshire, Herfordshire and Northamptonshire, Leigh Shaw-Taylor has estimated that only 15 per cent of 'southern' labourers had a right to keep a commonable cow.[76]

It is important to note that Shaw-Taylor's case studies were based on communities with commonable land. In large parts of south-east England, not least most of Kent and south-west Sussex, enclosure had long since created a landless 'proletariat'. There were significant pockets where commonable land survived in the south-east, the New and Holt Forests in Hampshire, Ashdown in Sussex, and the patchwork of large remnant commons around Hindhead and to the north of Folkestone (see figure 2.1).[77] In long enclosed parishes, customary, as opposed to commonable, rights could also provide useful supplements to the domestic economy. Peter King's studies of gleaning suggest that in the eastern and Home Counties it continued to contribute a significant proportion of household budgets in the early 1830s. Even nationally, King's figures suggest that gleaning contributed between 3 per cent and 14 per cent to labouring budgets.[78] In the south-east, if the evidence related in the 1832 *Rural Queries* is accurate, the figures were towards the lower end of this spectrum. But even here, it was recognised that it was an important practice. In the summer of 1830, Rev. Price JP of Lyminge, subsequently enmeshed in the trial of the first Swing machine-breakers, told the farmers of the parish not to mow their wheat because it was 'cruel to deprive the poor' of gleanings.[79]

Either way, household support from the exercise of common and customary rights in the south was in long-term decline. Indeed, income, as broadly defined, from non-wage and poor relief sources, with the arguable exception of illicit activities and friendly society doles, declined in absolute and proportional terms in late eighteenth- and early nineteenth-century southern England.[80] In its place, and against a backdrop of steadily declining real wages, the parish took

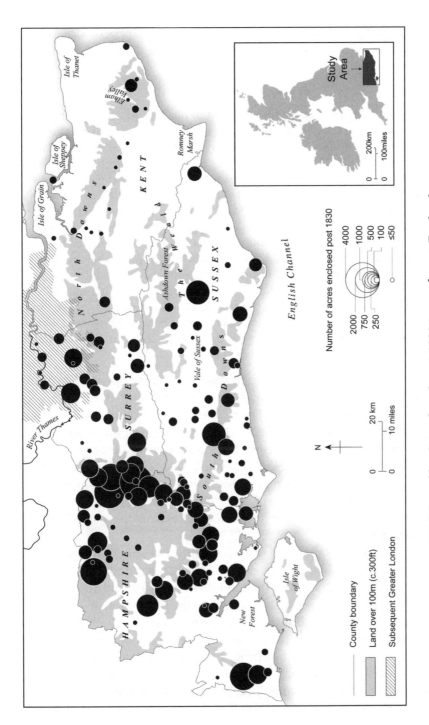

2.1 Map of lands enclosed post-1830 in south-east England

the strain. And those without access to wide networks of kin, as Sam Barrett has shown,[81] or charitable support, were the first to apply.

A life as well as a living

Richard Richardson, who, as we stated in our last, was found dead on the downs, in the parish of Alceston [*sic*], is supposed to have fallen a sacrifice to fatigue and want. He was in the habit of going every morning to the distance of four miles from home to work, at 12*s.* per week. On the fatal day he got up at his usual hours, and was about to start for his destination without taking any victuals with him – for all the food he possessed in the world consisted only of a three-penny loaf, and which he would fain have left for his family, as it was the only article of subsistence in the house, and he had no money or credit, and had been refused, as we understand, parochial support, when his wife, by repeated solicitations, induced him, though most reluctantly to accept the loaf, with which at length he departed. On his return, at night, it is supposed, he sunk exhausted, as he was found lifeless on the downs, with the loaf, almost untouched, in his bag, intending no doubt, to restore it to his half-starved wife and six children. The verdict returned was '*Died by the visitation of God*'.[82]

This tragic, perhaps apocryphal, case highlights the need to think about issues of labour, making do, welfare and the practice of everyday life in synthesis. Poor relief was only given after some investigation into income derived from work and other sources. If Richardson existed, then clearly the Alciston vestry thought his case did not warrant granting relief. That he had six children suggests that, at least in downland Alciston, scales were either not used or were not rigidly applied. Yet with the family's money having run out, and their lines of credit exhausted, he succumbed to exhaustion exacerbated by acute hunger.

Most southern labourers were born into the landless 'proletariat'. They were raised in an aggressive agrarian capitalist system that assumed they would labour for a living. In the 1810s and 1820s, as E.A. Wrigley asserted, there was an increase in the proportion of individuals engaged as artisans.[83] But the depression hit artisans with the perfect storm of tightening plebeian budgets, tightening poor law expenditure and reduced expenditure by farmers, forcing many to go labouring – or to the parish – to support their families. In many ways, artisans and labourers therefore became largely indistinguishable. The ranks of labourers were furthered swelled by the many small peasant proprietors – found by Mick Reed 'lurking' in the Weald but also surviving in large numbers in any area with commons – who were forced to supplement their declining incomes by resorting to paid labour.[84]

Young girls were similarly born with the expectation that they would either enter into domestic service, with all the drudgery and sexual exploitation that so often ensued,[85] or would combine work in the household with work in the farm yards, fields, gardens and orchards. The increased acreage of hops and orchards undoubtedly offered new employment opportunities for women, but at the same time, as Pamela Sharpe and Nicola Verdon have asserted, farmers employed fewer women on their arable fields in hoeing and weeding.[86] As already noted, falling prices and increasing poor rates meant farmers employed fewer men, when not directed otherwise by the parish. Farmers also cut back on task work. As one select committee interviewee pointed out, there was 'much work on farms [which] is currently undone' leading to 'bad cultivation'.[87]

Yet, to labour was to achieve a dignity of purpose. The persistence of wage disputes and protests directed at parsimonious (and often hard-nosed) employers and overseers refutes the myth that English field workers were resigned to a fate of exploitation. But as Jones has stressed, the demands of many activists were extraordinarily modest: work at remunerating wages. Labouring was exhausting and exacted a huge toll on labourers' bodies and health – at work at daybreak whatever the weather, toiling in the fields until dusk – but it was what was expected. All young men would replicate the social and economic roles of their fathers by labouring for the farmers. This was a simple agrarian equipoise: to offer one's labour in exchange for a living wage and the support of the parish when needed. When the system broke down, those who had to labour for a living reminded their social 'betters' of their responsibilities, sometimes through protest.

Such was E.P. Thompson's 'moral economy', a value system shared by all members of a community that encoded paternalist legislation in recognising the responsibilities of the rulers of rural England in protecting the poor from abuse and exploitation. The moral economy recognised that when these responsibilities were not exercised, the poor would react in certain well understood ways in reasserting moral economic values. In Thompson's formulation, the moral economy existed, and was enacted, in relation to the manipulation of food prices and quality by farmers, dealers, millers and bakers.[88] Yet, as

Jones, Randall and Wells, among others, have asserted, moral economic values also underpinned other realms of social action in rural England, from the use of machinery in the cloth industry, to the payment of sustaining wages.[89]

To quote Thompson, Speenhamland-style practices necessarily unsettled this 'field of force'. The timing of the initial Bench-sponsored scales and the coincident, but unconnected by way of formal policy, extension of relief, is instructive: 1795 was not only one of the worst food crisis years of the eighteenth century, but it also bore witness to the greatest wave of food rioting that England would ever see.[90] When similar conditions again plagued England in late 1799, the response of poor consumers was very different. By now, the reciprocal system that in essence offered relief in exchange for quiescence, meant that riotous forms of collective protest were ill-advised. Being seen to protest would jeopardise one's ability to claim relief. Moreover, the logic of the 'new' system, as Elizabeth Fox Genovese suggested, threw greater light on income rather than expenditure.[91] However, as 'wages' were no longer an accurate proxy for income, 'blame' became trifurcated. Should the aggrieved complain to individual farmers, the vestry or the Bench?

An analysis of the resort to protest in the first half of 1800 is instructive. The first south-eastern 'riot' during the crisis occurred at Petworth, but this was far removed from the 'classic' food riot. Fifty labourers gathered at Petworth to complain to the magistrates that owing to the high price of provisions their families were close to starvation. Sir Godfrey Webster, who was officiating, sent a summons to all parish officers to attend the next meeting of the Bench after which the men went home seemingly placated.[92] Ironically, the hitherto atypical nature of this incident perfectly typified the diverse repertoire of collective demonstrations in the first half of 1800. Other incidents during the spring and early summer of that year ranged from a very similar wages protest at Ardingly, to the 'traditional' act of stopping loaded wagons, as practised at Romsey. What is striking about this set of spring and early summer protests is the fact that in all eight recorded incidents, excluding protests at Romsey, Northchapel and Lewes (where the motives of the actants were not clear), food prices were juxtaposed with wages and/or poor relief. This juxtaposition, while evident in 1795, was now universal and more precisely articulated than before.[93] In addition, early targets of covert protests included a high proportion of poor law officials. If many rural vestries had been quicker to subsidise plebeian incomes than in 1795, the extended net of poor relief was neither universal, all-encompassing or without discrimination.[94]

As Wells has identified, the resort to incendiarism declined beyond the summer of 1801 (see figure 2.2),[95] but tensions between capital and labour were no less fraught. Indeed, it is telling that the first case of incendiarism after the grain harvest of 1801 was predicated by a dispute over piece rates in the hop fields of Farnham.[96] Tensions were most evident in the expanding Quarter Sessions and Assizes calendars, yet even expanding indictment roles mask the majority of crimes that never made it before a magistrate, let alone to the courts. In late 1802 it was reported that 'many' petty thefts had occurred in Southampton but that not a single person had been apprehended. Eight years later, a similar report was made about crime in the environs of Canterbury: '[n]umberless are the petty thefts of hay, roots, hop-poles, fences, etc which pass unrecorded'.[97]

Covert – and collective – protests continued, albeit at a lower level until 1815 when incendiarism assumed levels that surpassed those seen in 1800. While it is important to state that accurately assessing levels of incendiarism is fraught with complication,[98] it is worth noting that a single incendiary fire could have major repercussions not just for the victim but also for all those in the local area. Major fires were dramatic and devastating, and, in most rural areas, unusual enough as to remain in the collective consciousness for years, even decades. When in October 1823 Frith Farm in Newnham was targeted by incendiarists, it was noted that the same farm had been also been attacked 'about 60 years ago'. The archive reveals that Frith Farm had been torched in 1757, the last such reported fire in the parish until 1823.[99] The numbers may be small, but they hide a complex reality.

Before 1815, incendiarism was not a constant threat to farmers and other property owners in any area, but nor was the south-east free from collective protests. While agricultural workers appear not to have adopted unionist tactics, skilled and artisanal trades in both town and country undoubtedly did combine. The nationwide papermakers' strike in the winter of 1803–4 started in the villages surrounding Maidstone, journeymen tailors struck work at Brighton in June 1805 and at Sheerness in 1807, while journeyman shoemakers struck over wages at Southampton in June 1807 and at Brighton the following July.[100] Even the riots in London after the House of Commons voted to commit Sir Francis Burdett to the Tower for breach of parliamentary privilege on 6 April 1810 threatened to extend to the

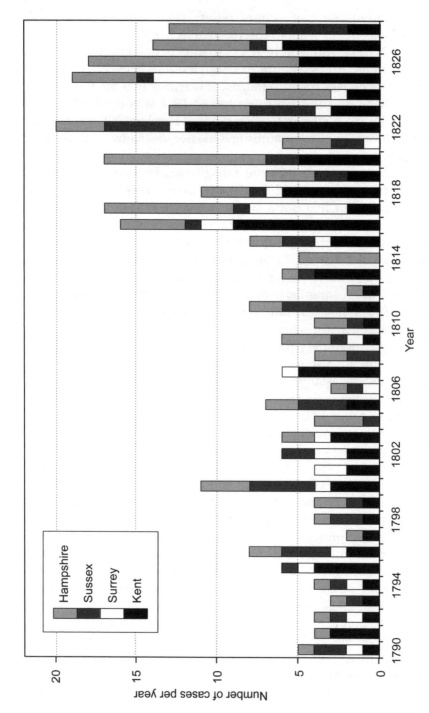

2.2 The resort to incendiarism, 1815–28

south-east. A letter sent on 9 April to the Collector of Customs at Deal, a notorious smuggling haunt, suggestively began: 'Since the Riot is now begun in London we have great hopes of reaching ... this Town.'[101] Chastened by the force of the metropolitan riots, an inquiry was instigated by Sir Francis Freeling, the head of the Post Office, as to the likelihood of provincial riots. Although this did not receive any positive replies from the south-east, it did provoke universal declarations that the disaffected were to be found everywhere. Yet, in the words of the Canterbury Post Office Deputy, these 'Men whose opinions differ materially on most Political Questions' would not 'endanger themselves and their connections by tumultuous rioting'.[102]

Limiting assessments only to acts of union and 'riot' though fails to grasp the complexities of collective action. We cannot, 200 years later, defiantly state that a group of labourers almost deferentially descending upon a rural vestry represented an act of overt protest while the activities of a violent poaching gang did not. As Thompson noted, the word riot 'can conceal what may be described as a spasmodic view of popular history' where the 'common people ... intrude occasionally and spasmodically upon the historical canvas, in periods of sudden social disturbance'.[103] In the early nineteenth century the arts of collective action and organisation, without which the Swing could not have happened, were learnt not in the occasional resort to riot but in the criminal, poaching and smuggling gangs that offered one of the only alternatives to immiseration under an unfettered agrarian capitalism.[104]

Between 1811 and 1813 food prices reached levels not seen during the previous grain crisis, yet the record reveals no cases of food rioting. However, an analysis of Home Office papers reveals that forms of collective protest were deployed. In November 1811 'about 10 women with 40 children in a very irritable state of mind' applied to Magistrate William Milford at Petworth to complain of 'a want of necessary relief' from their parish. The women were particularly fierce in their denunciation of the Tillington overseer – a tenant of Milford – who had pre-emptively refused them relief the previous evening. This report only reached the Home Office by virtue of the fact that the following night the barn of another of Milford's tenants was destroyed by an incendiary fire.[105] While there is evidence to suggest that incendiarism took on a relative importance hitherto not seen during grain crises, incendiarism levels would appear to have been no higher than in the previous ten years.[106]

The age of the (threshing) machine

As noted, it was the end of the Napoleonic Wars that prompted the greatest shift in protest practices. Notwithstanding a brief final flickering of food rioting and other food-related disputes in 1816,[107] mirroring the famed 'Bread or Blood' protests in East Anglia,[108] it was the increased resort to incendiarism that set the protest scene for pre-Swing period. The 1816 archive reveals sixteen cases of south-eastern incendiarism. That the geography of this is illusory, with the exception of a cluster of fires around Maidstone,[109] is largely unimportant. In more parishes than ever before, individuals were resorting to the weapons of covert terror to settle their grievances.

The incendiary fires of 1816 were also notable for the frequency of attacks on threshing machines. Despite the obvious resentments felt by workers displaced by machines, prior to 1816 such feelings find little voice in the archive. In 1791 the owner of the first machine in Surrey was threatened with arson, 'which was expected to be done'. In 1806 arsonists at East Dean in Sussex discussed whether setting fire to an oat stack would destroy the threshing machine kept in an adjacent barn.[110]

Intriguingly, the first two fires which targeted threshing machines occurred on the Hampshire-Surrey borders, the first at Froyle in July 1815, the second at Godalming in June 1816. The second led to the successful prosecution of labourer Andrews.[111] Elsewhere in Hampshire, the archive, alas, does not detail the parish where Harry Wright sent several letters threatening to set fire to threshing machines and murder 'their proprietors', for which he ended up in the county gaol.[112] Perhaps the most important fire occurred at the initial Swing centre of Elham the following year. 'For some time previous to the fire' the 'country people in the neighbourhood had shown a great dislike to the use of the threshing machine which had been lately introduced to the parish'. Farmer Fowler had signalled his intention in October 1817 of hiring the machine to thresh some oats and on the morning of 11 October, his oat barn was set on fire and destroyed. Not only is this fire critical in establishing a long-held antipathy to threshing machines in the very parish from which the first Swing gang came, but also because of the fact that the Kent press did not report the fire. That we know it occurred was due to the fact that under the Black Act, Fowler brought a civil action against the Hundred of Loninborough to recover his loss by the fire.[113]

While it would appear likely that many farmers turned to threshing machines as a cost-saving device to help combat falling grain prices,[114] many others had adopted machines during the Napoleonic Wars. In addition to the evidence already related from Surrey and Sussex, John Boys' *General View of the Agriculture of ... Kent*, first published in 1796, noted that he alone operated a threshing machine in the county. His revised edition of 1805 simply noted that there now 'several [threshing machines] introduced in different parts of the county'.[115] Abraham and William Driver's 1794 *General View of the Agriculture of ... Hampshire* makes no mention of threshing machines. Eight years later, R. Thompson of the small east Hampshire town of Wickham could not only boast of selling 'Scotch Thrashing Machines, with sundry improvements', but also that 'many' farmers were already using them and had provided 'certificates of their utmost satisfaction'. By 1810, Charles Vancouver's *General View...* directly mentions twelve threshing machines in operation in different parts of the county, and also states that in the Avon Valley, on the border with Wiltshire and Dorset, machines were 'getting into much use'.[116] As such, not all the incendiary attacks on threshing machines in 1816 were necessarily motivated by their recent introduction, for in many districts machines had long been in use. Rather, the wretched conditions of 1816 and the sharp upturn in unemployment meant that even in areas where threshing machines had only hitherto been grumbled about, their use now engendered bitter recriminations.

The next series of incendiary attacks on threshing machines in the south-east occurred in 1821–22, the period when the agrarian economy next launched into depression.[117] Fires again occurred on the Surrey-Hampshire borders, this time at Farnham, as well as at Gravesend, and downland Jevington in Sussex.[118] But although threshing machines were important generators of conflict in 1822, they were not the sole the initiators. Claims in the *Morning Chronicle* in early April that 'outrages ... among unemployed agricultural labourers' had occurred in Kent and Sussex were denounced as 'evil' by the *Maidstone Journal*. However, their counterclaim that the countryside was 'never in a more peaceful and tranquil state' was nonsense. Protests during the late spring and early summer of 1822 might not have attained the intensity of events in East Anglia but still attested to the disturbed state of the countryside. Pre-harvest cases of arson – including one supposedly accidental fire in which a threshing machine was destroyed at Bexhill, the receipt of a spate of threatening letters in south Kent, and an assassination attempt on a farmer at Stone-in-Oxney were all signs of foreboding.[119] Worse still were reports that the Sussex hay harvest was completed at 'scarcely any expense' by late June, while in Kent harvest wages – the main source of paying off accumulated debts – were cut, owing to the reduced price of agricultural commodities.[120]

As it turned out, the summer was hot and dry, and cereal, pulses and fruit harvest good. Protests – with the exception of Hampshire – though, assumed an unusual degree of intensity given the better than expected harvest, no doubt a function of the downward pressure on wages and localised unemployment during the harvest. This tended to focus rural workers' attentions on farmers, vestries and the competition – Irish migrant labourers. By late July, the arrival of Irish labourers on the Isle of Thanet provoked the resistance of both local and English migrant labourers seeking harvest work. The hop harvest in the environs of Maidstone traditionally employed many Irish labourers, acting to generate several bitter disputes in 1822. William Ledger, a substantial hop farmer at Ulcomb, near Maidstone, was in the unfortunate position of also being a parish officer. In mid-July, 400 hills of hops in one of Ledger's plantations were cut during the night. A week later a threatening letter addressed to Ledger was posted on the local pub door. Elsewhere, a Saturday night fire in one of Mr Ellis's oast houses at Barming, conjectured to be the result of a workman's candle falling among the hops, prompted a large crowd to gather and simply watch the flames. Ellis also lost another oast house at nearby Wateringbury, though the cause of the fire was not stated.[121] That year was plagued by a record number of harvest-time incendiary fires, an important fact considering that the harvest period in the years between 1790 and 1821 had represented the period of the year least blighted by incendiary fires.[122]

Attempts by rural vestries to cut costs, not least by the appointment of assistant overseers and the creation of select vestries, combined with low wages and unemployment (or underemployment) meant that the outlook for rural workers was bleak. It should not have been surprising then that parochial regulation was the key generator of rural protests in the winter of 1822–23. At Northiam, three days after a serious riot at a select vestry meeting that ended with three young men indicted at the Winter Assizes, Rev. Lord had his haystacks set on fire. At nearby Burwash, 'domineering' overseer Flurry had his barns fired, supposedly by 'a combination of paupers ... generally labourers out of employ'.[123] Other means of seeking redress – or revenge – were also adopted. In late October a body of labourers from Woodchurch, near Tenterden, journeyed to Union Hall Police Office, London, to complain about the 'manner in which they were set to work [by the parish officers], and their pay and allowances'. Notwithstanding the distance travelled, they were informed that such a complaint must be addressed to the magistrates in their neighbourhood. Unbowed, on 7 November 70 labourers travelled to Cranbrook to make their complaints to the divisional Petty Sessions. Again, they were dismissed.[124]

As figure 2.1 suggests, incendiarism declined in 1823 and 1824, and despite a harvest blighted by '40 days of rain' from the end of June,[125] the rural economy recovered slightly between 1823 and 1824. There were disputes, most notably in the building trades at rapidly expanding Brighton, but these were few.[126] Another wet harvest in 1824 halted the recovery, forcing up prices and leading to harvest rows between indigenous labourers and Irish migrants.[127] Post-harvest responses took four forms: an upturn in crime: strikes, an increased resort to incendiarism, and poor law disputes. Particularly telling was the letter posted on the Mayfield vestry door in early January 1825 addressed to overseer May: 'Wee do Intend Washing Our Hands inn Your Blood'.[128]

Better harvests in 1825 and 1826 helped to increase the demand for labour. However, the, by now, traditional wave of Irish migrant harvest workers generated conflict. In the summer of 1825 East Kent was reportedly 'swarming with Irishmen with wives and children in search of harvest work'. The next summer attacks on Irish labourers engaged in the hop harvest occurred at Barming, and in the hop parish of Boughton Monchelsea.[129] The following years followed the pattern of a severely cold winter (1826–27) followed by a good harvest, and a mild, if wet, winter (1827–28) followed by a disastrous harvest. The tensions that flared in this period established Swing's platform. Attacks on vestries, which ended up in court, occurred at Crondall, Westham and Hurstpierpoint,[130] while the Chartham overseer only narrowly survived an attempt on his life.[131] In Sussex there was, according to the *Brighton Gazette*, 'a clamour of evil tendency' against the payment of tithes.[132] The use of machinery in the paper industry around Maidstone prompted a flurry of threatening letters written in red ink, warning the owners that their mills would be destroyed unless they stopped using machinery. The extensive saw mills on the

Surrey side of the Thames were also destroyed by an incendiary fire, this following a long series of complaints by sawyers thrown out of employment by the introduction of new machinery.[133]

Notes

1 K.D.M. Snell, *Annals of the Labouring Poor* (Cambridge: Cambridge University Press, 1985), p. 104.
2 *Ibid.*, p. 108. Also see S. King, *Poverty and Welfare in England, 1700–1850* (Manchester: Manchester University Press, 2000), p. 155.
3 R. Wells, *Wretched Faces: Famine in Wartime England, 1793–1803* (Stroud: Alan Sutton, 1988), ch. 17; Wells, 'Social protest, class, conflict and consciousness, in the English countryside 1700–1880', in M. Reed and R. Wells (eds), *Class, Conflict and Protest in the English Countryside 1700–1880* (London: Frank Cass, 1990), p. 158.
4 *Reading Mercury* (hereafter *RM*), 6 May 1795.
5 *RM*, 11 May 1795; M. Neuman, 'A suggestion regarding the origins of the Speenhamland Plan', *English Historical Review*, 84 (1969), 317; Wells, *Wretched Faces*, ch. 17; and 'Social protest', pp. 135–8. The Buckinghamshire and the Oxfordshire justices at their 1795 Epiphany Sessions also devised scale-based systems of income subsidies: S. and B. Webb, *The Parish and the County* (London: Longmans, 1906), pp. 546–7; S. and B. Webb, *English Poor Law History: The Old Poor Law* (London: Longmans, 1927), p. 177; J. and B. Hammond, *The Village Labourer* (London: Longmans, 1913), p. 163.
6 See J. Huzel, 'The labourer and the poor law, 1750–1850', in G. Mingay (ed.), *The Agrarian History of England and Wales, vol. 6, 1750–1850* (Cambridge: Cambridge University Press, 1989), p. 775.
7 M. Neuman, *The Speenhamland County: Poverty and the Poor Laws in Berkshire 1782–1834* (London: Garland, 1982), p. 165.
8 L. Hollen Lees, *The Solidarities of Strangers: The English Poor Laws and the People, 1700–1948* (Cambridge: Cambridge University Press, 1998); King, *Poverty and Welfare in England*; A. Kidd, *State, Society and the Poor in Nineteenth-Century England* (London: Macmillan, 1999).
9 For instance see: S. Shave, 'Review forum', *Cultural and Social History*, 6:1 (2009), 110.
10 C. Griffin, 'As Lated Tongues Bespoke: Popular Protest in South-East England, 1790–1840' (PhD dissertation, University of Bristol, 2002), pp. 142–5, 147–8, 154–5 and 160–1; Wells, 'Social protest', pp. 135–6; *Sussex Weekly Advertiser* (hereafter *SWA*), 2 December 1799.
11 R. Wells, 'Poor-law reform in the rural south-east; the impact of the 'Sturges Bourne Acts' during the agricultural depression, 1815–1835', *Southern History*, 23 (2001), 53; *Kentish Gazette* (hereafter *KG*), 4 December 1792.
12 *Hampshire Chronicle* (herafter *HC*), 26 April 1802; Surrey History Centre (hereafter SHC), 6672/2/1, Coulsdon Vestry Minute, 23 February 1805,
13 Centre for Kentish Studies (hereafter CKS), PS/Ma/4, Malling Petty Sessions Minute, 3 August 1795; CKS P408/8/2, Yalding Vestry Minute, 1 November

1800. For an examination of the dynamics of out parish relief see: S. King, '"It is impossible for our vestry to judge his case into perfection from here": managing the distance dimensions of poor relief, 1800–40', *Rural History*, 16:2 (2005), 161–89.

14 A. Kussmaul, *Servants in Husbandry in Early Modern England* (Cambridge: Cambridge University Press, 1981). For a recent (re)assertion of the persistence of living-in farm servants in the south see: A. Howkins and N. Verdon, 'Adaptable and sustainable? Male farm service and the agricultural labour force in midland and southern England, c.1850–1925', *Economic History Review*, 61:2 (2008), 467–95.

15 J. Broad, 'Parish economies of welfare, 1650–1834', *Historical Journal*, 42:4 (1999), 1003.

16 M. Neuman, *The Speenhamland County; Salisbury and Winchester Journal*, 23 February 1795.

17 S. Hindle, 'Dependency, shame and belonging: badging the deserving poor, c.1550–1750', *Cultural and Social History*, 1:1 (2004), 15–16; S. Hindle, 'Civility, honesty and the identification of the deserving poor in seventeenth-century England', in H. French and J. Barry (eds), *Identity and Agency in England, 1650–1800* (Basingstoke: Palgrave, 2004).

18 E.P. Thompson, 'The moral economy of the English crowd in the eighteenth century', *Past & Present*, 50 (1971), 108–9.

19 C Griffin, 'Becoming private property: custom, law, and the geographies of 'ownership' in 18th- and 19th-century England', *Environment and Planning A*, 42:3 (2010), 747–62.

20 P. King, 'Gleaners, farmers and the failure of legal sanctions in England, 1780 1850', *Past & Present*, 125 (1989), 116–50.

21 J. Neeson, *Commoners: Common Right, Enclosure and Social Change in England, 1700–1820* (Cambridge: Cambridge University Press, 1993).

22 D. Vaisey (ed.), *The Diary of Thomas Turner 1754–1765* (East Hoathly: CTR Publishing, 1994), pp. 67, 238–9.

23 Hampshire County Record Office (hereafter HCRO), 4M69 PV1, Eling Vestry minute, 18 February 1819.

24 K.D.M. Snell, 'The culture of local xenophobia', *Social History*, 28:1 (2003), 21–3.

25 J. Archer, *By a Flash and a Scare: Incendiarism, Animal Maiming, and Poaching in East Anglia 1815–1870* (Oxford: Oxford University Press, 1990), p. 14; T. Richardson, 'The agricultural labourers' standard of living in Lincolnshire, 1790–1840: social protest and public order', *Agricultural History Review*, 41:1 (1993), 1–19.

26 For instance at Selsey and Siddlesham, on the West Sussex coastal plain, local labourers combined in the summer of 1831 to protest against the engagement of 'west-country men' in the harvest: *Brighton Gazette* (hereafter *BG*), 28 July 1831.

27 The critical study remains T. Sockoll (ed.), *Essex Pauper Letters, 1731–1837* (Oxford: Oxford University Press, 2001). Also see A. Levene (ed.) *Narratives of the Poor in Eighteenth-Century Britain*, volume 1 ('Voices of the Poor: Poor Law Depositions and Letters') (London: Pickering and Chatto, 2006).

28 P. Jones, 'Swing, Speenhamland and rural social relations: the 'moral economy' of the English crowd in the nineteenth century', *Social History*, 32:3 (2007), 271–90.

29 F. O'Gorman, 'The Paine Burnings of 1792–1793', *Past & Present*, 193 (2006), 111–56; R. Wells, *Insurrection: The British Experience 1795–1803* (Gloucester: Alan Sutton, 1983).

30 *SWA*, 31 December 1792; *HC*, 21 March 1793.

31 G. Williams, *Artisans and Sans-Culottes: Popular Movements in France and Britain During the French Revolution* (London: Arnold, 1968), p. 67.

32 *HC*, 10 March 1800.

33 For Thatcher: TNA, Assi 94/1387, indictment of John Thatcher, Kent Lent Assizes 1794. Other notable examples of rural sedition include the case of John Hollis of Wateringbury, Kent, at the Kent Lent Assizes 1793, found guilty and imprisoned for three months for uttering seditious and treasonable expressions against the King and Government; see TNA, Assi 94/1374. For urban cases see *KG*, 5 February and 11 November, and *Maidstone Journal* (hereafter *MJ*), 18 June 1793.

34 BPP. Commons, 'Report from the Select Committee on Labourers Wages' (1824), vol. vi, Evidence of Rev. John Pratt, Sedlescombe, Sussex, 12 April 1824.

35 Snell, *Annals of the Labouring Poor*, p. 27.

36 HCRO, 15M84/Z3/61, Rev. Henry Wake, *Abuse of the Poor-Rate!! A Statement of Facts* (Andover, 1818); *HC*, 26 April 1819.

37 BPP. Commons, 'Report from the Select Committee on Labourers Wages' (1824), vol. vi; Wiltshire County Record Office, 1551/48, Poulshot Vestry Minute, 3 January 1827; CKS P45/8/2, Brenchley Vestry Minute, 9 February 1829.

38 *RM*, 15 January 1827.

39 BPP. Commons, 'Report from the Select Committee elating to the Employment or Relief of Able-bodied Persons from the Poor Rates' (1828), vol. iv.

40 BPP. Commons, 'Report from the Select Committee elating to the Employment or Relief of Able-bodied Persons from the Poor Rates' (1828), vol. iv, Evidence of Henry Boyce, overseer, Walderslade, 10 June 1828.

41 CKS P339/8/3, Smarden Vestry Minute, 6 November 1829.

42 T. Malthus, *An Essay on Population* (London: Johnson, 1798), p. 83.

43 Quoted in M. Blaug, 'The myth of the Old Poor law and the making of the new', *Journal of Economic History*, 23 (1963), 152.

44 BPP, 'Report from His Majesty's Commissioners for Inquiring into the Administration and Practical Operation of the Poor Laws', Appendix (B.1), Answers to Rural Queries, pt. 1 (1834), vol. XXX.

45 Webbs, *The Old Poor Law*, p. 172.

46 Blaug, 'The myth of the Old Poor Law', 176; G. Boyer, 'Malthus was right after all: poor relief and the birth rate in south-eastern England', *Journal of Political Economy*, 97:1 (1989), 93.

47 S. Williams, 'Malthus, marriage and poor law allowances revisited: a Bedfordshire case study, 1770–1834', *Agricultural History Review*, 52:1 (2004), 82.

48 S. Shave, 'The dependent poor? (re)constructing the lives of individuals 'on the parish' in rural Dorset, 1800–1832', *Rural History*, 20:1 (2009), 67–97.

49 HCRO, 43M67/PV1, Amport Vestry minutes, 17 January and 6 November 1816.

50 D. Baugh, 'The cost of poor relief in south east England', *Economic History Review*, 28:1 (1975), 60–4; Boyer, 'Malthus was right after all', 96.

51 E. Hobsbawm and G. Rudé, *Captain Swing* (London: Lawrence & Wishart, 1969), p. 75.

52 Wells, 'Poor-law reform'; Jones, 'Swing, Speenhamland and rural social relations', 284–5.

53 R. Wells, 'Historical trajectories: English social welfare systems, rural riots, popular politics, agrarian trade unions, and allotment provision, 1793–1896', *Southern History*, 25 (2003), 89.

54 See P. Brandon and B. Short, *The South-East from AD 1000* (London: Longman, 1990), pp. 226–31.

55 K. Snell, 'Agricultural seasonal unemployment, the standard of living, and women's work in the south and east, 1690–1860', *Economic History Review*, 34:3 (1981), 407–37.

56 A. Armstrong, *Farmworkers: A Social and Economic History 1770–1980* (London: Batsford, 1988), p. 64; G. Gleig, *The Chronicles of Waltham* (London: R. Bentley, 1835), pp. 80–1.

57 HCRO, 4M69/PV1, Eling Vestry Minute, 11 July 1816; Aggregated annual average based upon: BPP. 'Abstract of the Answers and Returns, pursuant to Act 51 Geo. 3, for taking an account of the population of Great Britain in 1811' and 'Abstract of the Answers and Returns, made in pursuance to Act 1 Geo. 4, for taking an account of the Population of Great Britain, 1821' (1812) vol. xi, p. 299; and (1822) vol. xv, p. 298.

58 Gleig, *Chronicles*, p. 81.

59 BPP. Commons, 'Report from the Select Committee to whom several petitions complaining of the depressed state of the Agriculture of the United Kingdom were referred' (1821), vol. ix (hereafter 'Agricultural Report'), Evidence of Edward Wakefield, general land agent and steward, 5 April 1821.

60 BPP. Commons, 'Agricultural report', Thomas Barton, clerk to the Battle Magistrates, 16 March 1821.

61 Hobsbawm and Rudé, *Captain Swing*, p. 74; BPP. Commons, 'Report from the Select Committee on Poor Rate Returns' (1823), vol. v, Appendix E, Observations of parish officers from Burwash.

62 *SWA*, 21 January; *Sussex Advertiser* (hereafter *SA*), 26 August 1822.

63 BPP. Commons, 'Report from the Select Committee on Poor Rate Returns' (1824), vol. vi, Appendix F, Observation of parish officers from Southwick, Sussex.

64 BPP. Commons, 'Report from the Select Committee on Poor Rate Returns' (1823), vol. v, Appendix E, Observations of parish officers from Burwash and Rogate, Sussex; and, Bentley, Hampshire. Hobsbawm and Rudé, *Captain Swing*, p. 74.

65 See D. Eastwood, *Government and Community in the English Provinces, 1700–1870* (Basingstoke: Macmillan, 1997), p. 45; Wells, 'Poor Law reform', 80–9.

66 BPP. Commons, 'Report from the Select Committee relating to the Employment or Relief of Able-Bodied Persons from the Poor Rates' (1828), vol. iv, Evidence of John Coats, West Grinstead; Henry Boyce, overseer, Walderslade, all 10 June; and, Mr Richard Martin, Shipley, Sussex, 11 June 1828.

67 East Sussex County Record Office (hereafter ESCRO), PAR 360/10/2/3, Hartfield Vestry Minute, 21 May 1826.

68 Berkshire Record Office, D/P 38/8/1, Cholsey Vestry Minute, 16 October 1823.

69 West Sussex County Record Office (hereafter WSCRO), Add. MSS 39,858, Diary of William Hall, excise officer, Elham, 1819–20.

70 For instance the Hoath (Kent) Vestry agreed that if any parish officer did not attend a meeting they would forfeit 2 shillings and if the guardian was absent he would forfeit 5 shillings: Canterbury Cathedral Archives, U3/119/8/3, Hoath Vestry minute, 27 September 1827.

71 S. Williams, 'Earnings, poor relief and the economy of makeshifts: Bedfordshire in the early years of the New Poor Law', *Rural History*, 16:1 (2005), 21–2.

72 J.P. Kay, 'Earnings of agricultural labourers in Norfolk and Suffolk', *Journal of the Royal Statistical Society*, 1 (1838), cited in B. Reay, *Rural Englands: Labouring Lives in the Nineteenth-Century* (Basingstoke: Palgrave, 2004), p. 73.

73 D. Davies, *The Case of Labourers in Husbandry Stated and Considered* (London: Robinson, 1795); F. Eden, *The State of the Poor* (London: White, 1797), vol. 3, appendix 12.

74 S. King, 'Making the most of opportunity: the economy of makeshifts in the early modern North', in S. King and A. Tomkins (eds), *The Poor in England 1700–1850: An Economy of Makeshifts* (Manchester: Manchester University Press, 2003), pp. 247–50. Wells has highlighted the importance of shopkeeper credit to southern labouring families, something that was usually paid off using harvest wages: 'Social protest' p. 160.

75 J. Humphries and S. Horrell, 'Old questions, new data, and alternative perspectives: families' living standards in the Industrial Revolution', *Journal of Economic History*, 52:3 (1992), 849–90.

76 L. Shaw-Taylor, 'Parliamentary enclosure and the emergence of an English agricultural Proletariat', *Journal of Economic History*, 61:3 (2001), 654.

77 For southern enclosure, see: J. Chapman and S. Seeliger, *Enclosure, Environment and Landscape in Southern England* (Stroud: Tempus, 2001). For the increased regulation of the New Forest see: C. Griffin, 'More-than-human histories and the failure of grand state schemes: sylviculture in the New Forest, England', *Cultural Geographies*, 17:4 (2010), 451–72.

78 P. King, 'Customary rights and women's earnings: the importance of gleaning to the rural labouring poor 1750–1850', *Economic History Review*, 44:3 (1991), 461–76, esp. 474. These figures, as King points out, broadly mirrored those collated by Davies and Eden in the 1790s.

79 *KG*, 8 October 1830.

80 King, *Poverty and Welfare in England*. For friendly societies see: M. Gorsky, 'The growth and distribution of English friendly societies in the early

nineteenth century', *Economic History Review*, 51:4 (1998), 489–511.
81 S. Barrett, 'Kinship, poor relief and the welfare process in early modern England', in King and Tomkins (eds), *The Poor in England*, pp. 199–227.
82 *Hampshire Courier*, 28 August 1815.
83 E. A. Wrigley, 'Men on the land and men in the countryside: employment in agriculture in early-nineteenth-century England', in L. Bonfield, R. Smith and K. Wrightson (eds), *The World We Have Gained: Histories of Population and Social Structure* (Oxford: Oxford University Press, 1986), pp. 295–336.
84 M. Reed, '"Gnawing it out": a new look at economic relations in nineteenth-century rural England', *Rural History*, 1:1 (1990), 83–94.
85 For an excellent study of the lives of domestic servants see: C. Steedman, *Labours Lost: Domestic Service and the Making of Modern England* (Cambridge: Cambridge University Press, 2009).
86 P. Sharpe, 'The female labour market in English agriculture during the the Industrial Revolution: expansion or contraction?', *Agricultural History Review*, 47:2 (1999), 161–81; N. Verdon, *Rural Women Workers in 19th-Century England: Gender, Work and Wages* (Woodbridge: Boydell & Brewer, 2002), pp. 98–131; Verdon, 'Hay, hops and harvest: women's work in agriculture in nineteenth-century Sussex', in N. Goose (ed.), *Women's Work in Industrial England: Regional and Local Perspectives* (Hatfield: Local Population Studies, 2007), pp. 76–96.
87 BPP. Commons, 'Report from the Select Committee relating to the Employment or Relief of Able-Bodied Persons from the Poor Rates' (1828), vol. iv, Evidence of Mr Lester, Minster, Sheppey, Kent; John Coats, West Grinstead, Sussex; Henry Boyce, overseer, Walderslade, Kent: all 10 June; and, Mr Richard Martin, Shipley, Sussex, 11 June 1828.
88 Thompson, 'The moral economy', 76–136.
89 Jones, 'Swing, Speenhamland and rural social relations'; A. Randall, *Before the Luddites: Custom, Community and Machinery in the English Woollen Industry 1776–1809* (Cambridge: Cambridge University Press, 1991), pp. 254–62; R. Wells, 'The moral economy of the English countryside', in. A. Randall and A. Charlesworth (eds), *Moral Economy and Popular Protest: Crowds, Conflict and Authority* (Basingstoke: Macmillan, 2000).
90 See Wells, *Wretched Faces*; and Andrew Charlesworth, *An Atlas of Rural Protest in Britain, 1548–1900* (London: Croom Helm, 1983), pp. 97–100.
91 E. Fox Genovese, 'The many faces of the moral economy: a contribution to a debate', *Past & Present*, 58 (1973).
92 *SWA*, 24 February 1800.
93 Wells, *Wretched Faces*, p. 426; TNA, Assi 94/1499, Indictment of William Brookes, labourer, Kent Summer Assizes 1800; TNA, HO 42/49, fos 359–60, Lord Leslie, Dorking to Portland, 7 March 1800; HCRO, Q9/1/481, Calendar for Hampshire Easter Quarter Sessions 1800; *SWA*, 21 April 1800; *RM*, 16 and 23 June 1800.
94 *SWA*, 26 November and 9 December 1799, and 20 January 1800; *MJ*, 8 and 29 October; *Salisbury and Winchester Journal*, 9 December 1799 and 17 February 1800; *London Gazette*, 31 December 1799; *HC*, 27 January, 3 and 17 February 1800; TNA, HO 42/49, fos 26–8, John Latham, Mayor of Romsey to Portland,

26 February; *KG*, 21 February 1800. For the resort to such relief practices, see Griffin, 'As Lated Tongues Bespoke', pp. 160–1.

95 Wells, 'Social protest', p. 158.

96 *The Times*, 1 October 1801.

97 *HC*, 13 December 1802; *KG*, 23 January 1810.

98 See C. Griffin, 'Knowable geographies? The reporting of incendiarism in the eighteenth- and early nineteenth-century English provincial press', *Journal of Historical Geography*, 32:1 (2006), 38–56.

99 *The Times*, 8 October 1823; *Kentish Post*, 7 December 1757.

100 *SWA*, 13 February 1804, 10 June 1805, and 11 July 1808; *KG*, 2 June 1807; *HC*, 15 June 1807. For an examination of the broader context see J. Rule (ed.), *British Trade Unionism; the Formative Years 1750–1850* (London: Longman, 1988).

101 TNA, HO 42/106, fos 307–8, L. Richmond, Custom House, London to John Briket Esq., Secretary of States Office, 13 April; *KG*, 17 Apr, 1810.

102 TNA, HO 42/106, fo 412, J. Funley, Canterbury to Freeling, 18 April 1810. For other responses see TNA, HO 42/106 and 107.

103 Thompson, 'The moral economy', 185.

104 Studies by Archer and Shakesheff have shown that while poaching was normally the preserve of the lone labourer, poaching by highly organised gangs became relatively more important in the early nineteenth century: J. Archer, 'Poaching gangs and violence: the urban-rural divide in nineteenth-century Lancashire', *British Journal of Criminology*, 39:1 (1999), 25–38; T. Shakesheff, *Rural Conflict, Crime and Protest: Herefordshire, 1800–1860* (Woodbridge: Boydell & Brewer, 2003), ch. 6.

105 TNA, HO 42/117, fos 448–9, William Milford, Pin Hill, Petworth to Ryder, 18 November; *SWA*, 25 November 1811.

106 *SWA*, 21 January and 25 November; TNA, Assi 94/1662, Indictment of Jane Nye, 15, Sussex Lent Assizes 1811.

107 *KG*, 7 May and 25 October; *MJ*, 2 April; Wells, 'Social protest', p. 159; A. Charlesworth, B. Short and R. Wells, 'Riots and Unrest', in F. Leslie and B. Short (eds), *An Historical Atlas of Sussex* (Chichester: Phillimore, 1999), p. 75; *Times*, 14 October 1816; HCRO, Q9/1/543 and 545, Indictment of Uriah Palmer, John Allen and William Rose, East Woodhay, and Calendar listing charge against David Harper and John Fleming, Alverstoke, Hampshire Midsummer Quarter Sessions 1816, and Calendar listing charge against Robert Giles and William Woods, Emsworth, Hampshire Epiphany Quarter Sessions 1817.

108 See A. Charlesworth, 'The spatial diffusion of rural protest: an historical and comparative perspective of rural riots in nineteenth-century Britain', *Environment and Planning D: Society and Space*, 1:3 (1983), 251–63.

109 *Maidstone Gazette*, 21 November 1815, 13 February and 12 March 1816.

110 Wells, 'Social protest', p. 158; Wells, 'The moral economy of the English countryside', p. 232.

111 *HC*, 10 July 1815, 1 July and 26 August; *Hampshire Telegraph* (hereafter *HT*), 1 July; TNA, Assi 94/1740, indictment of James Andrews for arson, Surrey Summer Assizes 1816.

112 *HT*, 23 December; *HC*, 30 December 1816 and 3 March 1817.

113 *The Times*, 18 March 1819.

114 N.E. Fox, 'The spread of the threshing machine in central southern England', *Agricultural History Review*, 26:1 (1978), 26–8.

115 J. Boys, *General View of the Agriculture of the County of Kent* (London: Board of Agriculture 1796), p. 50; Boys, *General View of the Agriculture of the County of Kent* (London: Board of Agriculture, 1806), p. 56, note.

116 A. and W. Driver, *General View of the Agriculture of the County of Hampshire* (London: Board of Agriculture, 1794); *HC*, 28 June 1802; C. Vancouver, *General View of the Agriculture of the County of Hampshire* (London: Board of Agriculture, 1810), pp. 106–13.

117 For events in East Anglia see: Charlesworth, *An Atlas of Rural*, pp. 146–7; A. Peacock, *Bread or Blood* (London: Victor Gollancz, 1965). Outside of these 'peaks' of rural protest incendiary attacks on threshing machines occurred at Droxford (Hampshire) in May 1820; Folkestone in July 1825 – thereby offering further evidence of the depth and persistence of popular antipathy to threshing machines in the Elham Valley; and at Bromley in October 1828: *HT*, 15 and 22 May; *HC*, 5 June 1820; *KG*, 19 July; *Kent Herald* (hereafter *KH*), 21 July 1825; *County Chronicle* (hereafter *CCh*), 14 October 1828.

118 *HC*, 4 June 1821; *MJ*, 26 March; *SWA*, 1 April; TNA, HO 64/1, fos 205–8, J. Gell, Lewes, to Edward Curteis, 15 May 1822.

119 *Maidstone Gazette*, 9 April, 14 May and 4 June; *HC*, 22 April and 13 May; *KG*, 12 April and 5 July; *Times*, 28 June; TNA, Assi 94/1849, indictment of John Wraith, Kent Summer Assizes 1822.

120 *HT*, 24 June; *KG*, 5 July 1822.

121 *KG*, 26 July and 13 September; TNA, HO 52/3, Solicitor to the *Maidstone Gazette*, to Peel, 23 July; *Maidstone Gazette*, 23 July; *MJ*, 30 July and 17 September 1822.

122 *MJ*, 20 August; *KG*, 13 September; *Maidstone Gazette*, 20 August and 17 September 1822.

123 *SA*, 11, 18 and 25 November, December 23 and 30; TNA, HO 64/1, fos 46–7 and 310–3, Charles Jenkin, Northiam, E.J. Curteis, Battle, both to Peel, 13 November; TNA, Assi 94/1856, indictments of John Carter, David Saunter, and William Saunter for riotous assembly, Charles Weston and George Eastwood for arson, 'Complaint' against John Morgan for spreading fire, Sussex Winter Assizes 1822.

124 *MJ*, 12 November 1822.

125 *BG*, 4 September and 2 October; *Southampton Herald*, 6 October 1823; E. Jones, *Seasons and Prices: the Role of the Weather in English Agricultural History* (London: Allen & Unwin, 1965), pp. 162–3.

126 *HC*, 29 December; *BG*, 27 November 1823; *SA*, 24 March 1824. The exception that proves the rule occurred in the form of a harvest dispute at Aldingbourne: *Sussex and Surrey Chronicle*, 24 September 1823.

127 *BG*, 28 October and 2 December; *HT*, 5 July, 30 August, 6 and 13 September; *The Times*, 10 September 1824.

128 The use of rockets suggests the antagonists were smugglers, rockets normally being used to signal the landing of a cargo. *KH*, 11 November 1824; *SA*, 10 January 1825.

129 TNA, Assi 94/1956, indictment of Thomas Fulker for cutting hop bines, Kent Winter Assizes 1826; *KH*, 28 July 1825, 25 May, 6 and 27 July, and 15 September; *KG*, 2 and 15 September 1826.

130 *HC*, 11 December 1826; ESCRO, QR/E/796 and QR/E/798, Indictment of George Elphick, Francis Foord, Leonard Pearson and Levy Pearson for combination and assault, 3 May 1828, and Indictment of Jesse Gorringe and George Sayers for assault, 2 December 1828.

131 *KH*, 17 May; *MJ*, 7 August 1827.

132 *BG*, 20 September 1827

133 *KH*, 18 May 1826, 15 March; *CCh*, 22 May 1827.

3

Something before Swing or Swing itself?

When did Swing start? Such a seemingly straightforward question has produced several answers. What unites Swing's historians is an acceptance that the protests of 1830 represented something more than a random outpouring of feeling. The attacks on threshing machines, incendiary fires and 'mobbings' had different stimuli from place to place, but were all essentially driven by a desire to improve the rural worker's lot. While Swing deployed many different protest forms, there is something approaching unanimity among Swing's historians that the breaking of threshing machines was its most 'characteristic' form. From this position, it is possible to state that Swing started in the Elham area of East Kent in August 1830. Beyond this widely endorsed belief, similar claims could be made for series of attacks on threshing machines elsewhere. A wave of threshing machine-breaking in the early months of 1829 in the area between Finchingfield and Toppesfield (Essex) provoked considerable alarm among both the local and national authorities.[1] Threshing machine-breaking also occurred in the mid-Suffolk parishes of Ashbocking, Otley, Stonham Aspal and Wetheringsett during the autumn of 1829.[2] Despite his earlier pronouncement that these protests meant Swing 'started a year earlier in East Anglia', John Archer more recently suggested that these protests represented an intensification of protest activity rather than a coherent movement.[3] Elsewhere, an 'anti-threshing machine spirit' was manifested at Handsworth near Sheffield in November 1829, the 'flail users' being 'disconcerted' at the arrival of a travelling threshing machine.[4] Again, this was localised, neither diffusing beyond the vicinity nor inspiring protests elsewhere. Similarly, a wave of incendiary fires centred on the Essex market town of Witham did not stimulate protests beyond the locality.[5]

Seriously deficient harvests in 1829 and 1830 meant that the influx of migrant Irish workers represented serious competition for the reduced demand for harvest workers, and in a local 'culture of xenophobia' migrants were especially vulnerable to attack.[6] Indeed, such attacks were critical to Swing's pre-history. In the south-east (reported) attacks on Irish labourers occurred in the dockland community of Rotherhithe, presumably a place of entry for migrants, and repeatedly in the area between Brighton and Eastbourne. One attack at Jevington was particularly ferocious, the sleeping Irish being attacked at 2 a.m. by a volley of flints.[7] On the Kent-Surrey borders it was employers rather than the migrant labourers who were targeted, farmers employing Irish labourers in the early hay harvest were subjected incendiarism and violent threats.[8]

The next recorded attacks in Kent occurred in the Isle of Thanet, one of the places where reaping usually commenced in England.[9] According to Cobbett, at the start of the harvest 'several scores of … wretched slaves poured' into Thanet and quickly struck a bargain with the local farmers. Their agreement to reap the harvest at half the rate of their English counterparts was immediately seized upon by the local labourers:

> Feeling the injustice of this … took the giving of redress into their own hands. They armed themselves with what they called BATS; they went to the several barns, where the poor Irish fellows were <u>snoozled</u> … roused them up, and told them, that they must *march out of the Island*. The poor Irish fellows remonstrated, but remonstrances were in vain. At last it came to actual force; and though the attacked party had hooks and knives, these were of little avail against the <u>bats</u> … The invaders were thus marched in bands to a bridge at one corner of the Island … with an injunction not to return into the Island on pain of the <u>bat</u>, of which several of them had just had a taste by way of warning.[10]

Intriguingly, there is no record of attacks on the 'influx' of labourers from the Weald of Kent into Thanet, or on migrant harvest workers from other parts of East Kent. One such East Kent migrant to the Thanet harvest was Ingram Swaine, one of the seven Elham men subsequently prosecuted in the first machine-breaking trial. It was later alleged that while in Thanet, Swaine had received 'reports … from Men from the Weald' – an allusion to the protests in the vicinity of Sevenoaks – which emboldened him to instigate the machine-breaking campaign at Elham.[11] It is striking, though, that when the harvest started in the vicinity of Elham, the 'influx of reapers' from both the Weald and Ireland was greeted with 'perfect goodwill'.[12] John and Barbara Hammond and, more recently, John Rule and Roger Wells have repeated Cobbett's claim that the Thanet attacks represented 'Swing's first real manifestation'.[13]

Swing's most famous treatment, Hobsbawm and Rudé's *Captain Swing*, made several seemingly contradictory statements as to Swing's beginnings. Before analysing their pronouncements, it is instructive to consider their tabulations of protest incidents. While these tables are, as subsequent historians have related, deficient, they nonetheless offer some useful insights into Hobsbawm and Rudé's thinking. The first incidents detailed were the sending of threatening letters at Mildenhall, Brandon (both Suffolk) and Chipping Campden (Gloucestershire) in February, March and April, respectively. These events were followed by the destruction of mills used by the Orpington overseer to employ the parish poor on 10 April, and a political demonstration at Rye on 28 May. The first incident which is analysed in the body text of *Captain Swing* occurred on 1 June when farmer Mosyer of Orpington had his ricks fired.[14]

Mosyer's fire marked the first of Hobsbawm and Rudé's five phases of Kentish protest. It was a protest form, they claimed, that had 'been practised' before, 'even in this part of England', but was not the 'characteristic' form of unrest. If incendiary fires had recent precedence, the attack on threshing machines in Kent was a 'bolt from the blue'. These attacks, they suggested, marked the start of what would later be known as Swing.[15] Their interpretation has received support from Swing's most recent historians, including Archer who claimed that what marked these protests out as different was their sustained nature *and* their subsequent diffusion beyond the locality.[16]

Cobbett's prophecy

By the mid-1820s Cobbett had begun to prophesise 'a major rural rebellion'. By 1828 he placed a date on this insurrection: the winter of 1830–31.[17] This was not some off-hand, never-to-be-repeated assertion. Through the vehicle of his *Political Register*, Cobbett frequently returned to his prediction. For instance, in March 1830 on reporting the Kent county meeting calling for parliamentary reform, he noted that the efforts of the 'aristocracy' to prevent the adoption of a more strongly worded reform petition than that which had initially been mooted had failed. 'The haughty and oppressive hierarchy there got a blow, which ought to prepare it for other blows.'[18]

While other commentators did not have Cobbett's ability to accurately predict dates, many concurred that rebellion was likely. By July 1829, the Tory *Brighton Gazette* concluded a report on agricultural distress by stating that 'the evil day is not far distant'.[19] Such grandiose statements were grounded in observable phenomena. Although it is possible to take most years of the post-Napoleonic period and find pitiful accounts of unemployment, decay and depression, reports from late 1828 to the summer of 1830 were both more frequent and more severe. The harvest of 1828 had been an almost unmitigated disaster, with 'scarcely one dry day'.[20] Reduced opportunities for field work during the harvest and for threshing during the winter were further exacerbated by a deepening depression in rural trades.[21] This situation begat desperation, which in turn begat dire prophecies. A seemingly apocryphal case was reported from the Somerset Easter Quarter Sessions. When George Gray was sentenced to transportation for stealing some knives, he exclaimed to the judge, 'Thank ye, Sir; that's just want I wanted; I shall have now bread for life!'[22]

The situation in the English west was undoubtedly worse than in the south-east, but some areas of the south-east were hit particularly hard. Stockbridge and Whitchurch were important centres in the clothing trades, while larger south-eastern towns had pockets of industry, for instance the soon to be notorious Tasker's Iron Foundry at Andover and Baker's huge veneer saw mill at Southampton. Dockland communities also hosted a wide range of supporting manufacturers and services.[23] Doom-laden pronouncements were not made of the south-east until the second half of 1829, but parishes were, as was the case at Westbourne on the Sussex-Hampshire border, experiencing increases in unemployment.[24]

Another wretchedly wet summer brought the depth of depression in the English west to the south-east. In the 'lower parts' of Kent and Sussex the dismal harvest had left, according to the *Brighton Gazette*, the 'peasantry ... distressed beyond measure', a report echoed in the Kent press who noted that farmers were now subjected to nightly 'depredations'. Perhaps not surprisingly, there was thought to be a developing 'mania' for emigration among these small farmers, the Weald in particular was reportedly saw an 'exodus' of petty agriculturalists to America in early 1830. On the Isle of Wight the 'general want of employment' and 'extreme pressure of the times' had 'demoralise[d] the lower classes' and 'occasioned robberies and depredations'. The hop harvest also proved to be a disaster. Migrant hop-pickers were likely, in the apocryphal words of the *Hampshire Chronicle*, to get the 'ague and sickness' but no job.[25]

If the wet summer and autumn had contributed to universal distress and claims that applications for relief were at record levels, little prepared rural workers and vestries for the oncoming winter. It proved unremittingly cold, with 'extreme' frosts and snows that covered the last part of the 1829 harvest, and not clearing until the early spring. The freeze stopped all outdoor work, field workers and bricklayers alike were thrown off work. The impact of the prolonged cold also meant that the expenditure necessary to heat dwellings rose, forcing up the prices of coals and faggots, dramatically impacting rural workers' household budgets.[26]

Declining incomes and rising fuel costs acted to squeeze the poor to a point beyond subsistence. Town after town entered into subscriptions to set up soup kitchens, while the rural gentry's usual wintertime acts of beneficence were more extensive than usual. Typical were schemes at the 'open' and 'closed' Hampshire parishes of West Meon and Hursley. At the former, £40 was raised in a voluntary subscription – without gentry backing – and distributed to the poor in blankets, clothing and some little fuel. At the latter, Sir William Heathcote ordered the granting of several hundred pairs of blankets in addition to the 'usual' supply of wheat 'and other arts' to the 'most necessitous families'.[27] There is precious little evidence, though, that rural vestries tackled the (short-term) crises, despite their members successfully clamouring for lower tithes and farm rents. This apparent inhumanity of rural vestrymen – overwhelmingly farmers – refuted Cobbett's Old Englander assertion that 'it is not we [farmers] who are the cause of their sufferings'. Indeed, the merciless response(s) by vestries to the severity of the winter were invoked by many 'Swing' activists in justifying their actions. Support for such a view was expressed, albeit tacitly, by a Surrey magistrate to a meeting of fellow justices gathered at the County Epiphany Quarter Sessions. The Surrey gaol allowance was more than agricultural labourers could earn in a day, thereby provoking labourers to commit crimes for the sole purpose of being provided for in gaol. As the *Kentish Gazette* put it in July 1830, 'men are becoming daily more estranged from their masters and depredations are nightly committed on property'.[28]

Pauperism

At the root of this 'evil', according to one west Kent overseer, was idleness. Having no work for his 40 charges, he set them to play at cricket from 6 a.m. to 6 p.m. During the course of play, a village satirist anonymously published a notice:

> Now playing ... a match of cricket between twenty-two gentlemen ... to play till six o'clock this evening, and to conclude with *Grinning through Horse Collars* by those who have Poor Rates to pay; and *Jingling Matches* for those who have got any thing in their pockets to jingle.

If the match continued for several days, mocked the *Kentish Gazette*, 'the poor cricketers will find play is quite as fatiguing as work'.[29] Whether this report reached Cobbett is not known, but it would have added further weight to his belief that ratepayers viewed labourers 'not as men ... but merely as animals made for their service and sport'.[30]

If unemployment had not reached the catastrophic levels of western English towns, it nevertheless exacted a huge sociological, psychological and financial toll in the south-east. In February 1830 it was noted that even the parishes of Bosham, Bersted, Bognor and Felpham on the highly capitalised West Sussex coastal plains were spending on average £40 a month on supporting the unemployed. Here, a group of young men could be witnessed daily dragging gravel carts the two miles from the beach to the roads. 'Unfortunately', lamented the *Hampshire Chronicle*, 'many similar instances might be adduced'.[31] This situation was most acute in the Weald where labourers were in a deplorable state, openly declaring that so long as there was anything to eat they would steal it so as not to starve. To this end, rural workers were 'all now confederates, so that detection is scarcely possible'. Central to the formation of confederacies was the practice of employing men on the roads. By midsummer, the 'evil' had advanced to such an extent that the practice of working labourers in gangs was stopped in many parishes.[32]

It was not just the victims of plunder who viewed road working as socially dangerous. Cobbett, the labourers' champion, took a similar line. From the passing of Sturges-Bourne's Bill, Cobbett had persistently harangued government and county elites for not offering any palliative to ease field workers' sufferings. His campaign was stepped up in the winter of 1829–30. A speech given by the Duke of Richmond in the House of Lords on 25 February 1830 was effectively the first public admittance by the nobility that 'the once happy peasantry of England' were degraded to the state of the brute creation' through their being 'harnessed to wagons' to draw loads of stone on the roads. The Earl of Stanhope concurred: if labourers were unable to 'obtain a livelihood by the exercise of honest industry, nor support from the estate on which they were placed, [he] would at once endeavour to put an end to a state of things so intolerable and enforce through the power of their numbers, a division of the land'. Cobbett, keen to prevent this 'last stage', instead proffered that something should be done, for it was 'real madness; it is not error, but real madness, to imagine that the thing will *mend itself*. Revolution could not be held off by calls to the labourers' – in the words of the Bishop of Bath and Wells – 'Christian heroism'. Labourers' needed more than just 'a small piece of land' to 'make up for all'.[33]

Cobbett noted that the level of labouring protests against the operation of the poor law had already increased. One such incident at Bethersden, Kent, neatly expresses these immediate pre-Swing anxieties. Mr Lansdell, the assistant overseer, had already received several threatening letters before, while attending a parish meeting at the Bull Inn on the night of 16 February, being peppered with shot. Having turned his head to one side, Lansdell escaped unhurt. The parish had adopted a system of 'spade husbandry' to engage the unemployed labourers who were paid by the piece – a practice that generated 'much irritation'. Two months later the culprit was discovered. George Balcomb, a labourer whom the parish was assisting to emigrate to America, admitted on his departure that he had fired at Lansdell using a pistol he had stolen from a local gentleman. No attempt was made to detain him.[34]

Such protests were not confined to the Weald. One particularly instructive case occurred at Pevensey, near Eastbourne. For some time, overseer Hollands had been subject to abuse and threats by 'several single pauper men'. In January 1830 threats turned to bodily violence. As usual, several men employed on the roads went to Hollands' house to receive their weekly 'wages', this time, however, they forced their way into his house and refused to leave until he paid them at the rate set down in the vestry. A scuffle ensued, with Hollands being 'roughly handled' and subjected to 'very abusive' language. Although the vestry wanted to 'make an example' of the three men, they were discharged and proceeded to intimidate Hollands anew. Again, they besieged his house, refusing to leave until he set them to work or relieved them.[35]

Protest and politics

According to social movement theorist Sidney Tarrow, 'when we reconstruct cycles of protest from both public records and private memories, the peaks that leave indelible impressions in the public consciousness are really only the high ground of broader swells of mobilization that rise and fall from the doldrums of compliance to waves of mobilization more gradually than popular memory recognises'.[36] In relation to English rural protest, before and after the peaks of 'movement' activity – the Bread or Blood Riots of 1816, the East Anglian protests of 1822, Swing – we would expect a steady rise and a gradual fall in protest activity. Protest movements are, so the model suggests, defined by the point at which the level of protest activity begins to increase and the point when protest activity again assumes a steady level. These understandings have important implications for thinking through the start of Swing. While there might be a lead-in period to the existence of a fully fledged movement, this period can only be recognised retrospectively as laying its foundational conditions.

As noted in Chapter 2, incendiarism was a useful proxy for the level of protest, with the 'crisis' years of 1816 and 1822 witnessing record levels. However, in 1829, a total of 23 cases were uncovered compared to 20 fires identified for 1822. The archive for the period from the start of 1830 to 24 August details 26 fires. Clearly, in terms of trajectory from the 14 and 13 fires recorded in 1827 and 1828 respectively, the level of protest in the 20 months before the start of intensive machine-breaking in Kent would appear to be quantitatively different. And perhaps in terms of the deepening of social tensions, the period was also qualitatively different. Incendiarism, as will be detailed, with the exception of events on the Isle of Sheppey in the winter of 1829–30 and in the environs of Sevenoaks in the summer of 1830, was not the most reliable indicator of general tensions. While it occurred relatively more frequently than before, it is striking that of the cases recorded in 1829, ten occurred in the final three months of the year. When combined with the frequent acts of animal maiming and serious malicious damage, it is apparent that a widespread and deepening bitterness had befallen the south-east. Assaults on overseers, clergymen, farmers and tithe collectors, relatively infrequent occurrences in the earlier 1820s, now also occurred with greater regularity – at least during the early months of 1829 and 1830.[37]

Collective protests in 1829 and early 1830 were, taking the region as a whole, no more common than they had been during the previous ten years. Some protests were clearly outpourings of feeling, such as the actions of a group of lads who openly broke gas lamps, gratings and young trees at Lewes in May 1830. Other events used dates in the customary calendar to mask attacks on the property of odious individuals, such as at Romsey, when the customary Gunpowder Plot celebrations ended in a 'riot' and the destruction of many windows. Others betrayed specific socio-economic and community tensions, for instance an affray among the workmen digging a canal at Tunbridge Wells in May 1829 and a 'riot' between hop pickers at Chart Sutton five months later.[38] Behind these outbreaks of open protest lay a deepening sense that a tipping point was close. A petition forwarded to the Home Office from the dockland community of Queenborough on the Isle of Sheppey in August 1829 graphically demonstrated this creeping desperation: 'We can work, we wish to work, we will work, but we cannot work as slaves hired by the Man.'[39]

The East Sussex port of Rye was arguably the place where the balance between bitter recriminations and open protest tipped first. Landowners – many of whom were also commissioners of Rye harbour, despite living 'many miles from the town' – had recently erected a £2,000 sluice on the River Rother to prevent 9,000 acres from flooding at high tide. It also had the unfortunate side effect of lowering the water levels in the harbour to such an extent that it was impossible for Rye's extensive fleet of fishing vessels to navigate. During the night of 26 February, a body of men, accompanied by a band of music, marched to the sluice and all but destroyed it. They returned on the morning of 28 February to complete their work. Magistrate Herbert Curteis was soon on the spot to read the Riot Act. This was ignored until the Coastal Blockade (the dedicated anti-smuggling force stationed between Sheerness and Chichester), arrived, acting to disperse the sluice-breakers. In a state of dismay, Curteis wrote to Home Secretary Peel asking what he should do with any people he might take into custody, as 'they believe they have a legal right to do what they are doing'.

This 'right' was not something derived from customary practices but, as would later occur with threshing machine-breaking in Kent, from popular interpretations of a legal judgment. The erection of the sluice had been made possible by a private bill that had passed through Parliament in a 'hurried manner'. This, in turn, led to an application to the Court of Chancery by the residents of Rye who had no time to express any opposition to the bill. Chancery decreed that the sluice was 'a nuisance', and before any further legal proceedings were made, the parishioners of Rye, in the words of the Solicitor General, took 'the law into their own hands'.

Agitation was renewed on 28 April when a mob again descended on the repaired sluice. Once more, Curteis read the Riot Act and called for military assistance, a force stationed locally on Peel's insistence. Although the mob dispersed, the next day about 1,000 people reassembled near the harbour and, armed with various weapons, finally destroyed the sluice, filling the outer harbour with water. By the time the military arrived, the people had dispersed. A Bow Street officer was duly dispatched, and six 'ringleaders' apprehended for trial at the next Sussex Assizes. It was the intervention of the military on the 28 April rather than the arrests that prompted complaints. The Rye parishioners believing that Curteis had acted improperly in calling for military assistance, he being one of the landowners with an interest in the sluice, launched a petition which was presented to the House of Commons by Rye MP Colonel Evans. His involvement, and support of the petition in a speech to the Commons on 27 May, occurred against a backdrop of petitioning against his return to Parliament.[40]

A subsequent plan to blow up the Western Bridge at Rye in early June was foiled by officers of the Coastal Blockade who discovered a stash of explosives. The precise motivation for this planned attack remains unclear. Disturbance again erupted in July with a campaign by the so-called 'Free-Born Association' to widen the right to elective franchise. On Monday 12 July – coinciding with the dissolution of Parliament – the association paraded through the streets, later to be addressed by Dr Lamb, the Mayor and unsuccessful candidate. Lamb, somewhat foolishly, lavished the crowds with strong beer. The resulting fracas took a decidedly partisan turn with drunken quarrels between Lamb's supporters and those of the successful Colonel Evans.[41]

This combination of open demonstration and covert terrorism was also, albeit far less dramatically, deployed at Ardingly. Protests supposedly started in late September 1829 with the destruction of the windows of a cottage recently erected by Rev. Hamilton. For many years Hamilton had taken the tithes in kind but had recently 'farmed them out' to ex-army officer Mr Rogers whose subsequent zealous collection of tithes on garden produce made him obnoxious to the poor. The extent of popular revulsion to Rogers was made clear when he received several threatening letters, which were reinforced on the evening of 10 October as his stack-yard was set aflame. Rogers had done nothing to improve his standing in the parish by using a machine to thrash out his tithings – that the machine was destroyed in the conflagration was surely no coincidence. The crowd gathered at the fire basked in the reflected glory, refusing to assist in extinguishing the flames. Earlier on the day of the fire, 150 of the Ardingly poor had also marched, armed with bludgeons in a 'very threatening' manner, to the Cuckfield bench of magistrates to state their opposition to a vestry scheme. Their children, they related, were taken from their homes and placed into the care of the farmers for whom they would labour for their keep.[42]

The other major centre of agitation was the Isle of Sheppey. On 23 October 1829 a fire destroyed much of Mr Kemsley's Eastchurch farm, for which Kemsley was later indicted at the Kent Winter Assizes on a charge of attempting to defraud the Phoenix fire insurance office. One of Kemsley's labourers was actually on the farm when the fire broke out, attempting, so he claimed, to steal corn, and witnessed Kemsley setting fire to one of his own wheat stacks. The case, however, was thrown out by the grand jury as it transpired that this witness had quarrelled with Kemsley over pay before the fire. This was, suspicions suggested, a malicious prosecution. Moreover, it was no coincidence, claimed the *Kentish Gazette*, that Kemsley's barn contained a threshing machine. Between the Eastchurch fire and Kemsley's committal a further two fires occurred at neighbouring Minster, one on the farm of Baldwin Howe, and the other on the farm of Jeremiah Bigg. The fires prompted a meeting on 9 November to discuss what steps to take to guard against incendiaries. The meeting was too late, though, to prevent another two fires on 8 November: a second fire on Jeremiah Bigg's premises, and one on his father's farm at Minster. Moreover, in mid-July another incendiary fire had occurred at a Sheerness coal merchant's store. These pre- and post-harvest fires were, reckoned the *Kent and Essex Mercury*, all connected.[43]

Swing-like portents can be read in all three pockets of resistance. The Rye and Ardingly protests combined open and covert protest, customary ritual and a popular hatred of new technologies, the Sheppey fires also targeted machinery and unpopular employers. But none of the areas were centres of protest in the autumn and winter

1830. Indeed, all three areas were remarkable for their quiescence among the surrounding ferment. Still, Cobbett seized on such events as evidence that 'all is going on just as I anticipated', 'everywhere is the same, all is deadly ruin and misery'. And yet, as Monju Dutt correctly asserted, the gentry reacted with 'passive indifference' to these warning signs, being preoccupied with the continental revolutions.[44]

Evidence is mixed as to whether the gentry were alert to radical calls from even relatively small south-eastern parishes. A reform meeting at Buckland, near Dover, drew up a petition calling for the removal of all sinecures; an investigation into public grants; a reduction of tithes, taxes (including on newspapers), duties, and the standing army; suffrage for *all* taxpayers; and, for individuals to hold a maximum of one government post at once. This was a manifesto almost identical to Cobbett's, but, tellingly, predated the 'model' petition he circulated in September. There being a paper mill at Buckland, it is likely that notoriously political paper makers were instrumental in framing the petition. The same could not be said of a petition drafted by 'labourers' in defiantly agrarian Nether Wallop (Hampshire). As noted, even the Kent county meeting adopted a radically tinged petition calling for, among other things, the appropriation of all church property for 'national purposes'. The Kentish gentry might have failed to suppress the petition – but they tried.[45]

It is important to note that these coteries of radicals had not emerged overnight. While it is doubtful whether the wave of radical activity in the 1790s left a lasting legacy in the countryside, as it had in the larger towns, the experience of the post-Napoleonic depression acted to politicise some rural workers. As Ian Dyck noted in his study of Cobbett and rural culture, the 1820s were marked by a 'battle for the pedlar's pack', competition necessitating accessible and relevant writings for rural markets. That Cobbett's *Political Register* flourished and he found ready markets for his other outputs attests to both his success and the demand for radical political writings. Indeed, as early as 1821, the East Sussex Bench attempted to check the circulation of 'seditious publications' in its primarily agricultural realm. By 1830, many villages, if not every village as Cobbett claimed, contained committed Cobbettites and determined reformers.[46]

In addition to his widely circulated writings, Cobbett also energetically launched into a southern lecture tour to support his cause. Having only recently toured the west, his efforts were to be confined, starting in July, to Kent – 'to see how the lads come on there' – and then from mid-October starting at Battle and moving through Sussex and into Hampshire.[47] The latter tour was a direct response not to the reform crisis, but to the protests that had started in Kent. Before then, a series of fires occurred on the Kent-Sussex-Surrey borders, which would have widespread implications.

The Sevenoaks fires

In the late spring of 1830, Home Office attention was drawn to a series of incendiary fires in the vicinity of Sevenoaks. An initial fire at the Hasons Hill brewery of Messrs Tape and Davis on 29 May was not at first thought to be malicious, but when farmer Mosyer's ricks and barn were destroyed three days later at nearby Orpington, suspicions were raised. When three further fires in that parish occurred between 3 and 8 June, the County Fire Office offered a £100 reward, which levered the services of a London police officer and a 'pardon' from the Home Office. Phillip Porter, a wheelwright's apprentice, was subsequently charged with two counts of arson at the Kent Summer Assizes. The trial rested on the evidence of William Boxall, an unemployed labourer, who claimed that Porter had, a few days before one of the fires, stated in conversation that: 'There will be a damned good one in the middle of the place.' Boxall, on asking where Porter meant, was told 'up at Mayfield, where all the ploughs and harrows are kept'. Boxall's evidence was discredited – 'I say many things when I am tipsy, which I forget when I become sober' – and Porter was acquitted.[48]

Orpington was also the location of three earlier attacks on a corn mill used by the assistant overseer to employ those out of work. After a lengthy trial at the West Kent Easter Quarter Sessions, William Eldridge, who had been employed on the mill, was found guilty. Portentously, he was sentenced to nine months imprisonment 'to teach others by the example made of you, that ... if they attempt to interrupt the working of a mill or any machinery ... they will be visited by a severe sentence'.[49]

Before Porter's trial, a further fire occurred in the neighbourhood of Orpington, this time on Mr Lore's Shoreham farm on 29 June. The government added to the £100 reward offered by Lore, and – surely this was no coincidence – offered a pardon *after* Porter's acquittal.

Fires also occurred to the south of Orpington, the first targeting Mrs Fuller's barnyard at East Grinstead, the second Mr Swasland at Riverhead.[50] Three further fires occurred on three consecutive days from 1 August, at Chiddingstone, Caterham in Surrey, and magistrate Thompson's Sundridge farm. The investigation into these fires lasted well into 1831. Stephen Gower, the occupant at the time of the Caterham fire, was indicted at the Surrey Summer Assizes, 'creating a great sensation throughout the county'. It was alleged that Gower had set fire to the thatch of the threshing-machine house and a barn where many of the Irish labourers employed by Gower had taken up temporary residence. Other than the statement of a convicted sheep-stealer, given in an attempt to avoid the gallows, the evidence was purely circumstantial. The insolvent Gower did not help his case by selling the rest of his property and quitting his tenancy soon after the fire. On concluding the evidence, the jury immediately acquitted Gower.[51]

After a further fire on Thompson's farm while he was attending the Assizes on 9 August,[52] there were no more until the 20 August when magistrate Masters' farm at Sundridge was targeted. His premises, it was said, had been 'several times attempted to be destroyed', though no evidence exists detailing the earlier attacks. Four days later, Mrs Minet, 'a lady of fortune', became the latest victim in the area when her Brasted farm was fired. Reports that she was 'quiet and unlikely to have given offence' highlight the huge gulf between the way rural workers perceived the wealthy and how the wealthy *thought* they were perceived by the poor. Thompson and Masters, however, were thought to have been targeted for suppressing smuggling and poaching, 'the joint occupations' of 'many persons in the neighbourhood'.[53] Just as worrying as the fires – three more fires occurring on the night of 1–2 September – was the fact that many people were unprepared to help extinguish the conflagrations. As a Sevenoaks correspondent claimed:

> The expressions of the mob are dreadful: they said 'Damn it, let it burn, I only wish it was a house: We can warm ourselves now: We only want some potatoes, there is a nice fire to cook them by!'

At Minet's fire on 1 September, the pipes of the attendant fire engines were so badly cut that they were rendered useless, and pails had to be passed along a half-mile human chain.[54]

Further fires at Cowden and Brasted were followed by signs that plebeian discontent was not going to be confined to incendiarism.[55] In the first week of September, the 'peasantry' at Wrotham were reported to be in a state of 'turbulence', while several farmers in the vicinity of the fires received threatening letters. 'Poor' widow Huble of Ide Hill was threatened that if she was out late at night she would get a 'rap on the head' and that her house would be set on fire. Mr Morphew at Sevenoaks received a similar letter threatening not only to set fire to his house but also to also to set the town alight at both ends. Mr Nourvelle was warned that if he went to Mr Tong's fire – 'so that no doubt he will soon have one', lamented the press – he would have his head broken but that his house was going to be set on fire either way. Magistrate Manning in writing to inform the Home Office of Minet's second fire, claimed that he believed his farmyard was the next object of attack. Clearly, the fires and letters generated considerable alarm.[56]

The first letter to the Home Office requesting assistance from the local magistracy came from Manning who insisted that some 'effectual measures' were needed to stop the attacks. He was duly summoned to London to meet an (unnamed) Whitehall clerk. Their 'long conversation' established that the fear generated by the frequent fires would partially be overcome by the local billeting of a Bow Street officer. In return, the local magistracy would hold a meeting to discuss the developing crisis.[57] The meeting was held on 11 September and resolved that an association for the 'detection of incendiaries and the protection of property' be established – the first such society in the south-east. A subscription was established to fund a 'sub-committee' in every parish in the division, while Peel secured the offering of a pardon in all cases of arson in their jurisdiction.[58]

In mid-September two individuals were arrested at Maresfield, on the fringe of Ashdown Forest, on suspicion of being the Sevenoaks incendiarists. Committing magistrate William Day immediately informed the Sevenoaks Bench, who, unsuccessfully, wrote to the Home Office to request the dispatch of a police officer to assist Day.[59] The public invisibility of the judicial efforts generated considerable hostility towards the authorities, not least from the victims of incendiarism. Mr Nourvelle, ignoring the threats he received, went in person to the Home Office in an attempt to procure military support, while Mr Sandford of Farningham noted that 'the Magistrates seem paralyzed'. If the government did not 'take the lead and sanction the arming of the Bourgeois classes', he continued, the vacuum in authority would be filled with 'illegal' associations for the protection of property, 'especially with the example of the Continent before their eyes'.[60]

Despite the refusal, Day continued his enquiries. On 21 October, Day informed Peel that Charles Blow, a vagrant, and Mary Ann Johnson, a 10-year-old girl 'of intelligence and cunning far beyond her age', had been committed to Lewes House of Correction as rogues and vagabonds for three months. For, despite strong suspicions against Blow, the evidence was not sufficient to warrant a commitment for arson. Day believed that Johnson had used her extensive knowledge of several of the fires, including Minet's and Harvey's, to turn 'the full weight of her Evidence against Blow to shield her father and mother' who were, Day alleged, the principal perpetrators. On these suspicions, Day apprehended the girl's parents and a grown-up sister, all of who were also committed as vagrants. Unsure what to do next, Day asked Peel if a pardon could be offered and if the prisoners could be transferred to Bow Street to be interrogated there. Again, the answer was no: pardons were, Peel believed, ineffectual before confessions were extracted, while as Home Secretary he was powerless to remove prisoners already committed. Knowing that the Surrey magistrates had just apprehended a man called John Blakey on suspicion of incendiarism, Peel advised Day that he had best enrol the help of other local magistrates.[61]

Blakey had been witnessed displaying an unusual instrument in an Oxted pub and, allegedly, describing it as being able to fire agricultural property. The device was found laden with shot, while Blakey was found to be carrying bullets, receipts for various different combustible compounds, and several political writings – some written by him – which predicted revolution. Peel immediately sanctioned the sending of a police officer to rural Surrey to help foster 'a concert and unity of action in the attempt to unravel the mystery of the fires'. Chief Constable Hall and officer Curtis of Union Hall were dispatched, but on examining Blakey found no substantive evidence. The offending implement was, he claimed, a brass device intended to launch harpoons in the whaling fisheries. In a last-ditch attempt to secure evidence, several of the Kentish victims were called to Surrey in the a hope of identifying him. None could, and Blakey was committed as a rogue and a vagabond.[62]

Chief Constable Hall was duly dispatched to Lewes to assist magistrate Day. Peel's suggestion that Day should involve the Kent and Surrey magistrates in his enquiries was also acted upon, but by 25

October cooperation had turned to competition. The repeated, often contradictory questioning by the different magistrates had led to an irresolvable impasse. Lord Lieutenant of Kent Camden's post-mortem made unwelcome reading for Peel. 'Rows' had occurred between the Sussex and Surrey authorities: 'The Magistracy must be alert and not suffer any political feelings, or fanciful conceits to prevent them acting with vigor.' Magistrate Day had a different opinion, putting the blame squarely on the Government for their lack of assistance.[63]

Notes

1 *Kent and Essex Mercury*, 13 and 27 January, 3, 17 and 24 February, 3, 10, 17 and 24 March 1829; J. Gyford, *Men of Bad Character: The Witham Fires of the 1820s* (Chelmsford: Essex Record Office, 1991).

2 J. Archer, *By a Flash and a Scare: Arson, Animal Maiming, and Poaching in East Anglia 1815–1870* (Oxford: Clarendon Press, 1990), pp. 87–8.

3 *Ibid.*, p. 87.

4 *Sheffield Iris* quoted in *Devizes and Wiltshire Gazette*, 5 November 1829.

5 Gyford, *Men of Bad Character*.

6 K. Snell, 'The culture of local xenophobia', *Social History*, 28:1 (2003), 19, 15.

7 *Kentish Gazette* (hereafter *KG*), 25 June; *Sussex Advertiser* (hereafter *SA*), 23 August; *BG*, 26 August; *Kent Herald* (hereafter *KH*), 26 August 1830.

8 *KG*, 20 Aug.; TNA, HO 52/8, fos 261–2, Anonymous clerk, Whitehall, to Peel, 3 September; *The Times* (hereafter *TT*), 25 September. For other attacks on Irish labourers in the south see: *Devizes and Wiltshire Gazette*, 10 June; *KG*, 25 June 1830.

9 See R. Quested, *The Isle of Thanet Farming Community: An Agrarian History of Easternmost Kent* (Birchington: Quested, 2001).

10 *Cobbett's Weekly Political Register* (hereafter *CWPR*), 24 March 1832.

11 *KG*, 23 July; Centre for Kentish Studies (hereafter CKS), U951 C177/12, Interrogation notes of Sir Edward Knatchbull, no date (but September–October 1830).

12 *Maidstone Gazette* (hereafter *MG*), 24 August 1830. During the 1831 harvest Irish labourers were attacked in the area covered by the Elham gang: see Chapter 11.

13 J. and B. Hammond, *The Village Labourer* (London: Longman, 1978), p. 179; J. Rule and R. Wells, 'Crime, protest and radicalism', in Rule and Wells, *Crime, Protest and Popular Politics in Southern England 1740–1850* (London: Hambledon, 1997), p. 10.

14 E. Hobsbawm and G. Rudé, *Captain Swing* (London: Lawrence & Wishart, 1969), p. 312. Hobsbawm and Rudé's tabulations have been shown to be deficient, see: R. Wells, 'Social protest, class, conflict and consciousness, in the English countryside 1700–1880', in M. Reed and R. Wells (eds), *Class, Conflict and Protest in the English Countryside 1700–1880* (London: Frank Cass, 1990), pp. 165–6; C. Griffin, '"There was no law to punish that offence", Re-assessing

"Captain Swing": rural luddism and rebellion in East Kent, 1830–31', *Southern History*, 22 (2000), 131–63.

15 Hobsbawm and Rudé', *Captain Swing*, pp. 12, 97–8.

16 Archer, *Social Unrest*, pp. 16–17.

17 I. Dyck, *William Cobbett and Rural Popular Culture* (Cambridge: Cambridge University Press), p. 152.

18 *CWPR*, 20 March 1830.

19 *BG*, 16 July 1829.

20 *BG*, 14 August 1828.

21 *Western Flying Post*, 23 February; *Dorset County Chronicle* (hereafter *DCC*), 12 March and 2 April; *Sherborne Journal*, 2 April; *Devizes and Wiltshire Gazette*, 8 January, 2 and 9 April; *Western Flying Post*, 18 May 1829.

22 *Sherborne Journal*, 7 May 1829.

23 B.N. Raven, '"A humbler, industrious class of female": women's employment and industry in the small towns of southern England, *c*.1790–1840', in P. Lane, N. Raven and K. Snell (eds), *Gender and Wages in England c.1660–1840* (Woodbridge: Boydell & Brewer, 2004); P. Brandon and B. Short, *The South-East from AD 1000* (London: Longman, 1990), pp. 261–7, 306–7, 310–15.

24 West Sussex County Record Office (hereafter WSCRO), PAR 206/12/5, Westbourne Vestry Minute, 9 March; *Hampshire Telegraph and Sussex Chronicle* (hereafter *HT*), 4 May 1829.

25 *BG*, 16 July; *KG*, 24 July 1829 and 10 May 1830; *Hampshire Chronicle* (hereafter *HC*), 14 September and 7 December 1829; *County Chronicle*, 30 March; *Kentish Chronicle*, 20 April 1830.

26 *Devizes and Wiltshire Gazette*, 31 December 1829; *Brighton Herald*, 2 and 16 January; *MJ*, 5 January; *Kentish Chronicle*, 12 and 26 January, and 9 February; *Reading Mercury*, 8 February 1830.

27 *Sherborne Journal*, 7 January; *HC*, 11 January 1830.

28 *CWPR*, 2 January; *Reading Mercury*, 11 January; *Berkshire Chronicle*, 16 January; *Kentish Chronicle*, 19 January; *Rochester Gazette* (hereafter *RG*), 26 January; *MG*, 26 January and 2 February; *HC*, 2 February; *KG*, 2, 9 and 12 February, 23 July. The only discernible innovations to help ease labouring distress were allotments and assisted emigration schemes: *RG*, 12 January; CKS, P49/8/4 and U442 O22/1, Brookland Vestry Minute, 18 February, and Snave Vestry Minutes, 6 and 18 March; ESCRO, PAR 236/12/1/3, Battle Vestry Minute, 5 March 1830.

29 *KG*, 20 June 1828.

30 Dyck, *William Cobbett*, p. 153.

31 *DCC*, 6 May; *HC*, 22 February 1830.

32 C. Griffin, 'As Lated Tongues Bespoke: Popular Protest in South-East England, 1790–1840' (PhD dissertation, University of Bristol, 2002), ch. 2; *Brighton Guardian*, 14 October 1829; *KG*, 23 July 1830.

33 *Keene's Bath Journal*, 2 March 1829; *CWPR*, 6 March 1830.

34 *MJ*, 23 February, 2 March and 20 April 1830.

35 ESCRO, PEV 1259, Case for the opinion of and advise of Mr. Partington, May 1830.

36 S. Tarrow, 'Cycles of collective action: between moments of madness and the

repertoire of contention', in M. Traugott (ed.) *Repertoires & Cycles of Collective Action* (Durham, NC: Duke University Press, 1995), p. 96.

37 *Western Flying Post*, 5 January (attack at Albury); *HT*, 12 January (attack at Patcham); *KG*, 6 and 17 February, and 20 April (attacks at Elmsted, Westerham, and Sheerness); *MJ*, 23 February (attack at Bethersden); *Brighton Herald*, 18 April and 9 May 1830 (attacks at Pevensey and Hellingly).

38 *BG*, 3 June 1830; *HT*, 16 November; *MJ*, 26 May and 20 October 1829.

39 TNA, HO 40/24, fo. 18, Petition forwarded to the Home Office from Queenborough, 8 August 1829.

40 TNA, HO 52/10 fos 640–2 and 642–3, Herbert Curteis, Rye to Peel, 28 February and 9 May; *TT*, 27 March, 3 and 15 May; *SA*, 3 May; *KH*, 5 May 1830; R. Philip, *The Coastal Blockade: The Royal Navy's War on Smuggling in Kent and Sussex, 1817–1831* (Horsham: Compton Press, 1999); *Hansard*, House of Commons, 27 May 1830, vol. 24, cols 1142–5. Hobsbawm and Rudé claimed that an election riot had occurred in Rye: *Captain Swing*, pp. 105 and 312.

41 *HT*, 7 June; *Southampton Mercury*, 12 June; *Brighton Guardian*, 21 July 1830.

42 *Brighton Guardian*, 30 September and 14 October; *SA*, 12 and 19 October; *BG*, 15 October 1829.

43 *MJ* , 14 July; 3 and 10 November, and 22 December; *KH*, 29 October; *KG*, 6 November; *Kent and Essex Mercury*, 16 November 1829.

44 *CWPR*, 12 June 1830; M. Dutt, 'The Agricultural Labourers' Revolt of 1830 in Kent, Surrey and Sussex' (PhD dissertation, University of London, 1966), p. 282.

45 *KH*, 7 February; *County Chronicle*, 9 February; *CPR*, 20 March; *HC*, 14 March. A petition was drawn up at Rochester to specifically call for the abolition of tithes: *KH*, 29 April 1830.

46 Dyck, *William Cobbett*, ch. 4; Roger Wells, '1830: the year of revolutions in England, and the politics of the Captain Swing insurrection', www.canterbury.ac.uk/arts-humanities/history-and-americanstudies/histo ry/Documents/PoliticsOfCaptain Swing.pdf (accessed 20 May 2009), p. 4.

47 *CWPR*, 17 July and 2 October 1830.

48 *KH*, 3 June; TNA, HO 52/8, fos 89–90, 231–3, and 261–2, Joseph Berens, Kevington, Foots Cray, 8 June; Bromley Bench, 9 June; and, Clerk, Whitehall, 3 September, to Sir Robert Peel; *London Gazette*, 11 June; *MG*, 10 August; TNA, Assi 94/2066, Indictment of Phillip Porter, Kent Summer Assizes 1830.

49 *MG*, 27 April; *MG*, 27 April 1830.

50 *KG*, 5 July; TNA, HO 62/6, no. 778, Daily Report from the Metropolitan Police, 6 July 1830; TNA, HO 52/8, fo. 302, Undated list of fires (sent as an enclosure but has been detached from the original letter).

51 *MG*, 3 August; TNA, HO 62/6, no. 815, Daily Report from the Metropolitan Police, 18 August 1830; *TT*, 18 April and 10 August 1831; TNA, Assi 94/2100. Indictment of Stephen Stock Gower, Surrey Summer Assizes 1831.

52 *MG*, 17 August; TNA, HO 52/8, fo. 313, Managing Director of the County Fire Office, Regent Street to Peel, 31 August 1830.

53 *TT*, 8 September; *RG*, 14 and 21 September 1830.

54 TNA, HO 52/8, fos 313 and 259–60, Managing Director of the County Fire Office, Regent Street, 31 August, and, Mr Manning, New Bank Buildings, 3

September, to Peel; *RG*, 14 and 21 September 1830.

55 TNA, HO 52/8, fos 266–7, Manning, New Bank Buildings to Peel, 9 September; *KG*, 20 September 1830.

56 *KH*, 7 September; *RG*, 14 and 21 September; *KG*, 20 September; *MJ*, 19 October; TNA, HO 52/8, fos 259–60, Mr Manning, New Bank Buildings to Peel, 3 September 1830.

57 TNA, HO 52/8, fos 313, 259–60 and 261–2, Managing Director of the County Fire Office, Regent Street, 31 August, Mr Manning, New Bank Buildings, 3 September, and, Unnamed Clerk, Whitehall, 3 September 1830, all to Peel.

58 *MJ*, 14 September; TNA, HO 52/8, fos 261–2, Unnamed Clerk, Whitehall to Peel, 3 September 1830.

59 TNA, HO 52/8, fo. 270, Lower Division of the Lathe of Sutton-at-Hone Magistrates, Sevenoaks to Peel, 18 September; *TT*, 8 September 1830. The officer dispatched to investigate Minet's fire quickly returned to London, owing to a lack of evidence.

60 *TT*, 17 September; TNA HO, 52/8, fos 203–5, B. Sandford, Farningham, Dartford to John Irving MP, 8 October 1830.

61 CKS, U840 C250 10/4 and 5, Copies of letters from William Day, Maresfield, to Peel, 21 October, and Phillips, Whitehall to Day, 22 October; *MJ*, 19 October; *TT*, 22 October 1830.

62 CKS, U840 C250 10/3, Peel to Lord Camden, 22 October; *TT*, 22 October 1830.

63 TNA, HO 52/8, fos 19–20, 231–2 and 220–3, Camden, The Wilderness to Peel, 24 and 25 October, and William Day, Maresfield to Phillips, 7 November 1830.

Part II

Swing as movement

Social and political commentators predicated with greater frequency (and certainty) during 1829 and the early months of 1830 that rural England was a social time bomb. Increased levels of protest and the fervency of the protests in the period also generated considerable alarm. The physical breaking of threshing machines in Essex and Suffolk in 1829 and the flurry of incendiary fires targeting threshing machine users attest to the increased bitterness in which machines were held after the disastrous harvests and harsh winters of 1828 and 1829. But that these localised protests did not beget a pan-regional movement suggests that the start of threshing machine-breaking in Kent in August 1830 was not in itself portentous. And yet according to both the consensus in Swing's voluminous historiography and evidence from the physical contagion of protests, it is clear that machine-breaking in the vicinity of Elham provided the trigger for protests elsewhere.

This section systematically analyses this unfurling. It begins with the start of machine-breaking in East Kent, and ends with the start of the final major south-eastern Swing trial, the Hampshire Special Commission, on 18 December. This end date is chosen for the reason that, in the words of Hobsbawm and Rudé, the 'draconian punishments distributed' at the Winchester Assizes and the subsequent 'deportation of hapless men and boys to antipodean semi-slavery' helped to thoroughly demoralise rural workers.[1] Moreover, in the rest of the south-east, where Swing activists were not tried at government-sponsored Special Commissions but instead at the regular provincial courts of Quarter Sessions and Assize, Swing is supposed to have 'died a natural death' by mid-December. Swing, so such an analysis goes, was either stopped in its tracks or, instead, achieved its multifarious aims and therefore faded.[2] These contentions are explored in details in Chapter 11.

Beyond the analysis of the form and timings of revolt, Chapter 5 goes on to explore the mechanisms of diffusion, specifically the importance of mobile gangs and groupings in physically spreading protest and the role of communication and news. Chapter 5 goes on to examine the local and supra-local distinctiveness of south-eastern Swing. Finally, the chapter considers the relationship between incendiarism and 'overt' forms of protest, a 'connection' that has been problematised by scholars of Swing but which awaits its historian. For instance, Hobsbawm and Rudé' claimed that 'an element of mystery still remains . . . as to the part played by arson in the general labourers' movement'. 'Was it', they asked, 'an integral part, or was it a largely intrusive or alien element?'.[3] Chapter 5 seeks to answer their question.

Notes

1 E. Hobsbawm and G. Rudé, *Captain Swing* (London: Lawrence & Wishart, 1969), p. 281.
2 *Ibid.*, p. 233.
3 *Ibid.*, p. 200.

4

Movement dynamics and diffusion[1]

On 25 August 1830, while reaping at Ottinge in the parish of Elham, Ingram Swaine was approached by fellow labourer Selden Bayley. The previous evening, Bayley related, a threshing machine had been broken at Wingmore, a small hamlet on the border of the parishes of Barham and Elham, by a group of 'three or four and twenty' men. Bayley also declared that a group of 30 men were going that night to break another machine at Grimsacre. Swaine offered his assistance, and at 8 p.m. went to the arranged meeting point. Alas, nobody else was there. Swaine returned home and went to bed.[2]

Hobsbawm and Rudé famously stated that the first threshing machine was destroyed at Lower Hardres on 28 August. 'The precise date is worth recording', they claimed, 'as the breaking of machines was to become the characteristic feature of the labourers' movement of 1830'.[3] The precise date is still worth recording. But Bayley and Swaine's conversation, corroborated by farmer Dodds' deposition,[4] confirms that the first threshing machine was destroyed not on 28 August but four days earlier. Furthermore, the act of destruction occurred in the parish of Elham, not Lower Hardres. The now legendary status of Lower Hardres in nineteenth-century British social history – 'and now to Lower Hardres' Richard Cobb beseeched in his review of *Captain Swing* – might no longer hold, but Cobb's general point is still important.[5]

The machine destroyed on 28 August belonged to Collick, a substantial farmer, but was on hire to farmer Inge in the Upper Hardres hamlet of Palmsted. That same night the machine-breakers, initially 57 strong but now depleted to 24, also broke two threshing machines on Stephen Kelsey's farm at Eastleigh in Lyminge parish. Kelsey's threshing barn had been fired the previous year.[6] This protest precedent was also backed by a resolution earlier in 1830 by the Barham vestry that threshing machines should be put out of use because of their impact on employment levels and the poor rates. It also later transpired that Rev. Price JP of Lyminge had been in dispute with the 'most influential' local farmers, and another farmer, who had introduced a threshing machine. The open hostility of many farmers combined with Price's public intervention, the *Spectator* later claimed, led local labourers and artisans to believe that the destruction of the machines was a 'meritorious act, and, relying on the opinion of their betters, a judicious act'.[7] On this basis, a group of local labourers, artisans and small farmers had formulated a strategy. The men had approached local farmers and warned them that if they did not stop using their machines they would be broken. Evidence from depositions shows that some farmers heeded the warnings: for instance, the initial gathering on 28 August after some discussion, decided to go 'to Collicks, for Gilbert will not work his Machine'.[8] Machine-breaking was not, as Hobsbawm and Rudé suggested, 'a bolt from the blue'. It was predictable, and had precedent.[9]

The first four machines broken were all in relatively obscure locations in the maze of lanes and isolated farmsteads on the East Kent Downs, at some distance from the major villages of Barham, Elham, Lyminge and the smaller village of Upper Hardres. This sparsely-populated, undulating landscape was punctuated by large woods and remnant commons at Rhodes Minnis, Wheelbarrow Town and Stelling Minnis, with a huge common to the east of Elham at Swingfield Minnis (see figure 4.1). This was an area dominated by small farmers and squatters, independent peoples accustomed to traversing the country for work and, for some, to support criminal and smuggling activities.[10]

After breaking another machine belonging to a Lyminge carpenter but on hire at Newington-next-Hythe on 29 August,[11] the following fortnight appears to have been free from machine-breaking, though other attacks were planned.[12] By mid-September more members had joined the gang, many from parishes other than Elham, Lyminge and Stelling. Indeed, the next acts of machine-breaking occurred at a considerable distance apart: Brabourne on 16 September and Upper Hardres on 18 September. The latter episode ended with a return to Kelsey's farm to, reportedly, destroy his repaired machines.[13] Other farmers were more risk averse. On 15 September, Francis Castle had asked Daniel Woollett, a Paddlesworth publican and farmer, if he would bring his threshing machine to work at Stelling Lodge. Woollett declined, as he had heard that 'it was chatted about amongst the Stelling People that they would not let any Machine work in the Parish' and that 'there is a man in ... [Stelling] that says the first machine that comes into the parish shall be broken'. The identity of Woollett's informant was Henry Atwood, 'a small farmer who has no ploughing land' and kept '2 or 3 cows' who also happened to be the Stelling overseer.[14]

Hereafter their tactics changed. On 20 September, for the first time, two different parties were in operation on the same night. One group destroyed a threshing machine at Sellindge Lees, while another group destroyed at least four in the parishes of Barham and Womenswold. A bell stolen from one of the farms at Barham was taken two nights later on a return to Brabourne and Stanford where, joined by men from the immediate parishes, two more machines were destroyed.[15] The Elham gang's machine-breaking activities now covered the area between the fringes of Ashford, Canterbury, Hythe and Folkestone. On the nights of 24 and 25 September their area was further extended to the reaches of Dover, but although the archive details the movements of men from Barham and Elham to Hougham, near Dover, no acts of machine-breaking occurred. It is particularly instructive that the events on Saturday 25 September followed the examination of some suspected ringleaders earlier that day.[16] That they could still (and were prepared to) muster showed both their organisational strength and commitment. Machine-breaking even occurred again on the night of 27 September and on 1 October, both cases being machines on hire near Dover.[17]

After this date, their strategy shifted. On 5 October Rev. Price's farm was targeted by incendiaries, Price being, so he believed, victimised owing to his involvement in apprehending the Elham men.[18] On the following day, incendiary letters were sent by post to two individuals near Dover. Both were signed 'Swing', the first appearance of the word that became synonymous with the protests of 1830. On the same day, the 'dead walls' between Dover and Canterbury were also graffitied with 'the same significant word'. Two days later Widow Pepper, the occupier of farms at Hougham and Dover, also received a 'Swing' letter. Her threshing machine was to be destroyed, she was warned, so she should remove it to an adjoining field immediately. Pepper complied, and that evening her machine was broken and set on fire. Other farmers near Dover were reported to be 'so terrified

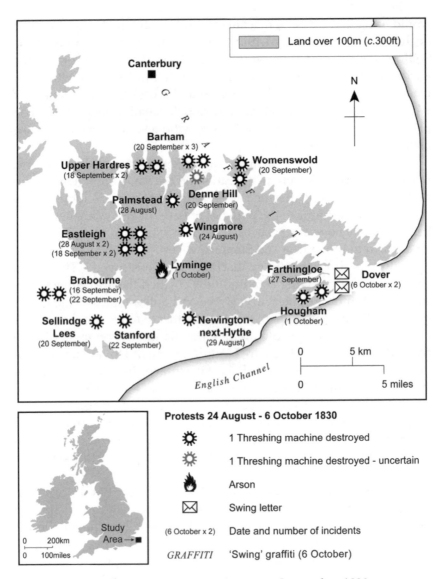

Protests 24 August - 6 October 1830

☀ 1 Threshing machine destroyed

☀ 1 Threshing machine destroyed - uncertain

🔥 Arson

⊠ Swing letter

(6 October x 2) Date and number of incidents

GRAFFITI 'Swing' graffiti (6 October)

4.1 Elham area protests, August – September 1830

[that] they have almost invited the men around to demolish their machines', farmers Coleman at Kearsney and Dell at Ewell placing their machines 'in the open fields, preparatory to their destruction'.[19] On 22 October, seven members of the gang were tried at the East Kent Quarter Sessions and sentenced to four days in the Canterbury gaol.[20]

The beginnings of a movement

Early October also marked a renewal of incendiarism on the Kent-Sussex-Surrey borders,[21] but the spread of machine-breaking was of greatest note. Even before the supposed cessation of the Elham gang's activities, protests occurred outside their area and without their involvement, as two threshing machines were broken and threatening letters received at Sturry to the north-east of Canterbury on 2 October. Elsewhere, on 5 October, a posse of twelve men appeared incognito at midnight and threatened Margate farmer Major Garrett's threshing machine with destruction. Whether they carried out their threat is unclear.[22] It is likely that news of the Elham gang's actions would have spread throughout much of Kent by early October. The first reports appeared in the Canterbury press on 3 September, while, according to Rev. Owen of Chislet, harvest gangs were 'in communication with each other throughout this part of the county'.[23] But until the night of the trial of the Elham men, these were, alongside cases of arson at Dumpton and Ash-next-Sandwich (against popularly-loathed overseer Becker) the only reported protests to occur in East Kent.[24]

The fortnight between the Ash and Lyminge fires and the trial of the Elham men was of greatest importance for the diffusion of machine-breaking and the receipt of Swing letters beyond East Kent. Moreover, these practices also made explicit reference to the Elham protests. On 12 October, William Chapman of Lenham had several of his 'agricultural implements' sawn to pieces. These acts of rural Luddism were, it was related, a punishment for Chapman having made vitriolic remarks about the Elham machine-breakers. This is the moment when the intensive, but geographically isolated, protests defiantly became a movement. The Elham gang had not only motivated others in their immediate vicinity but had also motivated others at a distance.[25]

It was at the notorious radical centre of Maidstone, nine miles north-east of Lenham, however, that 'Swing' as a complex more-than-East Kent movement was first forged. The meeting held on 1 October to congratulate the French 'on their Revolution' drew the mayor to remark on the events at either end of the county. He claimed that 'the fires and the machine breaking' were the result of grievances that would only be alleviated by a reform of Parliament. Cobbett's lecture, well attended by artisans, engineers and operatives, was followed by the receipt of threatening letters in the vicinity of Maidstone. One threatened to set Maidstone on fire, whereas two letters sent to 'Gentlemen' threatened to set their out-buildings alight unless they employed the parish poor. That all three were signed 'Swing' provided further evidence that the protests at Elham had not gone unnoticed, nor their implications unheeded, in Maidstone.[26]

While these protests were critical in establishing a movement, they were still tentative compared to those in East Kent. The trial of the Elham men provided the pivot on which this turned, the 'unparalleled lenity' of the sentences passed down to them acting to legitimise, and publicise, machine-breaking.[27] The popular response was immediate and unequivocal. Even the night before the trial saw a resort to protest in an area hitherto unaffected, presumably intended both to warn the farmers, gentry and magistracy gathered at the Sessions and to signal intent. Farmer Harnett at Newington-next-Sittingbourne and overseer Knight at Borden both had their farms set on fire.[28]

On the night of the trial, Mr Quested, the parish surveyor and a substantial farmer at Ash, had a gratten stack set alight,[29] and on 23 October a fire and an act of machine-breaking occurred at Sandwich. That a machine could be broken in broad daylight by men who made no attempt to disguise their identity was novel and evidence of a new degree of confidence.[30] This modus operandi continued at Ash, where two labourers who had been involved at Sandwich were again active. It later transpired that plans had been afoot for weeks.[31] Pressing other labourers to join them, over the course of the afternoon and evening the group destroyed nine different threshing machines on nine different farms between Wingham and Ash.[32] Unlike the Elham gang, the Ash machine-breakers did not stay at large for long. Later that night the magistrates, assisted by a troop of soldiers, took seven men into custody. A further two men were taken the following morning. Despite this hard-line approach, the 'labouring men' of Ash defiantly struck from work that morning, determined that married men should receive at least half a crown for a day's labour. If they did not secure this they would break the farmers' ploughs 'leaving them no alternative but the spade'.[33]

Notwithstanding their success, their actions were not replicated elsewhere in East Kent until late November, though a group of men – 'supposed not to have come from Elham' – assembled in the parishes of Bekesbourne, Patrixbourne and Barham and broke threshing machines on three different farms on 23 October.[34] While no large-scale or sustained destruction of machinery took place in the intervening period, there were isolated cases. On 28 October, the Mayor of Sandwich reported to Peel that threshing machines had been destroyed that day by 'tumultuous assemblages'. There is no corroborating evidence, but it is clear that a Sandwich farmer did become the victim of an incendiary fire that day, with 'threats of destruction' made the following day.[35] Also on the 28 October, farmer Noges at Crundale – in an area hitherto unaffected by Swing – had his machine destroyed. Finally, on 2 November three machines were destroyed on three different farms on the edge of Dover, presumably the residual work of the Elham gang.[36]

The spread of protests beyond East Kent was, as it would transpire, of greater significance. On the night of the trial, the tentative protests in the Swale area of the previous evening were intensified. A group of fifty men, some armed with guns and pistols, some with blackened faces, marched from Newington to Hartlip where they destroyed a threshing machine – the first to be destroyed by force outside East Kent.[37] At Ulcomb, to the south of Maidstone, not long after the parish officers had assembled for their 'usual business ... a number of people' entered the room, turned off the lights, broke the pay tables and compelled the officers to leave. The events in Hartlip and Ulcomb both demonstrated a strong degree of planning.[38]

As Sunday was not the most propitious day to press for higher wages and destroy machines, all appeared on hold, though after an incendiary fire at Stockbury the labourers paraded the village holding aloft a black flag. Then, on Monday 25 October, mid-Kent appeared to rise en masse. A 'mob' armed with staves gathered at Queenborough on the Isle of Sheppey to demand higher wages for their employment on the oyster grounds, a demand that was eventually conceded. Just over the Swale at Sittingbourne, the bricklayers, labourers and other journeymen struck from work for an increase in wages. The following evening, three different parties were also reported to be meeting at a Faversham beer shop, one of which was probably the '50 desperadoes' compelling other labourers at Ospringe to join them 'on a machine breaking episode'.[39] Another small group assembled from the hamlets around Wormshill and Frinstead compelling all other labourers they met to join them to intimidate the local farmers into meeting their demands. That evening the group proceeded from Frinstead towards Charing Heath where another 300 men were supposed to be joining them. The following morning (26 October) the Frinstead and

Wormshill men again gathered, this time setting off towards Lenham where they had arranged to meet the men from that parish and to destroy all the threshing machines in the area. Moreover, they were later to be joined, so they claimed, by 300–400 others at Wateringbury.[40] As at Elham, the early Swing risings around Maidstone and the Swale were planned and coordinated, the key difference being that the focus of protests had now shifted to embrace wages as well as attacks on machinery.

While these organised, mobile groups were important in diffusing protest, their activities paled into insignificance compared to a group led by Robert Price, a 48-year-old politically active Maidstone shoemaker. 'On or about' 25 October, Price was travelling between Newington and Chatham and, feeling fatigued, stopped to take refreshment at a Newington public house. Here, Price claimed, he was compelled to join a party who went on to declare their grievances and request an addition to their wages. He only joined the men on the stipulation that they must adhere strictly 'to what I should require of them which was to do no injury to anyone', that is, on condition that he led them. 'In their company' Price stayed until he was taken into custody on 16 November, having taken part in a series of 'risings' in an area stretching from Sittingbourne to Yalding. His involvement at Newington set the scene for their future protests. Some 150–200 labourers had left their work and proceeded from farm to farm to 'enforce certain demands on their employers'. They then assembled with a tricolour at that evening's vestry meeting. Price – 'a perfect stranger ... shabbily dressed but spoke ... most fluently' who had 'harrangued the populace' into action – went into the room to state their demands: 2/6 a day with a supplement of 1/6 a week for every child above two in number, and yearly rents of £3–10. All were granted.[41]

Over the following days, Price led an ever-changing group of men in a series of 'risings', often getting into heated politically charged parleys with farmers and members of the rural gentry. The form of these risings invariably followed the same pattern: the group, partially composed of 'pressed' men, would traverse the parish forcing farmers to increase wages while also calling for money and refreshments. As Price pronounced to Mrs Stacey at Stockbury, their object was simple: 'Now we have righted this Parish we are going thro' every other Village and Parish to do the same thing.' The farmers could afford to pay higher wages for, as Price claimed at Hollingbourne on 28 October, they had no need to pay their rents, taxes and tithes as the men would 'protect' them. Thus over the next few days, Hucking, Stockbury, Detling, Hartlip – where men from Rainham had joined the local men (27 October); Hollingbourne (28 and 29 October); East Sutton, Langley, Town Sutton/Sutton Valence (29 October); Town Sutton, Chart Sutton, Boughton Monchelsea and Linton (30 October) were 'righted'.

On 29 October, Price's group joined forces with another group centred on Hollingbourne, led by a fellow Maidstone radical shoemaker, John Adams, and accompanied by fellow Maidstone shoemaker Pitman and Southwark tailor Holloway.[42] Despite Adams's arrest on 29 October, Price went on to lead groups agitating for wage increases at East Malling on 2–3 November, reassembling at Cranbrook the following day. Thereafter, Price led a group collecting money 'from house to house between Yalding to Tonbridge', and on 11 November traversed Hadlow, East and West Peckham, Nettlestead, and Yalding calling for higher wages as well as a dole. Between then and his arrest five days later, it is unclear what part Price took in south-eastern Swing.[43]

The Weald and beyond

Beyond these risings, protests in mid-Kent were patchy and sporadic, comprised of otherwise isolated fires and threatening letters.[44] Instead, from early November Swing was most dramatically manifested in the Weald. In addition to Price's physical diffusion of protests into the Kentish Weald, there were two other parallel protest poles, Battle and Brede, both in Sussex. Protests in both locales were rooted in late October agitation, which, although inspired by events in Kent, was the product of indigenous Sussex activism. On the night of 30 October, some eighteen or nineteen Brede parishioners, 'principally smugglers' according to magistrate George Courthope, held a 'meeting of the poor'. No decisions were made, and the meeting adjourned to the following Thursday when fifty people met at Thomas Noakes's house. However, they 'could not very well agree about carrying assistant overseer Mr Abell away the next day, some wanted to do it and some didn't'. Initially thirty people gathered the next morning, but this soon grew to 'at least one hundred and fifty', including, for the first time in a Swing gathering, 'several women and boys and girls'. While at Abell's house, the party decided to call the gentlemen in the parish to meet them at the Red Lion, where some of the party 'made our price about what they were going to give us a day' before stating that they were going to remove Abell from the parish. The farmers present agreed to both plans. On leaving the pub, the crowd went to the workhouse and symbolically got the much-hated cart that Abell had constructed especially 'for the men to draw on the road', and after some resistance, Abell was placed in the cart and drawn to Vinehall.[45]

The circumstances at Battle were different. Cobbett's 16 October lecture, so thought the local magistracy, gave courage to the Battle poor to protest. A fortnight later one labourer did, openly threatening the overseer. The precise circumstances are unclear, but wages were the motivating factor. His arrest and examination before Sir Godfrey Webster on Monday 1 November prompted a group of labourers to assemble with the intention of rescuing him if he were committed. He was not. Moreover, Webster promised that 'something should be done to relieve the labouring class' from their distress, those gathered bursting into impromptu cheers of 'Sir Godfrey for ever'. Taking Webster's comments as a spur to action, the Battle labourers duly struck work, demanding that all men should be paid at least 12 shillings a week, threatening that if this was not agreed to they would take the money themselves. One 'ringleader' was seized, prompting an attempt by the men – some armed with clubs – to rescue him. A few days later, overseer Emary and assistant overseer Laincer received letters – the latter signed 'Swing' – threatening that, if the labourers' demands were not made good, their premises would be fired. On the night of 3 November, Emary's farm was set on fire.[46] The next day proved critical. Laincer left Battle, at 4 p.m. farmer Quaife had one of his barns set on fire, at 10 p.m. farmer Farncomb's stacks were set alight at nearby Icklesham, and at 11 p.m. a mass gathering at the George Inn prompted the authorities to send an express to Hastings for military assistance. Nothing transpired, but threats were openly made that the town would be burnt down that night. This did not occur, although farmer Watts's farm was set on fire.[47]

Over the next few days Battle remained tense. The assistant overseer returned to further threats that he would be 'treated like the one at Brede', which so worried the Battle authorities that no less a figure than Lord Lieutenant Egremont advised Peel that it was impossible to keep the peace. It was also reported that plans were afoot to remove assistant overseers at Ticehurst, Burwash, Heathfield and 'other places'.[48] Indeed, the examples of Brede and Battle made an almost immediate impact. Numerous threatening letters were sent to farmers in the vicinities of Lewes, Eastbourne and East Grinstead, some warning against using threshing machines.[49] The most tangible local impression was first manifest at Burwash where on Sunday 7 November the 'labouring population ... assembled *en masse*' and declared that they were going to remove the assistant overseer.[50] Monday 8 November proved the critical day in the diffusion of Wealden Swing. The Battle labourers sent a message to their brethren at Seddlescomb 'and other adjoining parishes', calling on them to join at Battle 'in organising a force to resist the military'. Several parties from different parishes did go to Battle, joining the local labourers at the meeting of the Petty Sessions. Their demands were heard and 'satisfactorily arranged'. The precedent was set and, with minimal delay, the attempt was made to enforce it elsewhere. Farmers at Robertsbridge, Seddlesomb, Guestling and Hooe readily agreed providing that the labourers support them in securing tithe reductions.[51]

The model was set for Wealden protests, and over the ensuing days the removal of assistant overseers, calls for higher wages and tithe reductions were made throughout the Weald. Threshing machines were also destroyed at Hawkhurst, Benenden, and later at Rotherfield and on an 'experimental' farm at Crowborough where all the machinery was destroyed. These 'risings' were all connected. John Beale, a 37-year-old carpenter, was a key instigator at Hawkhurst. Having attended the affray at Robertsbridge, on his return to Hawkhurst he and others traversed the parish and 'several of the adjoining parishes' calling on 'the poor and ill-disposed' to join them.[52] Protests at Rotherfield were indicative. On 12 November, having obtained money and victuals from several householders, the men succeeded in forcing Rev. Crawley to sign a paper agreeing to cut his tithes by half and made Mr Cochrane take down his threshing machine.[53] It had been feared that the same party, joined by a large 'mob' from Wadhurst and Frant, were to visit Tonbridge 'upon Tithes Taxes and Rents' or Tunbridge Wells, it being market day. In the end they chose Tonbridge.[54] The next day the 'Rotherfield mob' went, as planned, about Frant, Rotherfield, Groombridge, Withyham and Mayfield making their 'usual demands', threatening to return with 'additional strength' where they were unsuccessful.[55]

By 13 November, Swing had effectively been in control of the whole of the East Sussex Weald for a week. But other than the sending of threatening letters in the preceding fortnight in the areas around

Cuckfield, East Grinstead, Horsham, Lewes and Petworth, Mayfield was as far west in Sussex that 'mobbings' had occurred.[56] This now dramatically changed. On 13 November the *Brighton Herald* reported that the parish of Hurstpierpoint had for the past two or three days been anticipating a disturbance. Two days later, the *Sussex Advertiser* stated that an assemblage had now occurred, the date therefore being the either 13 or 14 November.[57] Fears that Swing would spread to West Sussex were certainly made real on the morning of 13 November, when an assemblage of over fifty men gathered at Kirdford – close to Coldwaltham where an incendiary fire had occurred during the night, but some forty miles distant from Mayfield – to force an increase in wages.[58] This example provided the trigger for much of West and Central Sussex to rise – after pausing on Sunday – on Monday morning, 15 November.

Four distinct areas in West Sussex 'rose' that day to press for higher wages and lower tithes: the area between Arundel, Pulborough and Bognor; the neighbourhood of Thakeham;[59] the vicinity of Worthing; and Shoreham.[60] The Bognor-focused protests drew in labourers from nearby Felpham, Yapton and Bersted, and publicly avowed to destroy all the threshing machines in the vicinity and force an increase in wages from 10 shillings to 14 shillings a week. Thwarted in their intention of marching to Arundel by the intervention of the Earl of Surrey, they reassembled, their numbers considerably augmented, the following day. This time they were more forceful, threatening to set fire to the premises of farmers who refused to destroy their threshing machines.[61]

Over the duration of the following week Swing would tighten its grip over much of West Sussex. Beyond several cases of arson and the receipt of threatening letters,[62] a new episode in the rapidly unfurling movement commenced in the vicinity of Chichester with the systematic breaking of threshing machines, the first place such sustained destruction occurred outside of East Kent.[63] Having spread through mid- and West Sussex in only four days, mobilisations now physically spilled over into neighbouring Hampshire. There were two poles of diffusion, one being machine-breaking around Chichester, the other being a wages movement around Petersfield, which spread from Rogate and South Harting on 17 November, and Compton and West Marden on the following day, before moving to Petersfield, inspiring protests at Warnford and Westmeon on 19 November.[64]

The Havant area protests were far more destructive. Around 11

November, farmers in the vicinity of Gosport had received threatening letters 'asking' them to remove their threshing machines, at least one of which was signed 'Swing'. By the middle of the following week a farmer at Nutbourne, to the west of Chichester, and farmers as far west as Hamble had also received threatening letters.[65] Notwithstanding the many, often conflicting, reports issued about these protests, it is possible to delineate some important aspects. Late in the afternoon on 17 November, 'a party of idle and dissolute characters' from Chichester began pressing the labourers of Fishbourne and Bosham, before stealing sledgehammers, hammers and saws from a blacksmith's shop. The party then proceeded to several farms, machine makers, public houses and beer shops in Bosham, Fishbourne and Westbourne, calling for money and beer as well as destroying at least six threshing machines during the night. At 8 a.m. on the following day, while eating and drinking at the White Swan in Westhampnett, eight of the men were arrested.[66]

Their arrest appeared to do nothing to quell further protests. Indeed, 20 other men had gone to Westboume, where from about 7 a.m., they started pressing the local labourers. Three hours later the party crossed the border into Hampshire and started destroying machines at Emsworth, Warblington and then Havant parish. The group returned to Sussex later that night, going on to destroy a further two machines at Funtington.[67] The men 'continued their destructive work' that morning, also visiting Woodmancote, Prinsted and Nutbourne (both in Westbourne parish).[68] Later that morning, a body of armed special constables accompanied Sussex and Hampshire magistrates to Westbourne where it was understood the group had a 'committee'. Here, a further nine men were taken into custody. Presumably as an act of defiance, the barn and ricks of a Westbourne farmer were set alight that evening.[69]

Although these protests might have inspired protests elsewhere in Hampshire, it would appear that Swing's continual westward spread occurred not through physical diffusion but instead, as it had initially in both East and West Sussex, through new protest poles. Before considering this westward spread, it is important to note that protests in Sussex and Kent continued. Indeed, a new wave of protests spread from Horsham into Surrey. A meeting had been arranged at Horsham for 18 November to appoint a new assistant overseer, the previous incumbent having resigned his position. On the evening of 17 November, a crowd had started to gather 'from all parts', and throughout the morning this 'strong and numerous' party pressed every man they could find in Horsham and the surrounding villages.[70] By 2 p.m. they numbered some 1,500 souls. They first visited Mr Hurst, Horsham's former MP and tithe proprietor, and demanded he attend the vestry, before calling on Mr Chapman, a wealthy old gentlemen, who, under 'violent' duress, gave them 30 shillings and a sovereign.

The church was now crowded, containing an estimated 3,000 people. In such an intimidating atmosphere it is not too surprising that the crowd's demands were 'listened to'. However Hurst's promise that their complaints would be considered at some later date enraged the men. Their 'violent' animation levered a concession: an increase in wages to two shillings a day in winter and 2/6 in summer, still short of their demand of a constant 2/6 a day. Now, having barricaded the church, the demand was finally acceded to, Hurst also agreeing to cut his rents and tithes. After resolving to meet again on Monday to petition Parliament for a remission of taxes and reform, the throng left the church tearing up the iron railings on their way. The rest of the day was spent calling at every house in Horsham demanding money, with those who refused having their windows smashed.[71]

Pre-empting the Monday reform meeting, many of the men reassembled on 19 November in an attempt to extract the same concessions in the surrounding parishes. Pressing all the labourers they could find, they first proceeded to Rev. Wood's Rusper tithe audit but on arriving found it had been postponed. In frustration, they stormed Wood's house and destroyed the dinner that had been prepared. From Rusper they crossed the county border to the Surrey parishes of Abinger, Wotton and Ockley, where the payment of tithes was prevented.[72] Evidence of direct agitation from Horsham was also clear at Woking, over 20 miles away, where that afternoon an 'immense magnitude of the peasantry' assembled to prevent the payment of tithes. On the intervention of magistrate Drummond, the crowd dispersed, several joining the travelling Horsham party, while others proceeded to Dorking to liberate several individuals incarcerated in the gaol.[73]

That weekend Swing was manifest in West Sussex and Surrey through a resort to incendiarism,[74] and tithe protests at Steyning and Upper Beeding.[75] On Monday almost every parish in a line north from Worthing to Reigate rose, with the Horsham-instigated gatherings in south Surrey recommencing and culminating in an invasion of a magistrates' meeting at Dorking.[76] Similarly combative were risings in Lancing, where the 'mob' called for the demolition of the poorhouse and increased wages, and at Hickstead where after barricading the farmers in the Castle Inn and berating them for starving the poor on 10*d.* a day, overseer Sharp's barn was set alight.[77] By way of contrast, the gatherings at Cowfold, Nuthurst, Steyning and Poynings were less aggressive but no less successful in their calls for wage increases and tithe cuts.[78]

Although protests had spread beyond the Weald they had by no means left it. Further Wealden parochial risings continued, including the attack at Crowborough on 15 November[79] while 16 November was the last day of intensive collective protest in the Kent and East Sussex Weald. Indeed, all recorded protests either exhibited the influence of events to the west – as at Hailsham where a successful wage demonstration attended by 800 people was clearly inspired by events at Ringmer on the previous day,[80] were attempts to conclude unfinished business or were responses to the unfurling repression. For instance at Cuckfield, the examination of a 17-year-old lad, apprehended on suspicion of having sent threatening letters to six local farmers, prompted a 'riot'. After breaking the windows of the Talbot Inn, the crowd marched over two miles to the residence of magistrate Cherry in a vain attempt to secure his release.[81]

Of greater concern than the continued Wealden 'mobbings' was the spread of protests eastward towards the hitherto unaffected eastern fringe of the Romney Marsh and wages agitation in areas previously affected only by machine-breaking. Until the night of 13 November, East Kent had been comparatively quiet – apart from several attacks on ploughs at Eastchurch and Westwell[82] – since the destruction of a threshing machine near Dover on the 2 November.[83] The event that broke the East Kent quiet occurred at Bridge (on the fringe of the area operated by the Elham machine-breakers) when a large party of labouring men passed through the village 'shouting and uttering threats against some of the neighbouring farmers'. Tensions had been running high since a dramatic 3 a.m. raid by several Bow Street officers and eight constables to apprehend Taylor, a shoemaker who – 'not being able to procure full employment ... ha[d] occasionally gone to agricultural labour' – was suspected of being a ringleader in the Bekesbourne protests.[84]

Wage assemblies (re)commenced in East Kent on 15 November,

both at Fordwich and Sturry and in the vicinity of Deal where a 'strong party of countrymen' visited the farms pressing any labourers they found to assist in their attempt to increase wages.[85] The most sustained wages movement, however, was not an indigenous East Kent creation but diffused from the Weald. Interconnected assemblages on the morning of 15 November at Biddenden, High Halden and Woodchurch – where a meeting with the farmers was co-organised by labourers from Appledore – extended to Ham Street in Orlestone parish. The men also expressed their intention of proceeding to Ruckinge and Bilsington to compel the farmers there to pay higher wages. That night two threshing machines were also broken in the area. This followed the receipt of threatening letters by several Romney Marsh farmers warning them not to use their threshing machines, and reports of strangers asking whether machines were in use.[86] On the morning of 16 November, the mobile party of wage protestors reconvened at Ham Street. Having successfully 'regulated' the wages, they made good their threat and departed for Ruckinge and Bilsington where they were finally checked by a civil and military force. Some of the men who escaped continued their journey to visit Chart, passing through Shadoxhurst, while others marched to Hawkhurst. This attitude of open defiance continued on 17 November when the men reassembled at Ham Street, Ruckinge and Bilsington where they were reportedly 'busily engaged in destroying the property of those who did not agree to their demands'. They 'seem more determined', a correspondent to *The Times* stated, 'than any [group] we have yet heard of'.[87]

The start of Swing in Hampshire

As Hobsbawm and Rudé noted, in the few days before the emergence of Swing in its overt forms in Hampshire, farmers in various parts of the county received threatening letters and were targeted by incendiarists. But other than those 'Swing' letters sent around Gosport around 11 November, and threatening letters received in the vicinity of Hamble around 17 November, nothing directly referenced protest elsewhere or could be taken as a harbinger of what was to come. Fires at Longparish (13 November), Strathfieldsaye (15 November), and Wallington (16 November) being met with the usual sense of misgiving.[88] The two poles from which protests physically spread into Hampshire did not directly diffuse further into Hampshire. Instead, the first series of protests that both presaged and defined Hampshire Swing occurred on 17 November in the parishes of Whitchurch, Laverstoke and Freefolk where money and provisions were levied, and the destruction of threshing machines and a reduction in rents demanded.[89]

The Whitchurch protests predated the hitherto recognised start of overt protests in Hampshire by one day. This in itself might seem insignificant, but these actions extend the 'life' of intensive protest in the county and help explain the intensive resort to protest on 18 November. Hitherto, our understanding of the start of Swing in the Dever Valley has rested on the activities of a 'Musical and Radical Society' that met regularly in local pubs and advocated universal male suffrage. An extraordinarily literate reform petition carried on foot to King William IV at Brighton that September shows the pre-existence of local plebeian solidarities, it being signed by 73 labourers, artisans, publicans and small farmers from the parishes of Barton Stacey, Bullington and Wonston. A few inspirational, well-organised individuals could use these solidarities – as well as networks generated through labouring – to coordinate simultaneous protests over multiple parishes. And so it occurred on 18 November.[90]

Three parallel risings occurred in mid-Hampshire that day: one centred on Bullington, another on Overton, and another on Micheldever, all adopting the form and discourses of the Whitchurch rising.[91] These protests, though important on their terms, set the scene for a far wider and more forceful uprising in rural Hampshire. Indeed, protests on 19 November, while following the same pattern as the previous day, covered more parishes and displayed a greater confidence. Beyond those protests at Warnford and West Meon, the protest area on 19 November represented an extension of 17 and 18 November. Now protests spread as far north-east as Basingstoke, as far north-west as Andover, and south to Alresford. In addition to the former places, protests were also – again – centred on Overton and Wonston.[92]

The Andover and the Wonston protests introduced machine-breaking to north and mid-Hampshire. At Andover, threshing machines belonging to Mrs Baker and Mr Callaway were destroyed. The arrest of some of the men and the rapid enrolling of a civil force – prompted by reports that the men were going to destroy the workhouse and loot the shops – gave the protestors renewed vigour. The gaol was broken into and those arrested earlier in the day liberated. Then, in an echo of Wealden Swing, the farmers agreed to increase the labourers' wages from eight to ten shillings a week providing that the men would 'render assistance in getting the rents, tithes, and taxes lowered'. This was agreed to, and several of the farmers marched off to see James Blunt Esquire, the holder of the great tithes and landlord to the farmers and the concessions were secured.[93]

The Micheldever protests – drawing in 700–800 field labourers, artisans and small farmers from Wonston, Hunton, Micheldever, Stratton, Barton Stacey, Chilbolton, Longparish and other places – combined calls for an advance of wages and machine-breaking.[94] Their undoing came when they started to attack the property of the Baring family, banking magnates, major landowners and leading members of the Hampshire judiciary. Having witnessed the men in action, William Bingham Baring sought assistance at the Grange, the seat of Alexander Baring. On returning, Bingham Baring asked to speak to the machine-breakers' spokesman. In the ensuing parley, Baring cornered spokesman John Silcock prompting someone to shout out 'Go to work!' Henry Cook stepped forward, demanding to Baring: 'God damn you, get out of my way' before raising his sledgehammer aloft and striking the rim of Baring's hat and his shoulder. Baring collapsed, only being spared from another blow by the intervention of George Harding who had accompanied Baring from the Grange. Baring and Harding were bloodied and bruised, but Cook suffered his life on the Winchester scaffold for his 'impetuosity'.[95]

Swing in north and west Hampshire

On Saturday 20 November there was a distinct shift in the poles of protest in Hampshire. Protests continued in the Dever Valley – at Barton Stacey, Bullington, Micheldever and Newton Stacey – but these were more modest affairs than before, levying monies and pressing home the demand for higher wages. As Sir William Baring related to Lady Baring, for the rulers of rural Hampshire 'things ha[d] taken a better turn'. The men had failed to invade Winchester, and the expected walk on the Grange by '1,400 men' failed to materialise. The farmers had been ready to desert their property but now troops had arrived and plans were afoot to arm the Grange. With the exception of an apparently modest rising at Bullington on 22 November, the 'world [was] at ease'.[96]

Or at least it was in that part of Hampshire. The protests at Andover on 19 November were restrained compared to the events of the following day. According to one letter writer to *The Times*, 'exasperated with defeat' on 19 November, the 'rioters' strengthened their numbers with the intention of destroying Tasker's Iron Foundry at Upper Clatford. This was a concerted plan, for on that evening the foreman at Tasker's 'received some information respecting the factory', in consequence it was decided to close the factory the next day. By 11 a.m. a 'small mob' had gathered in Andover, while another 'large mob' visited the 'justice room' where an accommodation regarding wages and child allowances was arrived at. The request that the men should go back to work was ignored, however, as they stayed in Andover and visited the shop of a printer to find out – unsuccessfully – whether he used any machinery. At 3 p.m., 300 men armed with pickaxes and bludgeons marched 'three deep', headed by a flag bearer, to Tasker's. On arriving, the padlock of the gates was smashed off, the men entered the yard and buildings, and exchanged their bludgeons 'for better tools'. The destruction now commenced. First the flasks (in which tools were cast) were broken, then the crane, then the water wheel, then iron rollers, 'machines for the plough, and various agricultural implements'. Not only were machines and moulds destroyed but the windows, chimney and some walls were also broken. Even the roof was mounted and partially destroyed. The intensity of the attack, hitherto novel in 1830, was the function not only of the hostility generated because they made threshing machines, but also because, in the words of the crowd, 'the foundry was ruining every one – carpenters, and wrights, and weavers, and every body'.[97]

The three other poles of protest that day all represented a further extension of Swing's envelope. One group that destroyed a threshing machine of Mr Davison and a winnowing machine of Mr White on Saturday afternoon at Martyr Worthy also levied monies at Avington, Easton, Headbourne Worthy and levied £20 from Rev. Sir Henry Rivers. At Selborne, in an area hitherto unaffected by protest that autumn, a group of labourers announced their intention to guardian of the poor and workhouse master Harris of 'going round' the farmers attempting to press them into raising the wages. Harris advised them not to or they would 'repent thereafter'. At midnight, three guns loaded with slugs were fired into Harris's workhouse bedroom window, presaging two days of workhouse-focused protests in that part of north-east Hampshire.[98]

The other protest locale that day, and over subsequent days, was the

Test Valley. The parishes of Houghton, Compton, Broughton, Mottisfont, Michelmersh, Lockerley, Tytherley, Kings Somborne, Little Somborne, Crawley and Littleton were all visited, representing a significant shift south-westwards in Swing's envelope. The protesters avowed intention was to destroy all the threshing machines in the Test Valley. Notwithstanding a report in the *Hampshire Chronicle* that this was accomplished on 20 November, the record does not relate the destruction of any specific machines that day. Instead, a formidable force was established and largesse sought.[99] In the early hours of Sunday morning it appears that either the group divided or a new group was formed. One 'gang' was reported to be active at Stockbridge and the neighbouring parishes, while another group of men from Littleton and Sparsholt 'ransacked' a farmhouse in the former place some time before 2 a.m. Even the intervention of the military did not totally quell the ardour for protest that day, as further protests occurred at Littleton and Crawley.[100]

Protests continued on Monday 22 November. Assemblages occurring at Kings and Little Somborne and in 'all adjoining parishes', machine-breaking at Broughton, money levying at East Tytherley, Lockerley and Mottisfont, and a combination of machine-breaking and levying at Timsbury, Kimbridge and Michelmersh village. This latter group, on returning to East Tytherley and East Dean that night, even 'took down' the tollhouses on the Broughton and Romsey turnpike. This was a mere precursor, though, for the night of 23 November when the tollhouses were again visited, the families 'dragged out', and the buildings set on fire.[101] Romsey itself was also the focus of protests on 22 November. Combining late on Sunday night, the group proceeded to destroy threshing machines before 'forcibly enter[ing]' Luzborough House and looting the pantry and cellar. A further group assembled on the following day, but the focus was no longer the parishes of the Test Valley north of Romsey. Instead, the New Forest fringe parishes of the county border with Wiltshire provided the locus of wages agitation and machine-breaking.[102] Other places in the area between Romsey, Stockbridge and Winchester did protest on 22 November, but thereafter open protests ceased.[103] Beyond 23 November, machine-breaking and the other activities of mobile gangs no longer occurred in the area around Romsey – with the exception of two partial risings at Romsey on 25 November and at Eldon on 26 November.[104]

Despite the lull on Sunday 21 November, one area that witnessed protests for the first time was the north-west border with Wiltshire.

These protests were almost certainly inspired by events in nearby Andover, perhaps even drawing in individuals who had been active there on 19 and 20 November. In the early hours of Sunday morning, a group, reportedly 200 strong, assembled at Shoddesden. After levying money and victuals from farmer Barnes, they fired his barn and a cottage on his farm. The tactic of combining assembly with incendiarism – and threats of incendiarism – was also deployed later that day by another 'mob' at Fyfield and at Weyhill.[105] The 100 or so men gathered at Vernhams Dean used somewhat more conventional Swing tactics: levying money – occasionally resorting to physical force – from various inhabitants and breaking farmer Fermor's winnowing machine. Fermor, among other parishioners, was visited again on the following day, the group threatening 'more mischief' if he did not give them a crown.[106] Vernhams Dean must have also been visited again on 24 November when a group of men from Buttermere in Wiltshire went to Hurstbourne Tarrant.[107]

Vernhams Dean was not alone among the north-west Hampshire risings on 22 November. In addition to the aforementioned levying of monies at Andover, money and victuals were also demanded at Hurstbourne Tarrant and Weyhill, while at Ashmansworth higher wages were demanded. Threshing and chaff-cutting machines were also destroyed at Penton Grafton and Thruxton. According to one man pressed by the Thruxton men, the group 'had been round two days before they met him, breaking thrashing-machines ... by an order of the Government', presumably a perversion of the news from the Canterbury trial.[108] This discourse was also evident at neighbouring Quarley on 23 November where a chaff-cutting machine and two threshing machines were destroyed 'by order of the magistrates'.[109]

This pattern was followed on 23 November at St Mary Bourne, Crux Easton and Woodcott. After destroying several machines, the men visited Rev. Easton to press for an increase in wages, only to be informed that the magistrates had pre-emptively increased wages and that a note detailing the arrangement had been 'fastened on the church'. Still, William Simms took the clergyman to task for a sermon on the preceding Sunday which was 'against the poor'. It also transpired that labourer John Simms had visited Easton a few days earlier to ask for higher wages. The conversation turning to 'these riots', Easton had told Simms to 'stick to the farmers for your rights that's the only way to get them'. The protests were not spontaneous, but the product of a concerted plan.[110]

North-west Hampshire remained a centre of Swing activity for the next two days. Rather than being indigenous Hampshire protests, the stimulus now came from neighbouring Berkshire. According to J.R. Gowen, the 'rioters' in this part of Hampshire first assembled at the Axe and Compasses at East Woodhay on the evening of 22 November, the 'signal of revolt' having been given by 'some people from Inkpen and Kintbury' in Berkshire, where protests had started on Sunday. At some point – the precise time is unclear – they were also joined by a group from Whitway in Burghclere parish. They started by levying 'contributions' from the inhabitants and pressing all the labourers they could find, though some allegedly joined 'for the sake of the guzzle', before moving to neighbouring Highclere. After an extended drinking session at the Crown, they proceeded at 4 a.m. to break machines and levy more money in Highclere, Burghclere and Sydmonton parishes before dividing. The East Woodhay group 'marauded' about their parish and Ashmansworth, before twenty of the party were captured at the Crown. The fortunes of the Whitway group were a little different. Some of the party dispersed in a panic on hearing what had happened at the Crown, the others, albeit further depleted by the desertion of the pressed men, continued breaking machines through the night at St Mary Bourne, Woodcott and Crux Easton parishes.[111] In two days their actions had, in the words of the Rector of East Woodhay, 'paralysed' the area.[112]

Wages demands, money levying and occasional machine-breaking also dominated protests in the area to the north and west of Basingstoke on 22 and 23 November.[113] Apparently, a different group was responsible for protests on the second day, traversing, according to the Duke of Wellington, 'a very lawless part of the county between here [Strathfieldsaye] and Kingsclere'. Before being captured, they had destroyed machines and levied monies at Pamber End, Sherborne St John, Wolverton, Tadley, Baughurst parish and then West Heath. Here they were ensnared by a pincer movement by a detachment of Guards heading south from Reading and a detachment of Lancers from Basingstoke. Fifty-seven (or fifty-eight depending on reports) of the men 'surrendered' 'without resistance'.[114]

Swing in south and east Hampshire

Events in mid and east Hampshire took a similar course, except in Selborne and Headley where, in addition to threshing machine-breaking and calls for higher wages and lower tithes, the focus of the assembled group was the workhouses. As noted above, on 20 November shots were fired into the windows of workhouse master Harrison after he advised a group of labourers not to go about the farmers and demand an increase in wages.[115] Between then and the destruction of Selborne workhouse on Monday afternoon, some of the farmers had consented to increase the labourers' wages, and in return the men had promised to 'get a reduction of tithes'. This they attempted to do en route to the workhouse by going to Rev. Cobbold's and demanding he cut his tithes by £300. The parley ended fruitlessly, for soon after a 300-strong group passed on their way to the workhouse. Some of the men stayed, Cobbold later relayed, 'so that they could watch my motions', but most went to 'turn old Harrison out'.

According to farmer Bridger of Oakhanger, the farmers had warned Harrison the previous evening of the Selborne men's intentions. Consequently, the governor was away on Monday morning but presumably had not mentioned the warning to his family as they were still in residence. Here accounts differ. Magistrate Henry Budd's account states that the 'mob' threatened to murder Harrison and his family, another account stating that they gave Mrs Harrison notice to quit before nightfall upon which she immediately fled to the Anchor in neighbouring Liphook. Either way, the men then started to destroy the house. Tiles were tossed off the roof, furniture was smashed up, doors and windows were broken. The remnants of the furniture, including a grandfather clock, and Harrison's clothes were also set on fire. Having partly demolished the workhouse, the men returned to Cobbold's. Several farmers were now present and although they did not intervene, they did warn Cobbold that he ought to agree to the men's demands or 'the mob' would pull down his house. The clergyman's bailiff drafted an agreement, and 'in fear' the clergyman signed it, with the farmers countersigning.[116]

Cobbold and Harrison's tormentors spent the rest of the day and night at Selborne, reportedly 'eating, drinking and rioting'. Ringleader Robert Holdaway, an unemployed carpenter and former publican, was an exception. He had been co-opted by the men and the farmers to visit the farmers in the neighbouring parishes to secure their assent to increase the labourers' wages. Signatures were obtained in Hartley Mauditt and Newton Valence, but plans to visit further farmers on 23 November were scuppered by the Selborne men who insisted that they come with him. They did, and the next morning in what was a preconceived plan, marched seven miles to Headley, calling at Empshott and Greatham levying money as they went. Perhaps knowing of the plan to visit Headley, the parish farmers had called a meeting to discuss the labourers' wages, presumably in an attempt to prevent any disturbance, while farmer Bennett removed his threshing machine to neighbouring Kingsley. This was not just an invasion by strangers. That morning the Headley men had also started to assemble, before forcing Rev. Dickinson under duress to reduce his tithes by £300 a year.

Sometime between 10 and 11 a.m., the group that started from Selborne arrived at Headley workhouse. They initially called at the workhouse, prompting governor Shoesmith to remove his goods, before going to the farmers' meeting at Headley Green. The farmers agreed to increase their labourers' wages and, according to a report in the Portsmouth press, a 'similar paper' to that signed by Cobbold at Selborne was now signed by Dickinson. A 'declaration' that the farmers would not assent to have any more 'hired guardians of the poor' was also signed. Before the meeting was over, some of the men returned to the workhouse and, according to Shoesmith 'rushed like a torrent into every room'. They began by breaking the windows, wooden wall partitions and the stair banisters. The floors, window frames, ceilings and rafters were next, some of the men also climbing onto the roof and throwing off the tiles. All but the sick ward was destroyed. Holdaway, who had attempted to prevent the destruction, then managed after much persuasion to get the men to accompany him to Kingsley in his effort to get other local farmers to sign up to the Selborne wages agreement. Whether all the men did follow Holdaway to Kingsley is unclear, but from Baron Vaughan's summary it is clear that representatives from ten parishes were present: Holdaway calling on representatives from all parishes to distribute the £23 levied that day. In addition to levying money, Bennett's threshing machine was also destroyed.[117] After going to Kingsley, the men dispersed, the threat to go to Alton and demolish the workhouse and breweries coming to nothing, though protests did occur elsewhere in the neighbourhood on 24 and 25 November.[118]

Events in the rest of mid- and east Hampshire took a more conventional form. On Monday 22 November, a large 'assembly' of farmworkers descended on Petersfield in a well-planned operation to demand an increase in wages from the local farmers. This was a gentle affair, no 'violence was offered' and only three protestors were arrested. How successful they were in their demands is not known. However, the protest presumably provided the inspiration for the labourers of neighbouring Buriton who 'intimidate[d]' the farmers into raising their wages, and those of Steep who called a meeting for the following day. According to a report in the Portsmouth press, the Steep labourers had been ordered by 'persons calling themselves delegates from the general committee', a notice being taken round the farmers for their signatures.[119]

Alresford was the other district of east and mid-Hampshire affected by protests on the 22 and 23 November. At a planned meeting at Alresford on 22 November to discuss the labourers' conditions it was agreed that field workers' wages would be increased, with the landowners and clergy promising to reduce their rents and tithes respectively. Rather than being pacified, several of those present went to New Farm where they destroyed a threshing machine and were only narrowly dissuaded from destroying a steam engine. The reason? They were persuaded that it did not reduce manual labour.[120]

Protests were also anticipated at Avington, the seat of the Duke of Buckingham. Not only had the Home Office had been prevailed upon to send down two 'of the new police' to 'help quell the riots in the vicinity of Winchester', the officers being stationed at Avington, but the Duke had barricaded his windows and commandeered canons from his yacht to be placed on the roof of his mansion. Such fears were well grounded. The group who had been machine-breaking and levying monies at Martyr Worthy, Avington, Easton, Headbourne Worthy on Saturday 20 November had an 'understanding' that they would meet again on Monday. They did, and carried on their previous plan of operations. After levying monies at Martyr Worthy and destroying a threshing machine at Itchen Abbas, the 'near 300 rioters, from Winchester and distant parishes' were met by Rev. Wright JP of Itchen Abbas. Here, on the intervention of the special constables and London officers, fifty men were arrested and the rest dispersed.[121]

The other major centre of protest on both 22 and 23 November was the area around Bishop's Waltham. As with many other areas of Hampshire, there had been some 'warning' protests: an incendiary fire at Droxford on the night of the 17–18 November and a series of Swing letters received at Southwick, Botley and Durley.[122] Machine-breaking at Durley and tithe protests at Upham occurred simultaneously on the 22 November, the two groups then joining forces to destroy more machines and extort money. On again separating, the Durley men went to Bishop's Waltham to demand of Rev. Scard and the landowners in their native parish (but resident in Bishop's Waltham) that they attend a parish meeting on 24 November to discuss the state of the poor.[123]

Protests on 23 November were more dramatic. At Soberton, having also risen on the previous day, a 'large body of labouring men' paraded through the streets. No more is known of this group, though it is at least likely that they joined together with a group that assembled on Shirrell Heath, who had already levied money at several farmhouses and broken at least one threshing machine at Droxford. On the heath they were met by a military detachment, and despite being armed and being determined to resist, several of the men were taken. Some of those who fled proceeded to Wickham, where, on being addressed by magistrate Major Campbell, spoke 'exceedingly rationally' about the impossibility of living on their current wages. On promising that their case would be 'fully considered', they dispersed.[124] Military intervention did not stop further risings on 24 November, and group of labourers successfully lobbied the Soberton vestry for higher wages and a guarantee of year round employment. At Droxford, despite promises that their 'situation would be looked into', the group went on to destroy a 'model' threshing machine at Swanmore.[125]

There were also links between the Monday and Tuesday risings in other south-east Hampshire parishes. An act of threshing machine-breaking at Exton on 23 November was reportedly the work of 'those who had assembled on Monday' – presumably at Preshaw – while individuals who had been present at Corhampton on 22 November were also involved in protests at Owslebury and South Stoneham on the following day. Indeed, the 'great party' responsible for destroying a winnowing machine and a threshing machine, levying £17, and compelling some of the farmers and landlords at Owslebury to sign an agreement to increase their wages and lower their tenants rents, were from 'the different villages'.[126]

This multiformity of motive and complex, pan-parish geography is best demonstrated by the actions of Abraham Childs, a 48-year-old labourer from Alresford. Not only was Childs involved in the rising at Corhampton, but he had also been active at Upham and Preshaw, calling out commands while wearing a handkerchief tied round his body like a sash. The following day – again adorned with the distinctive sash – he was part of a group that started at Durley before proceeding to various places in Bishopstoke and South Stoneham parishes destroying threshing machines and extorting money as they went. Their mission, in Childs's words, 'for our lawful rights, to break machinery, and get higher wages' ended at Stoneham Park, the seat of Fleming, the county MP. Fleming was ready, though, and with the assistance of a party of 3rd Dragoons took forty-five of the men into custody in a bloody scuffle.[127]

The area to the west of Southampton was the last part of the county to rise. As Hobsbawm and Rudé correctly asserted, most of the events on the fringes of the New Forest were either isolated affairs or thwarted by a now well-organised judiciary. While many of the reports from this area were rather vague – *The Times* printing an undated report from Lyndhurst stating that magistrate Buckly had been called up in the night to meet a mob of '2,000 people' marching from Ringwood and Poole[128] – some protests were recorded in detail. In particular, two episodes received detailed coverage. At coastal Fawley protests started on 25 November, the labourers going about the parish to attempt to effect an increase in their wages and, seemingly uniquely in Hampshire, to remove the assistant overseer from the parish. A parish meeting on the following day to discuss the labourers' situation, prompted the men to again mobilise. On being told by the magistrates that they were to meet with the farmers on Saturday to consider the case, a 'riot' ensued.[129]

By far the most dramatic events occurred in Fordingbridge parish on 23 November. Mr Shepherd's threshing machine manufactory at Stuckton was ransacked and Mr Thompson's sacking manufactory at East Mill was destroyed by a group 'under the guidance and direction' of Captain Hunt (a.k.a. James Thomas Cooper), an ostler from East Grimsted in Wiltshire. According to Sir Charles Halse of Breamore, once embodied, they 'proceeded to every house in the neighbour-hood' demanding drink and money, pressing every man they came across into their service. Many, he related, went willingly. From here they followed the Avon river, through Breamore, into Fordingbridge, and on to Shepherd's at some little distance from the town. As Cooper entered the factory, the men started knocking the machinery to pieces. Soon all was destroyed and much of the building wrecked. Their ends accomplished, they proceeded to destroy several threshing machines in Fordingbridge and to take beer and victuals at the public houses. At 4 p.m., they went to Thompson's. Again, all the machinery was quickly destroyed, part of it being thrown out of the factory windows, other parts being carried like trophies back into Fordingbridge. Some of the men, including Cooper, returned to the Greyhound, going on to levy money from the householders in the town during the evening, groups on three different occasions throughout the night also visiting Eyre Coote at West Park. Others went directly to Damerham, Rockbourne and Whitsbury where they 'continued their plunder and devastation' until they were finally dispersed at 2 a.m. by a part mounted civil force. By this time, Cooper had joined a group in a public house at Damerham where, in an alcohol-induced stupor, he was finally taken by two of Eyre Coote's gamekeepers.[130]

The end of Swing?

Swing in its collective forms had a short but intensive existence in Hampshire. Protests continued, though, in the form of occasional incendiary fires, the sending of threatening letters and the voicing of bitter recriminations against those who had incarcerated their friends and family members. The part of Hampshire most intensively subjected to such treatment during this period had not previously been impacted upon by intensive 'mobbings', but had only been subjected to occasional protests: this was the Isle of Wight. There had been protests on the island in the autumn of 1830, but these made no reference to the unfurling movement. The first sign of protest clearly inspired by 'Swing' occurred in the week starting 15 November, the Newport parish poor striking work and a 'Swing' letter being received by a farmer in the 'east end' of the island.[131] In turn, on 22 November small assemblages occurred at Newton and Parkhurst where the men set to work in the forest by the Isle of Wight poor law incorporation struck work. At the former place, fifty men – self-styled as the 'grand army' – left their employ with the intention of destroying Rev. Hughes's threshing machine. This was not achieved, the men quarrelling among themselves and only getting as far as levelling a wall of one of the overseers.[132] These partial risings were the only (recorded) instances of collective protest on the island. What followed in the final days of November were at least four fires (at Newport, Carisbrook, Ryde and Freshwater), a flurry of threatening letters – several targeting threshing machines users – and an open incitement at Newchurch to destroy threshing machines.[133]

The protest practices on the Isle of Wight in late November were the same as those deployed elsewhere in Hampshire. After fires and threats of fire on 28 and 29 November,[134] protests were sporadic until the start of the Special Commission on 20 December, with occasional fires interspersed by a labourers' strike at Twyford on 13 December, occasioned by an attempt to cut wages.[135] These dynamics did not hold elsewhere. Swing in Kent reverted to its initial forms of machine-breaking, threatening letters and incendiarism. In East Sussex, occasional poor relief and wages demonstrations also continued until late November. Plans by an assemblage of 'nearly a 1,000' people from Hellingly and Horsebridge to visit Lord Gage at Firle Place, and to compel the collector of the assessed taxes at Crowhurst to return the monies he had already collected both failed on military interventions. Equally unsuccessful was an attempt to force the Rector of Ewhurst to lower his tithes, the cleric absconding at 5 a.m. to avoid being followed.[136] Not all late Wealden protests were unsuccessful. On 19 November, an assemblage successfully demanded higher wages from the Ore vestry.[137]

The final week of November effectively saw the end of mass assemblages in Surrey and West Sussex, those that occurred being mild-mannered affairs. At Henfield on 24 November, a group, including a contingent from neighbouring Woodmancote, met with the farmers when their 'little difference' was accommodated. Other assemblages on 24 and 25 November were equally good natured. Protestors at Shermanbury and Slinfold had their demands readily assented to, thirty labourers gathered at Treyford disbanded without 'mischief', while a group from Kirdford and Wisborough Green went to Petworth to request that Egremont increase their wages. Finally, 100 labourers from Limpsfield marched to Oxted but offered no resistance when met by the magistrates.[138] If these were not the final acts of overt protest in Sussex and Surrey in 1830 – Kirdford rose (again) on 30 November,[139] and on 4 December a group of West Chiltington road workers marched to the Petworth Bench to complain that the parish had reneged on local agreements[140] – they effectively marked the end of 'new' protests. Now, as in Hampshire, protests took the form of incendiarism and incendiary letters, clustering in the downland strip stretching from Hastings to Newhaven on the coast and inland to Hellingly.[141]

A similar scenario played out in Kent. After the dramatic but brief protests on the fringe of Romney Marsh in mid-November, collective actions were few. A group of men who gathered at Herne on 18

November and proceeded to Mr Sladden's farm were thwarted in their attempts to destroy his threshing machine. With this in mind, a few days later, it was demanded that neighbouring farmer Harrison stop using his threshing machine. The aggravation caused by the frustrated visit to Sladden's farm was released on the night of 20 November when, as Harrison and Sladden accompanied each other on the parochial watch, they were shot at by some person(s) hiding behind a hedge.[142]

The other non-Thanet disturbances all occurred in north-west Kent. On 24 November at Wrotham, between 400 and 500 labouring people gathered at the Rector's mansion and, to cries of 'Bread or Blood', demanded that he cut his tithes to allow the farmers to increase labourers' wages. This demand was met by the defiant claim that the Rector 'would rather submit to be hanged on the first tree, than accede to such violent proceedings'. Eventually, both sides agreed to attend the scheduled vestry meeting. On their arrival, the labourers, in imitation of Wealden Swing, seized the assistant overseer, placed him in a cart and wheeled him to the edge of the parish, where they warned him that he must resign his position.[143] Some other wages-related disputes occurred in the area,[144] while an attempt was also made to force a tithe reduction at Sevenoaks.[145]

The last sustained campaign of machine-breaking occurred on the Isle of Thanet. On 15 November, magistrate George Hannam's Minster farm was targeted by incendiarists. This being interpreted as a warning against the use of threshing machines, farmer Hills-Rowe of neighbouring Margate stopped using his machine, placing it in a chalk pit preparatory to its destruction. News of Hills-Rowe's actions quickly spread, and on the night of Saturday 20 November a semi-inebriated group of labourers, artisans, sailors and tradesmen, descended on his farm and destroyed the machine.[146] Two nights later they visited Hannam, and proceeded to destroy three threshing machines and his steel-made implements.[147] Fears that machines at Birchington, Minster and Monkton were also vulnerable to attack were confirmed on 24 November when forty-six men regrouped under the lead of 'General' Moore and destroyed six threshing machines.[148]

The activities of the Thanet gang coincided with a renewed resort to arson and the sending of threatening letters. The environs of Faversham were particularly plagued by incendiarism, while Canterbury and Thanet farmers were reportedly bombarded with

Swing letters threatening destruction if they yielded to the demands of tithe collectors.[149] By the final week of November, the frequency of incendiary fires and threatening letters had considerably diminished. While 'only' seven fires were reported to have occurred in the county during December, there were ominous signs that Swing was not yet over. A fire on Mr Arnold's Aylesford farm was preceded by the receipt two letters: one warning that his premises would be fired, the other calling on the labourers to meet.[150]

Notes

1 For a tabulation of all recorded protest incidents between 24 August and 31 December 1830 see Appendix.
2 Centre for Kentish Studies (hereafter CKS), Q/SBe 120/11, Deposition of Ingram Swaine, 6 October 1830.
3 E. Hobsbawm and G. Rudé, *Captain Swing* (London: Lawrence & Wishart, 1969), p. 97.
4 CKS, Q/SBe 120/1, Deposition of William Dodd, 30 August 1830.
5 R. Cobb, 'Review of *Captain Swing*', *Times Literary Supplement*, 3254 (1969).
6 CKS, Q/SBe 120/11, 14b, 34 and 35, Depositions of Ingram Swaine, 6 October, John Collick, 8 October, Isaac Croucher and Thomas Larrett, both 19 October 1830.
7 Report from the *Spectator*, q.f. *Kent Herald* (hereafter *KH*), 6 January 1831. BPP Commons, 'Report from His Majesty's Commissioners for Inquiring into the Administration and Practical Operation of the Poor Laws' (hereafter 'Rural Queries') (1834), vol. xxxiv 237e, Response of John Pope, Barham, question 53; Hobsbawm and Rude, *Captain Swing*, p. 85.
8 For sources see note 6.
9 Hobsbawm and Rude, *Captain Swing*, p. 98.
10 *Kentish Gazette* (hereafter *KG*), 7 November 1823; *KH*, 24 May 1827.
11 CKS, Q/SBe 120/11, 4, 19a, 19b, 20 and 21, Depositions of Ingram Swaine, 6 October, John Hambrook, 25 September and 18 October, Norwood Woolett, George Hambrook and John Archer, all 18 October 1830.
12 TNA, HO 44/21, fos 241–2, 'A Kentish Farmer', Swingfield Minnis to Home Office, 13 September 1830.
13 CKS, U951 C177/4, Orders to High Constable of Bircholt Barony (Knatchbull) for summoning a Special Sessions, 18 September 1830; CKS Q/SBe, 120/2 f, b, c, a, d and e, 120/8b, and 120/11, Depositions of Richard Castle, John Fairman, Francis Castle, William Dodd, George Castle and Thomas Castle, all 19 September, James Whitnall, 5 October, and Ingram Swaine, 6 October; CKS, U951 C177/14, Deposition of William Hughes, 25 September; *Kentish Chronicle* (hereafter *KC*), 21 September 1830.
14 CKS, Q/SBe, 12012c and 3b, Depositions of Francis Castle, 19 September, and Daniel Woollett, publican, 22 September 1830. According to the Stelling tithe apportionment Atwood held just over six acres of pasture, being one of 58

land occupiers with under 10 acres out of total 83 landholders in the parish: TNA, IR 29/17/344.

15 CKS, Q/SBe 120/5 and 13, Confessions of George Youens, Lyminge, 29 September and 7 October; CKS U951 C177/11, 10 and 19, Deposition of William Forded, 24 September; Information of Edward Hughes and Richard Hills, 23 September; and, Information of Benjamin Andrews, 27 September; TNA, HO 44/21, fos 263–6, Edward Hughes, Smeeth Hill House, to Home Office, 23 September 1830.

16 CKS, U951 C177/18 and 13, Rev. Price, Lyminge to Knatchbull, 27 September, List of persons entered into recognisances (n.d. but 2 October 1830).

17 CKS, U951 C177/17, T.P. Junior, Denton to Knatchbull, Mersham, 26 September; *KG*, 28 September, 1 and 5 October 1830.

18 TNA, HO 52/8, fos 276–7 and 281–2, Knatchbull, Mersham to Peel, 6 October 1830 (twice). For a full treatment of the events surrounding Price's fire see chapter ten.

19 *KG*, 8 and 15 October; *Brighton Herald* (hereafter *BH*), 16 October 1830.

20 *KH*, 28 October 1830.

21 *Brighton Gazette* (hereafter *BG*), 14 October; *KG*, 19 October; *Maidstone Journal* (hereafter *MJ*), 21 October; *KH*, 21 October; TNA, HO 52/8, fos 338–9 and 216–8, Mr Moneypenny JP, 15 October, Camden, Canterbury, 22 October, both to Peel; *Sussex Advertiser* (hereafter *SA*), 22 November 1830. For cases see appendix 1.

22 *KG*, 5 October; *KC*, 5 October; TNA, HO 52/8, fos 209–10, John Boys, Margate to Peel, 17 October 1830. The evidence does not explicitly claim that they broke his machine. However, it does imply that an attack had occurred 'because of their [Garrett's labourers] suffering last Winter'.

23 *KG*, 3 September; TNA, HO 52/8, fos 370–1, Rev. Edward Owen, Chislet to Peel, 29 October 1830.

24 *KG*, 12 October 1830.

25 *Maidstone Gazette* (hereafter *MG*), 19 October; *KH*, 21 October 1830.

26 *Cobbett's Weekly Political Register* (hereafter *CWPR*), 2 October; *MG*, 19 October; *MJ*, 19 October; *KG*, 19 and 22 October; *KH*, 7 and 21 October; TNA, HO 52/8, fos 333–4, Maidstone Postmaster to Sir Francis Freeling, 14 October 1830.

27 *KH*, 28 October; CKS, U840 C250 10/6, Peel to Earl of Camden, 25 October 1830.

28 TNA, HO 52/8, fos 216–18 and 300–1, Camden, 22 October, Poore, Murston to Peel 23 October,; CKS, U951 C177/35, Poore, Murston to Knatchbull, 24 October; *MJ*, 26 October; *KH*, 28 October; *MG*, 9 November 1830.

29 TNA, HO 52/8, fos 216–8 and 359–360, Camden, Canterbury, 22 October, Rev. Gleig, Ash, 25 October 1830, both to Peel. A gratten stack was the name given in Kent and Sussex to a stubble stack.

30 *The Times* (hereafter *TT*), 27 October; *KG*, 29 October; TNA, HO 52/8, fos 359–60, Gleig to Peel, 25 October 1830.

31 TNA, TS 11/943, Prosecution Brief prepared by the Treasury Solicitor against Timothy Willocks (but not brought to trial).

32 TNA, HO 52/8, fos 363–4 and 359–60, John Plumptree and Mr Hammond,

Wingham, Gleig, Ash, both 25 October to Peel; CKS, Q/SBe 121/1–13, 8, 9 and 19, Various depositions, 26 October to 20 November; *KG*, 29 October 1830.

33 CKS, Q/SBe 121/1, 12a–c and 9, Depositions of James Dowker, 26 October and 19 November, James Petty, John Spain and William Euden, all 19 November; CKS, U951 C14/7, Poore, Murston to Knatchbull, 26 October; *MJ*, 2 November 1830.

34 CKS, U951 C177/36, George Gipps, Bekesbourne to Knatchbull, 24 October 1830.

35 TNA, HO 52/8, fo. 142, David Taylor, Mayor of Sandwich to Peel, 29 October 1830.

36 TNA HO 52/8, fos 22–3, Sharp, Faversham to Freeling, 31 October; *KG*, 5 November; *TT*, 2 November 1830.

37 TNA, HO 52/8, fos 300–1, Rev. Poore, Murston to Peel, 23 October; CKS, U951 C177/35, Poore to Knatchbull, 24 October 1830.

38 *MJ*, 26 October; TNA, HO 52/8, fos 361–2, Mr Sharp, Faversham to Sir Francis Freeling, 26 October 1830.

39 TNA, HO 52/8, fos 365–6, Poore, Murston to Peel, 25 October; CKS U951 C14/7, Poore to Knatchbull, 26 October; *MJ*, 26 October; *KH*, 28 October; *KG*, 29 October 1830.

40 TNA, HO 52/8, fos 365–6, 361–2 and 228–30, Poore, Murston to Peel, 25 October, Sharp, Faversham to Freeling, 26 October, and Camden to Peel, enclosing letter from Mr Scudamore, Wrotham Heath, 26 October; CKS, U951 C1417, Poor, to Knatchbull, 26 October; *KH*, 28 October; *KG*, 29 October 1830.

41 CKS, Q/SBw/124/7, Defence of Robert Price, 19 November; TNA, HO 52/8, fos 365–6 and 361–2 Poore, Murston to Peel, 25 October, Sharp, Faversham to Freeling, 26 October; Poore to Knatchbull, 26 October, CKS, U951 C1417; *KH*, 28 October. The *Rochester Gazette* (26 October 1830) also reported that 'large bodies of men armed with bludgeons' had over the last few nights been observed on the road below Rainham, occasionally going in different directions.

42 CKS, Q/SBw/124/7, 8 and 9, Defence of Robert Price, Depositions of Daniel Green, farmer, and Charlotte Stacey, wife of Courtney Stacey, all 19 November; CKS, U951 C14/8 and 6, Poore, Murston to Knatchbull, n.d. (but 28 October) and 29 October; TNA, HO 52/8, fos 367–8, 28–9 and 25–6, Poore, 29 October, Maidstone Bench, 30 October, and, Lt Col Charles Middleton, Cavalry Depot, Maidstone, 31 October, all to Peel; TNA, TS 11/1071, 5035, 943, Prosecution Briefs prepared by the Treasury Solicitor in the cases of *The King* v. *Edward Chapman, Mathew Waltz Walker and William Robinson*, and *The King* v. *John Adams*; *MJ*, 2 November; *KH*, 4 November *Hastings & Cinque Ports Iris* (hereafter *HIris*), 6 November 1830.

43 *TT*, 4 and 18 November; *KG*, 5 and 12 November 1830; CKS, Q/SBw 124/4,5,6 and 15, Depositions of Charles Chamley, John Luck, and Robert Tassel, all 19 November 1830, and Gaol Calendar, West Kent Epiphany Quarter Sessions 1831; *MG*, 9 and 16 November; *MJ*, 9 November; TNA, HO 52/8, fos 212–13; Mr Scadamay, Maidstone to Camden, 11 November; *KH*, 18 November 1830.

44 *MJ*, 26 October and 2 November; *Rochester Gazette* (hereafter *RG*), 26 October

and 2 November; *KH*, 28 October and 4 November; *TT*, 4 November; *KG*, 5 November; TNA, HO 52/8, fos 384–5, W. Lushington, WLCMO to Arbuthknot, 26 October; *HIris*, 6 November 1830.

45 TNA, HO 52/10, fos 369–70, 371–4 and 422–3 and 428, G. Courthope, Whiligh to Phillips, 6 November (twice), second enclosing deposition of Thomas Arcoll, Assistant Overseer and Governor of the Poorhouse, Brede, 6 November, Sir Godfrey Webster, Battle to Peel, 20 November, enclosing examination of Joseph Bryant, 19 November; *BH*, 6 November; *BG*, 11 November 1830; BPP Commons, 'Report from His Majesty's Commissioners for Inquiring into the Administration and Practical Operation of the Poor Laws' (1834), vol. xxxiv, 201a, appendix A, report of A Majendie, 'History of the Brede Riots'.

46 *CWPR*, 2 October; *Brighton Guardian*, 11 November; TNA, HO 52/10, fos 354–6 and 357–8, Freeling, General Post Office to Phillips, 4 November, enclosing Ticknoll, Battle to Freeling, 3 November, Barton, Clerk to the Battle Bench to Peel, 3 November; *BH*, 6 November; *MJ*, 9 November; *BG*, 11 November 1830.

47 TNA, HO 52/10, fos 363–4, 364–6, 359–60 and 361–2, Ticknall, Battle, Thomas Quaife, Battle both 5 November, Barton, Battle, 4 and 5 November to Peel; *TT*, 8 November 1830.

48 TNA, HO 52/10, fos 617–19 and 383–5, Earl of Egremont, Petworth, 7 November, enclosing Courthope, Whiligh to Egremont, 7 November, Godfrey Webster, Battle Abbey, 8 November to Peel; *MJ*, 9 November 1830.

49 TNA, HO 52/10, fos 582–3, Charles Ford, Sun Fire Office, London to Peel, 11 November; *BH*, 6 November; *TT*, 8 and 15 November; *SA*, 8 November; *BG*, 11 November 1830.

50 TNA, HO 52/10, fos 394–5 and 383–5, Battle Bench, 12 November, Godfrey Webster, Battle Abbey, 8 November to Peel; *RG*, 16 November 1830.

51 TNA, HO 52/10, fos 386–7, 383–5, 388–9 and 52/8, fos 160–70, J.C. Sharpe, Dormons, Northiam, 9 November, Godfrey Webster, Battle Abbey, 8 and 9 November, Messrs Collingwood and Young, Hawkhurst, 11 November, to Peel; East Sussex County Record Office (hereafter ESCRO), AMS 5995/3/10 and 13, Davenport, Robertsbridge, 8 November, and E.J. Curteis, 9 November, both to H.B. Curteis, Battle; *BH*, 13 November; *RG*, 16 November 1830.

52 Hawkhurst and Benenden: TNA, HO 52/8 fos 166–70, Collingwood and Young, Hawkhurst to Peel, 11 November; TNA, TS 11/943, Prosecution Briefs prepared by the Treasury Solicitor in the case of *The King* v. *George Barrow, John Ballard, John Tuckner, William Chrisford and John Beale*, Kent Winter Assizes. Rotherfield: TNA, HO 52/8, fos 16–17, Major General Lord Fitzroy Somerset, Tunbridge Wells to Peel, 16 November 1830. Crowborough: TNA, TS 11/1007, Prosecution Briefs prepared by the Treasury Solicitor in the case of the King vs. Richard Hodd and John Wickens alias Wicking. For other protests see Appendix.

53 TNA, HO 52/8, fo. 161, Earl of Liverpool, Buxted Park, 14 November to Peel; *BG*, 18 November; *BH*, 20 November; *SA*, 22 November 1830.

54 TNA, HO 52/8, fos 212–13 and 235–6, Mr Scudamay, Maidstone, J. Major,

Tunbridge Wells to Camden, both 11 November, forwarded to the Home Office; *BG*, 11 November 1830; Wells, 'Social protest', p. 161.

55 *BG*, 18 November; *HIris*, 20 November; TNA, HO 52/8, fos 11–12, W. Bremridge, Rusthall to Peel, 14 November 1830.

56 For details see Appendix.

57 *BH*, 13 November; *SA*, 15 November 1830.

58 *SA*, 15 November 1830; West Sussex County Record Office (hereafter WSCRO), QR/Q 51, Indictment of John Champion and Thomas Champion, West Sussex Epiphany Sessions 1831.

59 WSCRO, QR/W1758, fos 257–8 and 263, Deposition of Rev. Peter H. Moore, Thakeham, and Information of William Terry, Thakeham, both 27 December 1830; WSCRO, QR/Q/51, Indictment of Harry Robinson and William Smart, both West Chiltington, West Sussex Epiphany Sessions 1831; WSCRO, Add. Mss. 13,395, Charlotte Palmer, Sullington to her mother, 23 November; *TT*, 23 November; WSCRO, Goodwood 1477a, fo. 123, Letter to Duke of Richmond, 24 November 1830.

60 *BG*, 18 November; *BH*, 20 November; *HIris*, 20 November 1830.

61 *BG*, 18 November; *TT*, 19 November; *HIris*, 20 November; *Hampshire Telegraph* (hereafter *HT*), 22 November 1830.

62 *BG*, 18 and 25 November; *BH*, 20 November; TNA, HO 52/10, fos 410–12, Charles Howell, Hove to Peel, 17 November 1830.

63 TNA, HO 52/7, fos 31–2, Petersfield Post Office Deputy to Freeling, 18 November; *HIris*, 20 November; *BG*, 18 November and 23 December; *HT*, 22 November; *SA*, 22 November 1830.

64 TNA, HO 52/7, fos 31–2, Petersfield Post Office Deputy to Freeling, 18 November; Hampshire County Record Office (hereafter HCRO), 75M19/L3/9, Henry Howard MP, Petworth to Lady Porchester, Lynton, Devon, 20 November; *Hampshire Advertiser* (hereafter *HA*), 20 November; *Hampshire Chronicle* (hereafter *HC*), 22 November 1830.

65 TNA, HO 52/10, fos 7–9, Anon, Gosport to Peel, 12 November; *Southampton Mercury* (hereafter *SM*), 13 November; *HC*, 15 November; *TT*, 16 November; *Devizes and Wiltshire Gazette*, 18 November; *Salisbury Journal*, 22 November; *London Gazette*, 23 November; WSCRO, Goodwood Mss 1447A, R3, Draft letter by Duke of Richmond, Chichester, 24 November 1830.

66 For details see appendix 1. *BH*, 20 November; *SA*, 22 November; *HT*, 22 November; *BG*, 25 November; WSCRO, QR/W/758, fos 204 and 206, Examinations of John Dyer, victualler of the White Swan, Westhampnett, and Richard Caplin, Chichester, both 18 November; WSCRO, Goodwood 1477a R16 and 24, Examinations of Stephen Farndell, farmer, Bosham, 18 November, and Henry Meaden, machine maker, Bosham, 20 November 1830.

67 WSCRO, QR/W1758, fos 222, 221, 218 and 219, Examinations of David Bowman, yeoman, Westbourne, Thomas Ellman Thompson, Funtington, William Collins, Funtington, all 20 November, Francis Cronnsilk, Funtington, 15 December; WSCRO, Goodwood 1477a R27, Examination of John Gratwick, Westbourne, 20 November; *Portsmouth, Portsea and Gosport Herald* (hereafter *PHer*), 21 November; *HT*, 22 November 1830.

68 *PHer*, 21 November; WSCRO, Goodwood 1477a R30, Examinations of Henry

Walker, Navy Lieutenant, and Charles Lutman, Navy Lieutenant, both 22 November 1830.

69 *SA*, 22 November; *TT*, 23 November 1830; *BG*, 25 November 1830.

70 During the day Timothy Shelley, a neighbouring magistrate, had received a threatening letter imploring him that if he 'wish to escape the impending danger in this world and that which is to come' he should 'first go round to all your parishioners and return all the last years tyths and inquire and hear from there own lips what distresses there in and how of them are drove to part with the last shilling to pay you this shamefull manopely'. The letter was chillingly signed 'a Friend to all Mr Swing about – beware of the fate! Dagger and the are [air] gun'. TNA, HO 52/10, fos 532–3, Thomas Sanctuary, The Nunnery, Horsham to Peel, 17 November 1830.

71 *BG*, 25 November; TNA, HO 52/10, fos 534–7 and 538–9, Thomas Sanctuary, The Nunnery, Horsham to Peel, 18 November, and Mr Davis, Leystonstone, Essex to Peel, 20 November 1830, and enclosures.

72 *BG*, 25 November; TNA, HO 52/10, fos 542–3 and 204–5, Thomas Sanctuary to Peel, 19 November; and, William Crawford, Dorking to Peel, 19 November 1830.

73 *TT*, 22 November 1830.

74 WSCRO, QR/W 758, fos 224–5 and 226–2, Information of Sarah Mitchell, Petworth, 14 December, Deposition of John Andrews, Petworth, 18 December; *TT*, 24 November; *BG*, 25 November; WSCRO, Add. Mss. 13,395, Charlotte Palmer, Sullington to her mother, 23 November 1830.

75 TNA, HO 52/10, fos 216–17, G. Sawyer, Ham (Surrey), to Peel, 20 November; *BG*, 25 November; *BH*, 27 November 1830; *SA*, 28 March 1831.

76 *BG*, 25 November; TNA, HO 52/10, fos 226–7 and 237–42, Lord Arden, Nork, nr Epsom, 23 November, Clerk to the Reigate Bench, 26 November, enclosing various examinations and informations, taken 24 November, to Melbourne; TNA, Assi 92/2070, Surrey Winter Assizes 1830, Various indictments for riot and assault at Dorking.

77 *BG*, 25 November; *SA*, 29 November; *TT*, 24 November; *BH*, 27 November 1830.

78 Cowfold: *BH*, 27 November; Nuthurst: *BG*, 25 November; Steyning: *TT*, 25 November; *KG*, 26 November; Poynings: *TT*, 25 November 1830.

79 For protest events see Appendix. For Crowborough protests see note 52.

80 *TT*, 25 November 1830.

81 *BG*, 18 November; *TT*, 19 November. Despite the strength of community feeling the boy was indicted at the Assizes. All but one of the six letters he sent were signed 'Syng': TNA, Assi 94/2073, Indictment of John Pagden, labourer, Sussex Winter Assizes 1830.

82 One plough at Westwell on the 8 November with two other ploughs in the preceding days: *KH*, 11 November; three ploughs at Eastchurch on Sheppey, 14 November: *KH*, 18 November. These attacks followed earlier threats to destroy ploughs at Ash and the destruction of various farm implements of a Lenham farmer who had 'said something' about the Elham machine-breakers: *MJ*, 2 November; *MG*, 19 October; *KH*, 21 October 1830.

83 Gatherings had already occurred between Rye and Lydd: ESCRO, AMS

5995/3/15, Anne Mascall to H.B. Curteis, 10 November; *Kent and Essex Mercury*, 16 November 1830.

84 *KH*, 18 November; *TT*, 11 November. Small-scale disturbances among the residents of Canterbury workhouse on 14 and 15 November: *KC*, 16 November; *KG*, 19 November; *MJ*, 23 November 1830.

85 *KG*, 16 November; *KH*, 18 November; TNA, HO 52/8, fos 148–9, D. Bishop, Deal to William Rowley, no date (between 10 and 12 November 1830).

86 TNA, HO 52/8, fos 174–5, Charles Willis (junior), Clerk to Cranbrook Magistrates to Peel, 15 November; *MJ*, 23 November; *CWPR*, 27 November; *KG*, 19 November 1830.

87 *TT*, 19 November; *KG*, 19 and 23 November; TNA, HO 52/8, fos 2–7, W.R. Cosway, Sandgate to Peel, 17 November 1830, and enclosure.

88 Longparish: *HC*, 22 November; *Salisbury Journal*, 22 November; Strathfieldsaye: *TT*, 19 November; Wallington: *TT*, 19 November; *HA*, 20 November; *London Gazette*, 26 November 1830.

89 *HC*, 22 November 1830.

90 *SM*, 20 November; HCRO, 92M95/F2 8/3, Rev. Cockerton, Stoke Charity to Sir Thomas Baring, 2 December 1830; *Two-Penny Trash*, volume II, issue 12, July 1832.

91 TNA, HO 130/1, Hampshire Special Commission Calendar (hereafter Calendar): James Pumphrey for assault at Micheldever; *SM*, 20 November; *Berkshire Chronicle* (hereafter *BC*), 27 November; *Examiner*, 28 November; HCRO 10M57/03/8, Information and deposition of Charles Smith, victualler, Dean, information of James Hunt, Steventon, information of George Taylor, Steventon, all taken 2 December; HCRO, 92M95/F2/9/3, List of prisoners under the heading 'Mitcheldever, Stratton and Wonston Mobs', n.d. (but late November/early December); *TT*, 22 and 25 December 1830.

92 *HA*, 20 November; *SM*, 20 November; *TT*, 23 November; *BC*, 27 November 1830; TNA, 130/1, Calendar: John Gold, 29 and William Astridge, 43, for a riot and taking 1 sovereign from Cassandra Hankey, Basingstoke.

93 TNA, HO 52/7, fos 42–3, Andover JPs to Melbourne, 20 November; *Sherborne Journal*, 25 November; *SM*, 27 November; *HC*, 29 November; TNA HO 130/1, Calendar: John Hopgood for machine-breaking at Andover; *TT*, 23 November 1830.

94 *HC*, 23 November; *TT*, 22 and 25 December; HCRO, 92M95/F2/9/3, 11, 12 and 13, List of prisoners under the heading 'Micheldever, Stratton and Wonston Mobs', no date (but late November/early December), and depositions of Richard Collis, Micheldever, n.d. (but probably 1 December), William Pain, junior, Micheldever, 1 December, and William Pain, senior, Micheldever, 1 December 1830.

95 *HC*, 22 November; *PHer*, 28 November; *TT*, 22, 28 and 31 December; HCRO, 92M95/F2/9/11 and 12, Depositions of Richard Collis, Micheldever, no date (but probably 1 December) and William Pain, junior, Micheldever, 1 December 1830.

96 HCRO, 92M95/F2/9/3, List of prisoners under the heading 'Micheldever, Stratton and Wonston Mobs': details offence and names of prosecutors and witnesses; *HA*, 20 November; HCRO, 100M70/F1, Sir William Baring,

Winchester to Lady Baring, 21 November 1830.

97 TNA, HO 52/7, fos 42–3 and 53–4, Andover Bench, 20 November, and Rev. Henry Woke, Over Wallop, 21 November, to Peel; *TT*, 25 November; 23 and 24 December; *HA*, 26 November. A group from Longparish also descended on Andover on 20 November. Notwithstanding apprehensions in the town that these men were wracked with 'evil passions' and would join the Andover 'rioters', all remained calm: *BC*, 27 November; *HC*, 29 November 1830.

98 *PHer*, 28 November; *TT*, 30 November and 23 December 1830.

99 TNA, HO 52/7, fos 60–3, Mr Walton, Stockbridge to Mr Backam; 23 November; *SM*, 27 November; *HC*, 29 November 1830.

100 *SM*, 27 November; *PHer*, 28 November; *HC*, 29 November; Mr Sloane Stanley, Winchester to Peel, 21 November 1830, TNA, HO 52/7, fos 51–2; TNA, HO 130/1, Calendar: James Ford, Thomas Moody, Thomas Martin, Charles Kerby, Richard Holloway, John Turton, James Giles, and James Ford for riot at Crawley.

101 *Dorset County Chronicle* (hereafter *DCC*), 25 November; *BC*, 27 November; *HA*, 27 November; *SM*, 27 November; *PHer*, 28 November; *HT*, 29 November; TNA, HO 130/1, Calendar: William Noble, Henry Gale, John Lush, William Kelsey, Isaac Offer and Charles Forder for machine-breaking at Broughton, William Burbage and John Moody for machine-breaking at Mottisfont, Arthur Fielder for assault at Michelmersh, and John Tongs for machine-breaking at Michelmersh; *TT*, 29 December; Mr W Hay, Romsey to Mr Lockhart, nr Abingdon, 23 November, Isaac Goldsmith, Dulwich Hill House, Camberwell to Phillips, 24 November, TNA, HO 52/7, fos 65–7 and 93–4; *TT*, 29 December 1830.

102 *DCC*, 25 November; *HA*, 27 November; *PHer*, 28 November; *HC*, 29 November; *HT*, 29 November 1830; TNA, HO 52/7, fos 65–7, Mr W. Hay, Romsey to Mr Lockhart, nr Abingdon, 23 November 1830.

103 *HC*, 29 November; *TT*, 31 December 1830; TNA, HO 130/1, Calendar: John Baker and William Summerbee for assault at Leckford.

104 *TT*, 27 November; *HT*, 29 November 1830.

105 TNA, HO 52/7, fos 46–7, Sir L. Curteis Cart, Ramridge, nr Andover to Peel, 21 November; *HA*, 27 November 1830; TNA, HO 130/1, Calendar: Isaac Isles for assault at Kimpton, and William Conduit for machine-breaking at Kimpton.

106 *TT*, 23, 25 and 28 December 1830; TNA, HO 130/1, Calendar: Jacob Wilshire, George Hopgood, Thomas Neale, George Carter and Jeremiah Farmer for levying monies at Vernhams Dean, and James Collins alias Fisher and James Leader for riot at Vernhams Dean.

107 TNA, HO 52/7, fos 65–7, Mr W. Hay, Romsey to Mr Lockhart, nr Abingdon, 23/24 November 1830.

108 *TT*, 23 and 29 December; TNA, HO 130/1, Henry Masters for levying victuals at Weyhill, Joseph Hall for levying monies at Hurstbourne Tarrant, William Brackstone and John Allen for machine-breaking at Penton Grafton, and William Brackstone for machine-breaking at Thruxton; TNA, HO 52/6, fos 37–8, Anon, East Woodhay to C. Hodgson, Westminster, 23 November 1830.

109 TNA, HO 130/1, Calendar: Thomas Gregory for machine-breaking at

Quarley; *TT*, 23 December 1830.

110 *HC*, 13 December; *TT*, 24 December 1830; TNA, HO 130/1, Calendar: John, William and David Simms and John Tollard for levying monies at St Mary Bourne.

111 HCRO, 75M91/E26/15, JR Gowen, Highclere to Lord Porchester, Lynmouth, 9 December 1830; TNA, HO 130/1, Calendar cases 107–122 for various offences at East Woodhay, Burghclere, Highclere Sidmonton; Hobsbawm and Rudé, *Captain Swing*, pp. 137–8, 325–7.

112 TNA, HO 52/7, fos 70–1, Rev. Hodgson, East Woodhay to Peel, 23 November 1830.

113 TNA, HO 52/7, fos 85–6, W. Lewis, Mayor of Basingstoke to Peel, 21 November; TNA, HO 130/1, Calendar: Charles Pain, James Cook, John Keens, John Bulpitt, John Batten, George Clark, James Baker, Henry Bulpitt, Richard Rampton, Henry Day, Henry Keens, William Wareham and Charles Bulpitt for various offences at St Lawrence Wootton, Monk Sherborne and Pamber, William Farmer for levying monies at St Lawrence Wootton, and Thomas Bennett for riot at Basingstoke; HCRO, 10M57/03/33, Informations of Joseph Curtis, St Lawrence Wootton; Harris Bigg Esq, Mary Down House, St Lawrence Wootton; Harris Jervoise Bigg Wither Esq, Many Down, St Lawrence Wootton; William Lutley Sclater Esq., Tangier Park, St Lawrence Wootton; Gervaise Pennington Esq. of Malshanger House, Church Oakley, all 24 November; *TT*, 23 and 25 December 1830.

114 TNA, HO 52/13, fos 107–8, Duke of Wellington, Strathfieldsaye to Melbourne, 23 November; HCRO, 10M57/03/33, Informations of William Leavey, Monk Sherborne, Thomas Chandler, Monk Sherborne, John Follett, Pamber, all 24 November; *SM*, 27 November; *HA*, 27 November; *HC*, 29 November; TNA, HO 130/1, Calendar: William Burgess, Peter Norman, Mark Wiggens, Henry Wells, Richard Keens, and James Dibley for riot and levying monies at Monk Sherborne and Pamber; *TT*, 24 December 1830.

115 *PHer*, 28 November 1830; *TT*, 30 November 1830.

116 HCRO, 94M72/F15/8 letter 1, Henry Budd to J.B Carter Esq., Petersfield, no date (but 23 November); *TT*, 24 and 30 December 1830; TNA, HO 130/1, Calendar: John Trimming for compelling Cobbold to sign a paper at Selborne, William Hoor, Thomas Hoare, Henry Bone, Aaron Harding, John Cobb, Benjamin Smith and Robert Bennett for destroying the workhouse at Selborne; CKS, U127/c78/29, E. White, Newton Valence, Friday (precise date not detailed) 1831 to 'My Dear Sir'.

117 HCRO, 94M72/F15/8 letter 1, Henry Budd to J.B Carter Esq., Petersfield, no date (but 23 November); *PHer*, 28 November; *TT*, 28 and 30 December; TNA, HO 130/1, Calendar: John Heath, Thomas Robinson, Robert Holdaway, Thomas Marshall, William Bicknell, Henry James, James Painter, Matthew Triggs and Thomas Harding for destroying the workhouse at Headley, and Thomas Marshall and John Kingshott for theft of victuals at Kingsley. In addition to Selborne, Headley, Kingsley, Hartley Mauditt, Newton Valence, Empshott and Greatham and the ten parishes were competed by Bramshott, East Worldham and West Worldham.

118 TNA, HO 130/1, Calendar: William and Thomas Heighes for

machine-breaking at Binstead; *TT*, 29 November and 24 December; *HT*, 29 November; TNA, HO 52/7, fos 120–1, J.B. Curteis Esq., Petersfield to Phillips, 25 November 1830.

119 TNA, HO 52/7, fos 120–1 and 122, J.B. Curteis, Petersfield to Phillips, and R. Parsons, Petersfield Post Office Deputy to Freeling, both 25 November; *PHer*, 28 November; *TT*, 30 November and 25 December 1830; TNA, HO 130/1, Calendar: Henry Wells and Richard Hoar for assault at Buriton, and John Knight for theft of victuals at Greatham.

120 *HA*, 27 November 1830; TNA, HO 130/1, Calendar: Benjamin Bown and James Camis for machine-breaking at Petersfield.

121 TNA, HO 52/7, fos 89–92, Duke of Buckingham, Avington to Wellington, 23 November; *TT*, 25 November (copying a report from the Globe), 23, 25 and 29 December; *PHer*, 28 November; *HC*, 29 November 1830; Arthur Aspinall (ed.) *Three Early Nineteenth Century Diaries* (London: Williams & Norgate, 1952), p. 24; TNA, HO 130/1, Calendar: George Coleman for levying monies at Martyr Worthy, Henry Thorp and John Cooper for machine-breaking at Itchen Abbas, and cases 191–205 for riot at Itchen Abbas.

122 *HT*, 22 November; *HA*, 27 November; *PHer*, 28 November 1830.

123 *HA*, 27 November; *HC*, 29 November; *TT*, 30 December; TNA, HO 130/1, Calendar: Peter Houghton, James Houghton, Richard Etherington, John Stonegate and John Chalk for machine-breaking at Durley, and James Cropp, Baenjamin Harding and Charles Brummell for various offences at Upham and Corhampton.

124 HCRO, 92M95/F2/8/2, Statement by George Buttley, Soberton, Hants, in favour of his labourer Jesse Burgess, n.d. (but late November/December); *HA*, 27 November; *PHer*, 28 November; *HC*, 29 November; *TT*, 30 December 1830, TNA, HO 130/1, Calendar: Jesse Burgess for levying monies at Droxford, Charles Bryant for machine-breaking at Droxford, John Smith, William Abraham and William Varndell for riot at Wickham. According to the *Hampshire Chronicle* (29 November) machines were also broken in neighbouring Botley. Whether this was occasioned by the Droxford machine-breakers is unclear though.

125 *HA*, 27 November; *HC*, 29 November 1830; TNA, HO 130/1, Calendar: Thomas Stagg for machine-breaking at Droxford.

126 *HA*, 27 November; TNA, HO 130/1, Calendar: Nicholas Freemantle and Abraham Childs for various offences at Owslebury and Corhampton, William Adama, William Barnes, John Hoar, James Fussell and William Boyes for assault and riot at Owslebury, Benjamin Batchelor and Charles Churcher for assault at Owslebury, John Boyes for robbery at Owslebury; *TT*, 30 December 1830; *HT*, 7 March 1831.

127 *HA*, 27 November; *SM*, 27 November; *TT*, 29 and 30 November, and 30 December 1830; TNA, HO 130/1, Calendar: Richard Page, Thomas Smith, William Whitcher and William Scovey for riot and machine-breaking at South Stoneham, William Kinchin, Thomas Hooper, John Reeves and James Verndell for machine-breaking at South Stoneham.

128 Hobsbawm and Rudé, *Captain Swing*, p. 121; *TT*, 27 November 1830.

129 *SM*, 27 November; *HA*, 27 November; *HCr*, 29 November; *TT*, 29 and 30

December; TNA, HO 130/1, Calendar: Charles Bratcher alias Bracher, Richard Lane, William Lane and Samuel Bundy for riot at Fawley on 25 November, Henry Cavell, Josiah Cull, Andrew Mintram, John Webb, Henry Bundy, Robert Cull, and Samuel Bundy for riot at Fawley on 26 November 1830.

130 *SM*, 27 November; *HA*, 27 November; *HC*, 29 November; TNA, HO 52/7, fos 21–4, 29–30, 132–3, and 248–9, John Mills Esq., Ringwood, and W. Eyre-Coate, West Park, both to Melbourne, 26 November, Eliza Pleadon, Fordingbridge Post Office Deputy to Freeling, 26 November, Sir Charles Halse, Breamore House to Melbourne, 28 November; *TT*, 21 and 22 December; TNA, HO 130/1, Calendar: John Weeks, George Webb, John Newman and John Slade for riot at Rockborne, cases 44–52, 73–80, 85–7, and 140–146 for various offences at Fordingbridge, and John Harrison for levying victuals at Breamore.

131 *SM*, 18 September and 20 November 1830.

132 *PHer*, 28 November; *HC*, 29 November 1830.

133 *PHer*, 28 November; *London Gazette*, 3 December; *HA*, 4 December; *HC*, 6 December; TNA, HO 52/7, fos 168, 176–7 and 241–4, Mr Hearne, Guildhall, Newport, Isle of Wight to Melbourne, 3 December, Lord Yarborough, Newport to Melbourne, 5 December 1830, Sir Graham Hammond Bart, North Ledge, Yarmouth to Melbourne; HCRO, Q9/1/591, Various indictments and calendar, Hampshire Epiphany Quarter Sessions 1831.

134 TNA, HO 130/1, Calendar: Henry Howe for threatening to set fire to William Gunner's house at Bishop's Waltham; *HA*, 4 December 1830.

135 TNA, HO 40/27/5 fos 440–1, Lieutenant Colonel Mair, Winchester to Melbourne, 14 December; *Reading Mercury*, 13 and 20 December; *HA*, 18 December; *TT*, 18 December 1830.

136 *HIris*, 20 November; *TT*, 23 November; TNA, HO 52/10, fos 415–16, 417, 418–19 and 52/8, fos 54–5, G. Courthope, Battle, 18 November, enclosing deposition of John Birch, J.S. Hewett, Tunbridge Wells, 18 November 1830, both to Peel.

137 *TT*, 25 November; *HIris*, 20 November; CKS, U1127 C21, Sir Howard Elphistone, Ore Place to William Smith, Gravesend, 25 November 1830.

138 WSCRO, MP 1977, Note about Kirdford protest, 25 November; *BG*, 25 November; *SA*, 29 November and 6 December; WSCRO, Goodwood 1477A R3, Letter to Richmond, 24 November; WSCRO, QR/Q 51, Indictments of Thomas Puttock and Thomas Cooper, labourers; *HT*, 4 December; WSCRO, QR/W/758 f.274, Deposition of George Duncton, labourer, 30 November; TNA, HO 52/10, fo. 233, Godstone Postmaster to Freeling, 26 November 1830.

139 *HT*, 4 December; *SA*, 6 December; WSCRO, QR/W/758 fo. 273, Informations of Richard Goatcher, and Richard Hasler JP, both 30 November 1830.

140 WSCRO, QR/W/758 fos 280, 269, 270, 271 and 272, Informations of Timothy Town, 18 December, William Mates, 6 December, Examinations of John Pennicott, William Searle, and Robert Braby, all 27 December; *BG*, 2 December 1830.

141 For details of individual incendiary fires see Appendix.

142 *KG*, 23 November; *TT*, 23 December 1830.

143 TNA, HO 52/8, fos 237–8, Camden, Wilderness to Melbourne, 28 November; *TT*, 29 November; *RG*, 30 November; *KH*, 2 December 1830.

144 *RG*, 30 November; TNA, HO 52/8, fos 95–6, J. Bradley Esq., Gore Court, Sittingbourne to Melbourne, 1 December; *KH*, 9 December; *KG*, 10 December 1830.

145 TNA, HO 52/8, fos 134–5, General Dalbiac, Maidstone to Phillips, 2 December 1830.

146 *KG*, 26 November and 29 December 1830; East Kent Archives Centre, DO/JS/g/3, bundle 1, various examinations and notes.

147 TNA, HO 52/8, fos 33–4 and 97–9, John Boys, clerk to Margate Bench to Maule, 23 November, R. Cobb Esq., Solicitor, Margate to Melbourne, enclosing deposition of William Liley, both 28 November; TNA, TS 11/943, Prosecution Briefs for the King vs. George Moore, James Dunk, James Pointer and George Hollands, Kent Winter Assizes 1830; Evidence of George Hannam Esq., John Forster, James Pointer and George Hollands.

148 TNA, HO 52/8, fos 77–8, John Boys, Margate to Phillips, 26 November; *RG*, 30 November. Reports that the group were to reassemble at Margate on the following Saturday night (27 November) to pull-down the workhouse came to nothing.

149 *KG*, 22 November and 7 December; *MJ*, 23 November; *TT*, 29 November and 2 December 1830.

150 See Appendix. *RG*, 6 December; *KG*, 7 December 1830.

5

Movement mechanisms

The group of nouns used by reporters to describe Swing's 'overt' forms all presumed some degree of collective action but ascribed varying degrees of organisation and solidarity: gang, group, mob, crowd. Of course, this could simply be journalistic, or letter-writing, expediency. Either way, as social movement theory tells us, all forms of collective action are necessarily reliant on the coming together of individuals with broadly similar intentions.[1] It is in the forging of these collectivities that the form and outcome of Swing was shaped and determined. In Chapter 4, it was asserted that the very first 'Swing' incidents were the product of the Elham gang. But on what basis can such a claim be upheld?

Such a question is particularly pertinent given the apparent fact, according to Roger Wells, that over the previous forty years forms of collective protest declined in relative importance to individualised, covert forms of rural terror.[2] This analysis bears a striking parallel with that of Ulrich Beck on the fragmentation of late twentieth-century society. In the late eighteenth- and early nineteenth-century English countryside, so Wells has suggested, the bitter repression food rioting and the rise of surveillance systems led to a fundamental shift in protest practices. In Beck's thesis the response to increased 'risks' – crime, illness, pollution, economic instability and technological change – predicated a shift from 'the solidarity of need to solidarity motivated by anxiety'.[3] This theme of 'individuation' (the concept was developed by Friedrich Nietzsche but developed in social movement studies by Antonio Melucci) suggests that when society is governed by choice, the 'foundation of solidarity' is inevitably undermined.[4] In response, where solidarities have emerged as a response to anxieties they have tended to be more 'tribal' and identity based (for example environmental protest groups such as Earth First! and Reclaim the

Streets), and founded on narrow circuits of trust.[5] Yet, as Graham Crow has shown, even in unsettled times solidarities not only continue to matter but also emerge in different ways and forms, not least in families and communities.[6]

In many senses, the culmination of crises in 1830 represented the ideal crucible in which pre-existing solidarities – kinship networks, work groups, criminal gangs – could assume new forms and potencies. At the same time, individuals with no prior connection, even those from different communities, could be brought together through various mechanisms by virtue only of a shared experience of impoverishment and a shared desire for change. What follows seeks to examine these mechanisms and explores how new solidarities were forged in the white heat of the autumn and winter of 1830. Beyond the analysis of these techniques that helped to diffuse protests, the chapter goes on to consider the resultant local and regional patterns of protest, and, finally, the relationship between Swing activists' resort to covert terror and 'open' protest.

Organisation, solidarities and agents provocateurs

The initial machine-breaking episodes, though clandestine, reveal a clear mission, a strong degree of planning, clear leadership and the devolving of specific roles to different individuals. Although few of the meetings, liaisons and reconnaissance missions are mentioned in the depositions and confessions, the evidence of the machine-breakers having warned local farmers of their intentions attests to some initial meeting and planning. In some senses, even the relatively thinly documented protest episodes that occurred in the final days of mass mobilisations in Hampshire show similar organisational forms. What makes the Elham gang – and others – different is the existence of evidence which demonstrates the longer-standing nature of these organised solidarities.

In every respect, the Elham machine-breakers were a gang as opposed to a merely temporary alignment of like-minded individuals. Through personnel and kinship links it is evident that the Elham gang was, in part, born out of the collapse of the Aldington gang of smugglers, also known as 'The Blues' – the most notorious of all smuggling gangs in the post-Napoleonic period.[7] Initially formed in 1820, it was the Blues' activities in the mid- to late 1820s that set the blueprint for the machine-breaking gang. After the death of five members in an affray with the Coastal Blockade at Brookland on the Romney Marsh in 1821, their leader Cephas Quested was captured, tried and hanged. Then, under the leadership of George Ransley ('Captain Batts'), a labourer-turned-waggoner-turned-professional smuggler and unlicensed beer-house keeper, the Blues slowly morphed from a smuggling gang into a broader criminal gang. After the murder of one of the gang members, when an internal row degenerated into a vicious brawl, the Blues began to lose community support. Local farmers who had hitherto turned a blind eye to their activities now publicly resolved not to employ any known smuggler. The gang showed no sign of being intimidated and diversified into burglary. Simultaneously, the Coastal Blockade redoubled its efforts against the gang, resulting in a rising tide of injuries and even deaths.[8]

Matters escalated further on 30 July 1826 when Richard Morgan, a quartermaster in the Blockade, was shot dead at close range during an attempt to land spirit tubs at Dover. The subsequent offer of a 'large reward' and the King's pardon to any accomplice for information leading to the conviction of Ransley and his men prompted gang member Edward Horn to come forward. On the strength of Horn's evidence, two Bow Street officers accompanied by 120 armed Coastal Blockade men secured Ransley and seven others in a night-time raid. After the arrest of several further individuals, Ransley and thirteen of his men were tried and transported for life.[9] The rump of the gang attempted some 'desultory' smuggling missions, but most now turned their efforts to armed poaching, thereby combining their knowledge of the networks through which illicit goods could be fenced with their violent tenacity. A combination of armed raids – including one on Sir Edward Knatchbull's Mersham estate – and attacks on keepers proved their eventual undoing.[10]

Although evidence for the period when the Aldington gang became the Elham gang is somewhat limited, it is probable that they were almost responsible for the destruction of Kelsey's machine at Lyminge in May 1829.[11] Indeed, the coincidence between the recent widespread local adoption of threshing machines and the collapse of smuggling is surely significant.[12] From both the numerous depositions taken against gang members and Knatchbull's detailed notes, it is evident that the machine-breakers assumed both the Blues' strong internal discipline and their readiness to resort to acts of violence. Their activities betrayed a strong central organisation with members taking a formal vow to be 'faithful to each other'.[13] Furthermore, if any member provided evidence against the gang they were to be killed. Conversely, if any member were taken into custody the gang would rescue them.[14] Those labourers who attempted to prevent threshing machines from being destroyed (or even attempted to watch their destruction ceremonies) were warned that if they did not keep their distance the men would 'blow out their bloody brains'.[15]

Although the Elham machine-breaking gang was in many ways exceptional, other Swing groups deployed similar practices and discourses. The gang members centred on the East Kent parishes of Ash and Wingham – who were, incidentally, in communication with the Elham men – armed themselves with axes, pickaxes, sledgehammers and saws and toured the local farms compelling all labourers then at work to join them. Particular care was taken to make sure that those working on threshing machines were among their number in an attempt to promote a sense of community-endorsed opposition towards machinery. Only after discipline was relaxed, or rather drunk into oblivion at alehouses, did any of the pressed men manage to escape. Indeed, those who had attempted to flee before the effects of alcohol rendered order inviolate were seized and forcibly dragged along from farm to farm.[16]

Cohesion was thus achieved partly through impressment. Yet what made this group of machine-breakers a gang was their clear leadership ('Captain' Revell), a predetermined plan that had evolved over several weeks – not a quick-witted response to the unfurling movement – and internal discipline. Ash was also a notorious smuggling centre, and in all probability some of the machine-breakers had, as at Elham, learnt mobilisation and organisational techniques through necessity in the cat-and-mouse game 'played' with the Customs and Coastal Blockade.[17]

Through a strong reliance on impressment, the tactics deployed by other south-eastern Swing groups portrayed a greater resemblance to those of the Ash, rather than the Elham, gang. For instance, the initially small gathering who first met at Frinsted and Wormshill on 25 October used a combination of gentle persuasion and forceful impressment as they traversed an ever wider area. Indeed, by this tactic this highly mobile band physically diffused Swing into the Weald.[18] Labourers at Hawkhurst who refused to join the local agitants were dragged from their beds and either forcibly compelled or humiliated by having their backs chalked as deserters, a reference to the military practice of branding deserters with a 'D' below their left armpit.[19] Even the twenty or so, well-organised men, 'principally smugglers' according to a local magistrate, at Brede used compulsion to present a picture of a united community.[20]

With the exception of those at Brede, it is questionable whether these Swing groups were gangs. The problem partly relates to the thinness of the archive, the Elham gang in particular being exceptionally well documented. It also relates to the fact that as Swing entered the Weald its rapid physical diffusion meant that there was less need for organised gangs to diffuse protests: rapid contagion does not require organisation. Indeed, rapid contagion actually militated against organisation, with gangs having no time to decide on objectives, targets or strategies.

Elsewhere, there is little evidence to suggest that pre-existing protest groups utilised Swing's momentum and power to effect their own pre-determined local agendas. Instead, groups in much of West Sussex, Surrey and Hampshire were largely transient collections of men.[21] Such groupings relied, at least in part, on organisational understandings and networks forged through other solidarities. At Sixpenny Handley, a Dorset parish within the recently disenfranchised Cranborne Chase and near the Hampshire border, a long history of deer stealing was important in forging plebeian interaction.[22] Handley was notorious as a 'nest of Deer stealers, Poachers, Smugglers, & every variety of lawless characters', the men having a reputation as, in the words of local magistrate D.O.P. Okeden, 'wild and dissolute'.[23] Elsewhere, the protests in the Dever Valley of Hampshire were initiated and largely orchestrated by members of the 'Musical and Radical Society' based at Sutton Scotney.[24]

How were such organisational capacities and tactics learnt? If in small villages and hamlets most labourers and artisans would know one another,[25] kinship networks did not teach organisation and mobilisation. Instead, work, criminal, poaching and smuggling gangs all taught labourers how to organise and act. Much of the voluminous commentary generated by Swing referred to the central role of smugglers in diffusing radical analyses of social conditions in south-eastern rural communities. According to one Sandwich observer, 'many thousands of countrymen' were employed in gangs whose 'nightly visits' to the shores of the Continent invested them with 'French tastes and inclinations'.[26]

The reported firing of rockets in a line between Lyminge and Ash on the night of the fires on farms belonging to Rev. Price and overseer Becker also attests to the importance of communication in organising protest. While such a report might have been apocryphal, protests in Sussex on 15 November offer more certain 'proof' of the importance of communication in helping to diffuse protest. As noted in Chapter 4, some 100–200 'working people' assembled at Shoreham walked twenty miles to Ringmer to attend a prearranged meeting. While the precise connection between Ringmer and Shoreham remains obscure – perhaps the news diffused through the highway linkmen that Andrew Charlesworth has posited were important in diffusing Swing, or perhaps criminal gangs connected the two places – it is undeniable that some form of communication was central to the involvement of Shoreham labourers in Swing.[27]

As noted above, military (and military-inspired) tactics were often central to Swing mobilisations. That some 250,000 men had been demobilised from the armed forces after Waterloo also meant that it was inevitable that some of the older protestors had served in the military.[28] For instance, John Gilmor, indicted at the Hampshire Special Commission for destroying Taskers' foundry at Upper Clatford, was singled out at the trial as having been a soldier.[29] The similarities between some Swing groups and a mobilised army were not lost on farmers. In the first mass mobilisations beyond East Kent, it was 'represented' that 'the rioters ... marched about in great numbers [near Sittingbourne] ... many of them being armed with hatchets, hammers, saws, and even guns'.[30]

This was, by appearance, a plebeian army, extraordinarily similar in form to earlier Luddite gangs.[31] There is no evidence, though, that Swing groupings drilled by night.[32] At Brede, the village where 'overt' Swing was first manifest outside Kent, those who followed the cart in which assistant overseer Abell was ejected from the parish, marched 'with their Bats on their shoulders as if they were Guns'.[33] That many Swing ringleaders were known by military titles and that the pseudonymous leader of the movement became known as Captain Swing was surely no coincidence. Arguably, though, it was through work that organisation and the ability to mobilise was learnt by most Swing activists. Parishes and magistrates were particularly alert to this truth. In the summer of 1829, it was reported that 'in the lower parts' of Kent and Sussex the practice of working men on the roads had been discontinued so as 'to prevent them from forming confederacies'.[34]

Just as important in the diffusion of protests in the autumn and winter of 1830 were agents provocateurs; but it is necessary to exercise a degree of caution in thinking through their role in Swing. Magistrates were often keen to shift the blame of rebellion away from their local charges, instead blaming itinerant figures hell-bent on revolution. In late October, when several threshing machines were destroyed in Bekesbourne, George Gipps, a yeoman of considerable local influence, supposed the culprits 'not to have come from Elham ... but we must unfortunately conclude, that such persons are to be found in most places'. Still, Gipps was vehement that Bekesbourne labourers were not involved.[35]

Evidence for the involvement and actions of such agitators is often veneered with the authorities' paranoia. For instance, the *Morning Herald* reported in early October that provocateurs were going to public houses in unfrequented hamlets to 'get into conversation with the peasantry and excite their passions'. One 'of these fellows' was seen at Elham, dressed distinctively in a white silk hat and a striking blue coat. From the Reigate area Home Secretary Peel was warned that 'parties from London' – the correspondent implying political agitators – were 'stirring up' the labouring classes.[36] At Burstow on the Surrey-Sussex border, Richard Garson, a labourer employed by Mr W. Saunders, the proprietor of a large estate, was accosted on 6 October on his return from work and quizzed about Saunders. Garson was again accosted on 8 October, this time being dragged into some straw where three men stripped him of his clothes, for no apparent reason, and cautioned him 'you have been very quiet in these parts but we shall give you a turn before the Winter is out'. These threats may have been heeded, as local farmers kept a strict watch both day and night, but rather than being seduced into the cause Garston was petrified.[37]

Far more important than the shadowy figures from London in the spread of 'Swing' were motivated local activists. Within the Elham gang, Martin Carvill and other male members of his family were key provocateurs. Carvill, in tandem with two labourers from Brabourne, on the morning of the day previous to the destruction of machines at Barham and Womenswold, approached John Jefferey, a labourer from Lyminge, to go to destroy the machine at Brabourne. Carvill also went to Elmstead to incite the labourers there, and was actively involved in the destruction of the machines at Barham and Womenswold on 20 September, joined by his brother William, and at Brabourne on 22 September. Carvill's movements alone – the distance between

Brabourne and Barham is over ten miles – would have both spread news rapidly and given the impression to local labourers that machines were being destroyed everywhere. Henry Read, one of the ringleaders of the Elham gang, went even further, proclaiming: 'We shall destroy any machine about here   the law provided to break them all.' The importance of the Carvill family is intensified yet further by Price's fire on 5 October, for which Martin's brother John was suspected.[38]

Patterns of protest: local and regional distinctiveness

If the activities of gangs, agents provocateurs and the mobilisation of other solidarities was central to the diffusion of Swing, it follows that such processes would create locally distinctive protest patterns. That is to say that in certain locales the resort to particular weapons of rural protest would be determined not only by localised conditions and concerns but also by the protest memories and competencies of key individuals. Crudely put, the form of the movement would therefore also be a function of the past resort to protest wherever Swing was manifest. For instance, in East Anglia we would expect machine-breaking, in the Weald a resort to vestry 'mobbings', in the forested areas of Hampshire incendiarism. As detailed in Chapter 4, incendiarism and threatening letters were universally present wherever Swing was manifest. But to what extent do these crude geographies hide greater complexities? To what extent are the above extrapolations and suppositions supported by the archive?

While a large proportion of south-eastern parishes hosted Swing protests, many other parishes must have been at the very least passed through by mobile Swing groupings. For, just like the group from Shoreham who visited Ringmer, we will never know what happened en route. Were men pressed? Were monies levied? Were threats made? Or did mobile groups simply pass through other parishes without effect? It is clear from some quasi-judicial archival fragments that men from parishes for which I have found no record of protest activity did provide protest personnel. Again, whether this was for events elsewhere or for events that occurred in their settled parish but which have eluded the archive – or this author's archival searches – cannot be known. For instance, William Farmer of Brown Candover was arrested on 26 November for his alleged involvement in a riot. Of the Candovers, I have only found evidence that Preston Candover hosted a Swing protest. Elsewhere in the Basingstoke division, a printed handbill advertising the names of 'rioters' apprehended detailed men from Eastrop, Tunworth and Winslade. Only in the former parish have any Swing protests been identified, and this the receipt of a threatening letter successfully stating that if farmer Portsmouth did not 'remove' his threshing machine his premises would be fired.[39]

In Hampshire, where protest was most intense but shortest lived, local patterns are easiest to discern. Machine-breaking – often accompanied by incendiarism – dominated protests in the far south-western corner of the county, the border parishes with Wiltshire in the New Forest, the Test Valley to the north of Romsey, the Dever Valley, the area between Durley and Southampton, and the area to the north-west of Andover (see figure 5.1). This is not to say that machines were not broken elsewhere, but rather that these were few and not the defining protest feature. For instance, a lone threshing machine was destroyed at Kingsley during the height of the poor law-related protests in that part of north-east Hampshire.[40] The narratives of protest detailed in chapter four attest to the importance of highly mobile groups in all these machine-breaking areas of Hampshire. Indeed, it is notable that in areas where machine-breaking was not the defining feature of the local movement but did occur, it was invariably carried out by men from the immediate vicinity alone rather than by mobile groups.

The same dynamic is true for the machine-breaking areas of Kent and Sussex: the Elham Valley and its environs, the parishes surrounding Ash-next-Sandwich, and the coastal plains of West Sussex (see figure 5.2). Here, threshing machines were destroyed by highly organised and mobile groupings that combined men who had travelled often considerable distances with local labourers and artisans. Why these patterns and dynamics occurred is harder to ascertain. The spatial patterning of protest is probably a function of several factors: the use (and use histories) of threshing machines; popular attitudes to threshing machines; and, archival strengths and weaknesses. As detailed in Chapters 2 and 3, by 1830 threshing machines were in operation throughout south-eastern England, but it was in the major areas of grain production – the southern coastal plains, the north Kent coast, the Vale of Sussex, the Dever and Test valleys, and the Isle of Thanet – that they were most intensively deployed.

Most of these areas, with the notable exceptions of the 'closed'

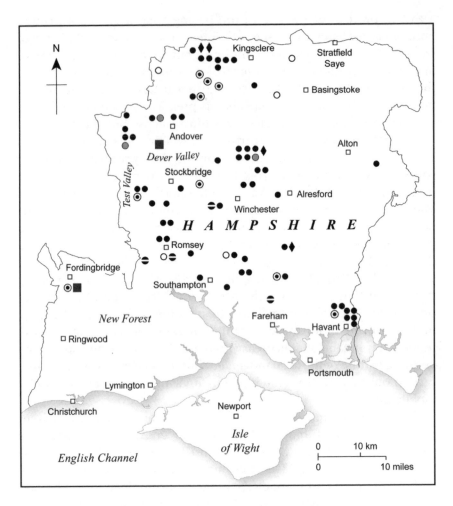

N

Kingsclere
Stratfield
Saye
Basingstoke
Andover
Dever Valley
Test Valley
Alton
Stockbridge
Alresford
Winchester
H A M P S H I R E
Romsey
Fordingbridge
Southampton
New Forest
Fareham
Havant
Ringwood
Portsmouth
Lymington
Newport
Christchurch
Isle of Wight
English Channel

0   10 km
0   10 miles

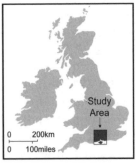

Study
Area

0   200km
0   100miles

Machine-breaking incidents

●   Threshing machine

◉   Several threshing machines

■   Machine works

●   Chaff cutting machine

○   Winnowing machine

◆   Hay-making / grass cutting machine

⊖   Machine-breaking

5.1 Hampshire machine-breaking, 1830

grandee-dominated the Vale of Sussex and the north Kent coast where the diverse agrarian economy kept field workers' wages relatively high,[41] became areas of machine-breaking. But this only occurred after the lead given by the men of the Elham Valley. Indeed, with the exception of farms on the estates of improving landlords and those of early adopting farmers, threshing machines had been used longest in the areas where, by 1830, they were most intensively deployed. Consequently, while threshing machines were never accepted by the labouring poor in these areas – the persistence of antipathy being demonstrated by repeated incendiary attacks – their intensive use was not new. However, this was not true of the Elham Valley. Here, despite their long usage, it was the recent widespread use of hired, portable threshing machines that generated huge resentment. Elham, as in so many other respects, gave the lead, and the judgement of Knatchbull at the Canterbury trial gave the impression that the destruction of threshing machines was, if not legally sanctioned, viewed with a degree of sympathy by the rulers of rural England. This signal lit the blue touch paper, it popularly legitimised machine-breaking.

So why were threshing machines not destroyed wherever they were present? The apparent absence of machine-breaking from mid-Sussex might in part be a function of poor press coverage, but this would only be true for the areas surrounding Horsham and East Grinstead. And yet here correspondence and legal documents relate a rich story of protests in 1830. The relative strength of estates in mid-Sussex is arguably a more important factor. As suggested in Chapter 2, while the power of 'closed' villages as regulators of social action has been subjected to critical scrutiny,[42] the relative paucity of protests in mid-Sussex and the large number of 'closed' villages would appear to be more than coincidental. For instance, at Ringmer Lord Gage took the lead in 'ordering' the protest and in regulating the behaviour of both the labourers and the farmers. Such regulation succeeded in preventing not only machine-breaking but all forms of crowd activity. Indeed, excluding the Ringmer meeting, the area between Hailsham and Hurstpierpoint was relatively protest-free.[43]

There is evidence as well that in areas controlled by grandees some pressure was put on tenants to either 'desist from using' their threshing machines, as on the Earl of Chichester's estate, or even 'break up' their threshing machines, as on the Marquis of Bath's estate. In some areas, such as around Farnham, farmers in a semi-coordinated manner voluntarily broke up their machines without prompting.[44] It is

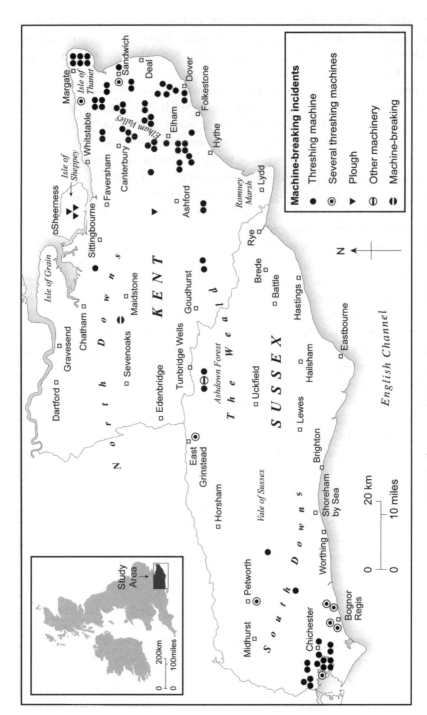

5.2 Machine-breaking in Kent and Sussex, 1830

also possible that in some areas where few threshing machines were in use, and so were not the key drivers of complaint in the autumn and winter of 1830, a conscious decision was made not to attack machinery as it might jeopardise field workers' bargaining position with farmers and the vestry regarding wages and poor relief. Hence, post-Elham, while the presence of threshing machines was a relatively good predictor of the likelihood of machine-breaking, this causal relationship hid many more complex factors.

The patterning of other forms of protest is even harder to explain. Although the predominance of incendiarism in the forests of Hampshire and west Surrey can perhaps partly be explained by the long and intensive history of fire-raising in these areas,[45] the primacy of arson in the rest of Surrey (see figure 5.3) and around Sevenoaks cannot be so explained. Instead, this pattern in the latter place reflects the fact that the protests started there outside the context of a movement and thus deployed the protest tool of choice in post-Napoleonic rural southern England. That incendiarism remained the key protest tactic resorted to in the vicinity of Sevenoaks even after the Elham machine-breakers had been released from gaol is, in all certainty, a reflection of the evident fact that once a particular protest form was established in one locale the inhabitants tended to persist with it. For instance, once wages and poor relief agitations were resorted to at Battle and Brede these forms dominated protests in the rest of the Weald.

The prevalence of incendiarism in much of Surrey, with the exception of the area around Dorking and the Sussex border, was the result of the same dynamic – but in reverse. As noted in Chapter 4, incendiarism heralded overt crowd actions throughout south-eastern England. In Surrey this dynamic occurred at Ockley where an incendiary fire on 15 November was followed by crowd actions there, and in neighbouring parishes, four days later.[46] Elsewhere in Surrey, such 'precursors' heralded nothing. The most striking example of this occurred in the area around Kingston-upon-Thames and Cobham on 10 and 11 November when at least six incendiary fires occurred. While no open protests followed, unlike elsewhere in south-east England, the archive does reveal the barely constrained sense of open hostility among some individuals. Not only did fires continue – at Cobham (again) on the night of 13 November and at East Molesey three days later – but at Cobham shots were also aimed at the owners of the fired farm.[47]

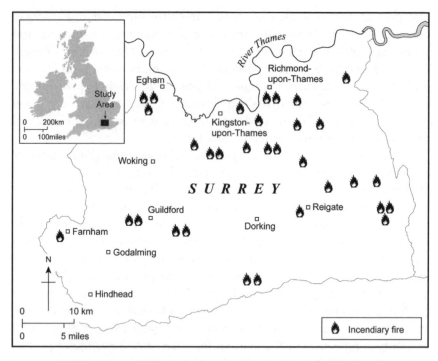

5.3 Incendiary fires in Surrey, 24 August–31 December 1830

The reasons for this relative quiescence remain obscure. Certainly, it is striking that even the few 'open' protests occurring in Surrey were instigated by the men of Horsham. But to state that the Surrey labourer was a more servile individual than his Hampshire, Kentish or Sussex counterpart is to fall into a logical trap: county boundaries determined allegiances not mentalities. Besides, the thirty-three incendiary fires I have recorded for Surrey from 24 August until 31 December attest to a readiness to adopt the weapons of rural terror by at least some Surrey residents. The conditions for an intensity and patterning of protest akin to that in the neighbouring counties certainly existed in Surrey. For instance, an attack on a paper mill at Albury was expected on 18 November, paper-makers from Cork 'who are on the tramp through Kent & Sussex, &' being 'sworn foes to Machinery of all kinds'. Yet nothing transpired. Moreover, wages in large parts of rural Surrey were no higher than in the neighbouring counties. In the Hindhead area, close to the disturbed Headley and Selborne district in neighbouring Hampshire, not only were wages low but a notoriously fiercely independent streak persisted among the commoners and squatters in the extra-parochial areas.[48] Yet the archive does not record any protests occurring in that part of Surrey. This could be a reflection of the absence of any large estates and gentry families and the relative paucity of magistrates, combined with the lack of any nearby newspaper, rendering the archive thin. The lack of a county press aside, this combination of factors was not true for the entire county.

Moreover, as will be shown in Chapter 9, the Surrey judiciary was no more ready or organised to deter protests. Indeed, a plan devised by Peel, in conjunction with Lord Hill, to 'reinforce' the military in Kent and Sussex, with troops stationed at various strategic places throughout the two counties, did not account for the physical spread of protests into Surrey.[49] The only central assistance offered to the authorities in Surrey during mid-November was the dispatch of a police officer to Egham to help in the investigation of a spate of incendiary fires.[50] Surrey, with some justification, was viewed as being peripheral to the movement.

The other sub-region defined by the overwhelming resort to one protest form was, as noted above, the Weald. Incendiarism and the sending of threatening letters had presaged open protests at Battle and Fletching and accompanied the initial risings in south-east Sussex, while threshing machine-breaking was resorted to at Benenden, Crowborough and Hawkhurst. But Wealden protests invariably took the form of open calls for higher wages and more generous poor relief payments, often supported by calls for tithe and tax remissions and reductions.[51] Here wages were at their lowest and living standards at their most depressed in the whole of the south-east. As noted in Chapter 2, the poor law had been a particular focus of Wealden protests post-1815, with overseers frequently subjected to incendiary attacks and vestries more frequently besieged by angry claimants than elsewhere in the south-east. That these tactics were replicated during the autumn and winter of 1830 is not therefore surprising. What was novel, however, was the tactic of expelling assistant overseers. Folklorists have suggested variously that this 'new' practice was based on 'mock Mayor' customs and an inversion of the rituals of justice. Thus while the expulsion of assistant overseer Abell at Brede was indeed novel, the practice was quickly adopted elsewhere in the Weald as the same hatred of hired overseers prevailed and the same cultural codes and understandings underpinned popular action.[52] What is more surprising is that, with the isolated exceptions of

Wrotham in north Kent and Fawley near Southampton, other equally loathed assistant overseers were not so treated.[53]

The removal of assistant overseers was not the only form of protest deployed during the course of south-eastern Swing that was truly confined to one locality. While threats of destruction were made against workhouses in several locales – interestingly in all recorded cases coinciding with areas of machine-breaking – and the partial destruction in Kent of the Birchington poorhouse by incendiarism,[54] it was only in north-east Hampshire that such threats were actually carried out.[55] Arguably, it is more telling that some protest forms widely practised in the post-Napoleonic south-eastern countryside were almost completely absent from Swing. Only at Hickstead (mid-Sussex) does the archive explicitly record any case of animal maiming, with the destruction of three pigs, though the provincial press claimed that there had been other 'similar instances', to cattle, in the vicinity. Moreover, that this instance occurred after Swing had effectively run its course in Sussex tends to marginalise animal maiming's place in southern Swing.[56] Plant maiming too was effectively absent from Swing's protest toolbox. Malicious attacks on flora occurred both before and after the autumn and winter of 1830, including a 'renewal of the offence' in October 1831 when 'young trees' belonging to Rev. Trebeck of Chailey were attacked.[57]

In most spaces of southern England, forms of agrarian capitalism and past protest patterns and practices were not, therefore, a perfect guide to Swing's form and diffusion. To what extent, though, did past protest practices hold during 1830 for spaces which supported ways of life that were not entirely dictated by agrarian capitalism? Specifically, how was Swing manifest in the forests, open fields and commons of southern England? These, with the exception of open fields, were notorious as lawless spaces. Yet, a cursory survey of the role of such spaces in Chapter 4 suggests no clear pattern. Indeed, Hobsbawm and Rudé's analysis offers no definitive conclusions. Some evidence adduced suggested that recently enclosed parishes were more prone to protests in 1830 than others, and yet in some other areas parishes with remnant commons were more likely to 'riot'.[58] Indeed, the Elham gang was based around, and partially populated by residents from, the remnant commons on the Elham-Lyminge-Stelling borders as well as that at Swingfield near Folkestone. Conversely, notoriously independent Hindhead, dominated by large remnant commons, appears to have been largely free from protest in 1830. To understand these dynamics requires a systematic survey of the spaces that remained unenclosed by late 1830.

The regional geography of enclosure in southern England is well understood, the localised pattern little so. Kent was little affected by parliamentary enclosure, the county having been largely enclosed by the seventeenth century. What remained in 1830 was almost exclusively common pasture and waste and was largely concentrated in East Kent, though substantial commons were yet to be enclosed at Brasted, Cliffe, Queenborough and Wouldham. After 1830, only 2,007 acres were enclosed by parliamentary act during the rest of the nineteenth century.[59] In comparison, in neighbouring Sussex 15,036 acres were similarly enclosed, in Surrey 19,095 acres, and in Hampshire 40,573 acres. These figures exclude lands subsequently enclosed by agreement – of which John Chapman and Sylvia Seeliger have identified two cases in Hampshire and five in Sussex; commons on the London fringe which became de facto parks; and those areas which survived unenclosed into the twentieth century, including the 93,670 acres of Crown land in the New Forest, Ashdown Forest and the substantial common at Chailey in East Sussex (see figure 2.1).[60]

What was the connection between Swing practices and these remnant open fields and commons? The largest concentration of these yet-to-be-enclosed spaces clustered around south-west Sussex, East Bere and Waltham Chase in Hampshire, the Hampshire-Sussex-Surrey borders, the New Forest fringe, the north Weald, the area between Arundel and Horsham, and East Surrey. The Hampshire-Surrey borders and New Forest fringe were also areas of remnant Crown forest. The north Weald was likewise dominated by the privately-held Ashdown Forest over which common rights still pertained. These areas, just like the parishes around Elham, had high numbers of the small farmers, commoners, dual occupationists and petty producers whose importance Mick Reed has powerfully reasserted.[61] They were also important Swing centres. But all deployed different protest forms: machine-breaking in west Hampshire, incendiarism and the sending of threatening letters in the north Weald, and poor law-related protests on the Hampshire-Surrey borders. In the latter place, the primacy of the poor law as a generator of conflict is suggestive of the fact that either Reed's independent peasantry were not those driving protests, or that the existence of remnant commons was no guarantee that the poor were sheltered from the ravages of agrarian capitalism. Also, the fact that north Wealden parishes were some of the most impoverished in southern England, with correspondingly high poor rates, suggests that even resource-rich commons – as Brian Short has emphatically proved Ashdown was – might keep only a few families from the parish. Besides, some commoners also combined exploitation of commonable resources in a mixed economy of welfare with occasional parish relief.[62] Whichever way the archive is consulted, the relationship is complex and uneven. The very largest commons in some locales – such as at Farnham and Frensham – might have offered genuine protection to the local poor, while others – such as Framfield (Sussex) and Kingsclere – appear to have provided a nest for the development of independently minded individuals.

As in Elham and at Sixpenny Handley, the acts of machine-breaking in New Forest fringe communities might have been the work of individuals partially reliant on the exploitation of commons and wastes, and also reliant on wintertime flail threshing. If this thesis is true, forests, as with commons, neither provided a perfect buffer against the effects of agrarian capitalism, nor an easy predictor of what protest form would be deployed. In the New Forest there was no (recorded) history of machine-breaking but instead a long history of 'covert' fence-breaking, maiming, incendiarism and threatening letter sending surrounding the regulation of common rights and their abuses.[63]

Arguably it was only in the parishes surrounding the not long since enclosed East Bere forest in south-east Hampshire – an area that still had several large surviving commons and common meadows, including over 1,000 acres in both Droxford and Hambledon – that Swing patterns were explained by past protest practices. As E.P. Thompson so vividly detailed in *Whigs and Hunters*, this was an area with a long history of collective organisation and covert terrorism that persisted beyond the 1720s.[64] And so was the case during Swing – these impoverished parishes hosting machine-breaking, other forms of collective bargaining by riot and incendiarism.

Combining protests: the relationship between incendiarism and collective protests[65]

The foregoing analysis shows the complex spatial patterning of the resort to protest. No one sub-region only resorted to one protest practice, instead different combinations of protest were deployed from one locale to another throughout the south-east. The most widely resorted to was incendiarism, and yet past studies of Swing have been equivocal as to the role fire setting played in the movement. According to Hobsbawm and Rudé, incendiarism was not the 'characteristic form of unrest' of either the period before Swing or of Swing itself. Only after 1830 did incendiarism become 'the characteristic form of rural unrest'.[66] Indeed, while to many contemporary observers incendiary attacks on farmers' property were 'the most notable and memorable of "Swing" activities', to Hobsbawm and Rudé 'an element of mystery' surrounded incendiarism's role. 'Was it', they asked, 'an integral part, or was it a largely intrusive or alien element?' They concluded that arson played a different role from place to place, only in East Kent was it closely associated with machine-breaking. 'It lay at the fringe rather than at the core of the movement.'[67]

John and Barbara Hammond were similarly equivocal. In analysing the Sevenoaks fires they posited that 'it was impossible to say' how 'far' the fires were 'connected with later events'.[68] The relationship between incendiarism (and other 'covert' protest forms) and the various forms of, to use Hobsbawm's phrase, 'collective bargaining by riot' was also central to the so-called Wells-Charlesworth debate of the 1980s.[69] Subsequent systematic research has highlighted the elasticity of these concepts when applied to the archive. John Archer has shown that incendiary fires could act as the focus for open, collective protest: plebeian communities joyously gathering by the light of the flames and refusing to assist putting them out.[70] Indeed, as Steve Poole has asserted, there could be much that was furtive about collective protest and much that was collective, even 'overt', about incendiarism.[71] Was it, as a protest practice, integral to Swing? Or was incendiarism merely incidental to the machine-breaking episodes, the wages demonstrations, and the levying of monies?

To be a Swing protest, as opposed to an isolated incident separate from any wider movement, the act had to occur in relation to other protest acts. Machine-breaking in one parish might therefore inspire a wages gathering in a neighbouring parish, which in turn might inspire an individual in another parish to fire a parsimonious overseer's stacks. Thus, the difference between said attack during the heightened atmosphere of late 1830 and, say, two years previously was that the author of the 1830 fire was at least in part inspired by other activists. One case of incendiarism, potentially at least, could encourage others to similarly attempt to effect change, amd to vent their frustrations.

Some commentators clearly believed this to be true. Incendiarism, fanned by the flames of Swing's open protests, was like a contagion. When farmer Westmore's barns and stacks were fired at Gosport on the night of 11 November in an act that predated the spread of collective protests in Hampshire by a week, one reporter noted that 'incendiarism is spreading'.[72] It was this fear that was particularly potent in the public mind beyond Swing's initial protest centres, not least because of the frequent reports in the southern provincial press of both the fires and machine-breaking in Kent. As the *Southampton Mercury* put it in early October, Kent was 'in a very agitated state by an organized system of stack-burning and machine breaking'.[73] Through such reports, incendiarism became associated in the public mind with rebellion, with open revolt.

Much of the uncertainty surrounding the connection between incendiarism and the open, collective protests of late 1830 relate not to whether it was possible for incendiarism to be part of Swing's repertoire of resistance but rather what the link was, if any, between covert fire-setting and the 'mobbings'. Some rulers of rural England believed there was no connection, either in terms of personnel or in terms of motive. Sir Edward Knatchbull was of this mind. When sentencing the machine-breakers of Elham he asserted that 'it was a species of consolation, that the great number, and a great number there were, Heaven knew, who had engaged in the breaking of machines, felt the same abhorrence as [himself] of the burnings'.[74] Yet of these men, and others in his own domain, this was palpably untrue. The primary motive of the Elham gang was to stop the use of threshing machines. As noted in Chapter 3, this had been twice affected through incendiarism, once at Elham in 1817 and once in neighbouring Lyminge in 1829.

This precedent was also followed directly during the early stages of Swing. As detailed in Chapter 4, after the arrest of several machine-breakers on 27 September and the voluntary surrender on 2 October of a further fifty Elham machine-breakers the tactics of the gang necessarily had to change.[75] On 5 October Rev. Price's Lyminge farm buildings were set on fire, clerical magistrate Price being targeted, owing to his involvement in the arrests,[76] while on the following day the very first 'Swing' letters were received by post by two individuals near Dover both, threatening incendiary attacks. Two days later farmer Pepper of Hougham and Dover also received a 'Swing' letter warning her that her threshing machine was to be destroyed so she should remove it to an adjoining field immediately. She complied, and that evening the machine was duly broken and set on fire. A reporter for *The Times* was under no illusions as to who the incendiarists were. Now that nearly all the threshing machines had been destroyed or put out of use, the 'labourers have begun to fire [the] barns and stacks of those who retain their machines'.[77] Here the culture of fire-setting, pseudonymous threats, and open, collective protest were intertwined and inseparable.

The next two Swing centres also deployed incendiarism (and incendiary threats) with machine-breaking and attempts to increase wages. On the night before the trial of the Elham machine-breakers Borden overseer Knight had his farm set on fire. A few days later a piece of chilling graffiti was scrawled on a nearby wall: 'Down with machines. Death to informers',[78] and the next evening a group of fifty men marched from nearby Newington to Hartlip where they destroyed a threshing machine.[79] At Ash-next-Sandwich, after overseer Becker had his stacks set on fire on 5 October – predating machine-breaking at Ash by twenty days – the parish surveyor also had his stacks set on fire.[80] When the machine-breakers were admonished for going about the parish in armed gangs, they sarcastically responded that 'they could not sleep quietly in their beds for fear of the fires' and as such 'were going to break all the threshing machines … then there would be no more fires'. In conversation, two of the machine-breakers also admitted that they had been machine-breaking the previous day at Sandwich and had been at a fire in the same town on the premises of a farmer who had refused to 'lay down his machine'. Subsequently, one of the machine-breakers was also charged with firing Becker's stacks.[81]

These early Swing fires were not simply coincident with machine-breaking, they were integral to the achieving of machine-breakers' goals. Incendiarism was also a vital component of campaigns for higher wages and more generous poor relief payments. The two poles of Swing protests in the Weald were typical. At Brede on the night of the expulsion of assistant overseer Abell, a farmhouse was destroyed by an incendiary fire in the parish. At the beginning of November in nearby Battle, strikes, threats of arson, demonstrations, the sending of threatening letters and incendiarism itself were used interchangeably.[82] In both places, incendiarism was therefore integral to sustaining pressure rather than simply being the lone protestor's tool of revenge.

In parts of Hampshire the connection between incendiarism and 'mobbing' was even more explicit. On 22 November, a group of machine-breakers in the Test Valley, on returning to East Tytherley that night, proceeded to 'take down' the tollhouses on the Broughton and Romsey turnpike at East Dean and Tytherley. This must have only been a partial success for the following night they returned, 'dragged' the families out and set the buildings on fire.[83] Similarly, a group initially embodied at Leckford to demand an increase of wages proceeded to Stockbridge to levy money. After failing to secure a reduction in tithes from the vicar, they sent a messenger to Rev. Cutlet, who lived some distance from the town, to warn that if he too refused to reduce the tithes they would set his stacks and property set on fire.[84]

Occasionally, threats were carried out instantaneously. In the early hours of Sunday 21 November, a group, reportedly 200 strong, assembled at Shoddesden in the parish of Kimpton. After levying money and victuals of farmer Barnes his threshing machine was destroyed and his barn fired. A cottage on his farm, occupied by an 'old woman' who was given 20 minutes to get dressed and collect her effects, was also fired. This tactic, combining assembly with incendiarism (and threats of incendiarism), was also deployed later that day by another 'mob' at Fyfield where threats were made to burn Mr Bishop and another individual's property, and at Weyhill where it was declared they intended to burn the booths of the famous sheep fair.[85]

Elsewhere in Hampshire, as occurred at Battle, open, collective protests during the day were often followed by incendiary fires by night. On 19 November alone fires at Barton Stacey and St Mary Bourne followed protests in the very parishes that day, and in the case of a Whitchurch fire only two days after the first mobilisation in the county. The night following the destruction of Taskers' Iron Foundry at Upper Clatford, the corn barn of South Park Farm in Andover was set fire, causing some £2,000 of damage. The very number of such occasions suggests the improbability that these were coincidences,[86] as an examination of the Barton Stacey fire shows. On the evening of 19 November, a small group of men visited the Newton Stacey farm of William Courtney. Claiming that there were 1,600 other men behind them and that the farmer should 'look over at the hills at Barton Stacey for a light' – a blatant threat of incendiarism – they managed to levy 15 shillings, bread, cheese, and beer from Courtney. The men had come from St Mary Bourne and had been breaking machines for which they had been given money. Less than two and a half hours later, the Barton Stacey farm of Sir Henry Wright Wilson Bt was ablaze.[87]

As Hobsbawm and Rudé noted, incendiarism heralded the start of open, collective protests in all counties west of East Sussex. In writing about Wiltshire, they claim that, 'there had been the usual preparatory "softening-up" by threatening letters and incendiary fires'.[88] But to what extent did these fires actually directly relate to other forms of movement activity? Or were they simply coincident precursors? What evidence do we have of incendiarism being used to 'soften-up' farmers and the rulers of rural England?

The first incendiary fire in West Sussex after the spread of protests into neighbouring East Sussex occurred at Coldwaltham on the night of 12 November. The next day the first 'rising' to occur in West Sussex happened at Kirdford, some 40 miles distant from Mayfield, previously the most westerly parish to rise. But this is crude geography, for there was no discernible connection between the events at Coldwaltham and 20-mile distant Kirdford.[89] In Hampshire, a flurry of incendiary letters were received at Gosport around the 11 November – at least one of which was signed 'Swing' – 'asking' the farmers to remove their threshing machines. The threats were carried out on farmer Westmore on that day. The subject and pseudonym of the letters were obvious a direct reference to the events in Kent, the Hampshire press hoping that the fire was not 'a prelude to the outrages which have for some time disgraced several neighbouring counties'.[90] These fears were well founded, but there was no connection between this localised conflagration and the sustained start of protests around Havant on 18 November. Nor was there any obvious connection between a fire at Longparish on 13 November and the start of open protests in that area on 18 November.[91] That no clear link existed suggests that the incendiarists, although they may have been inspired by events to the east or were potentially attempting to provoke others into collective action, were not part of any coordinated action to 'soften up' farmers to allow the machine-breakers and others to effect their changes without resistance.

Most of the fires were either attempts to consolidate the message (or even gains) from other forms of protest – as at Barton Stacey and Andover – or were the result of opportunist individuals. Indeed, many of the protest forms deployed by Swing's multifarious activists disavowed the attainment of public and symbolic goals and instead, influenced and emboldened by the urgency and confidence of the surrounding overt actions, sought to right personal wrongs. When Elizabeth Studdam, a young single woman, fired a hay stack in the grounds of the poorhouse at Birchington in the Isle of Thanet on 9 November, this was in revenge for *her* treatment at the hands of the parish poor law officials.[92] The atmosphere engendered by Swing not only emboldened some individuals to give a more public life to specific grudges but also to make more generic public statements. Brothers Henry and William Packman were found guilty of firing the farm of William Wraight at Hernhill on 20 November but their initial plan was to fire Mr Paven's faggot stack. On leaving the pub that Saturday night, the would-be incendiarists changed their minds. They would now fire Wraight's premises 'as it would not be so much trouble'.[93] Notwithstanding these personal motivations, their actions were probably toasted in public houses and beer shops throughout southern England.

Knatchbull's belief that the Elham machine-breakers viewed incendiarism with the same 'horror' that the rulers of rural England did might have betrayed a profound misreading of his local charges, but how true was it of other Swing activists? The resort to open incendiary threats suggests a willingness, at least on behalf of some Swing groups, to embrace fire raising. Further evidence is derived of support for incendiarism from Swing activists in mobile groups. Robert Price, the 48-year-old politically active Maidstone shoemaker, was one such individual. In a row with Mrs Stacey of Stockbury, Price launched into a tirade about the state of the poor. Stacey suggested they should wait to the new Parliament to see what the King did, in belief that he was going to 'take off five millions in taxes'. Price exploded: 'King, we have no King ... Five millions of heads will be taken off before that is done.' The 'burnings' were therefore 'necessary to bring people to their senses ... you are all too high and must come down from the Head'.[94]

Evidence is also provided by the refusal of plebeian parishioners to help extinguish incendiary fires. A Sevenoaks correspondent to the *Rochester Gazette* reported in relation to the wave of fires in the vicinity: 'The expressions of the mob are dreadful: they said "Damn it, let it burn, I only wish it was a house: We can warm ourselves now: We only want some potatoes, there is a nice fire to cook them by!"' At a fire on Mrs Minet's farm in early September the pipes of the attendant fire engines were also so badly cut that they were rendered useless, pails having to be passed along a half-mile human chain.[95] 'The most disgusting feature', wrote one Kentish correspondent, 'is to see the sangfroid with which the lower orders speak of their "Bonfires" and still more the exultation evinced by the Mob present at them.'[96]

Was Captain Swing an incendiarist? The answer is simple. Yes, whenever he – and occasionally she – needed to be. Many individuals drawn up in the euphoria of Swing, or pressed against their will into the movement, no doubt abhorred the actions of incendiaries. While, as many commentators were quick to point out, the political economy of rick firing was absurd, to many Swing activists the landlords and farmers were their tormentors, the reason their families' bellies were empty. There might be little economic 'logic' in firing the means and results of production but there was logic in intimidating farmers in the hope of increasing wages. Besides, protest does not always have to have a particular end in mind, its aims can be diffuse, its purpose psychological. In a practical and political sense, incendiarism was integral to the movement. It was deployed, and threatened, in tandem with other protest forms to achieve specific objectives. As Archer has suggested, rural workers were 'selective in their choice of tactics', combining 'open' and clandestine forms at will.[97]

Notes

1 For two fine surveys of theories of collective engagement see: R. Eyerman and A. Jamison, *Social Movements: A Cognitive Approach* (Cambridge: Polity Press, 1991); S. Tarrow, 'Cycles of collective action', in M. Traugott (ed.), *Repertoires and Cycles of Contention* (Durham NC: Duke University Press, 1995), pp. 89–116.

2 R. Wells, 'The development of the English rural proletariat and social protest, 1700–1850', *Journal of Peasant Studies*, 6:2 (1979), 115–39.

3 U. Beck, *Risk Society: Towards a New Modernity* (London: Sage, 1992), p. 49.

4 A. Melucci, *The Playing Self: Person and Meaning in the Planetary Society* (Cambridge: Cambridge University Press, 1996), p. 130.

5 M. Maffesoli, *The Times of the Tribes: The Decline of Individualism in Mass Society* (London: Sage, 1996); B. Doherty, 'Paving the way: the rise of direct action against road-building and the changing of British environmentalism', *Political Studies* 47:2 (1999), 275–91.

6 G. Crow, *Social Solidarities: Theories, Identities and Social Change* (Buckingham: Open University Press, 2002), esp. chs 3, 4 and 6.

7 M. Waugh, *Smuggling in Kent and Sussex 1700–1840* (Newbury: Countryside Books, 1998), pp. 81–4; R. Philp, *The Coastal Blockade: The Royal Navy's War on Smuggling in Kent and Sussex 1817–1831* (Horsham: Compton Press, 1999), pp. 75–6, 105–10.

8 Waugh, *Smuggling in Kent and Sussex*, pp. 82–3; *Kentish Gazette* (hereafter *KG*), 24 May 1822; *Sussex Advertiser* (hereafter *SA*), 20 February; *The Times* (hereafter *TT*), 30 October and 21 November 1826.

9 TNA, HO 77/28, Calendar of Prisoners for Trial in Newgate Gaol, 11 April 1821; *SA*, 20 February 1826; *Kent Herald* (hereafter *KH*), 18 January and 8 February 1827; Waugh, *Smuggling in Kent and Sussex*, pp. 81–4.

10 Waugh, *Smuggling in Kent and Sussex*, p. 83; *Maidstone Journal* (hereafter *MJ*), 3 December 1828 and 20 January 1829.

11 *KG*, 29 May; *Kent and Essex Mercury*, 9 June 1830.

12 There is little evidence of large-scale smuggling in late 1829 and 1830. Those operations undertaken – and reported – occurred in Sussex: Shoreham, December 1829; Fairlight and Bexhill, March 1830; Pevensey, September 1830. *Hampshire Telegraph* (hereafter *HT*), 9 December 1829 and 29 March; *TT*, 23 September 1830.

13 This tactic has parallels with both earlier Luddite organisation and trade union formation, most notably at Tolpuddle: E.P. Thompson, *The Making of the English Working Class* (London: Victor Gollancz, 1963, revised 1968).

14 CKS, U951 C177/22, Unsigned deposition, no date (late September – early October); *Kentish Chronicle*, 21 September; TNA, HO 52/8, fos 271–2, Charles Sandys, Clerk to Canterbury Bench of Magistrates to Peel, 22 September 1830.

15 CKS, U951 C177/11, 10 and 19, Deposition of William Forded, 24 September; Information of Edward Hughes and Richard Hills, 23 September; and Information of Benjamin Andrews, 27 September; TNA, HO 44/21, fos 263–6, Edward Hughes, Smeeth Hill House to Home Office, 23 September 1830.

16 TNA, HO 52/8, fos 363–4 and 359–60, John Plumptree and Mr Hammond, St Albans Court, Fredville, Wingham; Rev. Gleig, Ash, both 25 October, to Peel; CKS, Q/SBe 121/3a, 9 and 8, Depositions of John Sladden, labourer, 26 October, William Euden (a.k.a. Kingsfold), labourer, 19 November, George Quested, surveyor, 17 November 1830.

17 Captain was 'a nickname he [Revell] has had for years': TNA, TS 11/943, Prosecution Brief prepared by the Treasury Solicitor against Timothy Willocks (but not brought to trial).

18 TNA, HO 52/8, fos 365–6 and 361–2, Rev. Poore, Murston to Peel, 25 October, Mr. Sharp, Faversham to Sir Francis Freeling, General Post Office, 26 October; CKS, U951 C14/7, Poore to Knatchbull, 26 October; *KG*, 29 October 1830.

19 TNA, TS 11/943, Prosecution Briefs prepared by the Treasury Solicitor in the case of *The King* v. *George Barrow, John Ballard, John Tuckner, William Chrisford and John Beale*, Kent Winter Assizes 1830. For the marking of deserters see 'An Act for the Punishment of Mutiny and Desertion': 10 Geo. IV, c.6, s.10. This Act formalised earlier practices, including the branding of deserters' shoulders with gunpowder.

20 TNA, HO 52/10, fos 369–70, 371–4 and 422–3 and 428, G. Courthope, Whiligh to Phillips, 6 November (twice), second enclosing deposition of Thomas Arcoll, Assistant Overseer and Governor of the Poorhouse, Brede, 6 November, Sir Godfrey Webster, Battle to Peel, 20 November, enclosing examination of Joseph Bryant, labourer, 19 November; TNA, HO 52/8, fos 386–7, J.C. Sharpe, Northiam to Peel, 9 November 1830.

21 One possible exception was a group that was active in the environs of Salisbury on 23 November. The *Devizes and Wiltshire Gazette* (25 November 1830) reported that twenty-three of these men had been committed, but none were 'what are called "Farmer's Men", they belong to the class usually known by the title of the Salisbury and Fisherton Gang'.

22 C. Cheeseman, 'Geography and Modernity: Changing Land, Law, and Life on Cranborne Chase in the Nineteenth Century' (DPhil thesis, University of Oxford, 2008), ch. 6.

23 TNA, HO 52/7, fo. 225, D.O.P. Okeden, More Crichel, Salisbury to Phillips, 28 November; Dorset History Centre, D/ANG/B5/42, D.O.P. Okeden, More Crichel to Lord Uxbridge, 26 December 1830.

24 For a detailed treatment of this group, see: David Kent, *Popular Radicalism and the Swing Riots in Central Hampshire* (Winchester: Hampshire Record Office, 1997).

25 On community cohesion, see: K.D.M. Snell, *Parish and Belonging: Community, Identity and Welfare in England and Wales 1700–1950* (Cambridge: Cambridge University Press, 2006), chs 2, 3, 4 and 8.

26 *Brighton Herald* (hereafter *BH*), 30 October 1830.

27 *Brighton Gazette* (hereafter *BG*), 18 November; *BH*, 20 November; *Hastings & Cinque Ports Iris* (hereafter *HIris*) 20 November 1830; A. Charlesworth, *Social Protest in a Rural Society: The Spatial Diffusion of the Captain Swing Disturbances of 1830–1831* (Norwich: GeoBooks, 1979).

28 C. Griffin, '"There was no law to punish that offence." Re-assessing "Captain Swing": Rural Luddism and Rebellion in East Kent, 1830–31', *Southern History*, 22 (2000), 151.

29 Case of John Gilmor: *TT*, 23 December 1830.

30 *Rochester Gazette* (hereafter *RG*), 2 November 1830.

31 Thompson, *The Making*, p. 611. Adrian Randall has recently highlighted the multiplicity of Luddite forms of organisation, highlighting considerable variations between Nottingham and Yorkshire and the 'far more complex' protests in Lancashire and Cheshire: *Riotous Assemblies: Popular Protest in Hanoverian England* (Oxford University Press, Oxford), pp. 275–303.

32 As Katrina Navickas has noted, drilling Luddites were in the minority but still evoked an 'atmosphere of militarism' which impacted upon the 'general population': 'The Search for 'General Ludd': The Mythology of Luddism', *Social History*, 30:3 (2005), 289.

33 TNA, HO 52/10, fos 369–70, 371–4, 422–3 and 428, G. Courthope, Whiligh to Phillips, 6 November (twice), second enclosing deposition of Thomas Arcoll, Assistant Overseer and Governor of the Poorhouse, Brede, 6 November, Sir Godfrey Webster, Battle to Peel, 20 November, enclosing examination of Joseph Bryant, labourer, 19 November 1830.

34 *KG*, 24 July 1829.

35 CKS, U951 C177/36, George Gipps, Bekesbourne to Knatchbull, 24 October 1830.

36 *Morning Herald*, q.f. *BH*, 16 October 1830.

37 TNA, HO 52/10, fos 162–3, Glover and Hart, clerks to Reigate JPs to Peel, 19 October 1830.

38 For the Elham area protests and relevant sources see Chapter 4, pp. 87–90. For the Carvills see: CKS, U951 C177/31, 6 and 9, Information of Edward Gower n.d. (but early October), Miscellaneous deposition taken by Knatchbull, n.d. (but late September); information of John Jefferey, n.d. (but late September 1830).

39 HCRO, 10M57/03/10, Draft petition to the Treasury from Hugh Lawes, sheriff's officer, and John Hornsby, shoemaker, both Basingstoke, January 1831; *Southampton Mercury* (hereafter *SM*), 27 November; HCRO, 100M70/F2, 'WBH' to Lady Harriet Baring, Mayfair, 25 November; HCRO, 10M57/03/2, Handbill listing the rioters apprehended on 23 November in the Basingstoke Division; *Hampshire Advertiser* (hereafter *HA*), 20 November 1830.

40 *Portsmouth, Portsea and Gosport Herald* (hereafter *PHer*), 28 November; *TT*, 28 December 1830.

41 B. Short, 'Landownership in Victorian Sussex', K. Leslie and B. Short (eds) *An Historical Atlas of Sussex* (Chichester: Phillimore, 1999), pp. 98–9; G. Mingay, 'Agriculture', in A. Armstrong (ed.) *The Economy of Kent, 1640–1914* (Woodbridge: Boydell & Brewer, 1995), pp. 63–76; T. Richardson, 'Labour', in Armstrong, *The Economy of Kent*, pp. 235, 238, 241.

42 S. Banks, 'Nineteenth-century scandal or twentieth-century model? A new look at 'open' and 'close' parishes', *Economic History Review*, 41:1 (1998), 51–73.

43 *BG*, 18 November; *BH*, 20 November; *HIris*, 20 November 1830.

44 *SA*, 29 November; *Dorset County Chronicle*, 2 December; *Hampshire Chronicle* (hereafter *HC*), 22 November 1830. Farnham appears to have been a very early centre for hiring threshing machines. As such, while the recent adoption of portable, hired machines appears to have been a stimulus for machine-breaking elsewhere, such machines were already a part of the fabric of rural work to the labourers of Farnham. See: *HC*, 27 October 1817.

45 E.P. Thompson, *Whigs and Hunters: The Origins of the Black Act* (Allen Lane, London, 1975); C. Griffin, 'More-than-human histories and the failure of grand state schemes: sylviculture in the New Forest, England', *Cultural Geographies*, 17:4 (2010), 451–72.

46 TNA, Assi 94/2070, Indictment of James Bravery for incendiarism, Surrey Winter Assizes 1830; TNA, HO 52/10, fos 204–5, William Crawford, Dorking to Peel, 19 November 1830.

47 TNA, HO 52/10, fos 176–7, 178–9, 194–6, J.S. Elliott, Hampton to Sir James Campbell, 12 November, Charles Ford, Sun Fire Office to Sir George Clerk, 12 November, Attorney General, King's Bench to Peel, 15 November; TNA, Assi 94/2070, Indictment of James Ritchie for incendiarism, Surrey Winter Assizes 1830.

48 TNA, HO 52/10, fos 199–200, Henry Drummond, Albury Park to Peel, 17 November 1830; R. Wells, 'Historical trajectories: English social welfare systems, rural riots, popular politics, agrarian trade unions, and allotment provision', *Southern History*, 25 (2003), 92–3. For the 'unruly' culture of extra-parochial areas see: Snell, *Parish and Belonging*, pp. 375 and 377.

49 CKS, U840 C250/10/9, Peel to Camden, 12 November; TNA, HO 41/8, p. 37, Peel to Lord Egremont, Petworth, 13 November 1830.

50 TNA, HO 52/10, fos 206–8, E. Wyatt Edgell, Milton Place, Egham to Peel, 19 November 1830.

51 See Chapter 4, pp. 95–7, 101, 102.

52 A.W. Smith, 'Some Folklore Elements in Movements of Social Protest', *Folklore* 77:4 (1966), 241–52; G. Seal, 'Tradition and Agrarian Protest in Nineteenth-Century England and Wales', *Folklore*, 99 (1989), 159.

53 *TT*, 29 November and 30 December 1830; TNA, 130/1, Hampshire Special Commission cases 100, 134–5 and 268 (Fawley, 25 November) and 70–2, 136, 165–6, and 268 (Fawley, 26 November).

54 Birchington: *KG*, 8 November; *KH*, 11 November. Threats were made against workhouses at Andover (Finkley), Elham, and Margate: *HC*, 29 November; TNA HO 44/21, fos 241–2, 'A Kentish Farmer', South Kent, to Home Office, 13 September; TNA HO 52/8, fos 77–8, John Boys, Margate to Phillips, 26 November 1830.

55 For the destruction of workhouses in Hampshire see Chapter 4, pp. 108–10. In addition to these attacks, threats were also made to destroy the Liss overseer's house: *HT*, 29 November 1830.

56 *RG*, 6 December; *BG*, 16 December. In early September two cows and 'several' pigs were poisoned at the soon-to-be Swing hotspot of Shere (Surrey), but these occurred outside of the context of the movement: *HT*, 20 September 1830.

57 *BG*, 6 October 1831. For a detailed treatment of plant maiming before and after Swing see: C. Griffin, '"Cut down by some cowardly miscreants": plant maiming, or the malicious cutting of flora, as an act of protest in eighteenth- and nineteenth-century rural England', *Rural History* 19:1 (2008), 29–54.

58 E. Hobsbawm and G. Rudé, *Captain Swing* (London: Lawrence & Wishart, 1969), pp. 178–80.

59 C.W. Chalkin, *Seventeenth Century Kent: A Social and Economic History* (London: Longman, 1965), pp. 11–15; W.E. Tate, *A Domesday of English Enclosure Acts and Awards* (University of Reading: Reading, 1978), pp. 145–7; History Data Service, The Enclosure Maps of England and Wales, http://hds.essex.ac.uk/em/index.html (accessed 6 January 2010).

60 This data is derived from: J. Chapman and S. Seeliger, *Enclosure, Environment and Landscape in Southern England* (Stroud: Tempus, 2001), pp. 82, 103, 149–51; Chapman and Seeliger, 'Formal agreements and the enclosure process: the evidence from Hampshire', *Agricultural History Review*, 43:1 (1995), 35–46; A. Parton, 'Parliamentary enclosure in nineteenth-century Surrey – some perspectives on the evaluation of land potential', *Agricultural History Review*, 33:1 (1985), 51–8; Tate, 'Enclosure Acts and awards relating to land in the county of Surrey', *Surrey Archaeological Collections*, 48 (1942–3), 118–49; Tate, *A Domesday*, pp. 247–50; History Data Service, The Enclosure Maps of England and Wales, http://hds.essex.ac.uk/em/index.html (accessed 6 January 2010). For the battles to preserve commons on the London fringe for recreational purposes rather than for common rights see: A. Taylor, '"Commons-stealers", "land-grabbers" and "Jerry-Builders": space, popular radicalism and the politics of public access in London, 1848–1880', *International Review of Social History*, 40:3 (1995), 383–407.

61 M. Reed, 'Gnawing it out: a new look at economic relations in nineteenth-century rural England', *Rural History*, 1:1 (1990), 83–94.

62 B. Short, 'Conservation, class and custom: lifespace and conflict in a nineteenth-century forest environment', *Rural History*, 10:2 (1999), 127–54; Short, 'Environmental politics, custom and personal testimony: memory and lifespace on the late Victorian Ashdown Forest, Sussex', *Journal of Historical Geography*, 30:3 (2004), 470–95. For the exploitation of commons see: J. Neeson, *Commoners: Common Right, Enclosure and Social Change in England, 1700–1820* (Cambridge: Cambridge University Press, 1993).

63 Griffin, 'More-than-human histories', 451–72.

64 Thompson, *Whigs and Hunters*, pp. 229–31.

65 A more substantial version of this section appears as C. Griffin, '"The mystery of the fires": Captain Swing as incendiarist', *Southern History*, 32 (2010), 21–40.

66 Hobsbawm and Rudé, *Captain Swing*, pp. 98, 12.

67 *Ibid.*, pp. 200, 203.

68 B. Hammond and J. Hammond, *The Village Labourer 1760–1832*, 4th edition (London: Longman, 1978 [1911]), p. 179.

69 E. Hobsbawm, *Labouring Men* (London: Weidenfield & Nicolson, 1968), pp. 5–22.

70 J. Archer, *By a Flash and a Scare: Incendiarism, Animal Maiming, and Poaching in East Anglia 1815–1870* (Oxford: Clarendon Press, 1990), pp. 160–1.

71 S. Poole, '"A lasting and salutary warning": Incendiarism, Rural Order and England's Last Scene of Crime Execution', *Rural History*, 19:2 (2007), 164.

72 *Devizes and Wiltshire Gazette*, 18 November 1830.

73 *SM*, 9 October 1830.

74 *Cobbett's Weekly Political Register*, 30 November 1830.

75 CKS, U951 C177/18 and 13, Rev. Price, Lyminge to Knatchbull, 27 September, and, List of persons entered into recognizances, n.d. (but 2 October); CKS, U951 C14/9, Mary Tylden to Knatchbull, 1 November 1830.

76 CKS, U951 C177/31, Deposition of John Wakefield, bailiff, n.d. (probably 6 October); TNA, HO 52/8, fos 276–7 and 281–2, Knatchbull, Mersham to Peel, 6 October 1830 (twice). For a full treatment of the events surrounding Price's fire see Chapter 9, pp. 233–5.

77 *KG*, 8 and 15 October; *TT*, 9 and 10 October 1830.

78 *MJ*, 26 October; TNA, HO 52/8, fos 300–1, Rev. Poore, Murston to Peel, 23 October; *TT*, 30 October; *Maidstone Gazette*, 9 November 1830.

79 TNA, HO 52/8 fos 300–1, Rev. Poore, Murston to Peel, 23 October; CKS, U951 C177/35, Poore to Knatchbull, 24 October 1830.

80 TNA, HO 52/8 fos 216–8 and 359–60, Camden, Canterbury, 22 October, and, Rev. Gleig, Ash, 25 October to Peel; *TT*, 23 and 27 October; *KG*, 26 October; *KH*, 28 October 1830.

81 *TT*, 27 October; *KG*, 29 October; CKS, U951 C177/36, George Gipps, to Knatchbull, 24 October; TNA, HO 52/8 fos 359–360, Rev. Gleig, Ash to Peel, 25 October 1830.

82 For sources see Chapter 4, notes 95–7.

83 *SM*, 27 November; *PHer*, 28 November; *HC*, 29 November; *TT*, 29 December; TNA, HO 52/7 fos 65–7 and 93–4, Mr W Hay, Romsey to Mr Lockhart, nr

Abingdon, 23 November, and Isaac Goldsmith, Dulwich Hill House, Camberwell to Phillips, 24 November 1830.

84 *HC*, 29 November; *TT*, 31 December 1830; TNA, HO 130/1, Special Commission cases 216 and 217.

85 TNA, HO 52/7 fos 46–7, Sir L. Curteis Cart, Ramridge, nr Andover to Peel, 21 November; *HA*, 27 November; TNA, 130/1, Special Commission cases 98 and 154.

86 TNA, HO 52/7 fos 42–3, Andover Bench, 20 November to Peel; *HA*, 20 and 27 November; *PHer*, 21 November; *HC*, 22 and 29 November; *TT*, 25 November; 23 and 24 December 1830.

87 *HA*, 20 November; *HC*, 22 November; *TT*, 23 November, 23 and 31 December 1830.

88 Hobsbawm and Rudé, *Captain Swing*, p. 122.

89 TNA, HO 52/8, fos 621–2, Earl of Egremont, Petworth to Peel, 13 November 1830; WSCRO, QR/Q 51, Indictment of John Champion and Thomas Champion, labourers, West Sussex Epiphany Sessions 1831.

90 *SM*, 13 November; *HC*, 15 November; *TT*, 16 November; *Devizes and Wiltshire Gazette*, 18 November; *London Gazette*, 23 November 1830.

91 *HC*, 22 November 1830.

92 TNA, TS 11/943, Prosecution Brief prepared by the Treasury Solicitor in the case of *The King* v. *Elizabeth Studdam* for arson, Kent Winter Assizes 1830.

93 TNA, TS 11/943, Prosecution brief prepared by the Treasury Solicitor in the case of *The King* v. *Henry and William Packman* for Arson, Kent Winter Assizes 1830.

94 CKS, Q/SBw/124/9, Deposition of Charlotte Stacey, wife of Courtney Stacey, 19 November 1830.

95 TNA, HO 52/8 fos 313 and 259–60, Managing Director of the County Fire Office, Regent Street, 31 August, and Mr Manning, New Bank Buildings, 3 September, to Peel; *RG*, 14 and 21 September 1830.

96 TNA, HO 52/8 fos 203–5, B. Sandford, Farningham and Dartford to John Irving MP, 8 October 1830.

97 J. Archer, 'The Wells-Charlesworth Debate: A Personal Comment on Arson in Norfolk and Suffolk', *Journal of Peasant Studies*, 9:4 (1982), 86.

Part III

Chopsticks' politics

As Leonora Nattrass has observed, William Cobbett's 'Rural Rides' never took him to the city. Nor did he travel further north than Oxfordshire. Despite the fact that from 1832 the, by then, grand old man of English radicalism represented Oldham in the House of Commons, Cobbett's pre-Swing writings all but ignored the industrial revolution.[1] This was not simply because he found industry distasteful to the agrarian aesthetics and moral economic values he developed as a Surrey farmer's son but, more emphatically, because his mission was to restore the social bonds of *Old* England.[2] The chalk and sand ridges, verdant vales, rick yards and cottage tables were *his* spaces in as much as mechanics' workshops, factories,and city streets belonged to fellow radical journalist Henry Hetherington. The farmworkers were Cobbett's constituents and he alone would represent them: 'There is no man who knows the English labourers so well as I do. I not only know all their wants, but their dispositions, their tempers.'[3] To an extent, behind the bombast his claims were rooted in substance. When rick-burning and machine-breaking started in earnest in south-east England late in the summer of 1830, leading urban radicals were caught, as Ian Dyck has asserted, 'by surprise'. They had ignored both Cobbett's prophecies of a farmworkers' revolt, and the rising tide of rural protest. Tellingly, they even overlooked popular song:

Now when that the corn is cut the rakers the ground they run o'er,
And scarce leave an ear for a mouse, instead of a loaf for the poor,
Such doings they will have an end, and the devil he must have his due,
He'll shake them for robbing poor people, O what will old England
    come to.

Such confounded schemes and contrivances they do invent every day,
If a poor man he owes but a trifle, he cannot get money to pay,
And when that the cold winter comes on, what causes poor workmen to
   rue,
It's all through these machines, O what will old England come to.[4]

Cobbett, a master of self-publicity who was not prone to self-doubt, was quick to his task, stoking the flames through his soon to be notorious lecture tour of southern market towns. He also harnessed Swing's power in print for his broader parliamentary political ends, proclaiming that his *Political Register* and *Two-Penny Trash* were so widely read by rural workers that he was in part responsible for Swing's vehemence and had helped to shape its discourses.[5] Cobbett was not alone in this judgement. When asked for their opinion as to the causes of Swing as part of the 1832 Poor Law Commission, the rulers of rural England frequently mentioned Cobbett's lectures and writings.[6] Radical agitation was often invoked by others too. When the Earl of Carnarvon wrote to Melbourne in February 1831 to inform him of an incendiary fire on the Burghclere overseer's farm, he noted that notwithstanding that the 'poor' were now 'well paid and well employed' they were also 'sullen' and ill-disposed to work. At the root of this, according to Carnarvon, was the fact that 'Cobbett's papers are distributed all over the neighbourhood' leading to an 'incendiary spirit'.[7]

The *Bridgwater and Somersetshire Herald* went further. The 'unhappy wretches' found guilty at the Winchester Special Commission were not 'driven by the pressures of poverty' but by radical agitation. Yet, while the labourers had been tried, 'the old fox' Cobbett was not 'caught'.[8] So notorious was Cobbett – one of the few non-parliamentarians known nationwide by his surname alone – that when the clerk to the Battle Bench wrote to Peel to warn of the fire on overseer Emary's farm, he laconically related that the 'feelings of the paupers' were 'excited by a lecture lately given *by a person named Cobbett*'.[9]

To a point, Cobbett also believed this to be true. At his subsequent trial for seditious libel published in the *Political Register* of 11 December, Attorney-General Denman claimed that the *Political Register* had a 'prodigious effect' on the rural poor. The defendant replied: 'I hope in God it has.' At the height of southern Swing, Cobbett had gone as far as to pugnaciously profess that:

There is not one single village, however recluse, in England, where my name is not known as the friend of the working people, and particularly of the farming labourers, and if ever man deserved any thing, I deserve this character.

Cobbett realised though, as Dyck has suggested, that the revolt 'belonged' to the labourers themselves.[10] He had predicted, and in many ways encouraged, 'rural war', but he was not the leader of the revolt. Cobbett was not Captain Swing.

Such accounts, however suggestive, are little more than suppositions that 'radical' politics informed and motivated rural workers to protest in 1830. They are not evidence per se. Neither the Hammonds' nor Hobsbawm and Rudé's accounts of the movement make the jump from adducing gentry evidence of the almost total penetration of Cobbett's writings to proving their influence.[11] E.P. Thompson's review of *Captain Swing* berated the two esteemed historians for ignoring, as he saw it, clear evidence of the activities of political radicals in the mobilisation, reiterating claims made in *The Making of the English Working Class* that there was a 'Radical nucleus in every county, in the smallest market towns and even in the larger rural villages'. Hobsbawm and Rudé duly responded in the revised 1973 edition of *Captain Swing*, adding some few examples of radical influence and expression.[12] Yet the differences are slight, the overall argument unchanged.

It was not until Andrew Charlesworth's mapping of Hobsbawm and Rudé's tabulations of protest events that any credence was given to the idea that political radicalism was actually central to the diffusion of protests. Proposing that the linkmen of the road were responsible for the movement's rapid diffusion, this sophisticated reworking did not provide explicit evidence that such individuals were politically literate and motivated. Acknowledging the 'conjectural' nature of his argument, Charlesworth implored – much as Richard Cobb had done in his review of *Captain Swing* – that scholars must 'dig' into the archive of Swing's epicentres to prove or disprove his thesis.[13] Yet, according to Thompson, those market town and village radicals were 'in nearly every case … local artisans' who had been turned to the cause by 'Cobbett, Carlile, Hetherington and their newsvendors'. These were not fieldworkers.[14]

Given Thompson's influence, it is not surprising therefore that, as Katrina Navickas has recently claimed for northern England, the 'political views and actions of domestic servants and agricultural labourers remain largely undiscovered'.[15] Two scholars have, however, heeded Charlesworth's call. Dyck's fine contextual study of

Cobbett and rural popular culture considers, in detail, the interplay between Cobbett's writings, popular belief and mobilisation in the 'hard parishes' of the Dever Valley.[16] Wells, in a number of publications, has also explored popular political expressions in the countryside. In his essay on 'rural rebels' in the 1830s countryside, Wells identified artisanal (and schoolmaster) involvement in Swing mobilisations in southern market towns.[17] Subsequent analyses have extended this model to include politically literate farmworkers, and have reminded us that the distinction between artisans and agricultural labourers in the post-1815 depression was often rendered opaque any how by the latter groups' need to go labouring to supplement their incomes.[18] Wells's most recent interjections have argued that popular politics was central to Swing as a movement: the mobilisations drawing in not only politicised rural and urban artisans and operatives but also politically motivated fieldworkers and farmers too. Wells has therefore concluded that Cobbett's claim that the passage of the Reform Bill on the second time of asking 'owe[d] more to the COUNTRY LABOURERS than to all of the rest of the nation put together' has some credence. For Swing not only acted as the trigger for the collapse of the Duke of Wellington's government, thereby helping to install Lord Grey's pro-reform administration, but was also an integral part of the reform agitation.[19]

Wells's writings demonstrate that almost wherever one digs into the archive of the major outbreaks of rural protest in early nineteenth-century England it is possible to find evidence of 'radical' politics. Indeed, as Chapters 4 and 5 demonstrate, political placards, rousing speeches and the actions of highly mobile radical agents provocateurs all figured strongly in Swing. Despite Swing's coincidence with the reform crisis, this was not novel: the same had been true for the East Anglian risings of 1816 and 1822, and would also be true for the anti-New Poor Law protests of 1835–36.[20] Notwithstanding this vital, corrective work, beyond the, by now, well known radical centres such as Sutton Scotney, we still know remarkably little as to how important 'village Hampdens' were in the rising of 1830. Were Cobbett's 'chopsticks' – all rural manual workers – engaged in participatory politics? Or should we, aping innovations in political theory, place equal importance on 'instrumental' plebeian politics in the countryside? As Peter Jones's studies of Swing attest, fieldworkers actively participated in a sort of localised, non-parliamentary instrumental politics of everyday life.[21] A politics in which work and welfare provided the experiential context and the twin codas of responsibility and rights provided the rules.

As local agricultural labour markets were increasingly parochially focused post-1815, so the politicking of the parish became ever more important. It framed not only decisions about who was employed, and by whom, but also the terms and conditions of employment. This dynamic was further complicated by the fact that from the 1790s – at the very latest – poor relief in all its forms had come to be seen as a right. This paternalist theory of rural society was not, however, resistant to change, as E.P. Thompson's demarcation of the 'moral economy' so powerfully proved.[22] Indeed, if the vast majority of rural communities could usefully, if somewhat reductionistically, be described as having a working agrarian equipoise based on paternalistically protected natural rights in 1790, no such generalisation could be made by 1830. Thus, by definition, there was a shift, albeit temporally and spatially uneven, from a natural rights-based critique of the wrongs of agrarian capitalism to a politics of the parish that impacted upon all rural manual workers – a chopsticks' politics. While having great parallels and connections with the burgeoning reform and radical movements, this was a form of politics driven by – and grounded in – the specific experiences of rural labour conflict. It was, in essence, local, though experiences elsewhere were also important.[23]

This instrumental politics was not simply about 'the politics of the parish'. Rather, Swing was also informed and determined by changing gender and household relations, and found expression in the complex relationship between ritual and violence in rural communities. The following chapters suggest that both forms of politics were integral to Swing, with instrumental political understandings increasingly pushing rural workers of all forms to engage in 'radical' participatory politics. It also suggests that Swing was a response to changing household and community politics, and acted to help further refigure the social relations of the English countryside.

Notes

1 L. Nattrass, *William Cobbett: The Politics of Style* (Cambridge: Cambridge University Press, 1995), ch. 8.

2 For the importance of his upbringing in shaping his later mission see I. Dyck, *William Cobbett and Rural Popular Culture* (Cambridge: Cambridge University Press, 1992), ch. 2.

3 *Two-Penny Trash*, November 1830, p. 99.

4 'What will Old England Come to?' (Newcastle, Fordyce, printer), reproduced in Dyck, *William Cobbett*, p. 163.

5 For Cobbett's 'exploitation' of Swing see: R. Wells, 'Mr. William Cobbett, Captain Swing, and King William IV', *Agricultural History Review*, 45:1 (1997), 42–3.

6 BPP. Commons, 'Report from His Majesty's Commissioners for Inquiring into the Administration and Practical Operation of the Poor Laws' (hereafter 'Rural Queries') (1834), vol. xxxiv, pp. 475e, 478e and 503e, responses of Henry Drummond MP, Albury, George Holme Sumner, East Clandon, and William Beck, assistant overseer, and William Hilder, Ewhurst.

7 TNA, HO 52/13, fos 124–5, The Earl of Carnarvon, Grovesnor Square to Melbourne, 5 February 1831.

8 *Bridgwater and Somersetshire Herald*, 5 January 1831.

9 TNA, HO 52/10, fos 357–8, Barton, Clerk to the Battle Bench to Peel, 3 November 1830. My emphasis.

10 Dyck, *William Cobbett*, pp. 170–1.

11 J. and B. Hammond, *The Village Labourer* (London: Longman, 1978); E. Hobsbawm and G. Rudé, *Captain Swing* (London: Lawrence & Wishart, 1969).

12 E.P. Thompson, 'Rural riots', *New Society*, 13 February 1969, 251–2; Thompson, *The Making of the English Working Class* (Harmondsworth: Penguin, 1968), p. 806; E. Hobsbawm and G. Rudé, *Captain Swing*, 2nd edition (London: Penguin, 1973).

13 A. Charlesworth, *Social Protest in a Rural Society: The Spatial Diffusion of the Captain Swing Disturbances of 1830–1831* (Norwich: Geobooks, 1979); R. Cobb, 'A very English rising', *Times Literary Supplement*, 11 September 1969.

14 Thompson, *The Making of the English Working Class*, p. 806.

15 K. Navickas, *Loyalism and Radicalism in Lancashire 1798–1815* (Oxford: Oxford University Press, 2009), p. 11.

16 Dyck, *William Cobbett*, pp. 171–8.

17 R. Wells, 'Rural rebels in southern England in the 1830s', in C. Emsley and J. Walvin (eds), *Artisans, Peasants and Proletarians 1760–1860: Essays Presented to Gwyn A. Williams* (London: Croom Helm, 1985), pp. 134–7.

18 R. Wells, 'Social protest, class, conflict and consciousness, in the English countryside, 1700–1880', in M. Reed and R. Wells (eds), *Class, Conflict and Protest in the English Countryside, 1700–1880* (London: Frank Cass, 1990), pp. 183–7; Wells, 'Popular protest and social crime: the evidence of criminal gangs in rural southern England 1790–1860', in B. Stapleton (ed.), *Conflict and Community in Southern England: Essays in the Social History of Rural and Urban Labour from Medieval to Modern Times* (New York: St Martin's Press, 1992), esp. pp. 142–6.

19 R. Wells, '1830: The year of revolutions in England, and the politics of the Captain Swing insurrection' (unpublished internet paper), www.canterbury.ac.uk/arts-humanities/history-and-american studies/history/Documents/PoliticsOfCaptainSwing.pdf (accessed 21 April 2011); Wells, 'Mr William Cobbett', p. 48.

20 For the protests of 1816 and 1822 see: A. Charlesworth (ed.), *An Atlas of Rural*

Protest in Britain 1548–1900 (London: Croom Helm, 1983); A.J. Peacock, *Bread or Blood* (London: Victor Gollancz, 1965); P. Muskett, 'The East Anglian agrarian riots of 1822', *Agricultural History Review*, 32:1 (1984), 1–13. For southern anti-New Poor Law protests see: J. Lowerson, 'The aftermath of Swing: anti-Poor Law movements and rural trades unions in the south east of England, in A. Charlesworth (ed.), *Rural Social Change and Conflicts since 1550* (Hull: CORAL, 1983), pp. 55–83; R. Wells, 'Resistance to the New Poor Law in the rural south', in J. Rule and R. Wells, *Crime, Protest and Popular Politics in Southern England 1740–1850* (London: Hambledon, 1997), pp. 91–126.

21 P. Jones, 'Swing, Speenhamland and rural social relations: the 'moral economy' of the English crowd in the nineteenth century', *Social History*, 32:3 (2007), 271–90; Jones, 'Finding Captain Swing: protest, parish relations, and the state of the public mind in 1830', *International Review of Social History*, 54:3 (2009), 429–58.

22 E.P. Thompson, 'The moral economy of the English crowd in the eighteenth century', *Past and Present*, 50 (1971), 76–136. For the most recent examination of the changing dynamics of paternalism see: A. Randall and E. Newman, 'Protest, proletarians and paternalists: social conflict in rural Wiltshire 1830–1850', *Rural History*, 6:2 (1995), 205–27. Peter Jones, albeit from a different perspective, has also considered the moral economy of reciprocity: 'Swing, Speenhamland and rural social relations'.

23 In this sense the politics of the parish mirrored custom in that it was derived from local experience and precedence but did not exclude outside influence. For the classic examination of the politics of rural custom see: E.P. Thompson, *Customs in Common* (London: Penguin, 1993), ch. 3.

6

The politics of the parish

Sir,
Unless, you make some Alteration for the Better for the poor of Hadlow and to them justice your Life is in great Danger, for we are Determined Not to bare it any Longer for we have sworn ourselves by the powers above not to betray one another and you will feel the weight of Led before many more Sabbaths' is past but I sincerely hope that we shall not be oblidge to carry our Design in fact we beg it may be altered without but it will be carry'd in fact with some of the Farmers so no more

From your Deadly Enemys
H R N P F B
Z

J. Moneypenny of Hadlow, Kent, was so alarmed by receiving the above letter in early February 1831 that he wrote to inform the Home Office. Why, Moneypenny mused to Lord Melbourne, should he be the target of H R N P F B and Z's wrath? He did not own the tithes or any land in the parish, nor was he a 'member of the select vestry'. It must, he concluded, have been sent to him in his role as a magistrate. The evening before, a 'similar' letter had been left at the poorhouse, 'desiring' the assistant overseer to quit 'within six weeks', as well as threatening several farmers 'by name'.[1] These otherwise obscure acts neatly encapsulate the key features of 'the politics of the parish': the regulation of work, welfare and property. While issues surrounding property appear to have been only peripheral to Swing, the regulation of work and the way in which welfare was administered were arguably the major generators of resentments. They form the focus of this chapter. First, it examines the politics of regulating work as detailed by Swing's archive, and, second, the politics of administering welfare and work.

Regulating work

Threshing machines elicited opinions from everyone. On passing through the parish of Monckton during his 1823 rural ride from Sandwich to Canterbury, Cobbett noticed that there were seventeen men working on the roads even though the harvest was not yet finished. The cause? There were *'four threshing machines'* at work in the parish.[2] It was not only radicals that were of such a mind. The parochial return from Rogate, near Petersfield on the Sussex-Hampshire border, to the 1823 Select Committee on 'Poor Rate Returns' opined that 'the threshing machines are the occasion of [a] great many men being out of employ, and thereby increases the poor's rates'.[3] Parochial concerns about the use of threshing machines had a long history. In December 1816, the Odiham (Hampshire) vestry resolved unanimously that owing to difficulty in finding employment for the poor 'it would be expedient to discontinue the use of threshing machines within the parish'. Five years later, Basingstoke vestrymen similarly agreed – as part of a roundsmen employment scheme – to stop using their threshing machines.[4] While there was no way of enforcing such a policy, such pronouncements are important because they were made publicly.

As detailed in Chapter 4, before the first Swing incidents occurred, members of the Barham vestry had made such a resolution, while in nearby Lyminge, Rev. Price JP was in public dispute with the 'most influential' local farmers and another farmer who had introduced a threshing machine. The open hostility of many smaller farmers to the machines, combined with the Barham vestry and Price's pronouncements, led, the *Spectator* claimed, local manual workers to believe machine-breaking was 'meritorious ... and a judicious act'.[5] Threshing machines were never introduced – or deployed – without political consequences, pitting farmer against farmer, and farmworkers against farmers. If before 1830 expressions of this antipathy took the form of threatening letters and incendiarism, the actions of the Elham gang blazed a trail for all southern labourers.

While the destruction of machines en masse during the autumn and winter of 1830 obviously betrayed a deep and near universal antipathy on behalf of rural workers to the mechanisation of agricultural tasks, getting at the precise articulations of plebeian antagonisms to machines is more complex. As Adrian Randall's superb study of the reaction of manual workers to the mechanisation of cloth production between

1776 and 1809 shows, Luddism's archive details acts of machine-breaking rather than specific motivations. Utilising the few petitions and threatening letters that survive, Randall shows that custom was a key discourse mobilised by cloth workers to explain their actions, but the fear of unemployment and depressed wages played out rather more strongly.[6] The same documentary problems are true of Swing. As Judge Alderson declared at the Hampshire Special Commission, 'We do not come here to inquire into grievances. We come here to decide law.'[7] And for such reasons, articulations of motivations behind the destruction of threshing machines were related only in threatening letters – of which few survive – and occasional stilted snippets of conversation recorded in depositions. Again, as with Randall's evidence, these letters and depositions all (unsurprisingly) infer that machines supplanting manual labour provided the justification for their destruction. Thus, publican and petty agriculturalist Wollett noted, 'it was chatted about amongst the Stelling People that they would not let any Machine work in the Parish'. He had been 'laughed at about my Machine – that it would be broken and that there were several People in that Parish that would suffer a Machine to come in'.[8] The connection between machines and 'suffering' was also made in a threatening letter sent to the farmers at Fulking, Sussex: 'this is to inform you what you have to undergo ... providing you don't pull down your messhines and rise the poor mens wages'.[9] Nowhere was the connection more explicit than around Havant where magistrate Leeke reported to Peel that the machine-breakers exclaimed: 'we are out of employ – we have no work – Break the machines – we will have bread – we will not starve'.[10]

Perhaps the politics behind machine-breaking were so obvious to farmers and farmworkers that there was little need to articulate them. Actions spoke louder than words. A similar justification could be utilised to understand the discourses surrounding vestry-regulated employments, the other key generator of resentments at a parish level. Yet, these discourses *were* frequently given voice during Swing. Even otherwise loyal urban commentators occasionally betrayed a decidedly radical tone when thinking through the effects of post-Napoleonic parochial policy. In the words of one Gosport correspondent to the Home Office, 'by an illiberal, grinding system of impolitic grudging economy, [the farmer has] wickedly thrown his labourers on the Poor Laws ... hence has followed a reckless desperation of temper among the people'.[11]

The most coherent articulation of plebeian concerns surrounding parochial employment regulation came in the form of 'petitions' supposedly written by the poor themselves – though often betraying a technical literacy beyond that which could be expected of a labourer – 'requesting' changes in the parish. The example from Chithurst, Sussex, is particularly instructive:

> The humble petition of the labourers of the above Parish prayeth that the said Gentlemen ... will take into consideration the distress which as been in a same manner felt by the poor in general of this said Parish of Chithurst and requires who shall have occasion to employ either married man or a single man on their Premises or any other Employ whatever do give the value of two shillings per Day 12s per week and any Parish work shall have the same as if they were a work on the farms or other Premises and that Boys at the age of 16 years [?] have 6s a week or 1s a Day and Boys when first employed on Terms or Parish work be paid 6d a Day or 3s a week.

Beyond the deliberately deferential tone, the petition contained, as did many others, an implicit critique of the workings of the parish. Yet the Chithurst petition went further:

> And that every man shall be immediately employed in the Parish so some as be shall be out of employ at farms ... not be kept out of work as they have been until they have spent every farthing they have before they are not to work.

This was an explicit critique that, while acknowledging the undoubted distress felt by many agriculturalists, asserted that farmers had a moral responsibility to employ all men. Those engaged in 'Parish work' were, so the petition infers, not to be engaged in agricultural tasks but instead upon essential parish maintenance – unless the farmers had 'spent every farthing'.[12] Similarly emphatic was the 'violent' paper seized by Sir Godfrey Webster at Mayfield, Sussex: 'If a man has got any boys or girls over age for to have enough that they may live by there labour ... if ther is no alteration we shall proceed further about it.' While the petition acknowledged the importance of child allowances, that is, de facto wage supplements, it was an expectation that all men would perform meaningful labour.[13]

Much 'work' performed in the depression years before Swing was neither meaningful nor remunerating. As acting chairman Sir Thomas Baring admitted to the 1830 Hampshire Midsummer Quarter Sessions, the parochial policy of engaging all men of working age was not driven by the dictats of political economy but rather by the need to keep the 'poor' from idleness and crime. It was the 'incumbent duty' of the parish to 'find work where possible'.[14] This ideology was perhaps best expressed in early 1819 by the Framfield vestry: those men 'out of work' were to be sent to the surveyors and paid for 'what good they actually do'.[15] Few were the parishes like Milstead in Kent that, according to Richard Cooper and J.A. Tylden, paid able-bodied men 'a bare subsistence' from the poor rates 'for doing nothing'. A more typical, and perhaps honest, assessment came from Slaugham near Horsham: the fundamental cause of Swing was that the 'people' were out of 'proper employment'.[16]

While many Swing protestors were effectively out of gainful employment, they were still engaged in some form of work. Indeed, it is striking that Swing's archive invariably relates that when accommodations were arrived at between workers and employers, the following day everyone was back *at work*. Few individuals were, in the eyes of authority, actually idle. This epithet was normally reserved for those known, or rather suspected, of gaining their livelihood through illicit means: poachers, smugglers and members of criminal gangs. Even these statements were founded on moral judgements. For instance, when magistrate John Boys wrote to warn the Home Office of the 'planned' attack on the Margate workhouse, he noted that there were many 'smugglers and idle, bad characters' about the area. Similarly, the attack on threshing machines around Mottisfont was reported to be the work of local labourers joined by 'several idle and unprincipled fellows' from Romsey.[17]

Notwithstanding the entrenched nature of rural worklessness, that few 'Swing' activists therefore actually complained about unemployment per se should not surprise us. The plea of those assembled at Sutton Scotney came closest: 'we are half starved; we are willing to work, let us be paid what we earn, that's all we want!'[18] Yet even this was a tacit statement about the desire to do meaningful farm work. This is not to say that the condition of unemployment was not humiliating, robbing the labourer of that which defined him. Rather, in the words of the editor of *Keene's Bath Journal*, it was not so much unemployment per se that generated resentments but the fact that labourers were 'obliged to work harder by far than the worse treated slaves in the West Indies, for parish pay'.[19] No less a figure than Sussex grandee the Duke of Richmond concurred. Speaking in the House of Lords on 25 February 1830, he admitted that 'the once happy peasantry of England' were degraded to the state of the brute creation' through their being 'harnessed to wagons' to draw loads of stone on the roads.[20] It was, in short, the parish regulation of all labour that conditioned labourers' responses during Swing.

Employment schemes did not make easy targets for most had no physical manifestations. Workhouses were obvious exceptions. The Union workhouses at Elham and Margate were both threatened with destruction, while at Headley and Selbourne 'Swing' crowds made good such threats.[21] The problem with trying to adduce the importance of employment regulation precipitated protests is that it was impossible to delineate the precise motivations for attacks on individual overseers or vestry members. Those direct attacks on forms of employment regulation during Swing were largely symbolic. The carts used by the poor employed on the parish roads of Brede were symbolically used to remove the hated assistant overseer. The prearranged meeting at Ringmer workhouse between the labourers and the farmers ended with the pulling down of the grindstone that had been used to employ those otherwise out of work.[22]

The experience at Ash-next-Sandwich, while devoid of symbolism, was arguably more telling. Not only were the unemployed labourers put up for auction each week, but those settled to the parish yet resident elsewhere were forced to walk daily to the parish to collect their dole. Not surprisingly, after overseer Becker was targeted by an early Swing fire, it was relayed that he had 'greatly provoked the vengeance of the poor'. On the night after the fire, Timothy Willocks, a labourer and soon-to-be chief suspect, candidly admitted to a total stranger that he could not afford to pay the rent on his cottage and feared that he would be evicted. This made him defiant: 'he would as soon be hung as go to the Workhouse'.[23] Becker's fire was swiftly followed by an incendiary attack on the premises of the parish surveyor, farmer Quested.[24] A few days later when Quested was approached by a gang of machine-breakers, he pleaded that if it was a want of employment that had made them assemble he would employ them all on the roads from 1 November to 1 March at 2/6 a day, 'the same as his other men had'. The offer was ignored.[25] The following day the Ash labourers struck work, publicly stating their determination that married men should receive at least half a crown for a day's labour. If this were not granted, they threatened, the farmers' ploughs would be broken, 'leaving them no alternative but the spade'. Likewise, threatening letters sent to two gentlemen in the vicinity of Maidstone in mid-October threatened to set fire to their buildings unless *they* employed the 'parish poor'. These were explicit expressions of the universal southern belief that farmers should employ labourers directly, not the parish.[26] Moreover, labourers wanted steady employment. Hence, when the Soberton labourers were offered either 12 shillings a week when work was offered to them, or half a guinea for guaranteed year round employment they readily chose the latter option.[27] The dignity of labour was of even greater importance than the level of wages.

Manipulations of local labour markets through variations on the roundsmen scheme, and attempts to lower wages by placing the cost of labouring support on the wider community of ratepayers, had robbed the southern labourer of, as Cobbett saw it, their birthright. An agreement between the vestry, farmers and labourers of Owslebury, forged in the heat of Swing, acknowledged this inseparable politics of identity and work. 'All able bodied men' were provided with a minimum income guarantee, but any refusals to work would 'lead to withdrawal of parish relief and proceedings in law'.[28] Performing meaningful work should attract a fair and remunerating wage. Hence, the oft-repeated demand during Swing for 'pay' for breaking threshing machines. As Jones has suggested, even 'victims' 'implicitly acknowledged' that machine-breakers were 'engaged in labour, rather than in wanton destruction'.[29] Moreover, by asserting that other forms of protesting were also 'work', Swing groups could claim moral legitimacy in their actions. Thus, at Stockbridge, the protestors demanded of Rev. Cutlet four sovereigns as 'remuneration for their day's work',[30] while after destroying his threshing machine at Barham, the Elham gang shouted out to farmer Sankey to 'get up and bring us some Beer for we have been to work damn hard'.[31] Similarly, after destroying all the machinery on Sir Thomas Baring's farm at East Stratton, some of the 'mob' demanded of steward Francis Callendar: 'We've done our work, now we'll be paid for it.'[32] Some farmers also recognised that 'work' was being done. For instance at Brede, one farmer gave all those who helped removed assistant overseer Abell half a pint of beer for he 'never was better pleased in his life than with the day's work'.[33] In the words of E.P. Thompson, such payments were justified for they had been doing 'good work' for the community.[34]

Labouring in the fields and farmyards and in the coppices and coverts not only helped to give labourers their identity, but it also helped to define them as in some way sociologically different from other members of rural society. This notion of difference, of a distinctive social solidarity forged through work, was relayed both by those with capital – the 'labouring classes', 'those of the same classes' – and by rural workers themselves. If artisans and operatives endured similar conditions and privations to field workers and had often to turn to labouring, they were thought of as belonging to a different social group by both many labourers and their 'social betters' alike. Thus, as Wells has persuasively asserted, farm labourers formed a coherent self- and externally-identified labouring class. Protests surrounding issues of work thus were wrapped up in class politics, or rather a politics informed by class consciousness.[35] This was most clearly expressed in the widely resorted to practice of 'pressing' other labourers and servants in the parish: all members of the labouring class must be seen to be united in protest. As the Mayfield petition proclaimed, notwithstanding fissures and feuds, of labouring communities: 'we are all as one and we will keep to each other'.[36]

The dynamic of asserting labouring interests in direct opposition to the interests of employers was also expressed in the Swing tactic of 'leaving off' work to try and force an increase in wages. This form of proto strike had, as noted in Chapter 2, a long history in southern England, though organised striking was almost exclusively the preserve of those involved in rurally based trades and manufacture. Because of the entangled web of responsibilities for employment in the post-1815 countryside, not all strikes were targeted exclusively at employers. Overseers too were targeted. The first collective action at Battle was a strike of the 'poor', which targeted overseer Emary, while at Newport on the Isle of Wight those set to work in the forest also made their claims to the overseer.[37] But these were exceptions. In most cases the desire to assert the critical primacy of farmer-paid wages for an honest day's labouring meant that the employers were targeted. During the heat of Swing, a movement based on the ideals of unity and fair treatment, all farmers were invariably called upon to pay the same wages, hence the tactic necessitated calling on all farmers in the parish to make the demand.

One form of employment regulation that was relatively contention-free was the policy of refusing to employ those not settled in the parish, pandering as it did to labourers' 'culture of xenophobia'.[38] While such a policy flew in the face of political economic doctrines by limiting the local labour supply, it made some parochial economic sense. If the parish farmers employed only those who the vestry would otherwise have to support, demands on the poor rates would decline. Attempting to enforce this was effectively impossible without withdrawing wage subsidies for a recalcitrant farmer's employees. The archive of south-eastern Swing suggests though that this was not a major issue, only occasional archival fragments highlighting tensions over the employment of non-settled English labourers. For instance, farmer Farndell of Bosham was targeted by machine-breakers because, among other reasons, he 'employed persons not belonging to the parish'.[39] As Chapter 3 details, immediately prior to the start of machine-breaking, attacks on migrant labour and attacks and threats against those who engaged migrant labour were of critical importance. Yet such complaints do not figure again until the summer of 1831 when the politics of employing migrant labour became an explosive issue.

Administering work and welfare

Work was always political. It mediated the relationship between labourers, farmers and the vestry. But the provision of work was not the only way in which the politics of the parish played out. While, by 1830, arguably the most important role of the vestry was that of de facto labour market controller, its statutory functions remained of vital import too. Yet, as Jones has asserted, 'it was not simply the amount of wages or relief, or even the nature or quantity of work on offer, that provided the focus for the anger and, occasionally, the violence of Swing crowds'. Rather, Jones continues, it was the manner in which 'relief', and therefore by default 'work', was given that caused such a chronic dislocation between the poor and the parish.[40] As such, this section does not explore the specific relief demands made by Swing protestors, these are treated in context in Chapter 4, instead, it analyses the political critiques of welfare provision issued by Swing activists. It begins with a brief examination of the attitudes of labourers towards farmers and other members of the rural community, before considering the ways in which Swing protested at claimants' treatments at the hands of poor law officials. It concludes with an exploration of the vestry as an arena of conflict and a space of oppression.

The often deferential request for higher wages bore no hint of malice, nor was the destruction of threshing machines in itself evidence of a breakdown in relations between employee and employer. Indeed, as Chapters 4–6 demonstrate, in many locales small farmers were active members of Swing groups and gangs, in other places protests were encouraged by farmers, and in some locations farmers were hugely sympathetic to Swing's pleas. But while civilly asking for 'doles' from farmers and other well-to-do members of the community might appear to be evidence of an essential cordiality in parish social relations, its very (customary) form was rooted in subversion, turning the world topsy-turvy, reversing the chains of power. Doling and other processioning forms were, therefore, political acts: they inverted social relations and took 'payment' as a way in which the payee acknowledged past wrongs. Besides, acting civilly mocked the decidedly-lacking-in-civility acts of oppression experienced by poor workers. And yet, rural southern England was aflame with a malice that destroyed hundreds of farmers' stacks. Anomie also fired the bitter tone that broke in parleys between Swing groups and farmers when the protestors' civility was met with abuse. '[We have come] for our lawful rights, to break machinery, and get higher wages' answered labourer Abraham Childe to magistrate Jones's enquiry as to the reasons for having assembled. 'Have you got any machine?' Childe continued, prompting Jones to fire back, 'You rebel-ruffian, how dare you question me.'[41]

This dislocation between employer and employee might have been uneven, but according to Rev. Barter of Burghclere it was the primary cause of Swing. The 'rioting', he asserted, was attributable to the 'want of employment on the farms, in consequence of which many good Labourers are put on the roads, and all friendly intercourse between the Farmers and the poor ceases'.[42] If the lack of a daily dialogue between farmers and potential employees was not the only reason for this breakdown, Barter was clearly acutely aware that farmers and the parish had engineered this changed state of affairs. He was not alone. Answers to Question 53 of the so-called 'Rural Queries' were extremely telling. From Ash-next-Sandwich the respondent noted an 'absence of common courtesy' from farmers towards his labourers, similar to the claim of that the labourers had lost their 'good feeling for their Master's interest' at Faversham, and the 'want of good feeling … between the Farmer and the Labourer' at Minstead. Others were not so measured in their response. Rev. Henville of Wymering believed that labourers had been exposed to 'harsh treatment' by the farmers, while the Eastbourne correspondent believed the farmers had 'oppressed and degraded' their employees, forcing them upon the parish. The most graphic response came from the West Chiltington respondent who claimed that Swing was the product of 'the farmers by screwing the poor too severely in their wages'. The outcome of this mutual antipathy was, according to Robert Smith of Farningham, that the poor had turned to incendiarism 'out of spite'.[43]

Such responses are telling in that they record the beliefs of the farmers, middle classes, and rulers of rural England. But they are, presumably, part supposition, based on readings of Swing's vehemence as much as direct experience. The most direct record of the antipathy felt by labourers to their employers were the huge number of incendiary fires to occur against farming property in 1830. Interestingly, the few threatening letters sent to farmers that have survived in southern Swing's archive – with an exception, detailed below – do not articulate this mistrust, tending instead to only offer dire warnings about the use of threshing machines. This is probably mere coincidence, the few letters that survive not being representative of the oeuvre. After all, farmers were not likely to communicate the receipt of such a letter to the Home Office, or, for fear of sparking costly reprisals, seek prosecution, thus depriving us of two critical sources.

Clergymen, magistrates and grandees showed no such compunction. While the threatening letters they received represent a fraction of the overall number of letters recorded in the provincial press, they are still an important record of parish politics. The letter sent to the Earl of Sheffield on 25 October complained not only of his 'furren stuard and farmer' but also his 'balley' [bailiff]. If he did not 'git rid' of them, the letter warned, 'we will bourn him upt and you alomg with him'. 'My Lord', they continued, 'my written bad but my firen is good my Lord.'[44] John Ward, a minor gentry figure and master of the Squerries estate at Westerham, was similarly warned that his bailiff had been witnessed:

> bosting of his powr about Squerries of what he cane do and that he has dun ... and that he wood do A great dail more to Sume more About it yet but wee will take care of that if you not discharge him if you not send him wat alive we will send him did in a short time. Sir if our request is not atendet to wee are deteramend to burn the most of youre astats ... we have no thing to say againgst any of youre place but Tylor and if you not be atended to wee will put a end to him and blow you oup in youre carage and make you a exemple to outhers.[45]

Sir Harry Featherstone of Uppark was also warned in a letter brandished by a mobile Swing group about the actions of his 'grinders' (i.e. his bailiffs and steward).[46]

Gentlemen and members of the gentry themselves were also lambasted. Robert Price's mobile group expressed in a parley at Hollingbourne that one local gentleman was 'a damned bad one', and in conversation with Charlotte Stacey at Stockbury indignantly stated that: 'I understand you keep a great dog to bark at beggars.' William Tribe was called 'a damed rogue' for his 'conduct in Worthing' in a 'Swing' letter.[47] Sir Timothy Shelley, a former Horsham MP and father to poet Percy Bysshe Shelley, was the recipient of a threatening letter. It warned that '[If he] wish[ed] to escape the impending danger in this world and that which is to come' he should:

> first go round to all your parishioners and return all the last years tyths and inquire and hear from there own lips what distresses there in and how of them are drove to part with the last shilling to pay you this shamefull manopely.[48]

Nor were the feelings of the clergy spared. Indeed, they were especially vulnerable if they acted as clerical magistrates or officiously collected their tithes on all produce. One Horsham farmer who received a letter which accused him of 'gorg[ing] upon the vitals of the poor half starved labourer till he has sworn to wear the chains of slavery no longer', was also warned that the names of 'Parson Justices' were also 'down amongst the Black Hearts in the Black Book' and you ought 'make your Wills'.[49] Rev. Woodward of Maresfield, a notoriously unruly parish on the fringe of Ashdown Forest, received an even more vitriolic letter on 13 November:

> Sir, we have enquird into your tithe and find you join in eating the country up ... what business have you with the others ought not the poor labour to right have it that works for it who you starve you old Canible take it if you dare and we will rost you and your daughter in your bed.[50]

Parish officers were subjected to the greatest abuse and were most likely to feel Swing's full wrath. Vestry attendance, as Wells and others have shown, was notoriously poor, even some select vestries – the small cabals of concentrated self-interest – collapsed because of woeful attendance. The job of overseer was universally thought to be a poisoned chalice, huge responsibility without reward, with an increased chance of having one's farm fired for causing offence. This is not to say that all overseers had no sense of duty or care, but many rural parishes were administered by a small group of ratepayers most of whom neither had the time or the resource to properly attend to the liberal management of the parish. In the words of the Northiam respondent to the Poor Law Enquiry, this 'unwillingness' of occupiers to 'attend to parish affairs' combined with the acute financial pressure faced by many southern farmers led to a parochial system of governance based on expediency and political economy rather than a sense of duty and responsibility.[51]

At the forefront of Swing's concerns with the management of the parish and the poor laws were, therefore, the 'illiberal, grinding system of impolitic grudging economy'. The following example is instructive. On 5 December a small group of labourers came to request their pay from the West Chiltington surveyor. They were offered six shillings, but refused, claiming that having attended the Petworth Bench on the previous day the magistrates had promised an extra sixpence a day on top of the usual shilling, plus eighteen pence for any lost days. Surveyor Tourn then offered them five shillings, making a deduction of a shilling for their having taken the previous day off work. The men took this money and left 'abusing' Tourn 'very much'. Later that day the men repeated their demand when they met the surveyor on the way to church. Tourn promised to meet them in the vestry room where, again, they repeated their demands. The surveyor then placed the extra money on the pay table, and said that if the magistrates had said they were to receive 18 pence a day they would not be wrong in taking it, but if they had a said they were to receive a shilling a day and no money for lost days they would be wrong to take it. The men duly took the money. Tourn responded by saying that he would tell the magistrates, warning the men to 'take care' as what they had done 'should get them into prison'. Enraged, the men retorted: 'Damn your eyes take care that you do not get there yourself.'[52]

While the West Chiltington surveyor might have got off relatively lightly, compared to surveyor Quested at Ash-next-Sandwich,[53] his condescending and threatening attitude and the impetuous actions of the men is indicative of the broader breakdown in relations between many labourers and the parish offices. This was not only caused by stingy relief and 'wages' but also by the way in which plebeian families were increasingly subjected to minute enquiries into their circumstances by assistant overseers and select vestries, economy masquerading as sanctimonious moralising judgements and degrading treatment.[54] Such widely practised schemes that combined these most dubious of 'virtues' were many: the refusal of relief to those with dogs while farmers and the gentry kept guard dogs to scare the poor; the payment of relief in kind with low-grade flour, as occurred with rancorous results at Salehurst, while millers profited;[55] refusing relief to those who did not attend Divine Service.

While this is not the place to gazette the litany of woes and harassments experienced by rural workers in the months and years preceding late 1830, Swing's archive does reveal several cases of horrific maltreatment that generated specific resentments. At Ninfield, near Brede, during the attempted removal of the assistant overseer a giant pair of mocked-up scissors were paraded through the streets in a reference to the parochial policy of shaving the hair of all poor-house inmates.[56] This practice had first been uncovered in January when a report appeared in the *Brighton Herald* – and readily taken up by the London press – about the plight of the children of smuggler Ford, who was transported for his crimes. On Ford's transportation, his four daughters had been placed into service by the parish, but the 'stigma' attached to their father meant they were 'compelled' to leave their places. Notwithstanding their lack of resources, their application to enter the poorhouse was refused, prompting an application to the magistrates who overturned the parish officers' decision. Once domiciled in the house, the parish hired a man to cut their hair, but the girls' objections meant the barber shrank from his task. Three farmers duly forcibly held the girls, while a fourth cut off their hair with such violence that their clothes were 'literally torn from their backs'. Some friends of the girls – 'a gang of' of smugglers and prostitutes, in the words of the Earl of Ashburnham – commenced a prosecution, and the farmers offered £100 to settle the 'disgraceful affair'.[57] The Ninfield protest was seemingly unique in Swing's southern heartlands, for effigies were not deployed elsewhere.[58]

As detailed in the Hampshire press and later taken up by Cobbett, the combined parishes of Bosham, Bersted, Bognor and Felpham were spending £40 a month on employing 10–12 young men digging gravel from the beach at Bognor. From here they were 'harnessed like horses' to carts and had to drag their loads two miles. 'Unfortunately', reported the *Hampshire Chronicle*, 'many similar instances might be adduced'.[59] Also, as noted in Chapter 4, workhouse master Harrison at Selbourne had been the subject of a magistrates' inquiry into his practice of chaining 'the poor creatures' to the wall.[60] Respondents to the 'Rural Queries' from the Weald were particularly alert to this degradation. From Burwash, John Baldock advanced that the 'harassing manner in which they [the poor] were treated through various employment plans' had been instrumental to mobilisations there. Indeed, the 'petition' of the poor of the parish to the 'Gentlemen of Burwash' noted that:

> Sometimes If a Man any ways affronted [assistant overseer] Freeman he would send a man from one side or an End of the parish to the other to be revenged of him & then Laugh at him for his Slavery.

At nearby Eastbourne, labourers had been 'demoralised' by 'being employed unprofitably in degrading occupations'. According to the Slaugham rector, those employed by the parish in 'some pits or elsewhere' were paid 'a small and grudged allowance from the parish'. When overseers and surveyors were asked, not surprisingly, the response was rather different, invariably blaming low wages or politically motivated individuals.[61] And with good reason.

At the interface between 'grudging political economy' and degradation, the position of overseers and assistant overseers was particularly parlous. In, arguably, the first overt act of Swing beyond East Kent, a number of 'people' stormed the meeting of the Ulcomb parish officers on the night of 22 October, snuffed out the lights, broke the pay tables and compelled the officers to leave. Even though the vestrymen were not personally subjected to physical battery, there can be little doubt about the fearful impression imparted by the activists' demonstration.[62] Sometimes such displays actually turned to bodily violence. When a group of labourers assembled at Ringmer on 14 November with the intention of 'assail[ing] the principal farmers about wages', the exchange descended into chaos as the labourers surrounded the overseer, seizing his bridle and knocking him off his horse.[63] Overseers were also singled out by incendiarists, Messrs Becker of Ash and Knight of Borden being among the earliest victims of Swing fires.[64]

Assistant overseers, usually recruited from outside the parish and thus subject to suspicion and derision as 'foreigners', were subjected to even greater abuse.[65] As noted, the removal of assistant overseer Abell at Brede proved a decisive moment in the genesis of Wealden and Sussex Swing, the act spurring on others to similar protests. As Chapters 4 and 5 detail, threats to treat assistant overseers 'like the one at Brede' were widely made in the Weald,[66] and frequently carried out.[67] The expulsion of assistant overseer and poorhouse superintendent Sims at Fairlight, near Hastings, was typical, inverting the practice whereby the poor dragged carts of gravel from the beach. Sims was greeted at 5 a.m. by a group of labourers who informed him 'his time had come'. The men then placed a halter round his neck (un)ceremoniously placed him in a cart and drove him out of the parish to the sound of 'women and children, with fire-irons, bells and warming pans'.[68] All of this is best summed up in the words of a labourer speaking to a magistrate relaying the story of the expulsion of Abel from Brede: 'they [did] not mind being poor, if they could but be used with civility'.[69]

The space the poor found most lacking in civility was the vestry. While the vestry had no basis in the foundational Elizabethan Acts,[70] over time, it had become accepted as the key body in the parochial administration of the poor laws, only challenged by the boards of guardians, which were responsible for parishes under Gilbert's Act. However, because there was nothing to stipulate that the embodied vestry must meet in the church vestry, some parishes conducted their business in more comfortable public houses, while others met in specially constructed vestry rooms located in workhouses. The vestry was thus a space where claimants would tussle with the ratepayers, where those without were often confronted – and judged by – the wealthy. To many rural workers it was a space of oppression.

The exclusionary nature of the vestry was best highlighted by plebeian critiques of vestrymen's behaviour. Stephen Farndell of Bosham was chastised by those who broke his threshing machine because he 'never attended the Vestries', which one of the men 'did not think ... right'.[71] At Hickstead, after barricading the farmers in the Castle Inn and berating them for starving the poor on 10*d.* a day, while they were always 'boozing' at vestry meetings, overseer Sharp's barn was set alight.[72] While many rural workers might view the vestry in a dim light, its importance was not challenged. Instead, many Swing protests deliberately focused on the vestry as the administrative body and space of greatest political and symbolic importance in the parish.

The first examples during Swing of labourers assembling at vestry meetings occurred at Ulcomb on 22 October – the night after the trial of the Elham men – and at Newington-next-Sittingbourne on 25 October. Both cases relied on local protest precedent. The Ulcomb affray was preceded by a series of radical meetings in nearby

Maidstone and a series of 'Swing' threatening letters.[73] The Newington 'riot' followed a case of incendiarism four days previously in the parish, another incendiary fire against the overseer of neighbouring Borden, and widespread threats made to local farmers.[74] Instead of using the well understood and legitimising language of custom, both the Newington and Ulcomb protests relied on a display of force. Not long after the parish officers of Ulcomb had assembled for 'their usual business' – not held in the vestry of the parish church but in a house – a group of labourers entered the room and turned off the lights. They then, symbolically, broke the pay tables and compelled the officers to leave without finishing the meeting.[75] The Newington labourers paraded with a tricolour – a deliberate and provocative reference to the recent revolution in France – and were joined by non-parishioners, some of whom had possibly been active the previous evening at nearby Stockbury where, after setting fire to a farmer's clover stack they paraded the village wearing placards in their hats and carrying a black flag. Robert Price supposedly 'harangued the populace' before making the demand on the parishioners' behalf that wages should be increased to 2s. 6d. per day, that rents should be lowered to £3 10s. a year and that the labourers be instantly paid. This stranger was 'shabbily dressed but spoke ... most fluently'. The demands were acceded to.[76]

Notes

1 TNA, HO 52/13, fos 13–14, J. Moneypenny, Hadlow to Melbourne, 5 February 1831.

2 W. Cobbett, *Rural Rides* (London: Penguin, 2001), p. 164. Original emphasis.

3 BPP. Commons, 'Report from the Select Committee on Poor Rate Returns' (1823) vol. v, appendix e, p. 19.

4 Hampshire County Record Office (hereafter HCRO), 47M81/PV3 and 46M74 A PV1, Odiham Vestry minute, 31 December 1816, and Basingstoke Vestry minute, 5 October 1820.

5 Report from the *Spectator*, quoted from *Kent Herald* (hereafter *KH*), 6 January 1831; BPP Commons, 'Report from His Majesty's Commissioners for Inquiring into the Administration and Practical Operation of the Poor Laws,' (hereafter 'Rural Queries') (1834), vol. xxxiv 237e, Response of John Pope, Barham, question 53; E. Hobsbawm and G. Rudé, *Captain Swing* (London: Lawrence & Wishart, 1969), p. 85.

6 A. Randall, *Before The Luddites: Custom, Community and Machinery in the English Woollen Industry, 1776–1809* (Oxford: Oxford University Press, 1991), see chs 6 and 7.

7 *The Times* (hereafter *TT*), 21 and 29 December 1830.

8 Centre for Kentish Studies (hereafter CKS), Q/SBe, 120/2c and 3b, Depositions of Francis Castle, 19 September, and Daniel Woollett, 22 September 1820. According to the Stelling tithe apportionment Atwood held just over six acres of pasture. The overall land holding at Stelling was dominated by those with less than fifty acres: TNA, IR 29/17/344.

9 TNA, HO 52/10, fos 410–12, Charles Howell, Hove to Peel, 17 November 1830.

10 TNA, HO 52/7, fos 101–2, Henry J Leeke JP, Westleigh near Havant to Peel, 21 November 1830.

11 TNA, HO 52/7, fos 7–8, Anon., Gosport to Peel, 12 November 1830.

12 TNA, HO 52/7, fo 247, Petition from Chithurst, Sussex, n.d. (but November 1830).

13 TNA, HO 52/10, fos 397–9, Godfrey Webster, Battle Abbey, 12 November, and enclosure, to Peel; *Brighton Gazette* (hereafter *BG*), 18 November 1830.

14 *Hampshire Chronicle* (hereafter *HC*), 19 July; *Hampshire Telegraph*, 19 July 1830.

15 East Sussex County Record Office (hereafter ESCRO), PAR 343/12/1, Framfield Vestry Minute, 4 February 1819.

16 BPP. Commons, 'Rural Queries' (1834) vol. xxxiv, pp. 254e and 525e, Question 53, Answers of Richard Cooper and J.A. Tylden, Milstead, and respondents of Slaugham.

17 TNA, HO 52/8, fos 77–8; John Boys, Margate to Phillips, 26 November; *Hampshire Telegraph*, 26 November 1830.

18 *Southampton Mercury*, 20 November 1830.

19 *Keene's Bath Journal*, 2 March 1829.

20 Cobbett's Weekly Political Register, 6 March 1830.

21 See pp. 108–10, 157n.54, 173.

22 *BG*, 18 and 25 November; *Maidstone Journal* (hereafter *MJ*), 23 November 1830.

23 TNA, TS 11/943, Examinations of William Henry Clarke, Rochester, and Timothy Willocks, Ash-next-Sandwich, 8 October 1830.

24 *Kentish Gazette* (hereafter *KG*), 8 and 26 October; *MJ*, 12 October; TNA, HO 52/8 fos 209–10, 216–18 and 359–60, John Boys, Margate, Rev. Gleig, Ash and Lord Camden, Canterbury to Sir Robert Peel, 17, 25 and 22 October; *TT*, 23 and 27 October; *KH*, 28 October 1830.

25 TNA, HO 52/8, fos 363–4 and 359–60, John Plumptree and Mr Hammond, St Albans Court, Fredville, Wingham, Rev. Gleig, Ash, both 25 October, to Peel; CKS Q/SBe 121/3a, 9 and 8, Depositions of John Sladden, labourer, 26 October, William Euden (a.k.a. Kingsfold), labourer, 19 November, George Quested, surveyor, 17 November 1830.

26 CKS, Q/SBe 121/1, 12a–c and 9, Depositions of James Dowker, 26 October and 19 November, James Petty, John Spain and William Euden, all 19 November; CKS, U951 C14/7, Poore, Murston to Knatchbull, 26 October; *MJ*, 2 November; *Maidstone Gazette*, 19 October 1830.

27 *Hampshire Advertiser*, 27 November 1830.

28 HCRO 11M67 PV1, Owslebury Vestry minute, 9 December 1830.

29 P. Jones, 'Swing, Speenhamland and rural social relations: the 'moral economy' of the English crowd in the nineteenth century', *Social History*, 32:3 (2007), 276.

30 *HC*, 29 November; *TT*, 31 December 1830; TNA, HO 130/1, Calendar of the Hampshire Special Commission: John Baker and William Summerbee for riot and assault at Leckford.

31 CKS, Q/SBe 120/11, 12, 5, 13 and 15, Depositions of Ingram Swaine, and John Sankey, yeoman, both 6 October, George Youens, labourer, 29 September and 7 October, John Jefferies, labourer, 8 October 1830.

32 *TT*, 21 December 1830.

33 TNA, HO 52/10, fos 369–70, 371–4 and 422–3 and 428, G. Courthope, Whiligh to Phillips, 6 November (twice), second enclosing deposition of Thomas Akell, Brede, 6 November, Sir Godfrey Webster, Battle to Peel, 20 November, enclosing examination of Joseph Bryant, 19 November; *Brighton Herald* (hereafter *BH*), 6 November; *BG*, 11 November 1830.

34 E.P. Thompson 'The moral economy of the English crowd in the eighteenth century', *Past and Present*, 50 (1971), 111.

35 R. Wells, 'Social protest, class, conflict and consciousness, in the English countryside 1700–1880', in M. Reed and R. Wells (eds), *Class, Conflict and Protest in the English Countryside 1700–1880* (London: Frank Cass, 1990), esp. pp. 181–3.

36 TNA, HO 52/10, fos 397–9, Godfrey Webster, Battle Abbey, plus enclosure, to Peel, 12 November 1830.

37 *MJ*, 9 November; *Southampton* Mercury, 20 November 1830.

38 K. Snell, 'The culture of local xenophobia', *Social History*, 28:1 (2003).

39 West Sussex County Record Office (hereafter WSCRO), Goodwood 1477a R16, Examination of Stephen Farndell, farmer, Bosham, 18 November 1830.

40 Jones, 'Swing, Speenhamland and rural social relations', 287.

41 *TT*, 30 December 1830.

42 BPP. Commons, 'Rural Queries' (1834) vol. xxxiv, p. 416e, question 53, response of Rev. W.B. Barter, Burghclere.

43 BPP. Commons, 'Rural Queries' (1834) vol. xxxiv, p. 425e, 438e, 235e, 244e, 245e, 502e and 498e, question 53, responses of Anonymous, Minstead, and J. Henville, Wymering (Hampshire), Rev. Gleig, Ash-next-Sandwich, Robert Smith, Farningham and William Hills, overseer, Faversham (Kent); Rev. Pitman and Davies Gilbert, Eastbourne and Willaim Bailee, West Chiltington (Sussex).

44 TNA, Assi 94/2073, Indictment of Thomas Brown, Fletching, Sussex Winter Assizes 1830. Furren stuard: an allusion to an estate steward who was 'foreign' to the parish.

45 TNA, Assi 94/2067, Indictment of George Fairburn, Westerham, Kent Winter Assizes 1830.

46 *HC*, 22 November 1830.

47 CKS, Q/SBw/124/9, Deposition of Charlotte Stacey, Stockbury, 19 November; TNA, Assi 94/2073, Indictment of James Findel Boniface, Lancing, Sussex Winter Assizes 1830.

48 TNA, HO 52/10, fos 532–3, Thomas Sanctuary, The Nunnery, Horsham to Peel, 17 November 1830.

49 TNA, HO 52/10, fos 653–7, William Tribe, Worthing to Melbourne, enclosing two threatening letters, 3 December 1830.

50 TNA, Assi 94/2073, Indictment of William Bish, Fletching and Henry Bish, Newick, Sussex Winter Assizes 1830.

51 BPP. Commons, 'Rural Queries' (1834) vol. xxxiv, p. 518e, question 53, responses of Thomas Beale, assistant overseer, Northiam. For poor vestry attendance see: R. Wells, 'Poor law reform in the rural south-east; the impact of the 'Sturges Bourne Acts' during the agricultural depression, 1815–1835', *Southern History*, 23 (2001), 58, 63.

52 WSCRO, QR/W/758/280 and 281, Informations of Timothy Tourn, West Chiltington, surveyor, and Edward Butt, Petworth, taken 18 December 1830.

53 TNA, HO 52/8, fos 216–18 and 359–60, Camden, Canterbury, 22 October, Rev. Gleig, Ash, 25 October 1830, both to Peel.

54 See Wells, 'Poor law reform'; Jones, Swing, Speenhamland and rural social relations'.

55 TNA, HO 52/10, fos 388–9 and 52/8, fos 160–70, Godfrey Webster, Battle, 9 November, Messrs Collingwood and Young, Hawkhurst, 11 November 1830, to Peel.

56 ESCRO, AMS 5995/3/12, Gentlemen of Burwash to H.B. Curteis, 9 November; NA HO 52/10, fos 536–7 and 388–9, Sir Charles Blunt, Heathfield, 11 November, Godfrey Webster, Battle, 9 November, to Peel; TNA, Assi 94/2073, Indictment of William Isted, Sussex Winter Assizes 1830; *BG*, 11 November 1830 and 4 August 1831.

57 *BH*, 23 January; *Morning Chronicle*, 25 January; ESCRO, ASH 3261, 3rd Earl of Ashburnham, 9 South Andley Street, London to T. Barton, 11 February 1830.

58 Only at Banbury (Oxfordshire) does the archive relate that a human effigy was paraded by a southern Swing assemblage: Hobsbawm and Rudé, *Captain Swing*, p. 143.

59 *HC*, 20 February; *Cobbett's Weekly Political Register*, 6 November 1830.

60 *TT*, 24 and 30 December 1830.

61 BPP. Commons, 'Rural Queries' (1834) vol. xxxiv, p. 405e, 502e, and 525e, question 53, responses of John Baldock, Burwash, Rev. Pitman and Davies Gilbert, Eastbourne, and N. Barwell and Rev. Robert Elllison, Slaugham; ESCRO, AMS 5995/3/12, Gentleman of Burwash to H.B. Curteis, Beckley, plus enclosure, 9 November 1830.

62 *MJ*, 26 October 1830.

63 TNA, HO 52/8, fos 180–2 and 52/10, fos 526–7, Mr Hawkes, to Mabbot, Uckfield, 15 November, Charles Blunt, Heathfield to Peel, 11 November; *BH*, 20 November 1830.

64 *KG*, 8 October; TNA, HO 52/8, fos 209–10, John Boys, Margate to Peel, 17 October; *MJ*, 26 October 1830.

65 For an assessment of the role of assistant overseers in the 1820s see: Jones, 'Swing, Speenhamland and Rural Social Relations', 285–7.

66 TNA, HO 52/8, fos 171–2, 52/10, fos 617–19, 383–5, 397–9 and 394–5, Thomas Hodges, Hemsted, Benenden, 11 November, Earl of Egremont, Petworth, 7 November, enclosing Courthope, Whiligh to Egremont, 7 November, Godfrey Webster, Battle Abbey, 8 and 12 November, Battle Bench, 12 November, to Home Office; *MJ*, 9 November; *BG*, 18 November 1830.

67 ESCRO, AMS 5995/3/12, Gentlemen of Burwash to H.B. Curteis, 9

November; TNA, HO 52/10, fos 388–9, 536–7 and 394–5, Godfrey Webster, Battle, 9 November, Sir Charles Blunt, Heathfield, 11 November, Battle Bench, 12 November to Peel; TNA, Assi 94/2073, Indictment of William Isted, Sussex Winter Assizes 1830, *BG*, 11 November 1830 and 4 August 1831.

68 Hastings and Cinque Ports Iris, 13 November 1830.

69 BPP Commons, 'Report from His Majesty's Commissioners for Inquiring into the Administration and Practical Operation of the Poor Laws' (1834), vol. xxxiv, 201a, appendix A, report of A Majendie, 'History of the Brede Riots'.

70 According to Sidney and Beatrice Webb, under common law the inhabitants of the parish had the right to be summoned and assemble in the church as a 'town meeting' or 'vestry'. This meeting was held to check the expenses of the churchwardens, elect new churchwardens, and to decide on the Church Rate. When the hundredal and manorial courts began to decay from the sixteenth century, the vestry was, in the words of W.E. Tate, 'the natural successor to their duties'. The vestry thereby became a 'kind of parochial parliament', the jump from levying church rates to administering public welfare readily made. S. and B. Webb, *English Local Government from the Revolution to the Municpial Corporations Act: The Parish and the County* (London: Longmans, 1913), pp. 37–9; W.E. Tate, *The Parish Chest: A Study of the Records of Parochial Administration in England* (Cambridge: Cambridge University Press, 1946), pp. 13–14.

71 WSCRO, Goodwood 1477a R16, Examination of Stephen Farndell, Bosham, 18 November 1830.

72 *BG*, 25 November; *Sussex Advertiser*, 29 November; *TT*, 24 November; *BH*, 27 November 1830.

73 *Maidstone Gazette*, 19 October; *MJ*, 19 October; KG, 19 and 22 October; *KH*, 7 and 21 October; TNA, HO 52/8, fos 333–4, Maidstone Postmaster to Sir Francis Freeling, 14 October 1830.

74 TNA, HO 52/8, fos 216–18 and 300–1, Earl of Camden, Wilderness, 22 October, Rev. Poore, Murston, 23 October, to Peel; *MJ*, 26 October; CKS U951 C177/35, Rev. Poore, Murston to Sir Edward Knatchbull, 23 and 24 October; *TT*, 30 October 1830.

75 *MJ*, 26 October 1830.

76 TNA, HO 52/8, fos 365–6, Rev. Poore, Murston to Peel, 25 October; Rev. Poore, Murston to Knatchbull, 26 October, CKS U951 C14/7; *MJ*, 26 October; *KH*, 28 October 1830.

7

Radical participatory politics

Evidence of radical agitation in the southern countryside during the summer and autumn of 1830 is not hard to find. The acute economic distress felt in agricultural districts, given voice in countless meetings and petitions complaining about the assessed taxes,[1] combined with the developing reform crisis and the general election to offer the perfect platform for denunciations of the unreformed British state. These were not just utterances from the mouths of committed republicans but, increasingly, critiques articulated by otherwise loyal members of English society. According to Lord Carnarvon's steward on his Highclere estate, 'the whole rural machine is going wrong'. The labourers were 'not half employed', those who were received only 7 shillings a week, 'little better than a mere saloop from starvation'. The farmer, he continued, 'is half ruined by the withdrawal of the £1 notes and the subsequent depression in the price of dairy produce and livestock', while shopkeepers 'suffer from the poverty of their country customers'. All this led to a universal belief that the government ought to be reformed. He was convinced that the country was 'rife for change', needing 'only a spark to set it off'. A 'revolution', he concluded, 'is quite possible'.[2]

The dissolution of Parliament and subsequent electioneering provided a platform for such critiques to be publicly made. The Kent hustings on Penenden Heath attracted a particularly stinging critique from the electoral sponsor of sitting pro-reform Whig MP Thomas Law Hodges, even though the representation was not contested. Electors should, he urged, examine the 'state of the country ... Overwhelmed by debt, contracted ... by the convenience of those who called themselves the representatives of the people, but who were in fact nominated by the aristocracy ... That was the canker which consumed us, and while there was rottenness at the root, the branches could not flourish'. If the Kentish electorate 'wished to preserve themselves and their families from pauperism, and their country from ruin' they must support reform.[3]

The Hampshire representation *was* contested, the nomination meeting at Winchester marked with much 'clamour and confusion'. Notwithstanding the restricted nature of the Hampshire electorate, the *Hampshire Telegraph* believed that the crowd was so large that it would be 'impossible' to 'compute their number'. The 'many thousands' present represented the 'most numerous' assembly the county had witnessed in thirty years. After barracking the pro-government and anti-reform sitting MP, Sir John Fleming, the crowd gave a rapturous reception to the speech given by Lord Porchester's (Hampshire grandee the Earl of Carnarvon's son) sponsor:

> The County of Southampton, alas!, appeared for a long time to have been regarded as little better than an appendage to the Treasury, and classed amongst the Rotten Boroughs … Such indeed was the estimation in which it had been too often held.

It transpired, though, that Porchester had been nominated without his permission. Mindful of the probable expense of the campaign – estimated by Sir Thomas Baring at between £6,000 and £7,000 – and of the 'predominant influence which government possesses in the county', Porchester decided not to stand. News of this decision came after the hustings had been erected and the poll commenced. Uncontested, Fleming was duly elected, much to the disgust of many in the crowd who forced him to flee to the sanctuary of the White Hart Inn. Later that evening Fleming was burnt in effigy.[4] Elsewhere, the clash between reformers and the anti-reform Tory rump coalesced with local disputes about who was entitled to the electoral franchise, and found expression in riot, including at Rye where 'borough-monger' Lamb and his successful candidates were pelted with 'rotten eggs, mud and all the symbols of election vituperation'. While relatively modest, these election riots were a harbinger of the extensive reform riots in the south-west during the final months of 1831.[5]

That Cobbett's initial south-eastern tour – to 'see how the lads come on' – coincided with the election is surely no coincidence.[6] But this was not the 'spark'. Instead, revolutions in continental Europe, especially in France on 27, 28 and 29 July, sent convulsions throughout England and galvanised radicals into action. Cobbett abandoned his tour and returned to London to give a series of lectures on the French

Revolution at the Rotunda.[7] Cheapside and Ludgate Hill in London were reported in the Winchester press to be 'covered in tricolours'. If transplanted there from overseas, they suggested, one would 'certainly conclude that some great revolution had taken place in this country'. At Bristol a public meeting expressed 'admiration for the conduct of the French people' and their 'respect for social rights'.[8]

This was not an outpouring of support confined to the major towns of the kingdom. Many workers were presumably in the audience to hear Mr Marsh – Porchester's sponsor – deliver a speech at Winchester on 6 August. A mere week since the momentous events in France, Marsh, to general tumult, proclaimed that within the past month: 'a King had been found in a neighbouring state so tyrannical, so brutal, as to attempt the destruction, "at one feel swoop", of the liberties of a whole nation'.[9] A meeting at the County Hall in Lewes on 10 September called to 'address the French nation on their success in their recent struggle for liberty' offered a platform for similarly fulsome support. The chair of the meeting, the senior constable of the Borough, asserted that the 'success' of the 'French patriots' was particularly gratifying to the people of England who had seen 'their Constitution suspended by Sidmouth's gagging bills, and who had seen some of its best patriots suffer for asserting the birth-right of freemen'. Brightonians were reported to be wearing tricolours, with the pleasure boats sporting hoisted tricolour flags. A 'convention' at Maidstone sent £23 to the families of those killed in Paris, proclaiming that they had not forgotten that it was with English money that the Revolution had originally been suppressed.[10]

Country people were equally vocal and active in their support. A subscription was raised for the Parisian 'sufferers' at Wealden Benenden. At Battle – a place that was soon to become notorious for the intertwining of radical politics and popular mobilisations – the 'glorious actions' of the French people were juxtaposed with the treatment of the Levi Cohen, the tormented radical editor of the *Brighton Guardian*. Cohen was being tried for an alleged libel against the King, evidence, as his plebeian supporters at Battle saw it, of a lack of press freedoms in Britain.[11] As noted in Chapter 3, several radically tinged petitions emanated from rural communities before the spread of open protests beyond East Kent in 1830. Cobbett's publication of a model petition in September – and the industriously circulated 'Nice Pickings' handbill detailing the emoluments of various aristocrats and bishops – offering a useful template for would-be rural petitioners.[12]

The continental revolutions clearly offered a direct inspiration to southern radicals. According to Sussex magistrate George Courthope, the impact was profound in the countryside. In drafting his response to the 'Rural Queries' of the 1832 Poor Law Commission, he opined that the events in France 'gave rise to a very prevailing notion amongst the lower orders that the means of redressing their grievances was in their own hands'.[13] Several early Swing incidents provide direct evidence. In the first protest outing led by radical Maidstone shoemaker Robert Price, 150–200 labourers left their work and proceeded from farm to farm to 'enforce certain demands on their employers'. They then assembled with a tricolour at that evening's vestry meeting. Price – 'a perfect stranger ... shabbily dressed but spoke ... most fluently' who had 'harrangued the populace' into action – went into the room to state their demands: 2/6 a day with a supplement of 1/6 a week for every child above two in number, and yearly rents of £3–10. Radical politics combined, not for the last time during Swing, with modest material demands.[14]

The tricolour, accompanied by a black flag, reappeared on the morning of 27 October, the day of the Maidstone Michaelmas fair. A party of 'one or two and twenty' Hucking and Stockbury men equipped with sticks held the flags aloft and blew a horn as they proceeded to the Harrow pub at Debtling.[15]

Over the ensuing days, Price was frequently drawn into heated parleys with farmers and the rulers of rural England. In one such conversation with Mrs Stacey of Debtling, Price responded to Stacey's query as to their intentions by retorting that they had 'come to drink your health having righted the Poor of this parish ... [that they were] going round to the different houses to get something to drink and tomorrow all are going to work on two shillings and six pence a day'. Stacey offered them 2/6 but Price scoffed – 'all the farmers have given us as much and we expected this being the only gentleman's house at least a sovereign'. Stacey then offered three shillings, some bread and as much table beer as they wanted. Still not satisfied, Price launched into a tirade about the state of the poor, to which Stacey suggested they should wait for the new Parliament to see what the King did for it was thought he was going to 'take off five millions in taxes'. Price exploded: 'King, we have no King ... Five millions of heads will be taken off before that is done', even lending his support to the 'burnings' as:

> necessary to bring people to their senses, it is your dandy Houses and your dandy habits and your sinecure places that have brought the

Country to this state ... you are all too high and must come down from
the Head. If you go to Church you only go to look at the ... fashions ...
Now we have righted this Parish we are going thro' every other Village
and Parish to do the same thing.

On 29 October, Price's group joined with another local group led by
fellow radical Maidstone shoemaker, John Adams. Just like Price,
Adams was quick to issue political critiques whenever challenged.
When Adams's men were met by a combined military and civil force
at Boughton Monchelsea, he attempted to address the magistracy, led
by the Mayor of Maidstone. However, the Riot Act was read. Incensed,
Adams accused the government of being 'privy to the outrages ... as
an excuse for sending soldiers to spill the blood of these half-starved
men'. Adams and two others – Pitman, a fellow Maidstone shoemaker,
and Holloway, a Southwark tailor – were duly seized. According to
Lieutenant Colonel Middleton, commander of the military force,
Price's and Adams's actions were likely to attract the 'disaffected and
profligate scum of society' without being forcefully checked.[16]

These events occurred in a very particular local political context.
Maidstone had a long-held reputation as a radical centre. It was here
that the dual inspirations of machine-breaking in East Kent and the
events in France combined to first forge 'Swing' as a complex, more
than parochial, movement. On 1 October at a meeting held to congratulate the French 'on their Revolution', the Mayor remarked on the
events at either end of the county. He claimed that 'the fires and the
machine breaking' were the result of grievances that would only be
alleviated by a reform of Parliament. A further meeting was held a
fortnight later with the intention, as the correspondent to the Home
Office put it, 'to harangue the working classes'. The meeting was
chaired by Charles Waite, a 'person of no religion' who had sold his
commission in the army as Adjudicant Brevet Major for 'several
thousand pounds' to devote himself to radical politics. This meeting
was followed the next day by a lecture by Cobbett, the first on his
south-eastern tour. Admittance was only threepence so as 'that the
WORKING PEOPLE may not be shut out' – a price beyond the reach of most
field workers but affordable to Maidstone's many artisans, engineers
and operatives as some 200 individuals attended. Over the next four
days, at least three threatening letters were received in the vicinity of
Maidstone. One received at Maidstone threatened to set the town on
fire, two others were sent to 'Gentlemen' and threatened to set their
outbuildings alight if they did not employ the parish poor.[17]

Arguably the most dramatic display of radical feeling – and force – at Maidstone occurred on 1 November. A mass general meeting on Penenden Heath had been threatened for several days, sending the Maidstone authorities into a panic. The Maidstone Bench was minded to organise a large civil force to keep order, but soon realised that the task would be almost impossible as 'most [specials] have refused to be sworn'.[18] Troops were duly drafted into Maidstone from Chatham, Woolwich and Epsom but were said to be fatigued. The fact that many of the soldiers had to be billeted owing to lack of barrack accommodation hardly improved morale. On 1 November, the papermakers working in the many mills around Maidstone struck work to attend the meeting. While the crowd was not as big as expected, presumably the fear of magisterial or military intervention deterring some from attending, the 400 or so people present included a 'great number' of agricultural labourers from Thurnham 'and its neighbourhood', whose appearance 'was in the extreme of wretchedness'.

Amid placards with radical slogans and a tricolour flag, speakers called for 'Reform in the Commons House of Parl. Vote by ballot or 2 years or nothing', and the papermakers denouncing the 'paper machines'. Publican's son Stephen Crowte even ominously proclaimed: 'respect the soldiers as they are friends'. Indeed, Treasury Solicitor Maule – stationed at Maidstone to coordinate the government's response to the rapidly unfurling movement – had learnt that at Smithfield, in London, a penny subscription had been supposedly set up to purchase arms for the Kentish protestors.[19] Thus metropolitan and Maidstone radicals combined with politicised papermakers and labourers to make explicit the connection between Swing and the reform movement.

Maidstone was not alone as a notorious radical urban centre whose inhabitants were central to Swing mobilisations in the surrounding countryside. Chichester was another borough with a history of radical agitation going back to the 1790s.[20] Political 'feeling' had been running high throughout 1830, and even the March election for the thirteen guardians for the Chichester Poor Law Incorporation had been driven by politics. By September the 'Reform Society' was reported to be rapidly expanding its membership.[21] Swing mobilisations in the surrounding countryside had drawn in 'loose blackguards' from Chichester in machine-breaking groups, while Chichester radicals had been found – and incarcerated for – distributing 'seditious' handbills in the country parishes. As Wells notes, a plan to gather a posse of labourers to invade the city and call on the mayor to petition for reform was abandoned. Still, the mayor refused the radicals' demand. A meeting was eventually held on 15 December to petition for a radical reform of Parliament and the repeal of the malt and other taxes.[22]

Rather more dramatic was the interweaving of the city and the country, the participatory and the parochial politic, at Horsham. As detailed in Chapter 4, against a background of radically tinged threatening letters, the meeting arranged for 18 November to appoint a new assistant overseer prompted a mass gathering of workers from the town and the surrounding villages. Barricading the church, their demands of 2/6 a day and reductions in rents and tithes were conceded. This was not enough, though. Surgeon Rickward, a known radical politician, launched into a stinging critique of the status quo. The people 'had not half got over their grievances', for every 10 shillings they spent on the necessary articles of life, between 7 and 8 shillings were paid to the government in tax. A meeting was then swiftly called for the following Monday to petition Parliament for a remission of taxes and reform of the franchise. But before this occurred, the Horsham men were also responsible for instigating anti-tithe protests at Rusper, Abinger, Wotton, Ockley and Woking, and were also possibly behind a tithe protest at neighbouring Itchingfield.[23]

Preparations for the Monday meeting by the West Sussex judiciary were scuppered because 59 of the 63 individuals summoned to be sworn in as special constables refused to take the oath. That some of those involved in 'planning' the events of the 18 November were 'wealthy' residents of the town made it a 'very delicate subject to handle'. Eventually, troops arrived of and messages were sent out forbidding the country people from attending the meeting, countering the placards that had been widely posted. This had the result of limiting the attendance at the meeting held at the Crown Inn. It transpired in the subsequent investigations that the Horsham Radical Party had been behind all the protests, using their funds to support the actions of emissaries in the nearby villages and smaller towns.[24] By 26 November, Swing had effectively swept through and left West Sussex. Lord Lieutenant Egremont wrote to Melbourne to express his confidence in the 'safety' of the county – with the exception of Horsham. 'I am not surprised', he proclaimed, as there had been 'political feelings ... in the borough for the last forty years'. These fears were well grounded. Horsham continued to be the locus for politicking in the area into December, the indigenous Radical Party funding the flooding of the surrounding villages and towns with radical handbills (see figure 7.1). The printer of these bills was no less a Sussex radical than Levi Cohen, editor of the *Brighton Guardian*.[25] The Horsham radical platform embraced rural and urban workers, sought to use its power and funds to mobilise demonstrations that spanned parochial and participatory concerns, and knitted the area between Brighton and Woking together.

While Chichester, Horsham and Maidstone were notorious radical centres whose influence connected town and country together in political agitation, smaller south-eastern market towns had not been previously on the Home Office's radar. Despite the attempts of the local bench to suppress seditious publications in the early 1820s, Battle was one such 'unknown' place. And yet, as with Maidstone and Horsham, radical politics combined with parish politicking to further diffuse Swing into a previously quiescent area. As noted, as early as September a meeting was held in Battle to support Brighton radical publisher Cohen. If this was not evidence enough of radical activity in Battle, the fact that Cobbett chose to lecture there on 16 October as part of his tour of otherwise far larger towns was instructive, for Cobbett knew he had an audience at Battle. The Earl of Ashburnham, though not personally present, must have sent a spy to Cobbett's lecture, for he sent a précis of the speech to Kent Lord Lieutenant, the Earl of Camden. Cobbett, Ashburnham's report noted, had 'reprobated' the Sussex labourers 'for not shewing the example set' by their 'fellow sufferers' in Kent, who had asserted 'their rights by destroying the property of those who tyrannized over them'. Cobbett denied that he had offered any personal encouragement to incendiarism at his later trial. Labourer Thomas Goodman, who had been present at Cobbett's speech and was sentenced to death at the Sussex Assizes for firing farmer Atherton's barn on 2 December, thought otherwise. As Wells notes, this was probably Goodman's only chance of sparing himself from the gallows. Either way, Cobbett's influence on the labourers of Battle is beyond doubt. Indeed, Goodman also later admitted that publican (and overseer) Emary's barn had been fired on 3 November because he had refused a venue for Cobbett's lecture.[26]

This was not the only evidence for radical activity informing protests at Battle. On 7 November, Peel wrote to the Lord Mayor of

Conversation

BETWEEN

Two Labourers,

RESIDING IN THE

COUNTY OF SUSSEX.

A.—So Bob, you say as how if I and you and all the working men in the Parish go in a body to the Farmers, we shall make them raise the wages. Well, I thinks it is high time our distressed condition was attended to.

B.—I spoke to Tom Brown, Dick Smith and Jack Hodges, as they were leaving their work last night, when Hodges says " I'll just tell you a bit of my mind ;—we have been working all day for 8d., living on bread and potatoes, and as for me, I can be no worse off if they wont give us any more wages; but I can see how they may do it very well, and be better for our masters too."

A.—How will it be better for them?

B.—I'll tell you how.—In the first place, if they pays us better, we shall do more work, and not have occasion for Parish Relief, which is a thing I cant bear, and would as soon go to the Tread Wheel as be abused by that Assistant Overseer, because I cant live on 8d. a day. I met a chap from H———, who told me that felons was better off in jail than we poor labourers was.

A.—But did he not say that Farmers had agreed to give them 2s. 6d. a day.

B.—Yes, he did ; and I have no doubt they will be as good as their word, for they find at last that all of us who live by our labour have one common cause, and if they keep going on so, they must come to the parish as we have, and I am sure it is not their fault.

A.—But what do they say is the reason for their not being better off ?

B.—Why I'll tell you. The Rents they say is not the cause so much as the taxes; and they say the shopkeeper collects so much taxes in the charge of his goods that it takes his landlord's rent to pay them with, for a great part of his workmen's wages goes to the shopkeeper ; and one of them there shopkeepers at H——— told me his sugar and tea was half Tax ; and Ned Wright was told tother day that they had a Tax of 3s. a pound on his tobacco.

A.—What, then, becomes of all this money they collect in Taxes ?

B.—I'll tell you what that there shopkeeper said ;—That it was given to people who gave nothing in exchange for it, some fine ladies and gentlemen, who like to live without work, and all the time they make the working class pay the present amount of Taxes there will be no better times. He said a man the name of Grey was going to make a pretty big alteration, and if he done his duty and did not deceive us, we should have better times again.

A.—And do you think so ?

B.—Yes, I do; for that there shopkeeper said that it would put a stop to all that burning and mobbing that is going on at present.

December, 1830.

COHEN, PRINTER, BRIGHTON.

7.1 'A conversation between two Sussex labourers'

London to notify him that the King, on his ministers' advice, had cancelled his annual visit to the City. '[N]otwithstanding the devoted loyalty and affection born to his majesty by the citizens of London', Peel opined, 'advantage would be taken of an occasion which must necessarily assemble a vast number of persons by right to create tumult and confusion'. He continued:

> It would be a source of deep and lasting concern to their majesties were any calamity to occur on the occasion of their visit to the City of London, and their majesties have therefore resolved, though not without the greatest reluctance and regret, to forgo for the present the gratification which that visit would have afforded to their majesties.[27]

Reports of a 'conspiracy to cause confusion' by cutting off the gas mains, 'a general attack on the New Police', the sending of threatening letters to the bankers and merchants warning them not to 'illuminate', the influx of rural workers into London – a thousand more were reportedly prevented by the police from crossing the Thames, presumably from Kent or Surrey – and Cobbett and Henry Hunt's scheduled lecture at the Rotunda had certainly generated alarm. Carnarvon's steward, in London on business, reported to Porchester that 'everyone I meet ... thought the ministers were half mad', this was a 'deliberate scheme of Peel's to create alarm, rally the County gentlemen around the Government and arm it with fresh powers'. This occurred against the backdrop of Wellington's categorical refusal of any measure of reform, issued on 3 November, and the subsequent disintegration of his ministry. The impression was of a country on the edge of collapse: a constitutional crisis, the movements of the King dictated by the threats of London radicals.[28]

One individual caught up in this excitement was Charles Inskipp, a native of Battle who had joined 'A' Division of the London 'New Police' having received references from several Battle residents. In the wake of the London disturbances, Inskipp resigned his commission. Charged with fear by his inspector, Inskipp claimed that he had 'other motives' and wanted to go 'into the country', specifically that he would 'throw off his coat and join the mob'. By mid-November he had arrived back in Battle, where, on taking lodgings, he began to discuss the government and 'the disturbances' with anyone, whether they showed an interest or not. Taking his 'notoriously revolutionary principles' to the 'village' beer shops in the vicinity of Battle, he gave a series of lectures 'after Cobbett's fashion'. At noon on 22 November, the day of the Battle fair, Inskipp took his tour to Battle itself, delivering a lecture in a new beer shop. Dwelling on the disturbances and the revolution in France, Inskipp implored his audience that if they were like him they would 'fight for their rights at once', and as he 'didn't value his life one farthing' he would head them and teach them to fight for there 'would be a revolution here'. Four days after his speech, Battle farmer Quaife was targeted by arsonists for the second time that month, and within a fortnight of Inskipp's harangue a further three incendiary fires had occurred in Battle alone.[29]

Further evidence of a campaign by provincial and metropolitan radicals to promote revolutionary fervour in the East Sussex countryside abounds. James Taylor, like Inskipp, was a native of East Sussex and had until late October been engaged as an apprentice in London. Suspicions as to Taylor's radical connections – and therefore his motives for returning to rural Sussex – were aroused when he showed a letter he had in his possession to Joseph Fielder, the Salehurst farmer who in early November fell victim to an incendiary fire.

> I am glad to hear that you continue to pass without suspicion & and that you have accomplished your design so far so well at Battel & Bexhill & those other places ware you have been. I now advise you to continue the same course as you have been following. I think your apearance as a common working man is decidedly the best in a general way accept when you go from place to place & to bear all the fires in a common workenman dress is not a bad plan for then you hear what the people say & Gentalmen to & then you learn what Gentalmen are doing at ther own places & as people come from all Quarters you pass amongst others as Strangers so that there is no fear but carrey Nothing with you Lest you should be taken. The system of burning seems to work well we have gained all ready by its effects be carefull as to whose you burn do not burn the all of a poor man ... Great baits are laid by Government but its of no use if you will remain faithfull to your agreament Let not money be your whaut I shall be in Battel soon I will meet you at the place ware the barer meets you. I know not that I can say any more at present.[30]

Such a letter, whether evidence of a genuine radical conspiracy or simply a wind-up by local radicals, played straight into the hands of the rural gentry and aristocracy, who saw in every stranger and every fire signs of revolution. While the Home Office, under both Peel and Melbourne, advised that there had to be legal grounds to withhold 'strangers' for extended periods of time, they also actively supported the blanket policy of initially apprehending and questioning those travelling about 'under circumstances calculated to excite suspicion'.[31]

The 'County Correspondence' files of the Home Office are full of letters from magistrates and others reporting the movements of supposedly shadowy individuals. Many of the letters simply reflected the paranoia of the ruling class – in mid-November it was reported that 'many suspicious persons' had 'crossed and recrossed' on the different ferries to the Isle of Sheppey, coinciding with a spate of incendiary fires and the receipt of several threatening letters[32] – but other cases provided evidence of radical agitation. At Matfield Green in Kent, a publican, and a former servant to MP Thomas Law Hodges, received a visit in late October from a man who claimed 'things would soon be righted'. His brothers in London, Hodges related, had ordered him to collect all the firearms he could and send them to the capital.[33] Elsewhere, two men were apprehended for circulating radical handbills in the vicinity of Lewes on 19 November, the same day that two men were arrested at Glynde for questioning the servants of the nationally renowned Southdown sheep breeder John Ellman. Two men travelling in a gig who had made enquiries of labourers in the Uckfield area were believed to be a beer-shop keeper – and occasional preacher – and a journeyman carpenter, both of Lewes. The beer-shop keeper was apprehended and, although there was no evidence that he was one of the travelling agitators, he was fined £10 for allowing persons to remain drinking in his house throughout the night.[34]

Suspicions as to the involvement of mobile figures were also behind the apprehending of two men who had travelled from London, on 'strong evidence' that they had fired a hovel at Heighton, near Newhaven, on 28 November. In the last week of November, four farmers in the neighbourhood of Seaford received threatening letters, all in the same hand and written on the same paper. All also bore the Brighton postmark, 'where much mischief has emanated from'.[35] Suspicions regarding the involvement of Brighton radicals had already been raised on the night of 18 November when an attempt was made to break into the ammunition store of the Brighton barracks with the plan to steal 'eight 6 pounders' from the battery. Despite the seriousness of the attempt, the Brighton authorities made little reaction, infuriating one correspondent to the Home Office who claimed that effectively there was no authority at Brighton.[36]

The belief that mobile individuals were necessarily politically motivated agitants had some grounding in observed reality. As noted in Chapter 5, highly mobile individuals were important in diffusing Swing in several locales. Beyond coincidence, Swing's archive does attest to the importance of mobile politically motivated individuals such as Adams and Price of Maidstone. The large Wealden parish of Goudhurst was the scene of repeated mobilisations between 9 and 15 November, all led (or co-led) by Stephen Eves, a politicised sawyer. The first rising started with his initially small group 'proceed[ing] generally over the parish' compelling others to join them, and calling at the 'houses of the respectable for charity' while complaining about taxes, tithes, rents, sinecures and other 'state incomes'. The following day they met again, and, according to briefs prepared by the Treasury Solicitor, endeavoured to 'excite a friendly feeling, if not cooperation, [on] the part of the farmers by telling them tithes should no longer be paid and that if farmers would raise wages they would stop the tithes'. They then proceeded throughout Goudhurst and 'adjoining parishes', including Lamberhurst and Horsmonden, offering the farmers the same deal. The gathering on 15 November followed the now familiar pattern of the labouring force and the espousal of a distinctly Cobbettian political platform. Having called a 'general meeting' to discuss their demands of lower tithes, 2/3 a day in winter and 2/6 in summer, an allowance of 1/6 per week for every child above two in number, a reduction in cottage rents and the price of fuel, Eves's group called on Mr Springett, the 'owner' of the rectorial tithes, to demand his attendance. Just as the farmers and Springett were about to concede to Eves's demands, a military detachment arrived, under the control of Cranbrook magistrate Captain King. Rather than having the desired effect, the crowd started shouting and cheering and advanced towards the soldiers. The Riot Act was read, and a melee ensued. Defiant to the last, Stephen Eves, demanded that 'if the farmers can't pay the wages we demand let 'em give us up the land', on which he was seized by King.[37]

At Liphook on the Hampshire-Sussex-Surrey border, a wages demonstration on 22 November was led by Thomas Hamblin, a 'stranger to the county' who made use of the 'most inflammatory language' towards the magistrates. He was quickly seized and taken away by coach to prevent any attempt to rescue him.[38] Similarly, James Thomas Cooper, the Wiltshire ostler, one of two Hampshire Swing activists who would end their lives on the gallows for taking part in demonstrations, was prone to giving 'republican' speeches. When implored not to destroy Mr Shepherd's threshing machine manufactory at Stuckton, near Fordingbridge, because it employed sixty poor people who would otherwise be on the parish, Cooper claimed that all he was interested in was 'liberty'.[39] There were many others like Cooper. According to Richard Pollen, writing from Winchester Gaol, the various artisans and operatives active in Swing groups were 'always very eloquent' and 'universally politicians'.[40]

Outside of Maidstone's considerable sphere of influence, some other early Kentish Swing protests made the connection between the politics of the parish and indigenous radical politicians. At Elham, High Sheriff of Kent Edward Rice was reportedly told that: 'we will destroy the corn-stacks and thrashing machines this year. Next year we will have a turn with the Parsons, and the third, we will make war upon the Statesmen'.[41] Members of the other East Kent machine-breaking group at Ash-next-Sandwich also betrayed radical sensibilities. On the night after Ash overseer Becker's fire, labourer Timothy Willocks went with William Clarke, a Rochester wine merchant, to a nearby pub. Already much in liquor, Willocks began a tirade against the state of the poor man in England, 'he would as soon be hung as go to the Workhouse … the poor man's turn must come and will come along very soon'. Willocks then equated the state of the poor in England to that of the poor in France before the recent revolution, asking Clarke if he knew what the poor had been doing there, because before long England would soon come to the same state.[42]

The clearest expression of indigenous rural radicalism came from the Dever Valley in central Hampshire. As detailed in Chapters 4 and 5, a 'Musical and Radical Society' advocating universal male suffrage met regularly in local pubs in and around Sutton Scotney, even sending a petition to the King at Brighton in September demanding '*annual Parliaments, universal suffrage,* and *vote by ballot*'. Although the demands (and claims) of Swing protests in the immediate vicinity betrayed no evidence of a radical political agenda, evidence of their actions does demonstrate both a strong political understanding and a parochial agenda informed by participatory politics. According to farmer Pain of Micheldever, during a row with the group over their demand for money and beer, threats were made that: 'It will not end without Blood' and that 'It is not come to the worst yet.' Having only received a sovereign before departing, later that day the same group returned to Pain's farm to demand more money. Again, this descended into a heated exchange. One of the protestors reportedly professed that, 'We are going to Winchester to break the Tread Mill', another proclaimed that, 'We shall make Laws.' At Barton Stacey curate Rev. Joliffe's house, Robert Mason, along with brother Joseph, the notional leader of the mobilisations, responded to the clergyman's refusal to supply them with meat and drink with the class-conscious comment that, 'You have more than we have, and you must give us something.'[43]

As David Kent noted in his study of the Dever Valley protests, the men who signed the petition were a collection of publicans, shoemakers, sawyers, harness makers, shopkeepers, smallholders and labourers, a cross-section of the southern rural plebeian community. Truly they were Cobbett's chopsticks. They were also Cobbett's readers, discussing the latest issue of his *Political Register* at their meetings and, in the case of the 'Musical and Radical Society' leader Enos Diddams, also his correspondents.[44] Political understanding ran deep in the area. At Overton, on passing through the village on his way to the West Country, Henry Hunt was called on by the farmers to intervene in a wages dispute. That Hunt was asked suggests that the farmers believed that the labourers would know who Hunt was. That the labourers acted on his advice demonstrates that they did, presumably through Cobbett's reporting of his failure to secure the Lancashire industrial seat of Preston at the general election.[45] The destruction of the tollhouses on the turnpike at nearby East Dean and Tytherley was accompanied by the Cobbettian threat that they would soon destroy all 'Parsons, Excisemen, and Turnpike Gates'.[46] Radical politics, it would appear, penetrated all local communities in this part of Hampshire and informed the discourses *and* practices of Swing.

It was this fear that Cobbett's – and others' – writings had acted to politicise rural workers that prompted the Home Office to occasionally deploy spies in the countryside. Evidence from such sources is patchy. Police officer Johns, sent from London to act as an undercover agent in infiltrating the Horsham Radical Party, found plenty of evidence of indigenous popular politics. Indeed, radical politics was so entrenched in local society that after the arrest of three men in connection with the affray at the church, Johns feared for his safety and made a speedy return to London.[47] Conversely at Deal, Bow Street officer Bishop had 'gone to the different Pot Houses in the villages [around Deal] disguised among the labourers' only to find that 'all their talk is about the wages, some give 1/8 per day, some 2/-

some 2/3, all they say they want is 2/6 a day'. And yet the following year in investigations for a case of machine-breaking at Ripple, it was uncovered that *Cobbett's Political Register* was widely read in local pubs with copies even lent out to readers.[48]

It was the depth of the penetration of radical ideas that is particularly telling, for whether foregrounded or placed to the back of the minds of Swing protestors, radical ideas clearly informed their worldview. Hence at Lenham, no popular political expressions were made use of but the tactic of parading the parish with a banner stating 'Starving at 1s. 6d. a week' and demanding money or food from the parishioners was a fusion of rural custom and popular political iconography.[49] Similarly, the use of parochial petitions throughout the Weald aped the sending of pro-reform and anti-tax and tithe petitions. The petition of the Burwash poor – supposed to be avid 'readers of Cobbett' – to the 'Gentlemen' of the parish promised in the final line that 'We dont intend for any more Tythe to be paid in the Parish'. At nearby Guestling, the labourers offered to 'shake off the oppression of the tithes'.[50] Thus rural workers in many locations copied the tactics and style of radical politics and, critically, the agenda. Whether the connection between the radical political platform and rural workers' specific needs was made independently of farmers' coercive encouragement (or example) is not always clear. What is clear, though, is that the styles adopted by rural workers, whether fighting their own cause or that of their manipulative employers, were taken straight from the radical canon.

Of course, none of this proves that Swing was a participatory politically motivated movement. Outside a few areas where energetic and charismatic individuals managed to stir others into action, it was not. Yet there can be little doubt that radical political ideas penetrated much of the countryside prior to Swing, for wherever the archive is particularly rich we invariably find evidence of the impact of Cobbett's writings and radical expression. And these ideas informed the choices, actions and discourses of Swing protestors. Perhaps, given that the Dever Valley was the first part of Hampshire to 'rise' independently of the physical diffusion that had led to protests in the vicinity of Havant and Petersfield, the strongly held political views of individuals like the Masons and Diddams even acted as the trigger, and provided the conviction, to protest. The interconnections between the politics of the parish and participatory politics are clear, if impossible to untangle. Wherever radical ideas penetrated, there was always the possibility, even the likelihood, that at least one rural worker would be so struck with the language used and the critiques offered that they would, like Inskipp at Battle, act to draw others into the fold. Indeed, the rural radical platform espoused by Cobbett must have been hugely seductive to rural workers ground down by the economic and social degradation of the post-Napoleonic period: an end to oppression, fair treatment and living wages. The jump from issuing these universal parish politic demands to calling for tax cuts, parliamentary reform and vote by ballot was considerably greater than the jump from pauperisation to thinking that Cobbett was the saviour. But clearly many rural workers did. Swing was informed, and occasionally instructed, by both those village Hampdens actively advocating reform and those seduced by the idea espoused by Cobbett that there was an easy solution to their wretched state.

Notes

1 As Ian Dyck notes, Cobbett actually berated farmers for sending too few petitions: *William Cobbett and Rural Popular Culture* (Cambridge: Cambridge University Press, 1993), p. 159. For the use of petitions as a mode of communicating grievances with central government see: D. Eastwood, *Government and Community in the English Provinces, 1700–1870* (Basingstoke: Macmillan, 1997), pp. 75–7, 111.

2 HCRO, 75M91/E26/10, J.R. Gowen, Christian Malford to Lord Porchester, Lynmouth, 18 November 1830.

3 The other of the two Kent 'shire' seats was 'claimed' by fellow sitting MP, anti-reform Tory Sir Edward Knatchull, chairman of the East Kent Quarter Sessions: *Kent Herald* (hereafter *KH*), 12 August 1830.

4 *Hampshire Chronicle* (hereafter *HC*), 9 August; *Hampshire Telegraph* (hereafter *HT*), 9 August 1830; P. Salmon and H. Spencer, 'Hampshire', in D. Fisher, *The House of Commons, 1820–1832: Volume I, Constituencies part I* (Cambridge: Cambridge University Press, 2009), p. 422. For the role of the Barings in Hampshire county politics see: R. Foster, *The Politics of County Power: Wellington and the Hampshire Gentlemen 1820–1852* (Hemel Hempstead: Harvester Wheatsheaf, 1990); Foster, 'The decline and fall of George Hollis: "Old Corruption" and reform at the Hampshire Quarter Sessions c.1815–40', *Southern History*, 29 (2007), 59–82.

5 D. Fisher, 'Rye', in *Idem.*, *The House of Commons, 1820–1832*, p. 316. For a more detailed account of the events at Rye, see Chapter 3.

6 *Cobbett's Weekly Political Register* (hereafter *CWPR*), 10 and 17 July 1830.

7 W. Cobbett, *Eleven Lectures on the French and Belgian Revolutions and English Boroughmongering* (London: W. Strange, 1830).

8 *HC*, 13 September; *Sherborne Journal*, 16 September 1830.

9 *HT*, 9 August 1830.

10 *Brighton Guardian* (hereafter *BGu*), 15 September; *Brighton Herald*, 28 August; *CWPR*, 1 and 16 October 1830.

11 *Hampshire Advertiser*, 28 July; *Sussex Advertiser*, 13 and 20 September, R. Wells, 'Mr William Cobbett, Captain Swing, and King William IV', *Agricultural History Review*, 45:1 (1997), 35–6; *Maidstone Gazette*, 21 September 1830; R. Wells, 'Social protest, class, conflict and consciousness, in the English countryside', in M. Reed and R. Wells (eds), *Class, Conflict and Protest in the English Countryside, 1700–1880* (London: Frank Cass, 1990), p. 184.

12 *KH*, 7 February; *County Chronicle*, 9 February; *CWPR*, 20 March.; *HC*, 14 March; *Keene's Bath Journal*, 21 June; *Maidstone Journal* (hereafter *MJ*), 26 October 1830. For Cobbett's September petition see: Wells, 'Mr William Cobbett', p. 36.

13 *Ibid.*, p. 35.

14 CKS, Q/SBw/124/7, Defence of Robert Price, 19 November; TNA, HO 52/8, fos 365–6 and 361–2, Poore, Murston to Peel, 25 October, Sharp, Faversham to Freeling, 26 October; CKS, U951 C14/7, Poore to Knatchbull, 26 October; *KH*, 28 October 1830.

15 CKS, Q/SBw/124/7,8 and 9, Defence of Robert Price, Depositions of Daniel Green, farmer, and Charlotte Stacey, wife of Courtney Stacey, all 19 November; CKS U951 C14/6, Poore, Murston, to Knatchbull, 29 October 1830. For an examination of the role of flags and banners in radical politics see R. Poole, 'The march to Peterloo: politics and festivity in late Georgian England', *Past and Present*, 192 (2006), 109–53.

16 CKS, Q/SBw/124/7,8 and 9, Defence of Robert Price, Depositions of Daniel Green, farmer, and Charlotte Stacey, wife of Courtney Stacey, all 19 November; CKS, U951 C14/8 and 6, Poore, Murston, to Knatchbull, n.d. (but 28 October) and 29 October; TNA, HO 52/8, fos 365–6, 367–8, 28–9 and 25–6, Poore, 25 and 29 October, Maidstone Bench, 30 October and Lieut. Col. Charles Middleton, Cavalry Depot, Maidstone, 31 October, all to Peel; TNA, TS 11/1071, 5035, 943, Prosecution Briefs prepared by the Treasury Solicitor in the cases of *The King* v. *Edward Chapman, Mathew Waltz Walker, and William Robinson*, and *The King* v. *John Adams*; *MJ*, 26 October and 2 November; *KH*, 28 October and 4 November; *Kentish Gazette* (hereafter *KG*), 29 October; *Hastings and Cinque Ports Iris* (hereafter *HIris*), 6 November 1830. Similar radical language was also used at Prinsted (Westbourne) in West Sussex. On destroying a threshing machine on the farm of Mary Harfield, one man claimed he was the Captain of the gang, and in a politically charged parley asserted that 'if anyone was King he ought to be as he was Captain': WSCRO, Goodwood 1477a R30, Examinations of Henry Walker, Navy Lieutenant, and Charles Lutman, Navy Lieutenant, both 22 November 1830.

17 *CWPR*, 2 October; *Maidstone Gazette*, 19 October; *Maidstone Journal* (hereafter *MJ*), 19 October; *KG*, 19 and 22 October; *KH*, 7 and 21 October; TNA, HO 52/8, fos 333–4, Maidstone Postmaster, to Sir Francis Freeling, 14 October 1830.

18 TNA, HO 52/8, fos 28–9, Maidstone Magistrates to Peel, 30 October; *MJ*, 2 November; *HIris*, 6 November 1830.

19 TNA, HO 40/27, fos 54 and 56, Maule, Maidstone to Under-secretary Phillips,

1 and 2 November 1830; TNA, HO 41/8, pp. 12 and 22, Phillips to Rev. Dr Poore, Murston, 26 October, Peel to 'The Magistrates of Maidstone', 31 October 1830; *MJ*, 2 November; *CWPR*, 6 November; *HIris*, 6 November; *Maidstone Gazette*, 6 November 1830.

20 See C. Griffin, '"As Lated Tongues Bespoke": Popular Protest in South-East England, 1790–*c*.1840' (PhD thesis, University of Bristol, 2002), pp. 150–1, 153, 155, 159.

21 *BGu*, 17 March and 29 September 1830.

22 *Brighton Herald*, 20 November; *Portsmouth, Portsea and Gosport Herald*, 21 November 1830; R. Wells, www.canterbury.ac.uk/arts-humanities /history-and-american studies/history/Documents/PoliticsOfCaptainSwing .pdf (accessed 21 April 2011), p. 25; WSCRO, Goodwood 1477a R12, Letter to Richmond, 16 December 1830.

23 TNA, HO 52/10, fos 532–3, 534–7, 204–5 and 542–4, and 538–9, Thomas Sanctuary, The Nunnery, Horsham to Peel, 17, 18 and 19 November, William Crawford, Dorking to Peel, 19 November, Mr Davis, Leystonstone, Essex to Peel, 20 November; *The Times* (hereafter *TT*), 22 November; *Brighton Gazette*, 25 November 1830.

24 TNA, HO 52/10, fos 555–6, 557–8, 565–6, 569–70, and 573–5, Walter Burrell, West Grinstead Park to Peel, 21 November, to Home Secretary Melbourne, 28 November, Sir Charles Burrell, West Grinstead Park, to Melbourne, 5, 9 and 12 December 1830.

25 TNA, HO 52/10, fos 629–30 and 278–81, 285–5, Earl of Egremont, Petworth, 26 November, Mr Crawford, Dorking, and enclosures, 28 December 1830, both to Melbourne.

26 TNA, HO 52/8, fo. 219, Camden to Peel, 22 October 1830, forwarding a letter from the Earl of Ashburnhan; Wells, 'Mr William Cobbett', *passim*.

27 'Papers: 1830–1', London Radicalism 1830–1843: A selection of the papers of Francis Place (1970), pp. 8–15. At: www.britishhistory.ac.uk/report .aspx?compid=39480 (accessed 21 February 2010).

28 HCRO, 75M91/E26/13, J.R. Gowen, Athenean, to Lord Porchester, Lynmouth, n.d. (but *c*.9 November 1830). For an in-depth analysis of the impact of the cancellation of the King's visit see C. Tilly, *Popular Contention in Great Britain 1758–1834* (Cambridge MA: Harvard University Press, 1995), pp. 314–15.

29 TNA, HO 52/10, fos 312–13, 430, 435–6, 437, 431–2, 440–3 and 444, Mr Redgrave, Whitehall Place to Melbourne, 29 November, Battle Post Office Deputy, 26 November, Battle Post Office, 27 November and 1 December to Freeling, Clerks to the Battle Bench, 26 November, Thomas Bellingham, 2 and 3 December, to Melbourne; TNA, TS 11/1007, Prosecution Briefs prepared by the Treasury Solicitor in the case of *The King* v. *Charles Inskipp*, Sussex Winter Assizes; *Brighton Gazette*, 23 December 1830 (assize reports).

30 TNA, HO 52/10, fos 440–3, Thomas Charles Bellingham, Battle to Melbourne, 2 December 1830, enclosing Taylor's letter.

31 TNA, HO 41/8, fo. 83, Phillips to George Maule, Treasury Solicitor, Maidstone, 20 November 1830.

32 TNA, HO 52/7, fos 44–5, G.B. Chamling, Home Place, Sheerness to Beresford, 19 November 1830.

33 TNA, HO 52/7, fos 233–4, Thomas Law Hodges, Hemsted to Home Secretary Peel, 31 October 1830.

34 The drinking party was a group of journeymen tailors, supposedly 'very active in promoting discontent and tumult'. TNA, HO 52/10, fos 589–93: Lewes Magistrates to Melbourne, 30 November, enclosing Informations of William Kenward, Uckfield; James Catt, Little Horsted; John Batchelor, South Malling; and, John Jenner, Uckfield, all 27 November 1830.

35 TNA, HO 52/10, fos 324–5 and 603–4, Charles Verall, Seaford, 30 November, Lewes Bench, to Melbourne, 3 December 1830.

36 TNA, HO 52/10, fos 307–11 and 317–22, Brighton Ordnance Office to Peel, 23 November, plus enclosures, Mr Dinninar, Brighton, to Sir H. Taylor. G.C.H. (forwarded to Home Office), 25 November; *TT*, 20 November. Such fears were given further credence. On 26 November an (aborted) attempt was made to break into the office of the guardians of the poor. In early December a riotous assemblage gathered in front of the office of the Brighton guardians of the poor and in effecting a general rush to get into the office broke several windows. The result was that as there was no organised civil force in Brighton the guardians were intimidated into raising the wages of those employed by the parish. *Ibid.*, 27 November and 10 December 1830.

37 TNA, TS 11/943, Prosecution Briefs prepared by the Treasury Solicitor in the case of *The King* v. *William Standen, Stephen Eves and Richard Cutbush*, West Kent Epiphany Sessions 1831; TNA, HO 52/8, fos 248–53, Camden, Arlington Street to Peel, 12 November, and enclosures; *KG*, 12 November; *MJ*, 16 November; *TT*, 18 November; CKS, Q/SBw 124/1a, b and c, Depositions of Giles Miller, solicitor, Goudhurst, Captain James William Hay, Cranbrook, Rev. Phillip Legigt, Marden, all 16 November 1830.

38 HCRO, 94M72/F15/8 letter 1, Henry Budd to J.B. Carter Esq., Petersfield, n.d. (but 23 November); *Portsmouth, Portsea and Gosport Herald*, 28 November; *HT*, 29 November 1830.

39 TNA, HO 52/7, fos 21–4, 29–30, 132–3, and 248–9, John Mills Esq., Ringwood, and W. Eyre-Coate, West Park, both to Melbourne, 26 November, Eliza Pleadon, Fordingbridge Post Office Deputy to Freeling, 26 November, Sir Charles Halse, Breamore House, to Melbourne, 28 November; *TT*, 21 and 22 December; TNA, HO 130/1, Hampshire Special Commission cases 40–43 (Rockbourne), 44–52, 73–80, 85–7, and 140–6 (Fordingbridge) and 148 (Breamore).

40 TNA, HO 52/7, fos 25–7, Richard Pollen Esq., Winchester Gaol, to Philips, 26 November 1830.

41 *MJ*, 12 October 1830.

42 TNA, TS 11/943, Prosecution Brief prepared by the Treasury Solicitor against Timothy Willocks. Notwithstanding the drafting of the brief, Willocks was not brought to trial.

43 *Southampton Mercury*, 20 November; HCRO, 92M95/F2 8/3 and F2/9/13, Rev. D. Cockerton, Stoke Charity to Sir Thomas Baring, 2 December, Examination of William Pain senior, farmer, Micheldever, 1 December; *TT*, 22 and 25 December 1830; *Two-Penny Trash*, volume II, issue 12, July 1832.

44 D. Kent, *Popular Radicalism and the Swing Riots in Central Hampshire*

(Winchester: Hampshire County Council, 1997), pp. 5–6; *Two-Penny Trash*, volume II, issue 12, July 1832, esp. pp. 276, 278, 280–2.

45 *Hampshire Advertiser*, 20 November; *Berkshire Chronicle*, 27 November 1830; J. Belchem, *'Orator Hunt': Henry Hunt and the English Working-Class Radicalism* (Oxford: Clarendon Press, 1985), pp. 205–7.

46 *Portsmouth, Portsea and Gosport Herald*, 28 November 1830.

47 TNA, HO 52/10, fos 569–70 and 573–5, Walter Burrell, West Grinstead Park to Melbourne, 9 and 12 December 1830.

48 TNA, HO 52/8, fos 148–9 and 52/13, fos 75–6 and 81–2, D. Bishop, Deal to William Rowley, n.d. (between 10 and 12 November 1830), Deal Bench to Melbourne, 5 and 9 August; *KH*, 4 August 1831.

49 *KH*, 28 October; *KG*, 29 October 1830.

50 ESCRO, AMS 5995/3/12, Gentleman of Burwash to H.B. Curteis, Beckley, plus enclosure, 9 November; TNA, HO 52/10, fo. 525, William Stone, Mayfield to Home Office, n.d. (but 10 November); *Rochester Gazette*, 16 November 1830.

8

The gender politics of Swing

In the forty years since the publication of *Captain Swing*, while our understandings of Swing have evolved in a distinctly Hobsbawm and Rudé paradigm, our broader conceptions of rural life have been revolutionised. The opening chapters of their bestseller painted a picture of an English countryside where social relations were largely determined by the experience of pauperisation.[1] Since then, historians of work and 'the economy of makeshifts' have opened our eyes to the fact that while labouring life was underpinned by the aggressive vigour of agrarian capitalism, it was not reducible to it.[2] The centrality of women – and children – in supporting the domestic economy through paid work has been powerfully asserted by, among others, Joyce Burnette, Jane Humphries, Karen Sayer, Pamela Sharpe and Nicola Verdon. Women were not a 'hidden workforce' but an integral part of the rural labour market.[3] Similarly, the role of women in developing and instigating coping strategies through pulling together many resources – whether through exercising customary and common rights, applying for relief, taking lodgers, or tapping kinship networks – is also now viewed as a vital component of rural working life.[4] While the debate as to whether the intensification of capitalist agriculture in the late eighteenth and early nineteenth centuries meant more or less work for women continues, there is a an emergent consensus that the availability of agricultural work both varied between regions and within counties. Or as Verdon put it, the pattern of women's agricultural work in the nineteenth century was 'complex and contradictory'.[5]

Women's work appears to have been more important to plebeian household economies in the north-east than elsewhere, and relatively more important in the east than the west. In the south, so it has been suggested, some of the disparities are due to the persistence of domestic industry in the west reducing the female agricultural labour supply. Conversely, Robert Allen has suggested that the larger, more heavily capitalised arable farms more typical of the south-east than the south-west of England tended to employ fewer women, something repudiated by Burnette. Either way, Verdon's analysis of the (admittedly problematic) 1834 'Rural Queries', suggests that in the early 1830s not only was domestic industry irrelevant in most of the south-east, but that over 70 per cent of Hampshire, Kent and Sussex parishes mentioned the employment of women in the harvest (over 60 per cent for Surrey), and that over a third mentioned the importance of weeding.

There were other tasks that south-eastern farmers tended to engage female labour in too. Bridget Hill has noted that the growth of market gardening on the London fringe and that of other growing south-eastern cities generated a considerable demand for female workers. Similarly, the proliferation of small cow-keepers in the suburbs also increased female labour demands. The growth of the acreage under orchard fruits also created opportunities in weeding, pruning and fruit picking. The rapid turn to planting hops, not least in the Weald, the north Kent coast, and the area around Farnham and Alton, generated a highly varied demand for female labour in tying and weeding in the spring, picking in the late summer and early autumn, and helping strip and shave hop poles in the winter. On average then, according to Verdon's analysis of the 'Rural Queries', about 10 per cent of total household incomes throughout the south-east derived from female labour, the figure being nearer 20 per cent in Surrey, if only 7 per cent in Sussex.[6] Besides, even if women were not working in the fields and gardens, and clearly many did, they were always labouring for the household.

Protesting masculinities

Although the involvement of women in eighteenth- and early nineteenth-century food riots has long been understood as a direct function of their roles in running the domestic economy,[7] considerations of other protest forms or movements in the English countryside have tended to ignore gender relations altogether. Even the sole book-length study of the involvement of women in protest locates such activities almost exclusively in the city.[8] As Iain Robertson has noted though in relation to rural Scotland, crudely gendered models of protest have tended to brush over local gender roles, assuming instead that the same 'underlying legitimising ideology' applies aspatially whatever the cultural socio-context.[9] Thus, while Verdon's assertion that agricultural histories have suffered from 'gender blindness' is undeniable, John Tosh reminds us that we need to think of gender as a relation to one's body *and* as a disposition towards society as a whole is important here. Not only do we therefore need to think of male workers as gendered, but we need to think of gender as being one of the key ways in which rural social relations were regulated.[10] Such a perspective necessarily has profound implications for the way we think about all poor people's protest movements – including Swing.

From archival depictions of a brutish, lumpen mass of protesting labourers, to subsequent critiques of the brutal involvement of the masculinist state, representations of Swing and Swing's historians have hitherto not offered space for women, or for an explicitly gendered analysis of the movement. In many ways. by asking who Swing was – a function of the mystery of metonym answered almost reflexively by resort to the suggestive but essentially gender neutral language of 'rioter', 'pauper', 'machine-breaker', 'stranger'[11] – has tended to cloud the more immediate question of 'what was Swing?' The answer is seemingly obvious: a movement of impoverished labourers seeking to improve their lot by machine-breaking and calling for wage increases and more generous poor relief entitlements. But such a statement ignores a more profound set of realisations. To destroy winter labour-sapping machinery and gain higher wages was, as Peter Jones has persuasively argued, not just to triumph against seemingly almighty capitalists but instead to restore some semblance of 'balance' in rural social relations.[12] And this balance was not just about male labourers, though it will be shown that many Swing protestors were writ through with a desire to reassert an imperilled labouring masculinity, but about the community. Why else would Swing groups expend so much effort and risk in recruiting both the willing and the unwilling into their service?

Where women have made the historian's cut, they either exist as lone incendiarists or as enfeebled by the fear of the 'mob'. There is a massive difference though between stating, as the archive clearly and unambiguously does, that Swing groupings were overwhelmingly male and saying that women did not figure in the movement or that Swing had nothing to say about gender relations. Indeed, so much of our current reading of Swing is based on a series of assumptions based on impressionistic archival readings: that no women were present therefore Swing protestors had nothing to say about either gender relations or sexual politics. The following sections seek to move beyond such narrow readings. Instead, they offer a more nuanced reading of both the direct and indirect involvement of women in Swing and Swing's commentaries on gender relations in the post-Napoleonic English countryside. It considers the involvement of women in Swing – both directly and indirectly in the support of men's protests,[13] and the ways in which Swing protests represented an assertion of an imperilled masculinity.

Pauperisation and male primacy

Rural society in late Georgian England was undoubtedly masculinist and patriarchal, something most clearly evidenced in the resort to physical and sexual violence against women and girls.[14] Yet, it is foolhardy to deny that male labouring was underpinned, even made possible, by female labour. Male labour therefore also had a broader purpose. Labouring was not just about keeping body and soul together but about maintaining family unity. If the title of Ellen Ross's book is perhaps something of an overstatement, *Love and Toil* nevertheless neatly serves to remind us that male labourers could transcend being the mere applicators of capital.[15]

Before the opening of the Hampshire Special Commission, farmer Buttley of Soberton wrote to Sir Thomas Baring asking that he 'might admit of some lenity' on the case of his labourer Jesse Burgess, his wife having certified that he had been at work before being swept along by the large group of men traversing the parish. He had eight children who were 'dependant upon their father for support' and had not received 'support' from the parish for 'the last 9 years'.[16] Similarly, the extraordinarily literate Bullington dual-occupationalist Robert Mason, having been found guilty of 'robbery', wrote from his cell in Winchester Gaol to his prosecutor, Rev. Cockerton of Stoke Charity, to ask for assistance. His mother, having been 'comfortably supported' by him – and his brother – was now 'mortified' at having no support. 'God will support me in some way or other for he has promised by his servant David, to save all that put their trust in him. If we are cast into prison for 6 months my mother is nearly ruined, and if longer she will be obliged to depend on the parish for support.'[17] As one newspaper report relating to the arrest of machine-breakers in the area between Chichester and Havant related, 'the parting' between one man and 'his wife' at West Wittering 'was very affecting'.[18] To labour may have been to be degraded, especially if the labour was for, or arranged by, the parish, but to be a labourer was to struggle for self-respect, dignity and the family.

While not all Swing activists were 'pauperised', many labourers *were* effectively in constant subjugation to the vestry. As considered in Chapter 2, rural and poor law historians have long since argued that Speenhamland-type 'bread scales' and child allowances had become viewed by agricultural labourers as 'rights' by the time of Swing. The logical extension of these 'relief' practices into de facto wage subsidies, combined with multifarious parish make-work schemes, meant that in many south-eastern parishes all labourers were effectively pauperised.[19] Indeed, although many vestries adopted the policy of only allowing male heads of households to make claims, the pauperisation of labour represented a profound way in which powers of male self-determination were eroded. It is therefore instructive that many Swing groupings made claims both to employers for higher wages to help move beyond pauperisation as well as claims to vestrymen for more generous marriage and child allowances. The following 'violent paper … carried around the … adjacent parishes and … assented [to] by many occupiers of land' and seized by Sussex grandee Sir Godfrey Webster at Mayfield perhaps offers the clearest expression of this dynamic:

> Now gentlemen this is wat wee intend to have for a married man to have 2s and 3d per day and all over two children 1/6 per head a week and if a man has got any boys or girls over age for to have enough that they may live by there labour and likewise all single men to have 1/9 a day per head and we intend to have the rents lowered likewise … For we are all as one and we will keep to each other.[20]

By excluding women (whether actively or passively) from such negotiations, in the face of multiple onslaughts male primacy could be reasserted.

The exclusion of women as a deliberate symbol reasserting an imperilled masculinity was most vividly expressed at Owslebury, near Winchester, where a small group of Swing protestors, traversing the parish levying doles, were accompanied not only by 'respectable' farmer Deacle but also by Mrs Deacle riding a white horse. This Lady

Godiva-inspired incident represented the ultimate public performance of all power being inverted: the woman being literally and symbolically being placed over the men. The inversion was politically charged too, for in the post-Napoleonic English countryside 'normal' power relations were inverted. Hence the protest, as well as offering fantastical juxtapositions, also reflected a contrary reality.[21]

Beyond reasserting male economic primacy, there are other reasons why Swing groups in certain protest scenarios would only contain men. Claims for more generous poor relief entitlements mirrored a long-established protest practice of mass invasions by male labourers to vestries and magistrates' benches, a tactic frequently resorted to in food crises and during the depression of the early 1820s.[22] Similarly, there was no pre-history of female machine-breakers – though, as Adrian Randall has pointed out, women were often themselves disadvantaged by the introduction of machinery and thus joined anti-machinery protests – either in agrarian or industrial England.[23] It is also important to note that the aforementioned 'traditional' forms of female protest, most notably food rioting and enclosure rioting, were absent from Swing's repertoire apart from in the movement's outermost peripheries.[24] Swing activists were also quiet about piece rates, both as applied to male and female labour. Perhaps this reflected the desire of Swing activists to reassert the desirability and primacy of the idealised day-labouring occupation.[25] Nevertheless, this almost total silence also reflected the broader dynamic that male Swing activists shied away from commenting on or making claims that in any way diluted *their* claims and their reassertion of labouring masculinities.

The lack of female involvement in Swing's multifarious wages protests is much harder to understand from a past practice perspective, for, as Verdon has shown, female field workers necessarily had to enter into wage bargaining with potential employers.[26] Women used, albeit less commonly, the same proto-unionist tactics deployed by groups of male labourers. For instance, at the Wiltshire parish of Oaksey at the start of the 1830 hay harvest, some 60–70 female haymakers struck work after the farmers tried to reduce wages from 10*d.* to 9*d.* a day.[27] It is important to note though that in some localities even if men were trying to reassert their economic and household-political primacy, women clearly too had much to gain from Swing and therefore might support their husbands and brothers. Thus at Winfrith in east Dorset, the all-male Swing grouping were encouraged by local women from behind hedges.[28]

Masculinity and machine cultures

Close under the eaves of the stack, and as yet barely visible, was the red tyrant that the women had come to serve – a timber-framed construction, with straps and wheels appertaining – the threshing-machine which, whilst it was going, kept up a despotic demand upon the endurance of their muscles and nerves ... Tess was placed on the platform of the machine, close to the man who fed it, her business being to untie every sheaf of corn handed on to her by Izz Huett, who stood next, but on the rick; so that the feeder could seize it and spread it over the revolving drum, which whisked out every grain in one moment ... For some probably economical reason it was usually a woman who was chosen for this particular duty, and Groby gave as his motive in selecting Tess that she was one of those who best combined strength with quickness in untying, and both with staying power, and this may have been true. (Thomas Hardy, *Tess of the D'Urbevilles*, 1891)[29]

By the time of *Tess*'s publication, steam-powered threshing machines had replaced water- and horse-powered machines. They were more powerful than the two to four horse-power machines that were the norm in 1830, but otherwise operated on exactly the same basis with the same labour demands. Both necessitated the employment of a mixture of physically strong individuals, dextrous individuals, those able to work quickly and rhythmically, as well as someone to superintend the machine's operation. There was both good practical reason, then, to employ young women and lads alongside men in working threshing machines as well as obvious economic reasons. Pre-Swing reports of accidents with threshing machines in the southern provincial press demonstrate that farmers did employ a mixture of men, women and lads: of the twenty accidents I have uncovered, nine relate to lads, eight to men, and three to young women.[30] This probably underestimates the proportion of young women employed in working the machines, for women – like Tess – were employed in the most dangerous job of 'feeding' the machine, thereby in all probability being under-represented in the sample. Compared to flail threshing, machine threshing thereby displaced labourer power with a combination of horse, child, woman and (to a greatly reduced extent) man-power.[31] As Sonya Rose has put it, 'capitalist labour practices threatened to destroy ... men's power over women's labour'.[32]

As noted in Chapter 2, the diffusion of threshing machines largely coincided with the post-Napoleonic increase in rural unemployment, thus by not only dramatically decreasing employment opportunities for men but increasing them for women, threshing machines represented an affront to labourers' dignity and masculinity.[33] Destroying threshing machines would therefore not only provide more work for male labourers in the winter months but it would act to reassert the relative importance of men's work and invigorate labouring masculinities. Indeed, the very act of destroying a threshing machine was an overtly physical and masculine performance. As a deposition detailing one of the first acts of machine-breaking by the Elham gang testifies, the acts of destruction were ordered yet carnivalesque, rooted in solidarities and laden with machismo:

> About 20 of the company went to the Barn … and some brought out a Threshing Machine. The Party then broke it to pieces … There was a great noise and shouting all the while they were breaking the machine – they were engaged about 20 minutes or half an hour in breaking the machine. The company then assembled at the yard Gate and gave 3 cheers.[34]

These were men who worked and lived together, acting together. But beyond these immediate observations it is clear that the destructions made more profound comment about gender relations that the simple assertion of male solidarity in the face of agrarian capitalism. George Youens, one of the Elham gang, later recalled that during their second machine-breaking outing, 'The people made a great noise all the time – they called out – "Kill Her – More Oil! More Grease!"'[35] Similarly, the deposition of machine-breaker John Jeffereys gendered the machine as female.[36] To the Elham gang at least, threshing machines became proxies for female bodies, something they, as men, should control, dominate and discipline. Threshing machines were more than just proxies for female bodies, though, in the sense that the snippet of remembered speech in Yoeuns's deposition suggests that the female body was a sexualised one. Oil and grease were not needed to destroy threshing machines, instead, the allusion in the quote is in all probability to sex. Not only was a 'woman' going to be 'killed', but the machine-breakers also were going to rape 'her'.

This allusion makes a degree of sense. Not only were threshing machines clearly in some male labouring circles perceived as representing the high tide of female usurpment, but from a misogynistic perspective the machine's rhythmic action combined with the fact that it had to be 'served' through 'entry' meant that it was not unlike the objectified, sexualised female body. As Lerman *et al.* have asserted, 'gender ideologies play a central role in human interactions with technology' and, in turn, technology is a key way in which gender identities and structures are defined and formed in Western culture.[37]

Further evidence of threshing machines being bound up in complex gender politics comes from one of the last overt incidents of protest in Kent during the height of Swing. On the night of 24 November a party of machine-breakers led by the self-styled General Moore, who had two days previously destroyed two threshing machines and been involved in an assault on a farmer and a policemen,[38] again embarked on a destruction spree. That they destroyed six threshing machines in the Margate area and that the attacks occurred at night, a tactic not deployed since the first actions of the Elham gang, were obviously worthy of note, but that 'some' of the men were 'disguised in female attire' was an entirely new dynamic to Swing. Their exact motives are unclear, though the fearlessness that the gang had previously shown suggests disguise to avoid identification is unlikely. As with cross-dressing in Luddism, the invocation of the carnivalesque on what was a momentous day is a possibility. More likely still is that the threshing machines in question were being, at least in part, operated by women and the choice of female clothing a direct comment on the usurping of male labour.[39] Indeed, it is worth noting that a trawl of the south-eastern archive between 1790 and 1840 has found only a couple of instances of cross-dressing in relation to *any* form of protest or criminality, including in those forms of protest in which women were 'traditionally' involved, namely food and enclosure 'riots'.[40]

An analysis of pre-Swing gender politics in the Kentish machine-breaking heartlands shows the ingrained nature of sexual violence towards women. Indeed, acts of sexual violence against women were an integral part of labouring life. For instance, on 11 September 1822 a young Sellindge girl dictated a deathbed declaration:

> I Elizabeth Impett, with the prospect of Death upon me do most solemnly declare that John Hayward inflicted the wound in my side of which I expect to die, with a loaded in gun, in consequence of my refusal to yield to his embraces this morning.[41]

Eight years later, Sellindge was a parish in which the Elham gang destroyed several machines. Labourer, attempted rapist and murderer Hayward was evidently also a smuggler for he had in his possession a pistol, the owlers' weapon of choice.

Attitudes to women, or more particularly to the female body, were little different elsewhere in East Kent. In the area surrounding Ash-next-Sandwich – the second major area of Kentish machine-breaking – in the five years preceding Swing, of the cases brought before the Petty Sessions all attacks on women involved a sexual element. Two cases related to public attacks on women by groups of men involving sexual violence,[42] while a further two cases related to attempted rape, one against a nine-year-old girl, the other involving a young labourer who first attacked a married couple before attempting to rape the woman. The attempted rapist was convicted for twenty-one days' hard labour, and a year later was one of nine men indicted at the East Kent Quarter Sessions for machine-breaking in the vicinity of Bekesbourne and was subsequently sentenced to seven years' transportation.[43]

In a masculinist culture where violence against women was central to labouring life, it should come as little surprise to historians that threshing machines became proxies for female bodies. The destruction of threshing machines was not, therefore, solely an act of macho strength in a rural war against the unfettered action of capital against the interests of plebeian communities. Rather, it was a reassertion, as psychological as much as it was public, of male power at a time when labouring men's autonomy and powers of self, family and community determination were rendered ever less potent. Destroying a threshing machine not only restored an employment opportunity for labouring men but it also resurrected the totemic power of male labour in rural England.

Further evidence of the popularly embedded links between machine cultures and gender relations comes from an unusual source. Just before the trial of the Elham machine-breakers on 21 October, a Dover tradesman received an anonymous letter threatening to 'fire' his premises if his threshing machine were not 'put away'. Unsurprisingly, the man was much alarmed and with his neighbours kept a constant watch on his property that night. The following day he received another similar letter. The 'threshing machine' referred to was the tradesman's wife who had recently 'won' in a 'domestic recontre' with the letter writer. Again, a threshing machine was being compared to an assertive woman.[44]

Female activists

As Hobsbawm and Rudé showed, most Swing activists were young men and lads. These men were invariably in the most marginal of all social positions. Unmarried men, according to most relief scales, would get lower pay, would not benefit from other forms of relief-in-kind, such as rent or clothes, and were likely to be employed last after the farmers had hired married men. Being both socially excluded and without marital commitments, such men had both most to lose from widening female employment opportunities and least to lose from protesting their lot. A fictitious homogenised Swing group might, therefore, have little behind the scenes support from women and much to gain from altogether ignoring any claims that impacted upon women. In truth, though, there was no such thing as a homogenised Swing grouping that only reflected the most socially marginal members of rural society. Instead, most Swing groupings were constituted by a wide cross-section of labouring society, involving young lads, newly married men and wizened older labourers.[45] Claims to represent all the community were made possible by reflecting *all* domestic situations.

Although there are no instances where women were explicitly involved in negotiations over wages or poor relief, they were occasionally present in poor-law-related protests where it was necessary to present a deliberate face of community cohesion as opposed to male solidarity. At Brede, in the first expulsion of an assistant overseer, the crowd comprised some 150 people, including 'several women and boys and girls from twelve to fourteen years of age'. The women continued with the expulsion party and were, with the men, regaled with 'half a pint' by farmer Coleman at Broad Oak.[46] At nearby Fairlight, a copycat assistant overseer expulsion was also attended by women and children equipped 'with fire-irons, bells, and warming pans'. It is perhaps telling though that no reports detailed the presence of women at the 'meeting' to discuss wages that followed the removal.[47] At Ninfield during the same wave of expulsions, assistant overseer Skinner was removed to Battle by a procession of some 600 people. Although the archive does not relate the social composition of the group and the figure is probably an exaggeration, it would appear likely that in a far from densely populated Wealden parish the group must also have contained women and children. Their protest attacked not only the policy of employing intrusive assistant overseers but also the parish policy of shaving the heads of pauper women, suggesting that the men of Ninfield bitterly resented the maltreatment of their wives and daughters. Attacking the shaving of female hair therefore allowed for both the reassertion of labouring masculinity through the 'defence' of Ninfield women and also the defence of femininity in common cause against the vestry.[48]

According to the *Hampshire Telegraph*, women were also involved in Swing groupings that claimed 'doles' from local farmers and others. In the villages around Winchester, it claimed, 'women and boys take their share in these outrages'.[49] While the paper did not produce any explicit examples, it is telling that such protests, as with the expulsion of assistant overseers, closely mirrored customary 'processioning' rituals in which women would often be expected to participate.[50] It is quite possible that a Swing group containing a 'fair proportion of women and children', which visited the farmer's houses at Leckford did not primarily 'demand', as was reported, an increase of wages but instead demanded doles.[51]

All of this, however, is to conflate Swing only with the wave of machine-breaking and wages meetings that swept southern England rather than the equally intensive resort to incendiarism. John Archer in his study of Norfolk and Suffolk between 1815 and 1870 has suggested that incendiarism was a young man's protest,[52] as a protest practice it was not gendered in the ways in which machine-breaking was. Women could just as readily strike a Lucifer match and set fire to a hay stack as men. Indeed, in the spaces of domestic employment women were more likely to resort to incendiarism than men. Underpinning the shared objective of affecting an improvement in the rural poor's standard of living were a huge variety of individual and community grievances. To state that few women had deeply felt grievances because so few women appear to have been Swing activists is a tautological nonsense. Even though there was some suggestion that she was assisted by a husband and wife, Elizabeth Studdam, one of only two women to be transported for her involvement in Swing, set fire to the Birchington poorhouse in her own right.[53] Similarly, Sarah Mitchell, a domestic servant at Petworth, sent threatening letters to her master who had treated her cruelly.[54]

In all probability, the tally of female fire-setters and threatening letter writers brought before Swing courts grossly underestimates their actual proportionate involvement. Of the 1,976 Swing legal cases identified by Hobsbawm and Rudé, only twenty-two involved female activists, most of whom were charged with incendiarism and the sending of threatening letters. Five of these women, intriguingly, were charged with breaking agricultural machinery. It is important to note though that these female machine-breakers were from Gloucestershire, a county that Adrian Randall has vividly shown had a deeply entrenched cross-community hatred of all machinery.[55]

But such cases represent the dramatic peak of an iceberg of unknowable size. Many Swing groups might have contained women but their presence was, for whatever reason, not recorded. That many Swing incidents followed customary processioning forms suggest that women would have been familiar with the form – for as Alun Howkins and Linda Merricks have shown many 'subversive' customary rituals involved both men and women[56] – and presumably being excluded would act to undermine the customary claim to community. Moreover, when Swing groups marched on market towns members of the town populace might easily have joined the throng, including women. The following example from the Berkshire market town of Hungerford, about six miles from the north Hampshire border, is instructive. On 22 November, having broken all the threshing machines in the neighbourhood, 'a riotous mob of the lowest class of the poor' assembled in the town in their quest to have their wages increased from 8 shillings to 12 shillings a week. Refusing to leave without the offer of food and beer, the crowd grew to a reported 600 or 700 'men, women and children', many of whom got quite drunk.[57]

And herein lies perhaps the most important point about Swing. It was no more a movement of impoverished male labourers than it was a mass outpouring of emotion and collective frustration. While machine-breakers had explicit objectives, incendiarists and threatening letter writers wanted to frighten their target in the hope that they would see the error of their ways. Beyond these cases with observable, tangible outcomes, Swing also allowed for other even less explicit 'protests', the 'polyps' of 'everyday' resistance that make up James Scott's coral reef of protest.[58] One can only speculate what form these acts took during the unfurling of the Swing movement, but it seems highly unlikely that what Keith Snell has identified as 'deferential bitterness' would suddenly cease during the lifecourse of a protest movement.[59] All else being equal, it is probable that many scores were settled by women during Swing, and that many acts of psychological release were performed. Either way, for a movement whose public face was almost exclusively male, Swing was richly written through with an extraordinarily complex gender politics.

Notes

1 E. Hobsbawm and G. Rudé, *Captain Swing* (London: Lawrence & Wishart, 1969), chs 2, 3 and 4.

2 For an excellent overview of the field see: S. King and A. Tomkins (eds) *The Poor in England 1700–1850: An Economy of Makeshifts* (Manchester: Manchester University Press, 2003).

3 J. Burnette, 'The wages and employment of female day-labourers in English agriculture 1740–1850', *Economic History Review*, 57:4 (2004), 664–90; J. Humphries, *Childhood and Child Labour in the British Industrial Revolution* (Cambridge: Cambridge University Press, 2010); K. Sayer, 'Field-faring women: the resistance of women who worked in the fields of nineteenth-century England', *Women's History Review*, 2:2 (1993), 185–98; P. Sharpe 'The female labour market in English agriculture during the Industrial Revolution: expansion or contraction?', *Agricultural History Review*, 47:2 (1999), 161–81; N. Verdon, *Rural Women Workers in 19th-Century England: Gender, Work and Wages* (Woodbridge: Boydell & Brewer, 2003). Also see: E. Higgs, 'Women, occupations and work in the nineteenth century censuses, *History Workshop*, 23 (1987), 59–74; C. Miller, 'The hidden workforce: female field workers in Gloucestershire, 1870–1901', *Southern History*, 6 (1984), 139–53; and K.D.M. Snell, *Annals of the Labouring Poor* (Cambridge: Cambridge University Press, 1985).

4 For a recent example see: S. Williams, 'Earnings, poor relief and the economy of makeshifts: Bedfordshire in the early years of the New Poor Law', *Rural History*, 16:1 (2005), 21–52.

5 Sharpe, 'The female labour market', 161–2; N. Verdon, 'Hay, hops and harvest: women's work in agriculture in nineteenth-century Sussex', in N. Goose (ed.), *Women's Work in Industrial England: Regional and Local Perspectives* (Hatfield: Local Population Studies, 2007), p. 79.

6 Burnette, 'Female day-labourers', 677–8 and 684; R. Allen, *Enclosure and the Yeoman. The Agricultural Development of the South Midlands, 1450–1850* (Oxford: Clarendon Press, 1992); N. Verdon, 'The rural labour market in the early nineteenth century: women's and children's employment, family income, and the 1834 Poor Law Report', *Economic History Review*, 55:2 (2002), 305–13, and 317; B. Hill, *Women, Work and Sexual Politics in Eighteenth-Century England* (Oxford: Blackwell, 1989), pp. 164–5; Verdon, 'Hay, hops and harvest', pp. 84–5.

7 See E.P. Thompson, 'The moral economy of the English crowd in the eighteenth century', *Past & Present*, 50 (1971), 76–136, and Thompson, *Customs in Common* (London: Penguin, 1993), ch. 5 ('The Moral economy reviewed'); J. Bohstedt, 'The myth of the feminine food riot: women as proto-citizens in English community politics, 1790–1810', in H. Applewhite and D. Levy, *Women and Politics in the Age of the Democratic Revolution* (Ann Arbor, MI: The University of Michigan Press, 1990), pp. 21–60; J. Bohstedt,

'Gender, household and community politics: women in English riots 1790–1810', *Past & Present*, 120 (1998), 88–122; Lynne Taylor, 'Food riots revisited', *Journal of Social History*, 30:2 (1996), 483–96.

8 M. Thomis and J. Grimmett, *Women in Protest 1800–1850* (London: Croom Helm, 1982).

9 I. Robertson, 'The role of women in protests in the Scottish Highlands', *Journal of Historical Geography*, 23:2 (1997), 190. For an emphasis on the gendered nature of space in rural England, see B. Reay, *Microhistories: Demography, Society, and Culture in Rural England, 1800–1930* (Cambridge: Cambridge University Press, 1996), esp. pp. 199, 203–5.

10 Verdon, 'Hay, hops and harvest', p. 76; J. Tosh, 'What should historians do with masculinity? Reflections on nineteenth-century Britain', *History Workshop Journal*, 38 (1994), 179–80.

11 For instance see: P. Jones, 'Finding Captain Swing: protest, parish relations, and the state of the public mind in 1830', *International Review of Social History*, 54:3 (2009), 429–58.

12 P. Jones, 'Swing, Speenhamland and rural social relations: the 'moral economy' of the English crowd in the nineteenth century', *Social History*, 32:3 (2007), 272–91.

13 As Tosh has asserted, female work was essential to the public assertion of masculinity: Tosh, 'What should historians do with masculinity', 183.

14 Reay, *Microhistories*, esp. pp. 199, 203–5.

15 E. Ross, *Love and Toil: Motherhood in Outcast London, 1870–1918* (Oxford: Oxford University Press, 1994).

16 HCRO, 92M95/F2/ 8/2: Statement by George Buttley, Soberton, in favour of his labourer Jesse Burgess, n.d. (but early–mid-December 1830).

17 HCRO, 92M95/F2/8/4: Robert Mason, County Gaol to Rev. D. Cockerton, Stoke Charity, 3 January 1831.

18 *Sussex Advertiser*, 6 December 1830.

19 For these arguments see pp. 29–40.

20 TNA, HO 52/10, fos 397–9, Sir Godfrey Webster, Battle Abbey, 12 November 1830, and enclosure.

21 *Hampshire Advertiser* (hereafter *HA*), 27 November 1830. For an excellent micro study of the rising at Owslebury see: A. Howkins, 'The Owslebury lads', *Southern History*, 32 (2010), 117–38.

22 For this tactic during food crises see Chapter 2, pp. 29, 48–9.

23 A. Randall, *Riotous Assemblies: Popular Protest in Hanoverian England* (Oxford: Oxford University Press, 2006), pp. 243, 313. Five Gloucestershire women were charged during Swing of breaking threshing machines, something recorded by Hobsbawm and Rudé in *Captain Swing* (pp. 246–7) but yet to be fully analysed.

24 Hobsbawm and Rudé, *Captain Swing*, p. 195. The anti-enclosure dispute at Otmoor (Oxfordshire) does not count as it represented a long-running protest rather than something inspired by Swing's momentum: D. Eastwood, 'Communities, protest and police in early nineteenth-century Oxfordshire: the enclosure of Otmoor reconsidered', *Agricultural History Review*, 44:1 (1996), 35–46.

25 Some Swing agreements did set piece rates. For an example at Bredhurst see TNA, HO 52/8, fos 95–6, J. Bradley, Sittingbourne to Melbourne, 1 December 1830.

26 Verdon, *Rural Women Workers*, pp. 83–5.

27 *HA*, 19 June 1830.

28 K. Bawn, 'Social Protest, Popular Disturbances and Public Order in Dorset, 1790–1838' (PhD thesis, University of Reading, 1984), p. 89.

29 T. Hardy, *Tess of the D'Urbervilles* (London: Macmillan, 1912), 'Wessex Edition', pp. 414, 416 and 417.

30 *Salisbury and Winchester Journal*, 13 January 1812, 21 October 1816 and 17 November 1817; *Hampshire Chronicle* (hereafter *HC*), 10 May 1813, 8 August 1814, 18 November 1816, 17 November 1817, 8 July 1822, 15 August 1825; *Hampshire Courier*, 8 and 29 August 1814; *Hampshire Telegraph*, 5 September, 31 October 1814, 14 August 1826; *Sussex (Weekly) Advertiser*, 2 December 1816 and 20 December 1819, 10 December 1821 and 14 August 1826; *Kentish Gazette*, 24 August 1821 and 2 January 1829; *Brighton Guardian*, 24 October 1827; *HA*, 1 March 1828; *Brighton Gazette*, 3 September 1829.

31 Flail threshing was primarily a male occupation. However, as Helen Speechley has shown, women were also occasionally employed with the flail: 'Female and child agricultural day labourers in Somerset, c.1685–1870' (PhD thesis, University of Exeter, 1999), pp. 68, 73, 81 and 94.

32 S. Rose, 'Gender antagonism and class conflict: exclusionary strategies of male trade unionists in nineteenth century Britain', *Social History*, 13:2 (1988), 191.

33 For the ways in which early threshing machines were used see: E. Collins, 'The diffusion of the threshing machine in Britain', *Tools and Tillage* 1 (1972), esp. 16–19, 22–7; S. Macdonald, 'The progress of the early threshing machine', *Agricultural History Review* 23:1 (1975), 63–77; N. Fox, 'The spread of the early threshing machine in central southern England', *Agricultural History Review*, 26:1 (1978), 26–32. For the substitution of male labour see: C. Griffin, '"As lated tongues bespoke" Popular protest in south-east England, 1790– 1840' (PhD thesis, University of Bristol, 2002), pp. 136–7.

34 CKS, Q/SBe 120/34, 35 and 14b, Depositions of Ingram Swaine, labourer, Isaac Croucher, labourer, Thomas Larrett, labourer, both 19 October, and John Collick, yeoman, 8 October 1830.

35 CKS, Q/SBe, 120/13, Deposition of George Youens, labourer, 7 October 1830.

36 CKS, Q/SBe, 120/15, Deposition of John Jefferies, labourer, 8 October 1830.

37 N.E. Lerman, A.P. Mohun and R. Oldenziel, 'Versatile tools: gender analysis and the history of technology', *Technology and Culture*, 38:1 (1997), 1–8.

38 C. Griffin, 'The violent Captain Swing?', *Past & Present*, 209 (2010), 172.

39 TNA, HO 52/8, fos 77–8, John Boys, Margate to Phillips, 26 November; *Rochester Gazette*, 30 November; *The Times*, 29 November; *Kent Herald*, 2 December 1830. John Boys was, self-confessedly, the first farmer in Kent to use a threshing machine in 1793, its use being heavily on child labour: *General View of the Agriculture of Kent* (London: Board of Agriculture, 1796), pp. 50–2.

40 Farmer Peckham of Paternoster Hill near Canterbury having lost several sheep, placed his gardener to watch his flock. Two persons duly entered the field, one disguised as a woman, and endeavoured to catch a sheep. A violent

struggle ensued between the men and the gardener, in which the gardener received a pistol shot in the thigh. The shepherd then hit the 'female' with his gun so hard that the gun shattered to pieces (*Maidstone Journal*, 28 April 1812). The other case occurred in July 1826 at Chichester when two young military officers paraded the streets of Chichester 'dressed in female attire'. Their 'gait being rather un-Lady like' attracted the attention of the populace – 'who could also see their boots' – who then began to hoot and hustle them. An altercation took place and they were obliged to seek refuge in a confectioner's shop where a change of dress was procured for them before they were conveyed by the police back to their Barracks 'amid the clamorous revilings of an immense multitude' (*HC*, 17 July 1826). For the resort to cross-dressing in protest see: Robertson, 'The role of women'; and, G. Seal, 'Tradition and agrarian protest in nineteenth-century England and Wales', *Folklore*, 99 (1988), 146–69.

41 Griffin, '"As lated tongues bespoke", chapter 7; TNA, Assi 36/1, Depositions of Witnesses taken 11 September at Sellindge on view of the body of Elizabeth Impett, Kent Lent Assizes 1822, in the case of *The King* v. *John Hayward*.

42 CKS, PS/W4 and W5, Wingham Petty Sessions Minutes, 3 October 1826 and 7 October 1828. Similar attitudes amongst labouring men were found by Reay in the nearby Faversham Blean: *Microhistories*, pp. 104–5.

43 CKS, PS/W4 and W5, Wingham Petty Sessions Minutes, 1 March 1825, 4 August and 1 September 1829.

44 *Maidstone Journal*, 19 October 1830.

45 Hobsbawm and Rudé, *Captain Swing*, pp. 239–49. For an analysis of the social and demographic composition of part of a Swing group see Howkins, 'The Owslebury lads', pp. 124–5.

46 TNA, HO 52/10, fos 373, 369–70, 371–4 and 422–3 and 428, Deposition of Thomas Ackoll, Assistant Overseer and Governor of the Poorhouse, Brede, Sussex, taken before J.B.P. Micklewhaite, Richard Wetherall, and G. Courthope, 6 November 1830, G. Courthope, Whiligh, to Phillips, 6 November (twice), second enclosing deposition of Ackoll, 6 November, Sir Godfrey Webster, Battle, to Peel, 20 November, enclosing examination of Joseph Bryant, labourer, 19 November 1830.

47 *Hastings and Cinque Ports Iris*, 13 November 1830.

48 *Brighton Gazette*, 11 November 1830 and 4 August 1831.

49 *Hampshire Telegraph*, 29 November 1830.

50 For the dynamics of processioning see: T. Pettitt, '"Here comes I, Jack Straw": English folk drama and social revolt', *Folklore*, 95 (1984), 11–12.

51 *HC*, 29 November 1830.

52 J. Archer, '*By a Flash and a Scare*': *Arson, Animal Maiming, and Poaching in East Anglia 1815–1870* (Oxford: Clarendon Press, 1990), pp. 179, 214.

53 *Kent Herald*, 4 and 11 November 1830.

54 WSCRO, QRW/758, fos 161, 226–32, threatening letter sent to John Stoveld, gentleman, Petworth; depositions of John Andrews, servant, Mary Lawerence, servant, John Stoveld, and Sarah Mitchell, servant, all Petworth, 18 December 1830.

55 Hobsbawm and Rudé, *Captain Swing*, pp. 246–7; A. Randall, *Before the*

Luddites: Custom, Community and Machinery in the English Woollen Industry 1776–1809 (Cambridge: Cambridge University Press, 1991), *passim*.

56 A. Howkins and L. Merricks, '"Wee be black as Hell": ritual, disguise and rebellion', *Rural History*, 4:1 (1993), 41–53.

57 TNA, HO 52/7, fos 16–17, J. Westall, Hungerford to Sir Francis Freeling, 22 November 1830.

58 J. Scott, *Weapons of the Weak: Everyday Forms of Peasant Resistance* (Yale: Yale University Press, 1985).

59 K.D.M. Snell, 'Deferential bitterness; the social outlook for rural proleteriat in eighteenth- and nineteenth-century England and Wales', in M. Bush (ed.) *Social Orders and Social Classes in Europe Since 1500: Studies in Social Stratification* (London: Longman, 1992), pp. 158–84.

Part IV

Responses to Swing

By their very definition, protest movements attempt to effect change. In turn, their protests elicit responses, usually both in the form of attempts to suppress their actions, and in the form of policy responses. Before the publication of E.P. Thompson's 'moral economy' paper in 1971,[1] studies of protest tended to offer only brief treatments of the interaction between protestors, their targets and the authorities. Thus, John and Barbara Hammond cursorily detailed the actions of the first Swing trial at Canterbury and the subsequent special commissions, noting that these judicial actions 'crushed' the movement.[2] Hobsbawm and Rudé's *Captain Swing* contained one chapter entitled 'Repression', a breezy, statistically driven account of judicial efforts to repress Swing, focusing especially on the special commissions. This was followed by a somewhat impressionistic chapter examining the 'aftermath' of Swing.[3] What marked Thompson's paper out as novel was that it recognised that protests in the eighteenth-century market were enacted in a 'field of force' which balanced protestors' demands (and force) against the paternalistic and legal responsibilities of their targets and the magistracy, and the judicial force of the local and central state. Collective actions did not occur in an authority-less vacuum, rather, so Thompson asserted, protestors were always alert to how this 'stately gavotte' – the term is Charlesworth's – might play out. This is not to say that all collective protests were necessarily tightly choreographed, but rather that throughout the eighteenth century a system evolved in which all sides in a dispute knew pretty well how each other would react.[4]

While food rioting as a form of mass plebeian action had largely faded out by 1830, many recent protest historians have asserted, as noted in Chapter 6, that moral economy precepts underpinned Swing protests. Calls to 'fairness' – whether in the form of a right to labour, to a living wage, or more humane treatment under the poor laws – were clearly central to Swing, much like the eighteenth century marketplace. But to what extent did the other sides in Swing – on the one side the farmers, clergymen and landowners, on the other the local and national judiciary – continue to be driven by a paternalistic sense of duty and a responsibility to uphold the law (and protect capital)? The following chapters analyse both the nature of the response of the local and national forces of law and order, and the 'social policy' response of vestries and magistrates' benches. It ends with an examination of Hobsbawm and Rudé's contention that the 'draconian punishments distributed' by the government-sponsored special commissions stopped the movement in its tracks, while in those counties little affected by the 'active intervention of the government or magistrates' Swing 'died a natural death'.[5]

Notes

1 E.P. Thompson, 'The moral economy of the English crowd in the eighteenth-century', *Past & Present*, 50 (1971), 73–136.
2 J. and B. Hammond, *The Village Labourer* (London: Longman, 1978), p. 199.
3 E. Hobsbawm and G. Rudé (1969) *Captain Swing* (London: Lawrence & Wishart), chs 13 and 14.
4 Thompson, 'Moral economy'; A. Charlesworth, 'From the moral economy of Devon to the political economy of Manchester, 1790–1812', *Social History*, 17:2 (1993), 210.
5 Hobsbawm and Rudé, *Captain Swing*, pp. 281, 233.

9

Suppressing Swing

It has been understood since the Hammonds' initial analysis that the response to Swing took several forms: evolving from an initial 'lenience' to a centrally coordinated bloody repression. This broad interpretation is not in question – the increasing severity of the sentences and the quickening of the judicial response are self-evident – but there is much about the response that remains obscure. Indeed, only Roger Wells has significantly added to our understanding of Swing's repression.[1] No one has challenged *Captain Swing*'s thesis that it was the outbreak of 'riots' in the Kent and Sussex Weald in early November that provoked Home Secretary Peel into taking 'positive action'. Or that it was not until the election of Lord Grey's Whig government, and the installation of Lord Melbourne as Home Secretary on 23 November, that central government resolutely intervened in suppressing Swing.[2] Nor do we know much, besides Wells interventions and a recent paper by Rose Wallis,[3] about local responses. How did the magistracy react to protest (and the threat of protest) in their jurisdictions? How did the local and central authorities interact in responding to Swing?

This chapter begins with an analysis of the response to the initial acts of machine-breaking in East Kent, including the subsequent trial held at Canterbury. It then goes on consider the local and governmental response to the 'unparalleled lenity' – the words are Peel's – shown to the machine-breakers. It then examines how Swing's rapid westward diffusion was responded to, paying particular attention to the deployment of special constables, the military and yeoman cavalries. The chapter ends with an analysis of the role and impact of central government agents engaged to help procure evidence and prosecute Swing activists at the Hampshire Special Commission and other south-eastern Swing trials.

The response to the Elham machine-breakers

On Monday 30 August, farmer Dodd laid an official information before magistrates Richard Halford and General Mulcaster. Dodd stated that a 'riotous and tumultuous assembly' of one hundred people had already destroyed four threshing machines within his locality, and that he hoped the justices would take such steps as necessary to protect his property. Acting on this information, Halford and Mulcaster, accompanied by some specifically sworn special constables, proceeded to Dodd's farm at Hardres Court. Despite waiting on the premises for 'some hours', nothing occurred and the party returned home. Dodd believed, though, that an attack was still likely, and afraid that a civil power would not be strong enough against the machine-breakers, called for the 7th Dragoons to follow the magistrates from Canterbury. On their arrival, the thirty dragoons were placed at the rear of the farm and were to appear on being given a signal if the civil powers were overwhelmed. Nothing transpired.[4]

This was the first documented involvement of the magistracy and military in Swing. In the following acts of machine-breaking there was remarkably little intervention, one informer from Paddlesworth even claiming that the area was in anarchy and that the local magistrates 'encourage them on'. The Paddlesworth correspondent also requested that Peel should send down two 'Bow Street Officers', providing they 'avoid the County Justices'.[5] The first evidence of concerted action came in the form of a meeting of magistrates and 'gentlemen' held at the Halfway House, Womenswold, on 22 September. Chaired by grandee Sir Brook Brydges, it was resolved that the parish constables in the different hundreds were, prior to a meeting at Canterbury on Saturday 25 September, to send in lists of all individuals who might be called upon to be sworn in as special constables.[6]

Charles Sandys, clerk to the Canterbury Bench, duly sent a letter to the Home Office – the first official communication of events in East Kent to the Home Office. The magistrates, Sandys reported, were 'finding it difficult to procure any evidence' against the machine-breakers, and would be 'happy to receive any Communication or advice which you may think proper to offer them'.[7] Still, at the Canterbury meeting the enrolment of special constables went ahead, while a subscription was raised to offer a reward of £500 for sufficient evidence to convict the ringleaders. On the same day, the 'Farmers of East Kent' met at the Rose Inn,

Canterbury. This meeting was also attended by Knatchbull who, with ironic foresight, stated his belief that 'the laws of our country ought not to be violated in this disgraceful manner ... an end should be brought to these unlawful proceedings, or they might lead to more serious results'. The chairman was Edward Hughes, whose machine had been broken on 22 September. If 'the Magistrates ... had not taken those early steps which they might have,' Hughes proclaimed, 'they had certainly now come forward with great energy.'[8]

Sometime before 2 October, the exact dating being unclear, Bow Street police officer George Leadbitter was sent to Elham to investigate. There is no record of Knatchbull having called for the assistance of a police officer.[9] Leadbitter's role, it seems, was as a general go-between. He was deployed, by Price, to take the charged to the gaol at Canterbury. He also offered advice to the magistrates, something Price was only too happy to call upon to do, although he had 'not the slightest clue to [the protocol of] proceedings'.[10] Arguably more important was the intervention of Elham vicar Rev. Bramall between 22 and 27 September. Without being prompted, Bramall decided that it was his pastoral responsibility to attempt to convince the men to surrender voluntarily. Fifty men came forward, many of whom claimed to have been press-ganged into taking part in the machine-breaking outings. Some had been bribed beyond resistance with beer, while others had been genuinely under the impression that it was not illegal to break threshing machines. When told by Bramall that it was an offence punishable by law, they were persuaded that it would lessen their chances of conviction if they confessed.[11] Although the men had made a pact 'that if any constable came to take any of them the others were to rescue them' and that if any of them gave evidence against them 'the others would kill them', their statements were duly taken.[12]

Rev. Price was also spurred into action by a comment from the farmers that he did not view the events with the same horror. Attending a second meeting of the farmers, Price made it clear that he abhorred machine-breaking.[13] With some depositions now taken, he also began proceedings against the supposed ringleaders. On the morning of 27 September the constables caught Edward Read, one of the 'Head Men'. Later that evening, Price arrested Ingram Swaine, the supposed lead figure, but did not manage to capture Swaine's co-resident William Spicer who fled the house. Over the next few days the other ringleaders were also captured and the recognisances of thirty-seven men were taken to appear at the next Kent Assizes, if they were called.[14] Knatchbull duly wrote to Peel so as to give the impression that all was now well. The 'disturbances' had been 'confined entirely' to the destruction of threshing machines, the three 'very active' persons apprehended had confessed, and a 'great number of Persons implicated will voluntarily surrender themselves'. There was, in short, no need to offer the King's pardon for accomplices who came forward.[15] Undersecretary Phillips, writing on Peel's behalf, approved of the magistrates' actions, but tempered Bramall's Christian actions with clear formal legal advice: 'He [Peel] feels confident that the Magistracy will take as much care as possible in discharging persons, who may voluntarily surrender, on their own Recognizances'. The ringleaders though had to be made an example of.[16]

Price's change of tone and rediscovery of his magisterial brief were perceived as a betrayal by the machine-breakers. Price received intelligence in the afternoon of Monday 4 October that he might expect 'a Body of the rioters to wait on me ... to ascertain whether the machines shall be put down, if they will surrender themselves, and return, like Good Boys to their Duty'. Contacting Knatchbull for advice as how to respond, Price believed that he should make 'no concession – no compromise of course', but could not see what option he had but to give the labourers an affirmative answer. In the event, Knatchbull had no time to respond. On the night of 5 October, Price's barn, full of wheat and barley, and eight stacks in his farmyard were reduced to ashes.[17] Price had paid for his inconsistency. Bramall too feared reprisals, horrified that the men who volunteered themselves might feel that he entrapped them. 'I may have acted indiscreetly in what I have done', he admitted to Price, 'but I took no step without seeking that aid which a Christian ministry is bound to ask for in the hour of peril and difficulty.'[18] Knatchbull duly contacted Peel, who responded with an offer of a reward of £100 to capture the incendiarist. The offer was, Peel was at pains to point out to avoid setting precedence, made only because Price was a county magistrate.[19]

By the time of the trial, Knatchbull's hands were tied. He had even written in a state of desperation to Lord Lieutenant Camden in mid-October – and subsequently forwarded to Peel – stating a need for assistance. While Camden's request for a blanket reward in all cases of incendiarism was refused – 'the *invariable* practice of the

Home Department even in the worst of times' – a pardon would be extended to any accomplice offering sufficient evidence to convict incendiarists. Additionally, without specific prompting, Peel would seek the dispatch of extra troops to Canterbury to 'assist the magistracy'.[20]

At the East Kent Quarter Sessions, held at Canterbury on 22 October, both Price and Camden were present along with twenty-two other magistrates. Knatchbull, in his preamble to the Grand Jury, made the astonishing confession that he did not understand the nature of the evidence in support of the charges for he had not had enough time to read the lengthy depositions. The case was simple, though: anyone who was with the machine-breakers at the time of destruction was guilty of aiding and abetting. If the evidence was satisfactory, unusually none of the evidence coming from the victims of the arraigned crimes, Knatchbull reminded the Grand Jury that they must find the men guilty. Much turned therefore on the admissibility of two accomplices who had turned King's evidence against their fellow accused.

All the men, bar David Arnold, had admitted their guilt in being present. Pollock, the prosecution counsel, decided he would not trouble the court with the evidence, thus bizarrely acquitting Arnold despite his having admitted his guilt to a non-indicted offence. That the men had acted 'under ill and dangerous advice, and upon mistaken notions of your interest and welfare' were not mitigating circumstances, but, Knatchbull continued, because so many of their fellow villagers had also come forward to admit their also being present he could not sentence them to the maximum seven years' transportation. Instead they were each to be gaoled for four days without hard labour. By way of deterrent, Knatchbull concluded by warning that any future machine-breakers would, if found guilty, be subject to the full force of the law.[21]

After the trial

The day after the trial a further five machines were broken in East Kent, one being broken in broad daylight for the first time, while another was destroyed at Hartlip, some thirty miles distant from Elham. According to magistrate Rev. Poore, there was a regular 'intercourse with those concerned in breaking the machines (& and I fear the Incendiaries) at the two extremities of the county, as they in this neighbourhood have been heard to say, they could obtain the assistance of one Hundred men from either or both parts whenever required'.[22] This supposed confederacy came as no surprise to the farmers of East Kent, who were quick to point the blame at Knatchbull. George Gipps, a landowner at Bekesbourne, and subsequent first Governor of New Zealand, claimed that the sentences had led to 'nightly alarm and destruction of property'. Sir Henry Montresor, who had already lost his threshing machine to the Elham men, wrote in disgust to Knatchbull raging that: 'the subsequent outrages bear out [my] arguments ... temporizing with anarchists seldom succeeds; as a seditious and revolutionary spirit pervades the country nothing less than the extreme rigors of the law, will preserve social order'.[23]

Critically, Peel's tone underwent a dramatic change. 'I should have thought a severe example in the case of Destruction of farming property would have had a much greater effect', he wrote to Camden, 'than the unparalleled lenity shown to the Destroyers of Thrashing Machines.'[24] In reply, Camden related that Knatchbull would 'inflict the severest sentence' on any future machine-breakers, but did not defend Knatchbull: 'The County wants something to show that the authorities have not been asleep.'[25] Knatchbull made no initial response, declaring instead at a meeting of the Kent justices on 1 November that the sentences could not have been otherwise under circumstances that he was not at liberty to disclose, an allusion to the compromised position in which Brammall and Price had placed themselves.[26]

In responding to the protests that occurred beyond the area operated by the Elham gang, the local authorities showed an increased willingness to intervene directly. The outbreak of protests in the vicinity of Lenham on 25 October prompted the magistrates led by the Earl of Winchelsea to swear in special constables, though many of those called were unwilling to take the oath.[27] Poore also requested that a troop of Dragoons be stationed at Faversham. On the night of the mass machine-breaking at Ash and Wingham, 'soldiers' were likewise called out by the Wingham Bench to arrest seven of the suspects.[28] This was a palpably different, and considerably more urgent, response than to the events at Elham.

The authorities and local property owners were also far quicker in calling for central government assistance. After an incendiary fire at Borden near Sittingbourne, Poore requested that a reward be offered by the Home Office and that a police officer be sent to help investigate. Both were duly obliged. A few days later, Poore also requested that some dragoons should be stationed at Sittingbourne.[29] The Ash protests similarly prompted the local magistrates to request that 'active officers' be sent to help, one to be stationed at Ash and one at Canterbury. Knatchbull, reporting to Peel that 'strangers' were exciting 'the people' throughout the county, supported these calls: it was 'extremely probable that intelligent officers station'd as required, may render much service to the Magistrates'.[30] But there was still disquiet regarding the supposed inactivity of the local magistrates, Rev. Gleig of Ash warning the Home Office that the magistracy 'seem afraid to act' and that the case needed to be 'taken up' by the government.[31]

The extension of protests beyond the Elham area, and the evidence of unease regarding the ability of the magistracy to stop further protests, stiffened Peel's resolve. First, his anger was translated into action, informing Camden as early as the 26 October that he would 'adopt any Measures' and 'incur any Expense' in the 'suppression of the Outrages'. To this end, 'some-one well versed in Criminal Business & in the art of detecting crime' and supported by 'a certain number of Police Officers' would be placed at Camden and the 'most active' of the Kent magistrate's 'disposal'. In return, Camden had to promise that this intervention would not 'induce any relaxation' in the 'activity' of the magistrates. Camden assented, and suggested that as Kent was such 'an extensive county' the support should be sent to both Maidstone and Canterbury. This advice was ignored, and once Cabinet approval had been given, Treasury Solicitor Maule was sent to Maidstone, arriving on 31 October.[32]

Issuing Maule his charge, Phillips commented that 'there has been a good deal of inactivity or want of concert among the Magistracy in general' and in consequence that Peel 'attaches the greatest importance to your mission' – the 'mission' later being extended into Sussex and, four days before Peel was replaced, to act as the prosecutor of the machine-breakers at the Maidstone Winter Assizes.[33] Another direct response was Peel's summoning to Whitehall of the two magistrates who had requested the dispatch of police officers to help apprehend the Ash machine-breakers. In contrast to his earlier statement in relation to the Sevenoaks' fires – 'How can I *commence "a system of cooperation"* with the local authorities   they who have local knowledge   local experience [to] point out to me what way I can assist them?' – he now wished to impress on the Kentish justices the need for action.[34]

Reacting to rapid diffusion: civil forces

In the meantime, the Kentish magistracy was struggling to enrol special constables, there being a seemingly universal refusal to take the oath. At Faversham this refusal was attributed to 'fear ... attended with political prejudices' made worse by the fact that a fire at nearby Selling Court generated 'so great [a] ... panic that it appeared ... as if all men [were] paralysed'.[35] Attempts to swear in specials at Maidstone in advance of the mass general meeting on Penenden Heath also failed, necessitating calls for military assistance.[36] Likewise, a general meeting of the Ashford Bench was also met by the refusal of most of those called to be sworn, the *Kent Herald* noting a culture of 'dissent' in the area. Such was the heady blend of anti-government feeling, fear of reprisals and solidarity with the farmworkers' cause.[37]

The spread of Swing into the Weald created even greater problems. When protests broke out in Battle and Brede there were no troops stationed in an area that stretched from Maidstone to Brighton. Moreover, many farmers actively supported the men in helping to force tithe and rent reductions and refused to act in any repressive capacity. For instance at Robertsbridge, farmers were not only for the first time openly in support of the men but also directly opposed the magistrates.[38] Such refusals were integral to the form and discourse of Wealden Swing. Nowhere was this more clearly evident than at Cranbrook. After a week of 'mobbing' in the vicinity, on 16 November several hundred individuals were summoned from the nearby parishes to be sworn as special constables. All those from Staplehurst and Marden refused, while only three of those from Appledore and Woodchurch and two from Cranbrook took the oath. According to Cobbett, the farmers and tradesmen declared that they were 'not afraid of the poor' as they too were 'worn down' by tithes, taxes and rents and therefore had 'nothing to lose'.[39]

Against this backdrop there is some evidence that pressure was being used to compel the employees of local grandees to take the oath, for instance at Mayfield all those employed at the Castle were sworn under compulsion.[40] Pressure could also be applied more subtly. At Battle, substantial landlords George Courthope and Sir Godfrey Webster informed Peel that they had 'appointed' specials 'not under the compulsory scheme' to 'make them as friends instead of enemies', thereby placing considerable pressure on their own tenants to come forward and identity themselves as 'friends'.[41] Elsewhere, in those areas dominated by large estates, there is further evidence that tenants and employees of noblemen were treated as feudal retainers. Around Lewes, the Earl of Chichester and Lord Gage were reported in early December to have 'enrolled … some of their tenants' as potential members of a yeomanry force. Thirty of the Duke of Richmond's tenants in West Sussex were similarly enrolled and armed as part of a mounted force.[42]

As Swing moved westward beyond the Weald less resistance was made by those summoned to be sworn, essentially a function of the lower numbers of the economically marginal small farmers so predominant in the Weald and the Kentish downland and the greater influence of large landowners. But there is no sense in which the swearing in of special constables in East and mid-Sussex was being done proactively, instead incendiary fires, especially in parishes bordering market towns such as Arundel and Lewes, acted as the trigger.[43] This was a policy adopted not as a deterrent but as a tool of repression.

Under Peel's watch, the enrolment of special constables was not a de facto Home Office policy. Two days after taking office, Melbourne shifted the Home Office's policy to an active promotion of the Duke of Richmond's so-called 'Sussex Constabulary Plan'. For his native West Sussex, Richmond had proposed that a constabulary force comprising 'shopkeepers, yeomen, and "respectable" labourers'. Once enrolled, specials were to be organised into divisions with individual sections sent out 'after a manner of a military occupation by a hostile army' to the villages 'whether already rebellious or likely to become so', a system that was used to great effect in putting down protests in the vicinity of Chichester. Richmond could not, in the words of the *Portsmouth, Portsea and Gosport Herald*, be 'given enough credit' in 'restoring' the 'peace'. 'We hope to see the plan', commented the *Brighton Gazette*, 'generally adopted' and implemented in 'exact imitation' of the Richmond's 'manner of proceeding'.[44] Melbourne's recommendation came in the form of an official circular issued on 25 November by which time Swing had effectively fizzled out in the south-east. While the 'Sussex Plan' had been effectively deployed in the North Western and South Western divisions of Sussex,[45] the only (formal) application to the Home Office by south-east local authorities to adopt the plan was from the Lower South Aylesford Bench, Kent – and this as late as 8 December.[46]

Evidence for Hampshire also suggests that, with some exceptions, the plan was largely adopted after Swing had swept through the county. Particularly telling is the fact that the meeting of Hampshire magistrates chaired by Lord Lieutenant the Duke of Wellington did not mention special constables, merely that 'all occupiers of Land, and respectable Inhabitants of Towns and Villages, be called upon to co-operate with the Magistrates ... for putting down all unlawful assemblies'. Moreover, it was not until 2 December, a week the circular was sent out, that the Hampshire magistrates met regarding dividing the county into divisions.[47] The first explicit evidence that the plan was being adopted in Hampshire came in the form of official communications from Lieutenant Colonel Mair, dispatched by Melbourne to advise magistrates and help coordinate civil forces in Hampshire and the south-west in late November. Mair reported that the Mayor of Winchester 'cannot see the necessity of the organised system', but that he hoped to convince him and put in place a force to help in 'conveying prisoners and witnesses' to the Special Commission.[48] The use of special constables in Hampshire was similarly reactive, for instance at Fareham and Havant.[49] There is also evidence that in the other early Hampshire Swing centres of the Dever Valley and Andover that special constables were sworn in as a response to the emergent protests. Yet even after such augmentations, letter writers to the Home Office bemoaned the fact that their forces were inadequate to the strength of the protestors. Military support, it was asserted, was therefore essential.[50]

None of this is to say that the use of special constables could not be a successful strategy in putting down protests. Groups of Swing activists were put down by groups of special constables in the villages surrounding Romsey, Itchen Abbas and near Downton, where a large part of the group responsible for the destruction of the machine works at Fordingbridge were dispersed and the 'ringleaders' captured.[51] There is also evidence that in some rural jurisdictions specials were sworn in proactively. Thus at Odiham (22 November) and Hartley Wintney (23 November) in north Hampshire, specials were sworn in without any immediate resort to protest. The strategy appeared to be successful, for despite protests in neighbouring parishes, no protests are recorded as subsequently occurring in either parish.[52]

An alternative solution was to request the assistance of a London police officer, a practice going back to Henry Fielding's founding of the 'Bow Street Runners' in 1749.[53] As noted, requests for their dispatch during Swing were many, though not all requests were assented to, as at Ash-next-Sandwich, largely a function of availability. When available, both Peel and Melbourne readily dispatched police officers to assist the magistrates in investigating Swing cases. Sometimes police officers were used as spies to help infiltrate radical groups, as at Horsham. In other cases they were used to infiltrate Swing groups. At Deal, officer Bishop had 'gone to the different Pot Houses in the villages disguised among the labourers'. The Duke of Buckingham at Avington had secured the services of two officers, and, in anticipation of an attack on his mansion, had them disguised in labourers' dress to spend an evening visiting local public houses to ascertain the 'different plans'. On this information, several 'key individuals' were 'marked out' and a plan was adopted to arrest them.[54]

It is difficult to assess how many officers were deployed in the suppression of south-eastern Swing, owing to the fragmented nature of the evidence: some cases were recorded in the official record of officers' dispatch,[55] others in Phillips's letters, and some in records not of the Home Office's making – and the often clandestine nature of officers' missions – '[dispatched] into the country upon special business' being the favoured wording of the official register. However, London police officers were vital in arresting, and establishing cases against, many Swing activists. The many requests for such assistance attest to their perceived usefulness, and the repeated reports in the archive of their assisting the magistrates their actual importance.

Reacting to rapid diffusion: military

Beyond being reliant on their own horses for mobility and their own arms for protection, special constables' power was limited by, in the words of one Hampshire magistrate, a 'want of competence + the fear of retribution from the Mob'.[56] Even special constables who had just taken the oath were prone to be unreliable. One of the men arrested in connection with machine-breaking on the Isle of Thanet was a recently enrolled special.[57] Not only were military forces properly armed, they could also act in any jurisdiction, something not legally true of specials. Moreover, the very appearance of soldiers or cavalrymen would often cause fear or dread among protestors. As the respondent of the *Portsmouth, Portsea and Gosport Herald* related concerning an assemblage at Littleton, near Winchester, on the 'first appearance of the soldiers most of the mob fled.'[58]

As Swing unfurled beyond East Kent, correspondents to the Home Office emphatically – and with increasing frequency – did call for military support. And when there were troops to be shuffled from one supposedly quiescent place to a riotous place, Peel and Melbourne would often sanction their dispatch. Indeed, despite Melbourne's later criticism of Peel's pandering to those magistrates 'who saw in every burnt hay-stack a sign of bloody revolution' by agreeing to the dispatch of troops, he dispatched more troops than Peel ever did.[59] Initially such agreements were piecemeal. At the beginning of October in Kent, there were dragoons barracked at Canterbury and Maidstone, large numbers foot soldiers at Chatham and Sheerness, a substantial artillery and rifle presence at Dover, with a small number of riflemen stationed at Hythe and Winchelsea.[60] While mid-Kent and East Kent were well served with mobile cavalry troops, the Weald, south Kent, Thanet and the north Kent coast were either entirely bereft of troops or only had those units ill-suited to crowd control. Peel's response to this paucity of coverage was, in response to pleas from Poore and the Maidstone magistrates, to authorise the dispatch of a cavalry force from Canterbury to Sittingbourne on 26 October, and a further cavalry force assisted by two artillery pieces to bolster numbers at Maidstone on 31 October.[61]

Responses to requests for troops in the Weald might also suggest an as-and-when approach to troop deployments. Certainly letters to Egremont and Sir Godfrey Webster on 10 and 11 November respectively authorised sending additional troops into the Weald – even though this was 'not very easy to comply with'.[62] However, a comparison of the troop deployment registers of 1 October and 4 November in the papers of the Commander-in-Chief of the British Army Lord Hill demonstrates that there had been some apparently proactive movement of troops, most notably into the hitherto troop-free Weald. Fourteen troops of cavalry were now stationed at Tunbridge Wells, with small detachments stationed at Tenterden, Mayfield and Rotherfield, and Battle. Troops were also strengthened and dispersed throughout Romney Marsh, West Sussex, and east, mid- and north Hampshire.[63] This reorganisation seemingly predated Peel's 12 November announcement to Camden that he and Lord Hill had devised a plan to 'reinforce' the military in Kent and Sussex.[64] Either way, Hill realised the need to coordinate the military response and be proactive in the face of a now rapidly diffusing movement. Under the day-to-day command of General Dalbiac, initially stationed in Maidstone, the troops were to provide rapid assistance to any magistrate on application to their troop's commanding officer.[65]

On 18 November the plan was revised. Extra troops were drafted into Horsham from Dorchester, leaving the West of England without a cavalry force, and into 'West Sussex' from the garrison at Portsmouth. This support was offered with the proviso that the West Sussex magistrates met to devise a plan against further gatherings, and that a yeoman cavalry be raised.[66] A day later this force was augmented with an additional squadron of cavalry drafted into Dorking, who themselves were on sent to Guildford on 20 November in order to prevent an expected affray. The 2nd Surrey Militia had even been made available to prevent any disturbance in Guildford.[67] The threat of further violence at Horsham, not least a plot to force open the county gaol, prompted Peel to dispatch a further forty foot guards from London to act as an armed guard.[68]

As late as 18 November, the day after Swing first became manifest in overt form in Hampshire, Peel authorised the movement of cavalry troops from Dorchester and 100 infantrymen from Portsmouth to reinforce the military presence in West Sussex.[69] By the following day it had become obvious that troops could no longer be moved from the western counties to Sussex. Indeed, the simultaneous diffusion of Swing into several parts of Hampshire effectively rendered even revised versions of the Hill-Peel plan unworkable. The machine-breaking and wages demonstrations on the Hampshire-Sussex border could be dealt with, militarily, by the recent reinforcements in and around Chichester. The protests in the Dever Valley and around Alresford could not. The unravelling of the Hill-Peel plan was rendered complete by coincident demands for troops from Berkshire. As Phillips related on 20 November in response to a request for military assistance at Newbury, Peel wanted to 'help' but could not 'at present' send any troops to Berkshire. That mid-Hampshire was given priority was simply a function of the fact that detachments of the 41st Regiment barracked on the Isle of Wight and at Portsmouth could easily march to Winchester – ordered to so do by telegraph on 20 November – and the cavalry force currently marching from Dorset en route to West Sussex could more easily be diverted to Winchester than Newbury.[70]

Over the following days, further troops were drafted into Hampshire, most notably to Alton, Andover and Basingstoke, while troops already barracked at Portsmouth were 'dispersed' into south Hampshire. Most proceeded to their new stations by 'forced marches' but such was the perceived urgency at Alresford after the 'attack' on the Grange that soldiers were transported in carriages drawn by the post horses. Over the following days these troops were further shuffled around Hampshire. On 23 November, two extra troops of the 3rd Dragoons arrived at Winchester from Chichester accompanied by reserve companies of the 90th Regiment of Foot (a.k.a. the Perthshire Volunteers), in turn the detachment of the 47th Regiment that arrived in the county town on the previous Saturday left for Bishop's Waltham. On the same day, Major General Sir Colin Campbell, assuming the same role taken by Dalbaic but for the south-west district, arrived from Portsmouth with his staff to establish Winchester as his head quarters. On the following day further divisions of the 47th Regiment arrived at Winchester from Portsmouth.[71]

These troop movements provided the essential framework for the military suppression of the Swing in Hampshire. Besides, by the time these troops had reached their new stations the wave of open protest that had spread into Hampshire from Sussex had almost run out of steam. Indeed, by 26 November, Campbell had authorised the dispatch of 'about half' of the cavalry force hitherto stationed at Winchester westward to Wiltshire, Dorset and the Somerset borders. Further dragoons subsequently left Winchester for Fordingbridge on 27 November, followed the next day by detachments for Romsey, Ringwood and Blandford. Agreements that the Coastal Blockade and Preventative Water Guard assist the civil powers on the Isle of Thanet in Kent and the Isle of Wight were the last extensions of military power in the south-east.[72]

While demands for troops and a readiness to dispatch forces to assist the civil forces betrayed a belief in the effectiveness of the military in suppressing protests there were limitations. Certainly, some Swing activists thought that soldiers were unlikely to act against protesting groups. As detailed in Chapter 4, those attending the mass meeting at Penenden Heath on 2 November were asked to 'respect the soldiers for they are friends'. Similarly, the machine-breaking group active at Saint Lawrence Wootton, Hampshire, on 22 November when warned by a local gentleman that they ought 'to take care as soldiers were coming' retorted that 'the Soldiers won't fire upon us'.[73] Nor do we know whether the strengthened military presence acted to deter would-be protestors, though some commentators did make this connection. For instance, Sir Godfrey Webster reported to the Home Office on 8 November that the arrival of the military at Battle had made a 'big impact'. However, on the following day the 'farmer's men' gathered to 'intimidate' the Battle Bench, necessitating military intervention in the arrest of the ringleaders. Similarly, at Andover it was asserted that 'all reflecting men too plainly perceive, it is only the presence of the Military, that we can look to for permanent security'.[74] But such statements were just this, perceptions.

Assisting the civil forces in taking prisoners was by far the most important role assumed by the military, not least in Hampshire where troops were more readily available from the first appearance of protests. The experience in and around Havant was indicative. A civil force of magistrates and mounted special constables 'took' the ringleaders of the machine-breaking group at Westbourne, the military meeting the 'requirements of civil authorities in a ready manner', while at nearby Southwick 'a great body of men armed with bludgeons' lurking in the copses fled on 'the sight of the troops and other preparations in order "to give them a warm reception"'.[75] Similar claims were made at Andover. Beyond asserting that the military had helped to suppress the 'open violence + rapine' in the neighbourhood, the Andover Bench noted that the troops had been vital in apprehending several persons active at the destruction of Tasker's Foundry.[76] This pattern of military support to civil forces in arresting 'ringleaders', forcing all other protestors to flee, and duly escorting the prisoners to gaol proved effective throughout the county, with the cases at Littleton, Shirrel Heath near Wickham, Luzborough near Romsey, Kings Somborne, West Heath near Basingstoke, Fawley, Liss and South Stoneham providing a high proportion of all prisoners subsequently tried at the Hampshire Special Commission.[77]

By early December Hampshire no longer looked like a county under siege. Most detachments of the 47th Regiment had returned to Portsmouth, with Campbell also relocating the headquarters of the south-west division back to Portsmouth. Two troops of the 2nd Regiment of Lifeguards had left the city for Windsor, while the 90th Regiment were under orders to be ready to depart for Manchester.[78] A military force did remain in Winchester to guard against any attempt to liberate the prisoners (as had already happened at Andover) and to insure against any disturbance during the Special Commission, but as early as 10 December the Mayor had been told to ready the city for the withdrawal of the troops. The security of the city and the county at large was now to be secured by the civil constabulary forces.[79] A similar situation pertained elsewhere, with troops withdrawn to meet the perceived need for military assistance in the west and the Home Counties. Such was the sudden shift, that Lewes, the location of the forthcoming Sussex Winter Assizes, now had no troops, necessitating an application for assistance anew.[80]

Yeomanries

One quasi-military alternative to relying on troops was to call on yeoman cavalries first embodied during the Napoleonic Wars, a tactic successfully adopted in the south-east during the food crises of the 1790s.[81] While yeomanries in parts of Dorset, Somerset and Wiltshire had not been disbanded and took an active part in putting down Swing groups, in the south-east all yeomanry forces had long since been disbanded. Initially, in response to the spread of Swing beyond East Kent, Peel positioned the re-embodiment of yeoman cavalries at the heart of public policy. In response to an assertion by Sir J. Wrottesley in the House of Commons that the Home Secretary 'must go further' in assisting the local authorities, Peel stated that Knatchbull would say that he (Peel) had done 'all he could'. The Treasury Solicitor was at Maidstone, 'at considerable expense and much inconvenience to the public service', and every spare London police officer had been sent to Kent. As the House had previously supported the reduction/dissolution of local yeomanry forces, '[Peel] he did not think it a little unreasonable to say, when a disturbance broke out that the government ought not to leave it to the local authorities to quell the disturbance'. It was therefore the role of government, on behalf of the House, to provide military support, but that as the House had also supported reductions in the cavalry and the infantry, local forces should be re-established to take the pressure off the already stretched military forces.[82]

The first – recorded – call for the yeomanry to be reformed came in a letter from a landowner and an MP in the Darenth Valley in response to the late autumn wave of incendiarism in the locality. Fearful that as the 'Magistrates seem paralysed – & village constables are afraid to act', if government did not take the lead and 'sanction the arming of the Bourgeois classes illegal associations for the protection of property will spring up, especially with the example of the Continent before their eyes'. It was not until Peel's speech in the Commons and in a letter to Lord Lieutenant Camden on 2 November that the government supported re-embodiments:

> I cannot but think the re-organisation [of the Kent Corps of Yeomanry] would do more to check the spirit of outrage ... than the presence of a military force ... it appears to be the natural and most effectual check upon the organised mobs.

Eight days later, it now being apparent that the Sussex Weald was truly under Swing's hold, Peel also wrote to Lord Lieutenant Egremont, suggesting that in addition to the 'military aid' sent to East Sussex a yeomanry force should be organised in the Hastings and Battle districts.[83]

While the nobility and gentry enthusiastically responded to Peel's policy – the arrangements for embodying several troops in East Kent being already completed by 18 November – it soon ran into opposition. Echoing problems with swearing in special constables, the fledgling yeoman cavalries in Kent were running into difficulties recruiting enough privates, partly because many farmers supported the labourers' cause. Only *'feudal retainers'*, claimed the *Kent Herald*, agreed to 'a service so unpopular and useless'. Opposition in West Kent was equally entrenched. At a meeting of farmers at Rochester, convened by the High Sheriff to propose the re-formation of the yeomanry, no one came forward to enrol in the force. Mr Bentley, chairman to the Kent Agricultural Association, believed that while landlords, clergy and government extracted such high rents, tithes and taxes but 'contributed nothing' towards restoring tranquillity in the country, the farmers should not be expected to cooperate.[84] Similar oppositions were also made in Sussex and in Hampshire. Even Egremont, in response to the second appeal, believed that although it would be possible to raise such a force 'in West Sussex as far as Lewes' – an admission of the certain opposition of the Wealden farmers – such a force would not be ready to act on disturbances without arms, and then the process of arming must be done publicly for otherwise it 'might look like a declaration of war'.[85]

When Lord Grey's ministry took office, there was no public reassertion of Peel's promotion of the reformation of yeoman cavalries. Instead, Melbourne dealt with all suggestions that local yeomanries be re-embodied on a case-by-case basis, though he made it clear that 'it appears to me, that Associations of a more civil character would be better suited to the present circumstances'.[86] Ultimately, such problems were of no material consequence in the repression of south-eastern Swing, for none of the forces there were embodied in time to help in the suppression of open protests in 1830. The only role that these new yeomanries could – and did assume – in the south-east was the safe conveyance of prisoners and witnesses during the Swing trials.[87]

Prosecuting Swing I: beyond the trial of the Elham machine-breakers

The trial of the Elham machine-breakers was a pivotal moment in the unfurling of Swing. The response to Knatchbull's 'lenient' sentences and his promise that future machine-breakers would receive the most severe sentence available under law necessitated a different response.[88] On the resumption of machine-breaking in Kent, Knatchbull informed Peel that it would be necessary to 'speedily' hold a special sessions. Sir Edward's haste though was tempered by the time needed to build strong cases against those brought to trial. As such, depositions were taken in the case of the Ash machine-breakers as late as 20 November, the Sessions opening six days later.[89]

While Knatchbull remained in charge in East Kent, Maule oversaw the process in West Kent. In addition to trying to uncover evidence of a plot by metropolitan radicals to stir up discontent in Maidstone, Maule's brief was to 'to give spirit and courage to the Magistrates, by assisting them with your advice and by cordial cooperation', his first engagement being a meeting of some seventy county magistrates at Maidstone.[90] While the investigation of incendiarism was at the forefront of Maule's mission, much of his time was spent investigating the Robert Price and John Adams-led disturbances at Hollingbourne and the destruction of a threshing machine at Borden. Later he also went to investigate the events at Battle, his mission there supported by police officer W.B. Edwards, dispatched from London on 11 November, who stayed on when Maule returned to Maidstone.[91]

The myriad letters received by the Home Office stating that the respondents were to selectively pick those sent to the courts from the numerous Swing activists lodged in custody, on recognisances or on bail, received stock replies from Peel: it was up to the courts to decide who was actually prosecuted. The correspondence between Hawkhurst magistrate Collingwood and Peel provides a useful example. Collingwood had suggested to Peel that it 'would be expedient to prosecute artisans, carpenters, tailors, bricklayers and a smuggler because they have nothing to do with Threshing Machines'. This was also meditated by the same fear being investigated by Maule, specifically that the involvement of artisans and those known to live in total contempt for the law was symptomatic of a politically driven rural insurrection. Collingwood also suggested that he use his discretion as a magistrate in other ways. One man he had committed to trial, he subsequently discovered, was 'an excellent moral good boy' whom he regretted committing for he was 'now in Maidstone gaol with some of the greatest rascals in Kent. It will be his ruin,' Peel's response, issued by Phillips, was succinct. In future Collingwood was to 'make no such distinction[s]'.[92]

This was so much judicially correct bombast. Maule and the magistrates were given a totally free hand to decide whom to commit to trial, even the usual worries about the cost of bringing cases to trial was an irrelevance: 'you must not think of *expense* in considering the expediency of prosecuting', was the advice issued to Maule by Peel in the case of an alleged female arsonist. Beyond Peel's stipulation that the government would only fund cases of felony and those 'linked' to Swing, Maule effectively had complete discretion in deciding whose cases should be brought to trial, in which cases of felony the prosecution would be funded by the Treasury, and in which cases the prosecution would be funded by the county rates. Maule's brief was further extended on 19 November when Peel endorsed Maule's wish to act as the prosecution counsel in the case of those prisoners selected to be tried by the government at the East Kent Special Sessions on 25 November.[93]

While a few cases of assault and theft were also tried, the Sessions was dominated by Swing prosecutions. Eleven prisoners were indicted for breaking various machines in the Ash area; eight prisoners for cases of machine-breaking in the Bekesbourne area – a ninth man turned King's evidence; and five for riot and assault at Ruckinge. Of these 24 prisoners, 1 was transported for life, 6 were transported for seven years, 8 were jailed for twelve months, 2 for nine months, 1 for six months, 3 for three months, 1 for one month, and 1 for fourteen days. Only one of the 24 was found not guilty. Knatchbull had been unequivocal. On discharging the Petty Jury, he exclaimed that 'he hoped the sentences passed that day would be the means of deterring persons from engaging in those lawless acts'.[94]

Before the Special Sessions opened, Melbourne had been installed as Home Secretary under Lord Grey's new ministry. Beyond a change of tone, in matters judicial there were two dramatic shifts in policy. First, the proclamation of 23 November offering a £50 reward for information leading to convictions in cases of 'riot' and £500 in cases of incendiarism represented a profound break with Peel's sanctioning of rewards only in exceptional cases. The proclamation was issued in a specially published *London Gazette* and was circulated throughout the countryside over the following days.[95] Second, in consequence of a Cabinet decision, Phillips requested that Maule send copies of all depositions for cases where the government was acting as the prosecution to the Home Office for inspection by the Crown's law officers.[96]

While the Special Commissions held for Buckinghamshire, Dorset, Berkshire, Hampshire and Wiltshire were Melbourne's most violent innovation, there were still large numbers of cases to prosecute in Kent, Sussex and, to a lesser extent, Surrey. At the beginning of December Maule returned to London to coordinate attempts to prosecute Swing activists in Kent and Sussex and to help supervise the government prosecutions at the Special Commissions.[97] Although the magistrates were finding it difficult to secure evidence – such were the 'threats of vengeance against Informers', in the words of one Kentish clerical magistrate – by the time of Maule's return to London most of the depositions had been taken and the cases set. Securing any evidence beyond the circumstantial in cases of incendiarism was proving almost impossible.[98]

Still, the offer of the £500 reward for evidence leading to the conviction of an incendiary, and the dispatch of London police officers to assist in procuring evidence in cases of incendiarism had some impact. It was Maule's interventions, however, that proved decisive in bringing several fire setters to trial, though one alleged Kentish incendiarist – Alex Brown – fled to Calais to avoid prosecution.[99] Five cases, for which seven individuals were indicted, were heard at the Kent Assizes opening at Maidstone on Monday 13 December. Elizabeth Studdam was found guilty of setting fire to an outhouse and wood stacks of the Birchington poorhouse on 4 November, John Dyke was found guilty of setting fire to Bearsted overseer Stokes's barn on 10 November, and brothers Henry and William Packman were found guilty, partly on the confession of accomplice George Bishop, who turned King's evidence, of firing farmer Wraight's stacks at Blean on 21 November. Elizabeth was reprieved to life transportation, while labourers John, Henry and William were sentenced to death by Judge Bosanquet on the conclusion of the trials on Thursday 16 December.[100] At the Sussex Winter Assizes, opened at Lewes on Monday 20 December, four cases of incendiarism were scheduled to be tried, of which three produced guilty verdicts: Richard Pennells for firing his master's stacks at Bodiam on 13 November; Edmund Bushby for a fire at East Preston on 28 November and Thomas Goodman for a fire at Battle on 2 December.[101]

At the Surrey Winter Assizes, opened on 30 December, another three individuals were tried for incendiarism. Fifteen-year-old James Bravery was found not guilty of arson at Ockley on 15 November, while no bill was found in the case of 18-year-old James Ritchie for allegedly firing a stack at Carshalton on 11 November. Labourer James Warner was found guilty of firing James Franks's flour-mill at Albury on 13 November and duly sentenced to death. While there were calls for the execution to take place on Shere Heath or another convenient site close to the scene of the fire, shortly before 9 a.m. on 10 January 1831, at Horsemonger Lane Gaol, Southwark, Warner was launched into eternity.[102]

On Christmas Eve, in front of 'an immense concourse of spectators' on Penenden Heath, Dyke and the Packman brothers were the first Swing activists to be executed.[103] Edmund Bushby, the sole Sussex protestor to be executed that winter, was the next, his life ending upon the Horsham gallows on New Year's Day 1831. Pennells was spared on account of his age and an evident mental impairment, his sentence being commuted to one month's imprisonment. Goodman's case was more complicated. As Wells has uncovered, Goodman, while awaiting execution in Horsham Gaol, was interrogated as to Cobbett's actions at Battle. Notwithstanding claims by magistrate Francis Burrell that not 'the slightest hope ... [was] held out to him of any remission of his Sentence', Goodman made a full 'confession' in full knowledge that a statement incriminating Cobbett represented his only hope of avoiding the hangman's noose. King William IV, who took an active interest in Swing's suppression and Cobbett's involvement, approved a fortnight's respite for Goodman on 30 December. Within days his sentence had been commuted to life transportation.[104]

Incendiarists might have been the only Swing activists executed in

Kent, Sussex and Surrey but they were not the only protestors tried. At the Kent Winter Assizes, in addition to the seven charges of arson there were twelve charges for machine-breaking, one for sending a threatening letter and a further twelve for riotous assembly. The Dover Sessions – opened on 21 December – tried nine men for machine-breaking at Margate on 20 November. All nine were found guilty and sentenced to seven years' transportation. The final trial in Kent for protests committed in 1830 was the West Kent Epiphany Sessions opened at Maidstone on 13 January 1831. Charges of riot were brought against seven individuals, including radical Robert Price, all seven being found guilty. Price was found guilty on three separate charges of riot and was sentenced to a total of five years' hard labour, 'manifest[ing] not the slightest indication of feeling while receiving his sentence'.[105]

In Surrey, as well the trial of the arsonists, five charges of riot and one of sending a threatening letter were made at the Assizes.[106] At the Sussex Assizes there were also nine cases of machine-breaking, one of sedition (Charles Inskipp for 'sedition' at Battle), five for sending threatening letters, three for compelling others to 'join riotous mobs', and seventeen for riot. Among these cases 17-year-old Thomas Brown was sentenced to death for sending a threatening letter to Earl of Sheffield, John Pagden, also aged 17, was sentenced to seven years' transportation for sending a threatening letter at Cuckfield, John Barnes was sentenced to fourteen years' transportation for 'extortion' at Eastergate, and William Squires was sentenced to death for riot at Boxgrove on 14 November. Squires's sentence was duly commuted to transportation.[107]

Further Swing cases were also tried at the East and West Sussex Quarter Sessions. That for West Sussex opened at Petworth on 3 January 1831 before 'a very full Bench of Magistrates'. Of the several trials for machine-breaking, riot and one for sending an incendiary letter, ten individuals were sentenced to fourteen years' transportation and two individuals to seven years for machine-breaking – thereby transporting twelve out of the seventeen Sussex men so sentenced at the Sussex courts. The East Sussex Quarter Sessions were not so dramatic. Opening at Lewes on Friday 7 January, the only Swing cases tried were for riot at Mayfield and for riot and assaulting the East Grinstead overseer in a gravel pit, the most severe sentence being six weeks imprisonment.[108]

The recognition that Swing had already passed Kent, Sussex and

Surrey as much as the fact that trials had already occurred in Kent, meant that Special Commissions were considered superfluous in these counties. In Hampshire, though, a commission was necessary owing to fears that, as Hobsbawm and Rude put it, 'the over-tenderness of local magistrates' would rekindle the much fresher spirit of Swing, thereby replicating the impact of the trial of the Elham machine-breakers.[109] Compared to what followed at the Hampshire Special Commission, there can be no doubt that less government pressure was put on circuit judges Bosanquet and Taunton and the chairmen of the various quarter sessions to issue severe sentences. And yet, in deploying Maule to orchestrate the prosecutions in Kent and Sussex, in Maule's drawing up detailed prosecution briefs for several cases at the Kent and Sussex Assizes and the West Kent Epiphany Sessions, and in Maule's conducting the prosecution for the government in several cases at the Kent Assizes, Peel and then Melbourne wanted examples to be made. The clearest statement of government policy came in the form of a letter from Melbourne to Justice Bosanquet: Dyke and the Packmans were to be hanged 'earlier than usual', 'it may have the effect of making the example more striking'.[110]

Prosecuting Swing II: the Hampshire Special Commission

King William's assent for the holding of Special Commissions in Berkshire, Hampshire and Wiltshire was secured on 27 November, the Lord Chancellor being immediately empowered to issue the commissions.[111] The negotiations had taken several days. Hampshire magistrate Pollen had met with Melbourne on 23 November at which, a letter of the following days to Phillips infers, the issuing of a special commission was discussed. The letter stated that Pollen would use the opportunity of the meeting of Hampshire magistrates to be chaired by Lord Lieutenant Wellington at Winchester on 25 November to 'press the need' for the Special Commission on the government. The topic was duly discussed at the Winchester meeting, and it was then resolved that Wellington should be 'empowered' to inform the government that it would be 'expedient' if a Special Commission were held 'without loss of time'. It would appear, though, that Grey's ministry had already concluded that an application would be made to the King on 25 November, letters from the Home Office to Pollen, J. Baring and Sir Henry Wright Wilson all stating that a Special Commission for Hampshire was likely.[112]

Even before William IV's assent was given, preparations had been put in hand. On 25 November, J. Baring was informed that William Tallents, a 'gentleman ... of high character and great legal experience [being a solicitor]', would leave for Winchester on the following day to 'assist' the magistrates in preparing cases for trial. This news, Baring replied, had 'given great satisfaction to the magistrates'. No one was more relieved than Pollen, who was 'almost bewildered by applications, [and] questions over arrangements'. Tallents's mission was set out in letters to Pollen and Wellington. By examining the huge number of depositions already taken, Tallents was 'to select, arrange, and complete the cases to be tried under a Special Commission'. He was to make a special point in trying to put together a strong case against an incendiary, for, in Phillips's words, as 'very little has yet been done in that way, in any of the Counties' it would be a 'a grand point to catch an incendiary'.[113] Two 'committees' of magistrates had also been formed at Winchester to examine the depositions as divided into five different categories of case.

Only two days after his arrival in Winchester, Melbourne requested that Tallents proceed 'at the first opportunity' to Salisbury, 'and afterwards to Reading', to assist in preparing the Wiltshire and Berkshire Special Commission cases. But so heavy was the burden of work at Winchester – and Tallents's concern to avoid 'great dissatisfaction' among the judiciary in Hampshire if 'greater assistance' were given to Berkshire or Wiltshire – that Tallents spent most of his time in Winchester.[114] The sheer number of potential cases not only posed an administrative nightmare but also raised difficult questions as to which prisoners should be indicted at the Special Commission. There was also discussion as to who should act as (and pay the costs of) the prosecution. Indeed, notwithstanding the fallout from Knatchbull's earlier 'lenient' sentences, the sheer number of committals made to the gaols at Winchester and elsewhere in Hampshire – some 200 activists had been committed by the time of Tallents' arrival with 'many' warrants still out – made it impossible to try all arrested Swing. Instead, 'crimes of a serious nature' would be tried, while it was reported 'others of a lighter character will be allowed, perhaps, to depart upon their own recognizances'. The final printed calendar contained 325 cases with prosecutions against 305 individuals, rising to 345 cases with last-minute additions.[115]

Before the Special Commission opened, depositions in the cases for trial circulated between Tallents and the magistrates under Pollen's supervision at Winchester, Wellington, the Home Office, Maule and the Attorney General. Government involvement in arranging cases for trial created some confusion as to whether they would take the lead and cover prosecution expenses in all cases tried at the Special Commission. Maule had been informed on 30 November that the government would 'undertake' the prosecution in any case he recommended. Four days later, Tallents was asked to report to Melbourne 'on the nature of the cases concerned' so he could decide whether they were 'fit' for a government prosecution. Tallents duly prepared an 'abstract' of the cases for trial for Melbourne and the Attorney General's consideration. The response evidenced a shift in government policy:

> Some of the cases which are to be tried may not be of a very aggravated kind, some of them may admit of easy and not numerous proofs & many of them may be simple & ordinary cases, not involved in the least difficulty … [In such cases it appears to Melbourne that] to use Govt counsel may be viewed upon as a Species of apprehension or as an advantage taken by the Magistracy & by the Government against the accused.

While it was 'difficult to lay down a precise and definite rule' to 'carefully guard against' this, the Attorney General was asked to take 'the matter into his consideration', and Tallents was advised to 'select the most prominent cases of each class, considered with reference to their complexity, or the aggravated nature of the offence'. Tallents was also to inform Sir Thomas Baring and Sir William Heathcote, active on the committees set up at Winchester, that their suggestion that 'due to the great pressures of business' the King's Counsel should lead in all the prosecutions at the Special Commission, was 'not advisable'. The final arrangement was that where the government counsel held briefs, the Attorney General having selected 'from 40–50 cases' for the government counsel to prosecute, half the expense would be borne by the government and half by the county. The county would pay for copies of briefs made for their counsel and, as per a normal assizes, all witnesses' expenses. Attorney General Sir Thomas Denman, and solicitors Mr Gurney and Mr Dampier were to act as government counsel, while solicitor Mr Missing would prosecute for the county.[116]

There was also a widespread belief among the magistrates, so Phillips informed Tallents, that in all cases where Tallents had seen the depositions the cases were 'out of their hands'. This perception delighted many magistrates but generated concerns from petty session district clerks who feared the loss of their usual emoluments for drawing up cases, and needed to 'be corrected as soon as possible'.[117] Still, Tallents received the full support of Melbourne, both financially – the Lords of the Treasury being requested to direct Maule to 'advance' Tallents 'such sums as necessary' to carry out his mission – and in reducing his burden. When Maule was 'released' from the Sussex Assizes at Lewes on 21 November he was duly directed to assume Tallents' responsibilities for Berkshire,[118] so that when the courts of the Hampshire Special Commission opened on 20 December the vast majority of the cases were ready for trial.

On Saturday 18 December in a blaze of pomp, Judges Baron Vaughan, Sir James Parke and Sir Edward Hall Alderson arrived in Winchester, attended by Grand Sheriff George Purefoy Jervoise, a double flank of javelinmen and a large group of special constables. The Special Commission was then immediately opened, though it did not sit for the trial of the prisoners until 10 a.m. on Monday 20 December. On that first day all three judges would sit together, but on subsequent days cases would be heard in two courts. Even allowing for this and a mooted plan for the courts to sit after church on Christmas Day, it was not expected that the Special Commission would close until after Monday 28 December. This prediction proved correct, the commission not concluding its business – and then in a palpable hurry – until 30 December. That the savage sentences were handed out to the prisoners could be of little surprise given Melbourne's intentions and Judge Vaughan's sixty-five-minute long opening address to the Grand Jury, a body peopled by the landed gentry and nobility of Hampshire:

> It is of the highest importance to the good order of society that all classes of persons throughout the realm should be taught, by the awful lesson which may be afforded here, that whatever notions may be falsely entertained of the power of a riotous multitude, armed for rapine and plunder in defiance of the law, their success and triumph can be for the day only; that the law of the land, founded in wisdom, endeared to us by long experience of its benefits, and consecrated by time, must ultimately be found too strong for its assailants; that those who deride and defy its power, and continue in arms against it, will in the end be subdued by it, or compelled to submit to its justice, or to sue for its mercy.[119]

Armed with a detailed overview of the various statutes on which Tallents and the Winchester committees had drawn the indictments – most carrying the death penalty, including 'robbery' under 7 and 8 Geo. IV when money was given through 'fear and the reasonable apprehension of violence ... or by their numbers and alarming demeanour', c.29 and 'riot' under 7 and 8 Geo. IV, c.27 [120] – the Grand Jury were duly dispatched to their 'important business'. After all the cases were heard over the ensuing eleven days, the judges proceeded to pass sentence. Such was the overwhelming number of cases to be tried that by late on 28 December, already over a week into the trials, Heathcote, Baring and Attorney General Denman conferred as how to proceed. It was agreed to 'select' the 'worse' cases from those yet to be tried and to drop the 'lightest ones'. On the following day the plan was put into place. 'Many' prisoners were acquitted as Denman declined to offer any evidence 'in consequence of the slight nature of the evidence or other circumstances rendering that course expedient'. The final day of the Commission – 30 December – saw a similar course adopted, such was the pressure to move on to Salisbury for the Wiltshire Assizes and to release the Grand Jury. Many of the 'lesser offenders' pleaded guilty and were discharged on their recognisances, while other 'trivial cases' were quickly 'disposed of'. Several cases were also transferred to the next Hampshire Assizes, including one of machine-breaking at Stoneham and another of five men refusing to be sworn in as special constables.[121]

According to the final report submitted by Tallents to the Home Office, 101 capital convictions were made, 53 for non-capital felonies, and 94 for misdemeanours. Four cases were postponed, 3 passed over, 17 discharged for want of prosecution, 5 bills returned as 'igmoramus', 2 acquitted having turned King's evidence, while a further 67 individuals were acquitted. Of the 101 capital convictions, 6 individuals had been 'left for death'.[122] Mair's arrangements for the protection of the peace of the city had also proved effective, there having been 'not the slightest sign of disturbance' in the city.[123] On this conclusion, Wellington wrote to King William IV's private secretary, Lieutenant-General Sir Herbert Taylor, to inform the monarch of the outcome of the commission:

[Regarding the capital convictions] the law has been allowed to take its course in relation to six. Three of them concerned in the destruction of manufactories aided by machinery, one in the destruction of poor houses, one for a robbery by night, one for a robbery by day – this last is the man who struck Mr. Baring. It will be recommended that the others should be transported for life. Several have been sentenced during the commission to transportation for life, and some for terms of years ... Upon the whole this commission has worked well, and has already produced a good effect and I hope that its consequences will be long felt.

The King, Taylor replied, approved. The Special Commission had 'maintained its claims to his approbation and trust of the country'. It had given a 'proper tone to others and [had been] calculated to produce a good effect throughout the country'.[124]

While plans for the removal of those sentenced to transportation had already been put in place, a ship bound for Sydney being ready at Spithead by the New Year,[125] there was some debate as to where executions should take place. Mair believed that executions 'at a County jail are unfortunately too frequent to strike terror but such an occurrence intensified in an agricultural district, would never to forgotten and prove a lasting and salutary warning'. Having mentioned this to the judges, Mair believed that they would sanction staging any executions in 'different parts' of the county.[126]

He was to be disappointed. Robert Holdaway's execution was 'held over' until 5 February to allow for an investigation into an affidavit sent to both Vaughan and Wellington by Mr Cowburn, an individual who had assisted the magistrates and dragoons in arresting Holdaway. His life ought be spared, it asserted, for he had acted to save Selbourne workhouse master Cobbold's life, had forewarned Cobbold's opposite number at Headley, and at Empshott had 'stayed the fury' of the 'worst man in the parish' thus saving the chief farmer from injury. Cowburn continued, 'Executing him will have a bad effect at those places, provoking horror that one who is less guilty should pay the extreme penalty, while some of the most guilty escape with comparatively little punishment.' Having attended Holdaway's trial, Wellington believed that the 'preservation of the peace of the county and the protection of the lives and properties of His Majesty's subjects require that examples should be made'. He could not, therefore, recommend that the King's pardon should be conferred on Holdaway. His life was spared but his sentence was commuted to life transportation.[127]

The severity of the sentences passed down at the Commission had not provoked surprise, but that six people had been left for execution was, in the words of Rev. Dallas of Wontson, 'not expected': 'I fear that there is more of bitterness in the feeling with which the intelligence has been received than consisting with the continuance of the wholesome effect which has hitherto been produced.'[128] Immediately on the conclusion of the trials, a petition was prepared in Winchester, the Mayor not being one of the 700 signatories. A meeting at Whitechapel also prepared a petition to attempt to save the lives of the 'unfortunate and deluded individuals'. Within twenty hours, the petition had received 6,000 signatures. The Winchester press also reported the existence of petitions throughout Hampshire, one at Southampton having received 1,400 signatures in less than a day. The plethora of petitions, at least in the mind of the editor of the *Hampshire Advertiser*, worked as they were 'permitted' to have their 'natural influence on the Throne', as a respite was announced for James Annalls, Henry Eldridge, John Gilmore and Robert Holdaway on Thursday 15 January.[129] Henry Cook and James Thomas Cooper, found guilty of 'robbery' at Northington and rioting at Fordingbridge respectively, were not sparred. At 8 a.m. on 15 January at the County Gaol in Winchester before very few people, Cook and Cooper were executed.[130]

Notes

1 E. Hobsbawm and G. Rudé, *Captain Swing* (London: Lawrence & Wishart, 1969), p. 253; R. Wells, 'Mr William Cobbett, Captain Swing, and King William IV', *Agricultural History Review*, 45:1 (1997), 34–48. For a reinterpretation of the response of the local gentry to events outside Swing's initial theatre see: A. Randall and E. Newman, 'Protest, proletarians and paternalists: social conflict in rural Wiltshire, 1830–1850', *Rural History*, 6:2 (1995), 205–27.

2 Hobsbawm and Rudé, *Captain Swing*, pp. 254 and 256.

3 R. Wallis, ''We do not come here ... to inquire into grievances we come here to decide law': prosecuting Swing in Norfolk and Suffolk', *Southern History*, 32 (2010), 159–75.

4 Centre for Kentish Studies (hereafter CKS), Q/Sbe 120/1, Information of William Dodd, yeoman, Upper Hardres, 30 August; *KG*, 3 September; *Kent Herald* (hereafter *KH*), 3 September 1830.

5 The National Archives (hereafter TNA), HO 44/21, fos 241–2, Anonymous, (Paddlesworth), to Peel, 13 September 1830.

6 *Hampshire Chronicle* (hereafter *HC*), 4 October 1830.

7 TNA, HO 52/8, fos 271–2, Charles Sandys, Canterbury to Peel, 22 September 1830.

8 CKS, U951 C177/15, Notes of Justices meeting at Canterbury, 25 September; TNA, HO 52/8 fos 273–4, Edward Rice, High Sheriff of Kent, Wingham to

Peel, 25 September; *KH*, 30 September 1830.

9 CKS, Q/SBe 120/6, Deposition of George Leadbitter, 2 October; CKS, U951 C177/25, Rev. Price, Lyminge to Knatchbull, 6 October 1830. There is no record of Leadbitter being in the employ of the Bow Street office until 5 April 1831: TNA, HO 60/2, p. 541.

10 CKS, U951 C177/17 and 25, T.P. Junior, Denton, and Rev. Price, Lyminge to Knatchbull, 26 September and 6 October 1830.

11 CKS, U951 C177/26, 27, and 13, Rev. Bramall, Elham to Rev. Price, 6 October, and Reverend Price to Knatchbull, n.d. (probably 7 October 1830) and, 'List of 37 persons involved in machine breaking ...', n.d. (but after 22 September). TNA, HO 52/8, fos 276–7, Knatchbull, Mersham to Peel, 6 October 1830.

12 CKS, U951 C177/22, Unsigned depositions taken by Knatchbull, n.d. (but late September/early October).

13 *KH*, 7 October; *Kentish Gazette* (hereafter *KG*), 8 October 1830.

14 CKS, U951 C177/18 and 13, Rev. Price to Knatchbull, 27 September 1830, and 'List of persons involved sworn on recognizances'.

15 TNA, HO 52/8, fos 290–1, Knatchbull, Canterbury to Peel, 29 September 1830.

16 CKS, U951 C11/21 and 23, Phillips to Knatchbull, 30 September and 2 October. Peel also stated his belief that rewards encouraged agent provocateurs to stir up trouble and then claim the reward: CKS, U840 C250 10/2, Peel to Camden, 18 October 1830.

17 CKS, U951 C177/18, 24 and 25, Price, Lyminge to Knatchbull, 27 September, 4 and 6 October 1830.

18 CKS, U951 C177/26 and 29, Rev. Bramall, Elham to Price, Lyminge, 6 October and C.H. Hallett to Knatchbull, n.d. (but 6 or 7 October) 1830.

19 CKS, U951 C177/28 and 34 Knatchbull to Peel (draft), 6 October, and Phillips to Knatchbull, 9 October 1830.

20 TNA, HO 52/8, fos 243–4, Camden, Bagham Abbey, to Peel, 17 October; CKS, U840 C250/10/2, Peel to Camden, 18 October 1830.

21 *KH*, 28 October 1830.

22 TNA, HO 52/8, fos 300–1, Rev. Poore, Murston to Peel, 23 October 1830.

23 CKS, U951 C177/36, C14/4, George Gipps, Howletts, 24 October, Sir Henry Montresor, Barham, 27 October 1830.

24 CKS, U840 C250 10/6, Peel to Camden, 25 October 1830.

25 TNA, HO 52/8, fos 224–5 and 241–2, Camden to Peel, 23 and 27 October 1830.

26 TNA, HO 40/27, fo. 54, George Maule, Maidstone, to Phillips, 1 November 1830.

27 TNA, HO 52/8, fos 228–9, Camden to Peel, 22 October 1830.

28 CKS, U951 C14/7 and 8, Rev. Poore, Murston to Knatchbull, 26 and October; TNA, HO 52/8, fos 382–3, Gipps, Hallett and Mulcaster to Knatchbull, 27 October 1830.

29 TNA, HO 52/8, fos 300–1 and 354–6, Poore, Murston to Peel, 23 and 25 October; *Maidstone Journal* (hereafter *MJ*), 2 November 1830.

30 TNA, HO 52/8, fos 382–3, Knatchbull, Mersham to Peel, 27 October 1830.

31 TNA, HO 52/8, fos 363–4 and 359–60, and 382–3, John Plumptree and Mr Hammond, St Albans Court, Fredville, Wingham, 25 October, Rev. Gleig, Ash,

25 October, both to Peel, and Messrs Gipps, Hallett and Mulcaster, Canterbury to Knatchbull, 27 October 1830 (forwarded to the Home Office).

32 CKS, U840 C250/10/6 and 7, Peel to Camden, 25 and 26 October 1830; TNA, HO 52/8, fos 239–40, Camden to Peel, 27 October.

33 TNA, HO 41/8 pp. 24–5, 32 and 72–3, Phillips, Whitehall to Maule, Treasury Solicitor, Maidstone, 31 October, 11 and 19 November 1830.

34 TNA, HO 52/8, fos 363–4, John Plumptree and Mr Hammond, Wingham to Peel, 25 October; CKS, U840 C250/10/2 and 7, Peel to Camden, 18 and 26 October 1830.

35 CKS, U951 C14/8, Rev. Poore to Knatchbull, n.d. (but 28 October); *KH*, 4 November 1830.

36 TNA, HO 52/8, fos 28–9, Maidstone Magistrates to Peel, 30 October; *MJ*, 2 November; *Hastings and Cinque Ports Iris* (hereafter *HIris*), 6 November 1830.

37 CKS, U951 C14/2, Knatchbull to Camden, 29 October; *KH*, 4 November; *KG*, 5 November 1830.

38 TNA, HO 52/10, fos 166–70, Messrs. Collingwood and Young, Hawkhurst to Peel, 11 November 1830.

39 KH, 18 November; Cobbett's Weekly Political Register, 27 November 1830.

40 *KH*, 18 November; *Brighton Gazette* (hereafter *BG*), 18 November 1830.

41 TNA, HO 52/10, fos 401–2, Courthope, Battle to Peel, 16 November 1830.

42 *Portsmouth, Portsea and Gosport Herald* (hereafter *PHer*), 21 November 1830.

43 *Sussex Advertiser* (hereafter *SA*), 22 and 29 November; *The Times* (hereafter *TT*), 23 November 1830; Sussex Record Society (eds), *Lewes Town Book, 1702–1837*, vol. 69 (Lewes: Sussex Record Society, 1973).

44 *HIris*, 20 November; *PHer*, 21 November; *Hampshire Telegraph* (hereafter *HT*), 22 November; *KG*, 23 November; *BG*, 25 November 1830.

45 TNA, HO 52/10, fos 576–7, W Twyford, Angel Inn, Midhurst to Phillips, 27 November 1830.

46 TNA, HO 52/8, fos 206–7, Messrs M. and J. Scoones, Clerks to the Lower South Aylesford Bench, to Melbourne, 8 December 1830.

47 TNA, HO 52/7, fos 137–8, Henry Flight, Winchester Post Office Deputy to Sir Francis Freeling, 27 November, enclosing printed copy of the resolutions passed at the Winchester meeting; *HC*, 6 December 1830.

48 TNA, HO 40/27(5), fos 440–1 and 443–4, Lt Col Mair, Winchester to Melbourne, 14 and 16 adj. 17 December 1830.

49 *PHer*, 21 November; *HT*, 22 November 1830.

50 TNA, HO 52/7, fos 42–3, 44–5 and 105–7, Andover Bench, 20 November, Robert Wright, Henry Tichbourne and John Dutby, magistrates, Alresford, 19 November, to Peel, Andover Bench to Melbourne, 24 November; *Southampton Mercury*, 27 November 1830.

51 TNA, HO 52/7, fos 57–8, 21–4 and 248–9, W.S. Stanley, Romsey to Peel, 23 November, John Mills JP, Ringwood, 26 November, and Sir Charles Hulse, Breamore House near Fordingbridge, 28 November, to Melbourne; *HC*, 29 November 1830.

52 *Hampshire Advertiser* (hereafter *HA*), 27 November 1830.

53 David Cox, *A Certain Share of Low Cunning: A History of the Bow Street Runners 1792–1839* (London: Willian, 2010).

54 TNA, HO 52/8, fos 148–9, D. Bishop, Deal to William Rowley, n.d. (between 10 and 12 November 1830); *PHer*, 28 November 1830.

55 The official record was the filed as TNA HO 60/2.

56 TNA, HO 52/7, fos 178–81, Sir Theophilius Lea, Bedhampton House, Havant to Melbourne, 6 December 1830.

57 TNA, HO 52/8, fos 310–11 and 52/13, fos 32–5, Rev. Jones, Brasted to Peel, 6 November, Sir J. Grey, Ramsgate to Melbourne, 17 November 1831.

58 *PHer*, 28 November 1830.

59 P. Ziegler, *Melbourne: A Biography of William Lamb* (London: Atheneum, 1978), pp. 133–4 and 137.

60 TNA, HO 50/14, Commander-in-Chief correspondence, Distribution of Troops in Great Britain, 1 October 1830.

61 TNA, HO 41/8, pp. 12, 22 and 23, Phillips, Home Office, to Poore, Murston; Peel to Maidstone Magistrates; and, Peel to Colonel Middleton, Cavalry Depot, Maidstone, 26 and 31 October and 1 November.

62 TNA, HO 41/8, pp. 29–30 and 30–1, Phillips to Lord Egremont, Petworth, 10 November, and to Sir Godfrey Webster, Battle, 11 November 1830.

63 TNA, HO 50/14, Distribution of the troops in Counties, 1 October and 4 November (corrected) 1830.

64 CKS, U840 C250/10/9, Peel to Camden, 12 November 1830.

65 CKS, U840 C250/10/9, Peel to Camden, 12 November; TNA, HO 41/8, p. 37, Peel to Lord Egremont, Petworth, 13 November 1830.

66 TNA, HO 41/7, fos 5–8, Peel to Sir Walter Burrell, West Grinstead Park, Horsham, 18 November 1830.

67 TNA, HO 41/7, pp. 77 and 79–80, Phillips to W. Crawford, Pipbrook, Dorking, and Magistrates of Guildford, 19 and 20 November. Both dispatches were made in response to specific pleas, see: TNA, HO 52/10, fos 204–5 and 212–13, William Crawford, Dorking, and Guildford Bench to Peel, 19 and 20 November 1830.

68 TNA, HO 41/7, pp. 80–1, Phillips to W. Henry Hunt, Horsham, 20 November 1830.

69 TNA, HO 41/8, pp. 57–8 and 68–9, Peel to Walter Burrell, West Grinstead Park, Horsham, 18 November, and to Sanctuary, Horsham, 19 November 1830.

70 TNA, HO 41/8, pp. 84–5, 78 and 78–9, Phillips to W. Mount Esq. and J. Cove Esq., Newbury, R. Wright Esq., Sir H.T. Tichborne and John Dutty Esq., Alresford, and to Mayor of Winchester, all 20 November; *HC*, 22 and 29 November 1830.

71 TNA, HO 41/8, pp. 89, 91, 92–3, 118–19 and 117, Peel to Andover Division magistrates, 21 November, Phillips to Sir Lucious Curteis, Bremridge, and to Mayor of Basingstoke, both 22 November, and to J.C. Harrison, Alton, and Lieutenant General Sir Colin Campbell, both 24 November; *HA*, 20 and 27 November; *HC*, 22 and 29 November; *HT*, 22 November; *PHer*, 21 and 28 November 1830.

72 TNA, HO 41/8, pp. 157–8 and 159, Phillips to John Boys, Margate, and to Isle of Wight magistrates, 26 November; TNA, HO 52/7, fos 25–7, Richard Pollen Esq., Winchester Gaol to Phillips, 26 November; *PHer*, 28 November; *HC*, 29 November 1830.

73 HCRO, 10M57/03/33, Information of William Lutley Sclater Esq., Tangier Park, Saint Lawrence Wootton, 24 November 1830.

74 TNA, HO 52/8, fos 383–5 and 52/7, fos 116–17, Webster, Battle Abbey to Peel, 8 November, and C.W. Foster, Andover, 26 November, both to Melbourne; *KG*, 12 November 1830.

75 *PHer*, 21 and 28 November;

76 TNA, HO 52/7, fos 105–7, Andover Bench to Melbourne, 24 November 1830.

77 *Dorset County Chronicle*, 25 November; *PHer*, 28 November; *HA*, 27 November; *HC*, 29 November; *HT*, 29 November 1830.

78 *HC*, 6 and 13 December 1830.

79 TNA, HO 41/8, pp. 460–1, Phillips to Mayor of Winchester, 10 December 1830.

80 TNA, HO 52/10, fo. 579, Thomas Sanctuary, Horsham, to Melbourne, 14 December; TNA, HO 41/8, p. 50, Phillips to Thomas Sanctuary, Horsham, 15 December 1830.

81 R. Wells, *Wretched Faces: Famine in Wartime England, 1793–1803* (Stroud: Alan Sutton, 1988), pp. 253–60. Also see A. Gee, *The British Volunteer Movement 1794–1814* (Oxford: Oxford University Press, 2003), pp. 231–61.

82 *KG*, 12 November 1830.

83 TNA, HO 52/8, fos 203–5, B. Sandford and John Irving MP, Farningham and Dartford to Peel, 8 October; CKS, U840 C250/10/8, Peel to Camden, 2 November; TNA, HO 41/8, pp. 29–30, Peel to Egremont, Petworth, 10 November 1830.

84 *KH*, 18 November; J. L. Hammond and Barbara Hammond, *The Village Labourer* London: Longman, [1911] 1978, p. 188; *TT*, 13 November 1830.

85 TNA, HO 52/10, fos 625–6, Egremont, Petworth to Peel, 19 November 1830.

86 TNA, HO 41/8, pp. 322–3 and 387, Melbourne to the Earl of Digby, Sherborne, 3 December, and to Sir G.H. Rose, Southampton, 6 December 1830.

87 For instance see: TNA, HO 40/5, fos 440–1, Phillips to Lt Col Mair, Winchester, 14 December 1830.

88 *KH*, 28 October; TNA, HO 52/8, fos 224–5, Camden, Wilderness to Peel, 23 October 1830.

89 TNA, HO 52/8, fos 382–3, Knatchbull, Mersham to Peel, 27 October; CKS, Q/Sbe 121/13, Deposition of Caroline Matson, Wingham, 20 November 1830.

90 TNA, HO 41/8, pp. 24–5, Phillips, Home Office to Maule, Maidstone, 31 October 1830; TNA, HO 40/27, fos 54–5, Maule, Maidstone to Phillips, 1 November; Wells, 'Mr. William Cobbett', 37–8.

91 TNA, HO 40/27, fos 58–9 and 66–7, Maule, Maidstone, 5 November, and Battle, 12 November, to Phillips; Wells, 'Mr. William Cobbett', 37; TNA, HO 41/8, pp. 29–30, 31 and 32, Peel to Egremont, Petworth, 10 November, and Phillips to Sir Godfrey Webster, Battle Abbey, and to Maule, both 11 November; *MJ*, 16 November 1830.

92 TNA, HO 52/8, fos 91–2 and 41/8 fos 73–4, W. Collingwood, Hawkhurst to Phillips, 18 November; and Phillips to Collingwood, Hawkhurst, 19 November 1830.

93 Peel would not sanction the government acting as the prosecution in the case

of Elizabeth Studdam, in custody for allegedly setting fire to the Birchington poorhouse, for her supposed motive was not 'linked' to the 'burnings': TNA, HO 40/27, fos 77–8, Maule, Maidstone, to Phillips, 18 November; TNA, HO 41/8, pp. 59–60, 72–3 and 82, Phillips to Maule, 18, 19 and 20 November 1830.

94 CKS, Q/Sbe 121/14, 15 and 16, Rough list of sentences given to thirty machine breakers, n.d. (but 25 or 26 November), Rough assessment of destroyed machines, and list of twelve prisoners' sentences, n.d. (but 25 or 26 November), Gaol Calendar, East Kent Special Sessions November, with notes of verdicts and sentences, 25 November; *KH*, 2 December 1830.

95 The last case sanctioned by Peel was the case of the incendiary fire on Borden overseer's farm on the night of 22 October. *London Gazette*, 26 October and 23 November 1830 (nos. 18738 and 18749).

96 Grey to William IV, 23 Nov 1830, Earl Grey (ed.), The *Reform Act 1832. The Correspondence of ... Earl Grey with ... William IV and ... Sir Herbert Taylor, vol. I* (London: Murray, 1867), pp. 3–5, cited in Wells, 'Mr. William Cobbett', 38, n.26.

97 TNA, HO 41/8, pp. 361–2. Phillips to Lewes Bench, 4 December 1830.

98 TNA, HO 52/8, fos 30–2, Rev. Morrice, Betshanger House, nr Sandwich to Melbourne, 24 November 1830.

99 TNA, HO 52/8, fos 139–40, John Boys, Margate to Melbourne, 12 December 1830. Boys sent a constable to Dover with a warrant for Brown's arrest, but believed that it would be necessary to secure a state warrant to bring him back to Britain for trial.

100 *TT*, 15, 16, 17 and 18 December; *KH*, 16 December; TNA, Assi 94/2067, indictments of Elizabeth Studdam, John Seaman, John Jull, Jo Field alias Dyke, William and Henry Packman and George Bishop, Kent Winter Assizes 1830. A further case of incendiarism relating to the autumn and winter of 1830 was subsequently tried at the Kent Lent Assizes in 1831. This case, the destruction of the Queen's Head pub at Northfleet on 7 November, it was uncovered, was motivated by an attempt to defraud the Kent Fire Office by landlord Merrefield: *MJ*, 9 November 1830; TNA, Assi 31/26, p. 369, Kent Lent Assize 1831 Agenda.

101 TNA, Assi 94/2073, indictments of Richard Pennells, Edmund Bushby and Thomas Goodman; *BG*, 23 December; *HT*, 27 December 1830.

102 TNA, Assi 94/2070, Indictments of James Bravery, James Ritchie and James Warner; *TT*, 1 and 3 January; *Morning Chronicle*, 3 January 1831; TNA, HO 52/12, fos 367–9, G. Holme-Summers, Hatchlands, Guildford to Melbourne, 4 January 1831, enclosing letter from G.W. Onslow, Guildford, n.d. (late December 1830 or early January); *County Chronicle*, 18 January 1831.

103 *MJ*, 28 December; *TT*, 29 and 30 December 1830.

104 *TT*, 24 December 1830 and 4 January; *SA*, 6 December 1830 and 16 January 1831; *BG*, 23 December 1830; TNA, HO 52/10, fos 614–16, Francis Burrell to Melbourne, enclosing a confession from Goodman, January 1831; Wells, 'Mr William Cobbett', 43–6.

105 *KH*, 16 December; TNA, Assi 31/26, pp. 289–95, Agenda for Kent Winter Assizes; *KG*, 29 December 1830; *Rochester Gazette*, 18 January 1831.

106 *TT*, 31 December 1830 1 and 3 January 1831.

107 TNA, Assi 94/2073, various indictments, Sussex Winter Assizes; *TT*, 22 December; *BG*, 23 December; *HT*, 27 December 1830.

108 *HT*, 10 and 7 January 1831; ESCRO, QR/E/806, various depositions against James Norman, John Simmonds, William Simmonds sen. and William Simmonds jun., November 1830.

109 Hobsbawm and Rude, *Captain Swing*, p. 258. As Wells states, this was also partly motivated by the need for Lord Grey's administration to maintain the support of William IV for parliamentary reform, something that would have been jeopardised by numerous trials throughout the country highlighting the depth of popular republicanism: 'Mr. William Cobbett', 44–8.

110 TNA, HO 41/9, pp. 101–2, Melbourne to Justice Bosanquet, Maidstone, 18 December 1830.

111 TNA, HO 41/8, pp. 179–80, Phillips to the Lord Chancellor, 27 November 1830.

112 TNA, HO 52/7, fos 112–13, Richard Pollen Esq., Winchester to Phillips, 24 November; *HC*, 29 November; TNA, HO 41/8, pp. 127, 128–9 and 130–1, Phillips to J. Baring Esq., Pollen, and Sir Henry Wright Wilson Bt, all 25 November 1830.

113 TNA, HO 41/8, pp. 127 and 128–9, Phillips to J. Baring Esq., and to Pollen, both Winchester, 25 November; University of Southampton Special Collections (hereafter USSC), WP4/2/2/22, Melbourne to Wellington, 26 November; TNA, HO 52/7, fos 16–18 and 25–7, J. Baring and Pollen, both to Phillips, 26 November. Tallents was the Newark town clerk: *Derby Mercury*, 22 December 1830.

114 TNA, HO 41/8, pp. 380–1, Phillips to Tallents, Winchester, 6 December, TNA, HO 40 27(6), fos 580–5: Tallents, London to Melbourne, 13 December 1830.

115 *PHer*, 28 November; *HC*, 29 November and 6 December; USSC, WP4/2/2/20, Copy of the resolutions of the Hampshire magistrates assembled at Winchester, 25 November; TNA, 40/27(6), fos 546–9, Tallents, Winchester to Phillips, 28 November 1830.

116 TNA, HO 41/8, pp. 257–8, 356–7 and 466–7, Phillips to Maule, Maidstone, 30 November, and to Tallents, Winchester, 4 and 11 December; USSC, WP4/2/2/24, Wellington to the Lord Chancellor, 26 November; TNA, HO 40/27(6), fos 560–5 and 601–2, Tallents, Winchester to Phillips, 9 December (enclosing a letter from Thomas Baring, Winchester, 8 December) and 21 December; *Morning Post*, 20 December 1830.

117 TNA, HO 41/9, pp. 59–60, Phillips to Tallents, Winchester, 15 December; TNA, HO 40/27(6), fos 594–5, Tallents, Winchester to Phillips, 16 December 1830.

118 TNA, HO 41/9, pp. 30 and 103, Phillips to Tallents, Winchester, 14 and 18 December; TNA, HO 36/22, pp. 145–6, Melbourne to the Lords of the Treasury, 14 December 1830.

119 *HC*, 6 December; *Morning Post*, 20 December; *HA*, 25 December 1830 and 1 January 1831; *HT*, 27 December 1830.

120 The 'Criminal Statutes (England), Repeal Act' (7 and 8 Geo IV, c.27) was invoked because it changed some of the conditions of the 115 year-old Riot Act (1 Geo I, Stat. 2, c.5) but it left 'the full force' of the original clause against individuals still assembled after the Riot Act was read.

121 TNA, HO 40/26(6), fos 617–18, 618–20 and 621–3, Tallents, Winchester to Phillips, 28, 29 and 30 December 1830; *HC*, 3 January 1831.

122 *TT*, 21 December 1830; TNA, HO 40/27(6), fos 623–4, Tallents, Winchester to Phillips, 2 January 1831.

123 TNA, HO 40/27(5), fos 450–1 and 458–9, Mair, Winchester to Melbourne, 19 and 23 December 1830.

124 USSC, WP4/2/2/58 and 4/3/4/1, Wellington to Lt Gen. Sir H. Taylor, 30 December 1830, and Taylor, Brighton to Wellington, 2 January 1831.

125 TNA, HO 41/9, pp. 112–13, Phillips to Sir Thomas Baring, Stratton Park, 20 December 1830; *HC*, 3 January 1831.

126 TNA, HO 40/26(6), fos 458–9 and 461, Mair, Winchester to Melbourne, 23 and 24 December 1830.

127 USSC, WP4/3/4/3 and 4, W. Cowburn, Tavistock Square, London to Wellington, 3 January (enclosing copy of Cowburn to Vaughan, 1 January), and Wellington to Cowburn, 7 January; *HA*, 22 January 1831.

128 TNA, HO 52/13, fos 113–5, Rev. Dallas, Wonston to Melbourne, 8 January 1831.

129 *HC*, 3, 10 and 17 January; *TT*, 6 January; *Morning Chronicle*, 10 January; *HA*, 15 January 1831.

130 *HC*, 17 January; *HT*, 17 January. Cooper's corpse was left at the Sun Inn for six days before being removed to West Grimsted in his native Wiltshire by his friends and family: *HC*, 24 January 1831.

10

Swing and social policy

In the wake of the wave of 'risings' that swept through the Weald, magistrate Collingwood sounded a warning to the Home Office: 'Let the Hampshire Magistrates & Vestries raise the wages, before the Row gets to their county'.[1] This was part rhetoric and part pre-emptive social policy, for however Swing is conceptualised its one universal aim was to improve the living standards of rural workers. One possible strategy was therefore to prevent the further diffusion of protests by parishes either unilaterally increasing wages or acting in concert and multilaterally raising wages. Concession and repression, as Newman and Randall's study of protest and paternalism in Wiltshire attest, often went hand in hand.[2] But with the exception of the few pages of their article devoted to the events of 1830, and Roger Wells's several contributions to Swing's historiography, there has been no systematic study of the ways in which Swing effected changes in employment and other parish policies. In short, we still know remarkably little about how successfully Swing's multifarious activists actually were in achieving their one shared goal.[3]

This chapter addresses this imbalance through an examination of the responses of farmers, vestrymen, magistrates, landowners and poor law officials. What follows shows that not only were rapid revisions made to parochial policy but also that the response to Swing was innovative and, despite the importance of local precedent, wide-ranging. As Swing diffused westwards, responses were often pre-emptive, either in an attempt to prevent protests by predicting the likely demands of protestors, or by making public statements about the unaffordable nature of increased wages and poor relief payments. Often, it is shown, the ability to come to a speedy compact might have sought to diffuse tensions but could set a precedent that acted to encourage other nearby parishes to seek similar demands. These local innovations, this chapter contends, were in part responsible for several key legislative developments in rural social policy before the imposition of the New Poor Law between 1834 and 1836.

The chapter also builds on recent developments in poor law studies focusing on the ways in which the poor were active agents in framing their own relief. Hitherto, this emerging field has been driven by the 'discovery' of pauper letters and other pauper 'narratives', which has had the effect of focusing attentions on the effects of individual actions as opposed to collective protests.[4] As E.P. Thompson's seminal study of interactions in the eighteenth-century marketplace makes plain, crowd actions often helped to frame local policy formation. His – and subsequent – studies also remind us that as employment, wages and poor relief were increasingly juxtaposed we must be alert to whom claims were being made and by whom shifts in policy were being approved. Taking its lead from these literatures, what follows is framed by different social bonds and institutional responsibilities. It starts with an examination of the unilateral and multilateral social policy responses to Swing by farmers and other ratepayers. It then considers the importance of public meetings, before ending with an analysis of the mediating role of magistrates.

Policy at the farm gate and in the vestry

As Chapter 4 shows, demands for higher wages and more generous poor relief payments were not integral to the first Swing mobilisations. Still, the anti-threshing machine pronouncements of the Barham vestry and Lyminge clergyman Rev. Price set the initial precedent for institutional policy responses to Swing.[5] While the rapid diffusion of protests after the 'lenient' sentences handed down to the Elham machine-breakers warned other vestries against making statements regarding the deployment of threshing machines, it was the response to post-trial demands for higher wages that are arguably more telling. The machine-breakers active at Bekesbourne on the night of 23 October 'talked to' one farmer of 'having 2/6 a day', a demand that had also been made to Knatchbull in his investigations into the earlier machine-breaking cases. The farmer made no such promise, but it prompted magistrate Gipps to warn Knatchbull that wages 'ought' be raised 'before the labourers ask'.[6] This refusal to change policy at the farm gate but to consider wages (and relief) at subsequent vestries and meetings set the agenda for southern Swing.

Reports of farmers unilaterally increasing wages in response to the immediate demands of mobile Swing groups are indeed few. The clearest unambiguous report came from the earliest sustained indigenous mobilisations in Hampshire in and around the Dever Valley. Having assembled at Sutton Scotney claiming that 'we are half starved; we are willing to work, let us be paid what we earn, that's all we want!', the reportedly 500-strong group were known to be proceeding to Stratton. On route, they were met by county magistrate Rev. Dr Newbolt, who, having 'always been a friend to the poor', enquired as to their 'wishes'. On their saying they wished to have 12 shillings a week, Newbolt replied saying he thought this 'extremely reasonable' and though he had no jurisdiction to so do, acceded to their demands. Their further demand of his signing an order to their respective overseers to pay them for the two days they had been active destroying threshing machines was also eventually assented to, though only after they had refused to return to work unless it was agreed. Under subsequent questioning, Newbolt admitted that as there was 'a most determined resolution to do great mischief', the men being armed with sledgehammers, saws, axes and bludgeons and threatening to march on Winchester, he felt that if 'the peace of the country was to be preserved conciliation must be resorted to'. If the precedent set by his actions was ill-received by Hampshire landowners and his fellow judiciary, his actions did receive public support from the influential *Hampshire Chronicle*.[7]

An alternative was to first approach large landowners and landlords. On 17 November a group of (reportedly) 300 men went to Uppark to demand of Sir Harry Featherstone that he increase the wages of the men employed on his estate. Under threats that they would destroy the house, Featherstone assented to their wishes. This precedent established, the labourers from the nearby parishes of Harting and Rogate proceeded to visit all the farmers and, again, received promises that their wages would be increased.[8]

Most other reports though tended towards ambiguity. The following cases are typical. At Wadhurst on 10 November, it was reported by the Battle Bench that the labourers had 'riotously assembled' and 'intimidated' the farmers into raising their wages. Five days later, it was reported in the Brighton press that 'most' of the farmers visited by a group of labourers in the vicinity of Lewes had 'complied' with the labourers' demand to increase wages to 2/6 a day.

From Ham Street in Kent, it was noted that the assembled party were successful in 'regulating' the wages. Similarly, a report from Leckford in Hampshire related that a group of men 'with a fair proportion of women and children' proceeded to the farmers' houses and successfully demanded an increase in their wages.[9]

It is, of course, impossible to judge from these reports whether farmers were acting immediately and unilaterally or whether they subsequently came together informally or at a vestry meeting and then acted. Beyond the obvious extrapolation from political economy models that, all else being equal, labourers' wages would tend to the same level in a district, there were very good reasons why farmers would not act alone. As noted in Chapter 2, post-1815 there was a tendency for farmers to act together when changing wages. Thus at Ilminster in Somerset, it was reported that farmer Loaring offered to increase his labourers' wages from 7 shillings to 9 shillings a week if other farmers in the neighbourhood did the same. Conversely, farmer Oakley at Cooling (Kent) responded to the demands of his labourers who struck work for higher wages on 30 October that there was no need for him to increase their wages as he already 'often paid more than his neighbours'.[10]

Labourers knew well that farmers acted collectively. Besides, the juxtaposition between wages and relief – going back to at least the pronouncements of 1795 – was so firmly entrenched in the labouring mind that it was the received practice to make all appeals to either the vestry or the Bench, the latter option being reserved for when pleas to the vestry failed. As the evidence in Chapter 2 shows, during the grain crises of the 1790s and early 1800s groups of rural workers were more likely to descend on the vestry or the Bench than to resort to food rioting. The tactic was also the key way in which collective claims for higher wages and more generous poor relief payments were made in the post-Napoleonic depression.

What, therefore, was the logic behind approaching individual farmers, the process adopted by many southern Swing groups? Machine-breaking groups had to physically traverse the parish from farmer to farmer to break threshing machines, and while in the farmyard they could also ask for higher wages. The group at Ash-next-Sandwich, for instance, had declared their intention of visiting the farmers to ask them to put 'their Machines down or pay more money for labour'.[11] Overwhelmingly, the tactic appears to have been under-written by a desire for legitimacy by forcing *all* employers to act.

Other groups, most notably in the Weald and in mid-Hampshire, carried 'papers' from farm to farm to gather all the farmers' signatures to give collective legitimacy to any promised increase. The wording of the document proffered by the labourers of Steep is instructive:

> From the poor of Steep to the farmers of Steep. Our complaint is that we have not a sufficient maintenance to support our famleys, and as theare a geving more wages in the joining Parishes we do request that you will consent and sine your hands to this Paper that all labering men married and singel abel to a do a day's work to have 2s. per day ... Consented to and signed by ...[12]

By calling on all farmers in the parish, garnering their signatures on a quasi contract thereby engendering a sense of legitimacy and ersatz legal force, unity and order, both within the parish and with other neighbouring parishes, could be restored.

While there might be specific reasons why individual farmers might be visited, especially if they were the incumbent overseer, the critical dynamic in calling upon all farmers in the parish was to force them into collective action by calling a public meeting or a vestry. Refusals to return to work unless wages were increased helped to reinforce the sense of urgency and meant that there was little need to issue violent threats or threaten incendiary attacks, though this did occur at Battle and Waltham (Kent).[13] Turning out from work might have a dubious legality, but there was a sense in which it was accepted as a lesser evil during Swing. Indeed, I have found no case in the south-east where a Swing activist was so prosecuted in 1830. In part, turning a blind eye to turn-outs was a function of the fact that this resembled the customary form of processioning, the response therefore being in keeping with the expected playing out of the ritual. While promises that grievances would duly be attended to did not quell the ardour of all Swing activists,[14] responding to the demands of Swing groups by using ritualised forms – such as offering doles of money, food and beer – was to reference a well understood social code. It admitted paternal responsibility and acted to revivify trust.

Once summoned to meet at the behest of the labourers, vestry meetings invariably agreed to increase wages. This was hardly surprising, for to refuse the earlier demands which predicated the holding of the vestry would be explosive. Thus at Ringmer, the vestry held after Lord Gage intervened in the wages affray after Divine Service of 13 November, agreed to increase the men's wages. This 'determination' to 'give the men what they required' was made possible by Gage reducing his tenants' rents. By force and intimidation, paternalism had been made to work.[15]

What is striking about the deals agreed – for there is a sense of negotiation at these hastily arranged vestries – is that the vestry was acknowledged as a hybrid giver of welfare and regulator of the local labour market. The experience at Soberton was particularly telling. A vestry meeting was called for 24 November after several days of repeated mobilisations in Soberton and the neighbouring parishes. The labourers of the parish attended and were given the option as to whether they wished to receive 12 shillings a week when work was offered, or half a guinea a week and constant employment. The latter option was chosen. Indeed, the formal vestry minute notes that the agreed wage of 10/6 a week should be deemed adequate to support a man, wife and two children, all additional children earning the family an extra gallon loaf and sixpence a week. Moreover, the farmers were to employ the labourers 'according to their rates' – the classic allocation scheme.[16] Likewise at Hailsham, a meeting made 'by appointment' with the labourers for 16 November was attended by 700–800 people where it was agreed that wages would be increased and that an allocation scheme would be adopted so that full employment was restored.[17]

If it was acknowledged that the vestry had a critical role in regulating the labour market and therefore ensuring that work was always available for rural workers, there was also a shared understanding that labourers so engaged were not to be considered as paupers. A meeting at Newick near Lewes on 26 November, held in 'consequence of a notice given to an assemblage of labourers by Frederick Frankland Esq one of the JPs for the Lewes district to consider the state of labouring class', concluded that 'embroiling' the 'question' of wages and poor relief had 'had a pernicious effect'. The agreement between the labourers and the ratepayers allowed for the creation of a 'committee' to help allot out-of-work men to employers, but stated that the 'parish fund' was to deal 'exclusively' with the 'aged, women and children'. Moreover, all able-bodied men over the age of 20 were to be paid 2 shillings a day, an enforcement of the political economy understanding that labour should be 'valued on the basis of production'.[18]

An alternative tactic was to lobby already arranged vestry meetings, though this relied, of course, on the coincidence of the diffusion of Swing through that parish coinciding with a scheduled meeting. This tactic tended to precede wider localised risings. While not making any specific demands, the 'riot' at the Ulcomb vestry meeting on 22 October predated the mobilisations in the neighbouring parishes. Similarly, Robert Price's first involvement in Swing occurred when the group he fronted descended on the nearby Newington vestry on 25 November. Their demand of 2/6 a day with a supplement of 1/6 a week for every child above two in number, and yearly rents of £3–10 were all agreed to.[19] What is even more striking about this concession is that labourers from Newington, before making their wage demands at the vestry meeting, had been actively engaged in destroying threshing machines in nearby Hartlip. This episode of destruction followed an extended drinking session with the Hartlip assistant overseer and two farmers in a new beer shop. A professional poor law officer was, to quote clerical magistrate Poore, complicit in their 'combined plan'.[20] A variation on this theme was practised further along the north Kent coast at Boughton-next-Faversham. The day before a scheduled vestry meeting, a large group of labourers traversed the parish visiting the farmers – a small delegation only entering the farmyard – to demand 2/6 a day. Their plan was then on the following day to reinforce their demand 'in the neighbourhood' before then attending the vestry.[21]

Arguably the clearest expression of the role of the vestry in protest strategies came just over the north Hampshire border in the parishes around Newbury in Berkshire:

> On Monday last [15 November] the labourers of Thatcham parish began to assemble at an early hour, for the purpose of inducing their employers to raise their wages. A sufficient number of them gathered together, they marched off (preceded by one of their company blowing a horn) to visit each of the farms, for the purpose of compelling the labourers to unite with them. By this means their numbers increased, and at noon they amounted to two or three hundred. They then marched into the churchyard and, the select vestry being convened, presented to the gentlemen assembled a verbal request that they might be provided with work, and have their wages advanced. To the former of these requests a favourable answer was returned, but no hope was held out of an improvement in the latter.[22]

The following day the men reassembled, and started to destroy threshing machines. By Friday it was reported that they had destroyed some 43 threshing machines in the area.[23] But the vestry had been their first port of call.

The following morning (Saturday, 20 November), a group of labourers began collecting at the parish of Speen, only four miles distant from Thatcham. Again, the instigators marched from farm to farm imploring all those at work to join them with the purpose of attending a meeting of the select vestry scheduled later that day, rather than launching straight into a machine-breaking campaign. Unlike at Thatcham, it was 'previously known' that the labourers would make an application to the select vestry to increase their wages beyond the meagre 9 shillings a week they were currently receiving. The result was very different. The select vestry, who had a month earlier adopted a so-called Labour Rate to regulate the number of labourers employed by each farmer, resolved to advance all labourers' wages by a shilling a week whether married or not, and any attempt by the labourers to force higher wages would be resisted. Rev. Majendie was delegated to inform the labourers of the decision, though the farmers and the magistrates from Newbury who had heard 'exaggerated reports' about the events at Speen also joined him. The labourers formed a ring – a symbolic performance of unity, deliberately excluding any non-parishioners – and agreed to the select vestry's pronouncement 'disavow[ing] every intention of provoking riot or disorder'.[24]

Not long after the meeting had broken up, 150 labourers gathered at Speenhill where they were swiftly met by the Hungerford Troop of Yeomanry Cavalry and several of the magistrates who had attended the Speen meeting. The men were surrounded by the Yeomanry as magistrate Rev. Fowle – who had been at the earlier meeting – called on the Speen men to come forward and state their reasons for rioting. The response was that they wanted more wages. The select vestry decision was relayed and the men, apparently, dispersed.[25] The effect of iterating the decision to a group of labourers of whom few actually came from Speen was to inspire those from other parishes to force an increase in wages. On Monday – Sunday being a day of rest for Berkshire protestors – the area surrounding Speen rose in unison destroying machines and demanding higher wages.[26]

Cases of applying pressure at vestry meetings in areas where Swing was already established might have been more unusual – for once

Swing was established in the locale all normal 'business' ceased – but they tended to be more dramatic, relying on the possibility of bodily violence to exert terror over the vestrymen, as occurred at Horsham and at Wrotham.[27] In most cases concessions were easily won from vestries, with no need to issue threats and posture violently. At Billingshurst, a Sussex parish plagued by unemployment and with notoriously poor living conditions for labouring families, 100 labourers assembled at a prearranged vestry meeting and sent in a letter to the vestrymen demanding 2 shillings per day for married men and an extra 2 shillings a week for each child over and above the second born. The demands were immediately assented to and the labourers dispersed. Likewise, at Ore near Hastings, those gathered requested higher wages, a demand to which the vestry 'immediately acceded'.[28] In areas on the fringes of Swing activity, approaches to scheduled vestries could be decidedly more modest. On 25 November, three men employed on the Great Mongeham roads approached the vestry for 'an advance of wages'. Not only was this agreed but the vestry resolved to increase wages for all labourers in the parish.[29]

Some parishes tried to prevent Swing protests from occurring in their parish by calling vestry meetings and pre-emptively arranging employment, increasing wages and poor relief. Nowhere was this dynamic more complex than in the parishes contiguous to the Elham and Ash machine-breaking area. For instance, on 27 October the Crundale vestry decided that the recently appointed assistant overseer should purchase 'some wood' in which the poor were to be employed in felling timber.[30] Whether such a scheme was directly motivated by the fear of Swing is perhaps a moot point, but in some cases this uncertainty is removed by the wording of a vestry minute or a report. Thus, *The Times* reported that at Hamsey near Lewes the farmers had met to 'advance' the labourers wages to 'avoid a rising of the peasants'. Similarly, the Petworth Vestry met on 13 November '[i]n consequence of the outrages which have been committed at various places' to not only devise a plan to watch the town but also to increase the wages of the labourers employed on the roads.[31]

In areas where Swing was already established, there was a sense of inevitability, even resigned hopelessness, that vestries must act to meet localised demands. This was best summed up by events in and around Liphook. On 21 November, a paper promising an increase in wages had been signed by several gentlemen at Liphook, despite the protestations of several farmers that they would employ *no* labourers at the 'agreed' wages. Writing to Melbourne, Samuel Twyford, Sussex magistrate and resident of Trotton, believed a similar attempt would be made in the neighbouring parishes. The following day, Twyford again wrote to the Home Office. That morning he had met with a small group brandishing a copy of the paper at Hollycombe and demanding an increase of wages. Having refused to sign the paper, Twyford asked to know what the men meant to 'make of' the paper. They replied that they thought that as it had been signed by Sir Charles Taylor, a major local landowner, that the document 'might be of service at the Vestry' to be held that day. Despite his opposition, he still declared that: 'I am to attend the parish vestry tomorrow at Trotton, which is my place, and we are to decide what is to be done: no doubt we must advance the wages + approach the demands of the paper as near + as long as we can.'[32]

Assuaging the immediate threat of protests in the parish amid intensive local protests was also the motivation at Alton on 22 November. The select vestry noted: 'That the Poor of Alton appear desirious, as far as in them lies, of providing for themselves and their Famlies, by their own labour and exertions, and merit the assistance and support of the Inhabitants at large in the performance of this duty'. Whether the fear of protests stoked the collective conscience of the select vestry or the vestrymen had taken a gamble that increasing wages now would prevent the destruction of property witnessed in the neighbouring parishes is debatable. For either way, the result was an increase in wages to 12 shillings a week and more generous child allowances.[33]

The rapid diffusion of Swing through West Kent after 22 October, through the Weald in early November, and throughout Hampshire after 17 November, without any clear advance sign, meant that parish vestries had little opportunity to act pre-emptively. Indeed, Collingwood's prophecy and the upturn in incendiarism in Hampshire before 17 November provided no warning of what was to come. The only part of the south-east where the diffusion of Swing was more predictable was also the sole area where there was a clear sense that vestries were attempting to prevent protests: West Sussex. In addition to the above mentioned vestry at Petworth on 13 November, vestries at Pulborough on the 10th, Cuckfield on the 11th, and at Worth on the 13th all attempted to find work for the 'unemployed poor'.[34] Subsequent reported protests in all these parishes, with the exception of Worth, attest to the limited understanding of the nature of Swing and the fact that individual vestries were powerless to prevent the diffusion of Swing.

By far the most important way in which vestry policy was impacted upon by Swing though was in a post hoc way, either giving formal sanction to policies agreed at non-legally binding 'meetings' (for which see below) or acting to address a perceived need. The example of Owslebury is instructive. On 23 November, an agreement drafted by farmers Smith and Deacle in the hope that, according to Justice Parkes at the Hampshire Special Commission, the rents and tithes might be reduced, was taken by a 'great party' to all the farmers in the parish for their signatures. Sixteen days later, the very farmers that had signed the agreement met at the vestry and now resolved that all men over the age of twenty would be paid 10 shillings a week with a sliding scale for younger men and those at work on the roads with additional allowances for those with four children or more. All refusals to work, though, would 'lead to withdrawal of parish relief and proceedings in law'. Moreover, having 'removed all causes of discontent' the vestry would 'not yield to intimidation or threats on the part of the men.'[35]

There was no sense at Owslebury, or elsewhere, that such agreements were to carry on indefinitely. Indeed, few were the places where, as at Amport, policies agreed during the heat of Swing were subsequently extended. At East Woodhay, for instance, the ratification of earlier Swing agreements by a vestry meeting on 2 December acknowledged that all wage and allowance rates were 'subject to revision and alteration the 2nd week in January'.[36] As early as 15 December at Hurstpierpoint, it was minuted that the 'system was not working', while a vestry meeting at Alresford a fortnight earlier resolved to abandon a policy agreement made 'at the Alresford [magistrates] meeting', instead agreeing 'upon the principle of reducing the weekly wages to 10/- including an allowance of the price of a gallon loaf to every child above two in number'. Battle vestry even agreed to the potentially explosive policy of reinstating the office of assistant overseer, a post that would now also entail acting as the workhouse governor.[37]

Multilateral agreements meant little though if a particular farmer had already, in the words of the Chithurst petition, 'spent every farthing'. As the *Hampshire Advertiser* noted of the protests at Fawley, while the pronouncement of the magistrates that a commensurate reduction in farmers' rents and tithes would help ease the cost of higher wages, small farmers could not find the money to pay the previous level of wages. Instead, they were reduced to partly paying their labourers in truck with corn and potatoes.[38] Attempts to make sense of, implement, and even amend agreements forged in the heat of the mo(ve)ment were also problematic, all such vestry minutes betraying the same sense of despondency in dealing with issues of unemployment as pre-Swing vestries had. This frustration is perhaps best expressed by attempts at Frindsbury, near Rochester, to find employ for those out of work. The vestry met on 4 December and resolved to hold a further meeting five days later to consider the issue. The meeting never occurred.[39] Those parishes that could come to some resolution invariably turned to roundsmen-type labour allocation schemes.

While experiences – and resolutions – varied across the south-east, the policy machinations of the South Bersted vestry effectively sum up the problems faced. On 26 November, it was resolved that all 'out parishoners' (i.e. those not chargeable to the parish) were to be discharged by the farmers. A week later, it was decided that the farmers should employ two able-bodied men (or one man and two boys) for each £100 rate, with the 'surplus' labourers 'divided' amongst the rate-payers. Reporting the implementation of the scheme, on 9 December it was noted that thirty-six parishioners over the age of sixteen were still unemployed.[40] This age-old problem of farmers refusing to employ their 'quota' of labourers even resulted in the Battle vestry threatening to summon refuseniks to attend the next meeting of the local bench.[41]

As Monju Dutt and, more recently, Jeremy Burchardt have noted, Swing also acted to give impetuous to the nascent allotment movement, vestries acting to provide allotments to labourers *before* the passing of 1 and 2 William IV, c.42 in mid-1831 which gave legal sanction to such parochial provision.[42] While such schemes could be variations on pre-Swing 'parish farms' – the Wallington (Surrey) vestry employed 'a professional man' to set the poor to work digging a piece of ground[43] – many were genuine allotment schemes which sought to make labouring families independent of parish support. The earliest scheme I have found in response to Swing occurred at Lindfield in mid-Sussex. Here, a vestry considering how to 'more effectively employ the labouring poor' resolved that instead of relieving labouring families with money, or in kind, decided to allot land 'at a fair rent'. This though was an extension of an earlier policy that itself had been extended the previous February from 6 to 30 labourers.[44]

Hampshire was the south-eastern county where allotment provision as a vestry policy was most frequently adopted, with a cluster of adopting parishes in the south-west of the county.[45] This is perhaps a reflection of the fact that, as Burchardt has found, many of the earliest allotment schemes were in the neighbouring counties of Dorset and Wiltshire, the 'local' example being publicised in the provincial press.[46] However, as the pre-history of the Lindfield allotments attests, some schemes in the south-east already provided an inspiration to vestries trying to respond to Swing's objectives. For instance, in the spring of 1830, Hampshire MP Fleming 'originated' an 'experiment' at North Stoneham wherein he granted allotments rent free to labouring families, with the overseers providing free seeds, on the proviso that they did not make any subsequent claims on the parish. This scheme was soon copied at nearby Romsey, while the Bishop of Winchester offered to enclose forty acres of 'waste' to the Bishop's Waltham vestry to provide allotments.[47] Indeed, the turn to allotments as an immediate response to Swing was only possible because of existing local examples and supportive large landowners.

Public meetings

As shown in Chapter 9, throughout the south-east magistrates and mayors called public meetings to discuss Swing's suppression and to swear in special constables. Many of these meetings also considered wages and welfare responses to Swing. In addition to planned and publicised meetings, many were held at very short notice and at the behest of protestors. Meetings were an integral part of rural life for many labourers, not least through attending the vestry and being summoned to the Bench. Demanding the attendance of farmers at a meeting was therefore both an attempt to secure legitimacy and a way of asserting that the labourers were now in control of the levers of parish government. Indeed, while the word 'meeting' was used indiscriminately to describe all sorts of Swing gatherings, rural workers did have recent form for organising their own meetings. Beyond smuggling – the missions only made possible by the key organisers meeting together – the protestors at Brede had been holding meetings to discuss their grievances, while at Sutton Scotney the 'Musical and Radical Society' boasted many Swing activists among its number.[48] Critically, such hastily convened parish meetings, unlike vestry meetings, had no legal status and would often conflate matters of wages and poor relief with farm rents and tithes. This section explores how both types of meetings were key ways in which the social policy demands of Swing were addressed.

Hastily arranged meetings initially assumed a prominence in mediating the social policy demands of labourers in the Weald of Sussex, an area where farmers became active supporters of the labourers' cause in the hope that the terror created by a labourers' movement would help to win concessions on rents and tithes. The second such meeting occurred at Robertsbridge on 8 November and was as much organised by the farmers with their objectives in mind as it was with improving the conditions of the labourers whose low wages were supplemented with very low grade flour that many were forced to sell to finance other purchases. This was a concerted plan. Several farmers had lent their support to the labourers' call for higher wages in return for the labourers helping to intimidate the tithe holder into making a considerable reduction. Both were achieved.[49] In neighbouring Hawkhurst, the 'success' of the Robertsbridge meeting prompted a similar one to be arranged for the following morning. From midnight, John Beale, a carpenter who had been present at Robertsbridge, returned to Hawkhurst and, with a group of artisans and labourers, began traversing Hawkhurst and 'several of the adjoining parishes' calling on 'the poor and ill-disposed' to join them. After destroying a threshing machine on a Hawkhurst farm, the growing band headed to the village to demand higher wages and more generous relief 'work or no work'. At the meeting, fixed for 2 p.m., their demands were put to a vote, the great majority of ratepayers being in favour of increasing the wages. The men then left, giving three cheers to the King and declaring that they were loyal and would not be seduced by persons going about the country.[50]

Not all meetings relied on a shared compact. For instance, at Guestling near Battle the 'paupers' had given notice to the 'heads of the parish' to meet at 10 a.m. on 8 November, threatening that if they did not they would be 'fetched'. At the well attended meeting, an increase in wages was agreed to, with the 130 or so labourers present advising the farmers to 'shake off the oppression of the tithes'.[51] Sometimes the promise of a meeting could also act to temporarily assuage a Swing group, either prompting them to disperse, as occurred at Freefolk, or to turn their attentions elsewhere, as occurred at Whitchurch on the afternoon of 17 November in the first Swing mobilisation in mid-Hampshire.[52] Another variation on this theme occurred at Etchingham where a pre-planned meeting of the 'occupiers of land' to consider the level of wages and how to best employ the parish labourers was beset by a group of labourers. Their 'petition' calling for a raft of changes to both employment and relief scales was assented to by the farmers, even though 'in the present distressed state of agriculture they are totally unable to continue for any length of time to pay the same'.[53]

Conversely, rural workers could determine all aspects of a meeting: the location, the day, the time and who attended. The best example occurred at Steep where 'persons calling themselves delegates from the general committee' ordered all the labourers in the parish to meet in the churchyard on the morning of 23 November. Magistrate Quarrier duly alerted the farmers as to the labourers' plan and requested that they should 'not allow' their workmen from attending the scheduled meeting. This had no effect. The meeting went ahead, forcing Quarrier, the overseers and some of the farmers to also attend. While no promise of higher wages was given, Quarrier did make the concession that, provided the men did not go to a planned meeting the following day at Petersfield market, he would meet with all the farmers and would also report their condition to Lord Lieutenant the Duke of Wellington.[54]

Sometimes, though, the concessions offered at hurriedly arranged meetings were later denied. For instance, on 20 November a group of labourers assembled at Lower Wallop in Hampshire and were soon met by the farmers in a large field. A promise to raise their wages from 8 shillings a week to 10 shillings was duly given but only on the proviso that the labourers must go to the tithe proprietor and demand a 30 per cent reduction on the threat of his house being set on fire if he refused. Proprietor Blunt 'resisted' this 'illegal demand', prompting the farmers to retort in a letter to the editor of the *Hampshire Chronicle* that they had never made any deal with the labourers.[55]

Elsewhere, resolutions at meetings were quickly regretted. For instance, at a meeting at Alton on 24 November, it was agreed that the workhouse mill where the poor were put to work would be destroyed, something that was accomplished in a 'wanton manner'. When the vestry met two days later they expressed their 'entire disapprobation' at the results of the earlier 'meeting' but 'as it has been represented to this Vestry that a Misconception prevailed on the Subject, they do not wish to notice if farther than by their most decided reprehension'.[56] Similarly, when the labourers gathered at Ashmansworth in north Hampshire on 22 November, the rector went out to speak to the 'civil ... but apparently determined' men and assured them that the farmers would redress their grievances. On this promise, a meeting was arranged for that evening where the farmers effectively compelled the Rector to return 15 per cent of his tithes to facilitate their increasing the men's wages by 50 per cent to 12 shillings a week. 'If there is room in Winchester gaol', lamented the rector, 'I shall probably occupy a place there this year [as a debtor]'.[57]

If the Ashmansworth rector felt compelled to make some concession to Swing's broadening constituency, many of his fellow clergy together with landlords, magistrates and mayors felt a sense of duty to meet together to discuss their response to the unfurling protests. While the *Hampshire Advertiser* self-righteously proclaimed in early December that 'we have long raised our voice on behalf of the suffering poor, and endeavoured to avert the certain serious consequences of reducing the lower orders of the people to a state of pauperism', there was little sense that before the protests started such calls were being heeded. Indeed, the wave of rent and tithe reductions in the winter of 1829–30 were not met by a corresponding increase in wages.[58] Only the threat of protests – or protests themselves – prompted the rulers of rural England to act. Thus, as the protests threatened to spread from Wiltshire to south Somerset in late November and early December, magistrates and landowners acted to enforce wage increases. For instance, Dorset county MP Edward Portman reduced his tenants' rents in Somerset on the 'instruction' that they then proportionately increase their labourers' wages. A similar instruction was also issued by landlord Stanley to his tenants in South Petherton.[59]

The response in the south-east was usually made in direct response to protests in the vicinity. A meeting at Lymington on the southern coastal fringe of the New Forest was held on 23 November, it having been called before Swing had spread to the area. The purpose was publicly stated to be the adoption of measures to protect 'property from the diabolical acts of incendiaries, who ... are making their way through this and the adjoining counties'. It was observed though that as the problem was labourers' poverty, nothing would 'appease them but an advance of wages'. Notwithstanding their concerns regarding affordability, the farmers from Lymington, Boldre, Brockenhurst,

Hordle and Milford (with only one dissenting voice) agreed to raise the men's wages to 9 shillings a week, with the parish to provide a gallon loaf and sixpence extra per week per child. A small group of labourers then turned up to the meeting and, on being told about the agreement, expressed their 'great gladness' at the news. Only then did the meeting proceed to discuss the swearing in of specials, the creation of a nightly watch, and the raising of a subscription to pay for any future rewards in cases of incendiarism.[60]

Similarly at Millbrook on the edge of Southampton, a meeting was held on 24 November in response to the 'risings in Kent ... that would spread gradually throughout the country'. By then the parish had already hosted a wages rising, but the meeting had been planned since the previous week. Having considered that the claims of the poor were 'by no means unjust', Sir George Hewett determined that his tenants on the Freemantle Estate should increase their labourers' wages to 12 shillings a week, a sum that Lord Lisle was already paying on his farm. Despite objections that many labourers currently receiving 10 shillings a week were 'perfectly happy', it was agreed that on such wages labourers could not possibly 'morally live'.[61]

If the Lymington and Millbrook meetings tried to pre-empt – and prevent – further protests, elsewhere in the south-east meetings were reactive rather than proactive. For instance, at Havant on 22 November, a meeting was held to consider measures to prevent the 'reoccurrence of tumults and to relieve [the] poor by finding them work' in the district. Those in attendance resolved to ascertain the 'number of poor in each parish not in constant employ', secure them work, and to increase wages if it was 'thought necessary'.[62] Likewise, at a meeting held in Winchester on 20 November 'to adopt measures to preserve the peace in consequence of the excitement which has been manifested in the neighbourhood', after agreeing on the need to enrol special constables, the Mayor also remarked that the wage demands of the protestors were not 'unreasonable' and that if their 'wishes were acceded to tranquility would be restored'.[63] Even at the most notorious Swing meeting of all, that convened by the Duke of Wellington in the Great Hall at Winchester on 25 November, among all the discussion of raising yeomanry and volunteer corps, swearing in special constables, and holding a special commission, many magistrates were 'anxious ... to relieve the distresses of the labouring classes who had paid obedience to the laws'.[64]

Magistrates' mediations

As the above example from Alresford shows, in many parts of the south-east, vestry responses to Swing were impossible to separate from magistrates' reactions. This response could take three forms. First, single magistrates who were also substantial landowners might use their influence in their home parishes to alter policy, as occurred at Herriard under the auspices of JP Jervoise.[65] Second, lone magistrates could act in direct response to events. And third, magistrates acting together – usually in the form of the Bench – could intervene in the setting of wage and relief scales. Explicit evidence of interventions by magistrates in their home parishes is scant, as such this section analyses the latter two interventions.

As noted in the introduction to this chapter, from the first social policy interventions of magistrates in relation to Swing, concession went hand in hand with repression. A meeting held at Ashford on 30 October to 'preserve the peace' combined an attempt to swear in special constables with efforts by the magistrates to 'set' the labourers, in Knatchbull's words, 'at proper wages'.[66] This early precedent might have been in part responsible for the relative quiescence of the environs of Ashford, but it was in the vicinity of Battle that magistrates' policy interventions first transformed the course of Swing. In response to the events at Brede and Battle itself, the Battle Petty Sessions met on 5 November and adjourned until Monday 8 November. On this fact becoming known locally, a group at Burwash were prevented from removing the assistant overseer on 7 November, being told of a meeting scheduled at Battle the following day 'to raise wages'. The Battle labourers then sent a message to their brethren at Seddlescomb 'and other adjoining parishes' calling on them to join at Battle. Several parties from different parishes did go to Battle, joining the local labourers at the meeting of the Petty Sessions. Their demands were heard and 'satisfactorily arranged', or rather, in the words of *The Times*, the 'mob of farmers' men' acted to 'intimidate the magistrates into some concessions'. Critically, it would appear that the magistrates' arrangement referred only to the Battle labourers. However, the precedent now set, attempts were made almost immediately to enforce it elsewhere.[67]

The example, it would appear, acted across the whole of the Battle Petty Sessions district. On 18 November, the Home Office received a petition from the farmers of Dallington parish complaining of the level of taxation. Having raised their workers' wages and relief, as 'wished' by the magistrates, they were reduced to a state of 'common ruin' and could not continue without some relief. That same day, Phillips informed Petty Sessions chairman George Courthope of the petition, Peel thinking that he ought 'be informed of the contents'. This brought a swift retort: 'we [the Battle Bench] have never resolved to raise wages'.[68]

The problems in the Battle district set the scene for subsequent magistrates' interventions in regulating wages and relief. The next major interventions occurred in West Sussex. Wages risings (and the destruction of threshing machines) had started around Arundel on 15 November, with protests spreading to the edge of Chichester on the following day. Initially, showing 'much firmness', the groups had gone from farmhouse to farmhouse refusing to leave without a promise of higher wages, something *The Times* reported they achieved. Fears that a party of 1,000 labourers would descend on Chichester on 17 November, it being the market day, prompted a group of magistrates headed by Lord George Lennox to meet the men at Eartham. A promise was then made that they should address their concerns to their respective parishes and that if they then did not get redress they should send a delegation to the Chichester Bench. On Thursday 18 November, the Upper Division of the Rape of Chichester held an emergency Petty Sessions at Chichester.[69] In addition to reasserting their intention of putting down all assemblages and punishing all those involved in 'outrages', they promised that they were 'perfectly ready to give every attention to any grievances the labouring classes may individually bring before them'.[70] A similar understanding as to the power (or lack) and politics of magistrates in setting wages was demonstrated at Horsham, the magistrates acknowledging that they could not legally increase wages.[71]

The approach of the Arundel Bench was rather different. On 18 November, one group of protestors had even entered Arundel, only dispersing after the Earl of Surrey promised them their grievances would be 'redressed'. Meanwhile, a call to the Home Office for military assistance met with Peel's suggestion that the magistrates should meet to swear in special constables. A 'full' bench duly assembled on 19 November and proceeded to swear in all 'respectable and trustworthy' people. Moreover, notwithstanding that 'in all other places where rioters have made their appearance they have frightened the farmers into their demands' of receiving 2/6 a day, the parish, at the magistrates intervention, would only increase their wages to 2 shillings a day but with an allowance of 1/6 per week per child. Having, in the words of mayor and magistrate William Holmes, made a 'stand' against their demands, they were fearful that it would 'no doubt create Disturbances for weeks to come'. However, Surrey promised that, on behalf of his father the Duke of Norfolk, that he would 'extend assistance' to the farmers to allow them to increase their wages. Consequently, it was reported in the London press that the following day most of the men were back to work at increased wages.[72]

It thus appeared that the Bench had sanctioned an increase in wages for the whole district, the scale 'adopted' soon being used in other parishes, including at Steyning on Monday 22 November. By 7 December, the Bench was forced to backtrack. They again met and acknowledged that they 'had no power by law to fix wages between farmers and their servants' but could only appoint the rate of wages to be paid to those directly employed by the parish. They duly set a scale for parish pay and at the same time produced a parallel scale of 'recommended' wages for farmers' men at the previously 'agreed' rates.[73]

Similar problems were also encountered in Hampshire, the need to prevent further protests – not least incendiary fires – and to address the immediate demands of a potentially turbulent group of men potentially placing many magistrates in a compromising position. Clerical magistrate Newbolt's intervention at Bishops Sutton near Winchester might (though of course there is no way of telling) have prevented an 'invasion' of the city but provoked criticism. He had had to deal with, so Newbolt reported to Melbourne, the first rising in the county and therefore had 'no precedence to follow'. Through his 'conciliation', eight parishes had returned to work, a farmer's property had been saved from destruction, and he had saved himself from a violent attack. Melbourne was in no mood to receive apologies. The 'tranquillity which has been purchased', Phillips replied on his behalf, 'is likely to be a very treacherous & uncertain character', for concessions made in fear were not 'likely to be long adhered to'.[74] Elsewhere, at Liphook the aforementioned problems caused by 'gentlemen' signing a wages agreement were further exacerbated on 22 November when some of the Petersfield Bench met with a group of Swing activists on their way into the town. After a *'promise* of an increase in wages' (original emphasis) the men appeared satisfied and went off in the opposite direction to Petersfield.[75]

The most notorious of all the well intentioned but misdirected magistrates' intercessions in Hampshire occurred at Andover on 20 November, an area of intense early protests in the county. This was not the first emergency meeting of a Hampshire Bench during Swing, though: on the previous day the Alton Bench met at Alresford to consider the 'most effectual measures ... to put down a riotous + tumultuous assembly'. Whatever their initial intentions, 100 men descended on the Bench to 'clamorously demand' an increase in their wages. Having taken their demands into consideration, the Bench publicly pronounced an increase in wages and 'the multitude' departed after giving three cheers and chanting 'God Save the King'. The Bench's policy decision was subsequently advertised by a poster detailing a complex scale of payments (see figure 10.1), presumably an institutional legacy of the long history of bread scales in north Hampshire.

The pronouncement did nothing though to save Tasker's Iron Foundry from attack later that day, nor from Andover remaining the focus for protests the following day. When the protests had finally passed, C.W. Foster wrote to the Home Office to communicate what had occurred. There had been a 'great want of unanimity' among the authorities, which had allowed the labourers to impose 'such a rate of pay as they conceive to be their due', setting a precedent that in any future difficulties they could 'renew their extortions'.[76] Either way, local vestries acted on the policy. Amport Vestry met on 22 November and adopted the scale. Captain Pringle in his report to the Poor Law Commissioners noted that at Weyhill the labourers had at the time 'swallowed this new law evidently with some misgivings as to its duration', while the farmers 'grumbled, but submitted to it' in the belief that their rents and tithes would be reduced. Three years later, the policy was still in operation.[77]

Effects

The destruction of a threshing machine was absolute. And in the context of the heightened atmosphere of the autumn and winter of 1830, it was a foolhardy act to repair or purchase a new machine. Despite the risks involved in machine-breaking, as an objective, securing an increase in wages and more generous poor relief payments was altogether a less certain proposition. Still, throughout the south-east, Swing's multifarious activists were remarkably

ANDOVER, HANTS.

At a Meeting of the Magistrates for the

Division of Andover in the County of Southampton, and also at a Meeting of the Magistrates for the Borough and Parish of Andover, respectively held on Saturday, the twentieth Day of November Instant, the undermentioned Resolutions were proposed and agreed to, viz:

THAT they would recommend the several Occupiers of Land, in the different Parishes within the said Division, to allow the Labouring Class within their respective Parishes, the following rate of Wages, that is to say,

EVERY able bodied Man above the age of 20 Years, the sum of twelve Shillings per Week.

EVERY able bodied Man above the age of 16 and under 20 Years of age, the sum of nine Shillings per Week.

EVERY old and infirm Person, the sum of three Shillings per Week.

THEY will also recommend that a Gallon Loaf of Bread and Sixpence be allowed to a married Man for every Child above the number of two, after such Child shall have attained the age of one Month.

IN consequence of the above Resolutions and impressed as we are with the Conviction of the impossibility of our Labourers existing on their present rate of Wages, WE, the undersigned Occupiers of Land in the Parish and Neighbourhood of Andover, are induced to agree to the above Resolutions, trusting that our Landlors and Tithe Proprietors or their Agents will meet us on Saturday the twenty seventh Day of November Instant, at eleven o'Clock in the forenoon, at the Star and Garter Inn, in Andover, to enter into such Arrangments as will enable us so to do.

John Sweetapple	William Sweetapple	Thomas Longman	Robert Longman
Philip Henry Poore	Samuel Guyatt	William Child	Henry Poore
Richard Fortesque	William Dowling	Mary Lawes	George Marshment
Henry Tredgold	Robert Dowling	John Young	Henry Simes
Thomas Dowling	Abraham Goater	John Chandler	James Cole
Joseph Wakeford	Henry King	George Chandler	Robert Tilbury
John Lywood	Henry Cordery	William Chandler	William Hilliard
Robert Pickering	George Dowling	George Young	John Knowles
Charles Cheyney	Thomas Spencer	William Leveredge	Robert Tilbury, Jun.
George Guyatt	Nicholas Cole	Susan Batt	William Cooper
George Dawkins	William Attwood	Thomas Baugh	Robert Martin
Edward Ranger	John Holloway	John Cole	Robert Cole
Charles Holdway	Charles Mundy	Harry Church	Hugh China
John Reeves	Hugh Mundy	Charles Church	Ann Cole
William Longman, Sen.	William Moon	John Herbert	Mary Farley
Robert Pocock	Thomas Biggs	William Moore	Anthony Kersley
William Goodall	John Kellow	Thomas Sutton	John Hooper
George Dowling	Thomas Hutchins		

Andover, November 23, 1830.

KING, PRINTER, BOOKBINDER &c. HIGH STREET, ANDOVER.

10.1 Poster advertising the resolutions of the Andover Bench,
20 November 1830

successful in securing these objectives. No standard wage was demanded, the increase generally mirroring previous differences: as a rule, wages in the Weald and south-west Hampshire rose to 10 shillings; in mid-Sussex, east, mid- and north Hampshire 12 shillings and occasionally 13 shillings; and in east, mid- and north Kent and coastal West Sussex, to 14 shillings. Child allowances, where they had previously been paid, were also invariably part of the negotiation concerning wages, an explicit acknowledgement that Swing was not always concerned with establishing the absolute independence of wage labourers from dependence on the poor rates. Ultimately, though, Swing activists' demands were about the remuneration of male labour, the payment of parish pensions to the old and infirm were hardly ever raised by Swing groups. That the new Andover scale even detailed pensions was simply a reflexive act, a complete guide to overseers as to how the new system was to work.

Rural workers' triumphs were clearly a function of many different dynamics: farmers' fear, successful threats and a reinvigorated paternalism, partly stoked by landlords' fear that their property would otherwise go up in flames. But there is also a sense that Swing engaged vestrymen, landlords, the clergy, the nobility and magistrates in open negotiations to reconsider the value of labour and the social and political place of labourers in rural society. But, as noted in Chapter 4, within weeks farmers acting in collusion in rural vestries sought to reduce wages and allowances to pre-Swing levels. Such almost immediate retrenchments begat further protests. A group of West Chiltington road workers marched on the Petworth Bench on 4 December to complain that their parish had reneged on a local agreement,[78] while the labourers of Twyford threw off work nine days later after an attempt to cut their wages.[79] Were such protests an attempt to protect Swing's hard-won gains or the start of something post-Swing? The following chapter attempts to answer these questions through an analysis of what happened in the period between the end of 1830 and the initial attempts in early 1834 to construct the New Poor Law unions that would, in many parts of the south-east, fundamentally change rural social relations.

Notes

1 TNA, HO 52/10, fos 448–52, G.R. Collingwood Esq., Battle to Phillips, n.d. (but mid-November 1830).

2 A. Randall and E. Newman, 'Protest, proletarians and paternalists: social conflict in rural Wiltshire, 1830–1850', *Rural History*, 6:2 (1995), 205–27.

3 Ibid., *passim*; R. Wells, 'Social protest, class, conflict and consciousness, in the English countryside', in M. Reed and R. Wells (eds) *Class, Conflict and Protest in the English Countryside, 1700–1880* (London: Frank Cass, 1990), pp. 121–214; and Wells, 'The moral economy of the English countryside', in A. Randall and A. Charlesworth (eds), *Moral Economy and Popular Protest: Crowds, Conflict and Authority* (Basingstoke: Macmillan, 2000), pp. 209–72.

4 See T. Sockoll (ed.), *Essex Pauper Letters, 1731–1837* (Oxford: Oxford University Press, 2001). Also see A. Levene (ed.) *Narratives of the Poor in Eighteenth-Century Britain*, volume 1 ('Voices of the Poor: Poor Law Depositions and Letters') (London: Pickering & Chatto, 2006).

5 Report from the *Spectator*, q.f. *Kent Herald* (hereafter *KH*), 6 January 1831. BPP Commons, 'Report from His Majesty's Commissioners for Inquiring into the Administration and Practical Operation of the Poor Laws' (hereafter 'Operation of the Poor Laws') (1834), vol. xxxiv 237e, Response of John Pope, Barham, question 53; Hobsbawm and Rudé, *Captain Swing*, p. 85.

6 CKS, U951 C14/5 G. Gipps, Howletts to Knatchbull, 28 October 1830.

7 *Southampton Mercury* (hereafter *SM*), 20 November; *Hampshire Chronicle* (hereafter *HC*), 22 November; TNA, HO 52/7, fos 191–3: Rev. Dr Newbolt, Winchester to Melbourne, 10 December 1830.

8 TNA, HO 52/7, fos 31–2, Petersfield Post Office Deputy to Sir Francis Freeling, GPO, 18 November 1830.

9 TNA, HO 52/10, fos 394–5, Battle Bench to Peel, 12 November; *Brighton Gazette* (hereafter *BG*), 18 November; *Kentish Gazette* (hereafter *KG*), 19 November; *HC*, 29 November 1830.

10 *Keene's Bath Journal*, 6 December; *Rochester Gazette* (hereafter *RG*), 2 November 1830.

11 CKS, Q/SBe/121/9, Deposition of William Euden, labourer, 19 November 1830.

12 *Portsmouth, Portsea and Gosport Herald* (hereafter *PHer*), 28 November 1830.

13 *Maidstone Journal* (hereafter *MJ*), 9 November; *The Times* (hereafter *TT*), 11 November 1830.

14 *Hampshire Advertiser* (hereafter *HA*), 27 November; *HC*, 29 November; TNA HO 130/1, Hampshire Special Commission case 159 (Droxford). For example a Swing group at Droxford on being promised that their 'situation would be looked into' directly proceeded to destroy a model threshing machine at neighbouring Swanmore.

15 *BG*, 18 and 25 November; *Brighton Herald*, 20 November; *MJ*, 23 November; *TT*, 25 November 1830.

16 HCRO, 50M73 PV1, Soberton Vestry Minute, 24 November; *HA*, 27 November 1830.

17 ESCRO, PAR 353/12/1/25, Hailsham Vestry Minute, 16 November; *TT*, 25 November 1830.

18 ESCRO, PAR 428/12/2, Newick Vestry Minute, 26 November 1830.

19 *MJ*, 26 October; CKS, Q/SBw/124/7, Defence of Robert Price, 19 November; TNA, HO 52/8, fos 365–6 and 361–2, Poore, Murston to Peel, 25 October,

Sharp, Faversham to Freeling, 26 October; CKS, U951 C14/7, Poore to Knatchbull, 26 October; *Kent Herald* (hereafter *KH*), 8 October 1830.

20 Rev. Poore, Murston to Peel, 23 October, TNA HO 52/8, fos 300–1; same to Knatchbull, 24 October 1830, CKS U951 C177/35.

21 *TT*, 4 November; *KG*, 5 November 1830.

22 *Reading Mercury* (hereafter *RM*), 22 November 1830.

23 *Berkshire Chronicle*, 20 November; *RM*, 22 November 1830; NA TS 11/849–2900A/39 and 24, Prosecution brief and Treasury Solictor's notes in the case of *The King* v. *James Burgess, George Williams, Edward Harris and John Nash* for machine-breaking, Aldermarston.

24 TNA, HO 52/6, fos 10–13, Frederick Page, Deputy Lord Lieutenant of Berkshire, Goldwell House, Speen to Peel, 21 November 1830.

25 TNA, HO 52/6, fos 47–8, Captain Liddendale with co-signees, Hungerford, 22 November, to Sir Charles Dundas, Barton Court near Newbury, forwarded to Melbourne, 24 November 1830.

26 TNA, HO 52/7, fos 16–17, 25–6 and 27–30, J. Westall, Hungerford to Sir Francis Freeling, Post Master General, John Pearse, Childon Lodge, near Hungerford, and Fred Page, Speen to Peel, all 22 November 1830.

27 For Horsham references see note 11. Wrotham: TNA, HO 52/8, fos 237–8, Camden, Wilderness to Melbourne, 28 November; *TT*, 29 November; *RG*, 30 November; *KH*, 2 December 1830.

28 *BG*, 18 November and 23 December; *KH*, 24 November; *TT*, 25 November; *Hastings & Cinque Ports Iris*, 20 November; CKS, U1127 C21, Sir Howard Elphistone, Ore Place to William Smith, Gravesend, 25 November 1830.

29 CCA, U3/128/8/1, Great Mongeham Vestry Minute, 25 November 1830.

30 CCA, U3 U3/116/8/1, Crundale Vestry Minute, 27 October. The following day a threshing machine was destroyed in the parish: TNA, HO 52/8, fos 22–3, Sharp, Faversham to Freeling, 31 October 1830.

31 *TT*, 25 November; WSCRO, PAR149/12/1, Petworth Vestry Minute, 13 November 1830.

32 TNA, HO 52/7, fos 142–3 and 215–16, Samuel Twyford Esq., Hollycombe, Liphook to Melbourne, 21 November, same, Petworth House to Phillips, 22 November 1830.

33 HCRO, 21M71PV2, Alton Saint Lawerence Select Vestry Minute, 22 November; TNA, HO 52/13, fos 111–12, Wellington, Strathfieldsaye to Melbourne, 24 November; HCRO, 199M70/F2, J.J. Hugonin, Alton to J. Bonham-Carter, 24 November 1830.

34 WSRCO: PAR 153/12/2, Pulborough Vestry minute, 10 November; PAR 301/12/2, Cuckfield Vestry minute, 11 November; PAR 149/12/1, Petworth Vestry minute, 13 November; PAR 516/12/4, Worth Vestry minute, 13 November 1830.

35 *HA*, 27 November; HCRO, 11M67 PV1, Owslebury Vestry minute, 9 December; *HC*, 20 December; TNA, HO 130/1, Hampshire Special Commission cases 185–186, 206–210, 266–7, and 333; *TT*, 30 December 1830; *Hampshire Telegraph* (hereafter *HT*), 7 March 1831.

36 HCRO, 27M77 PV1, East Woodhay Vestry minute, 2 December. A meeting at Amport on 15 December agreed to continue with an 'agreement' made on 22

November and also agreed that labourers with four or more children would now also have their cottage rents paid by the parish, a 'proportion of fuel during the winter', and a 'piece of land for cultivating gratuitously: HCRO, 43M67/PV2, Amport Vestry minute, 15 December 1830.

37 WSCRO, PAR400/12/1/9, Hurstpierpoint Vestry minute, 15 December; HCRO 44M69 JP/77a, Alresford Vestry minute (though in the Herriard vestry book), 1 December; ESCRO, PAR 236/12/1/3, Battle Vestry minute, 2 December 1830.

38 *HA*, 27 November 1830.

39 Medway Studies Centre, P150/8/1, Frindsbury Vestry minute, 4 December 1830.

40 WSCRO, PAR 19/12/1, South Bersted Vestry minutes, 26 November, 2 and 9 December 1830.

41 ESCRO, PAR 236/12/1/3, Battle Vestry minute, 23 December 1830.

42 M. Dutt, 'The Agricultural Labourers' Revolt of 1830 in Kent, Surrey and Sussex' (PhD dissertation, University of London, 1966), pp. 332–3; J. Burchardt, *The Allotment Movement in England, 1793–1873* (Woodbridge: Boydell Press, 2002), pp. 71–3.

43 Surrey History Centre, P56/5/1, Wallington Vestry minute, 21 December 1830.

44 WSCRO, PAR 416/12/1, Lindfield Vestry minute, 27 November; *HC*, 9 February 1830.

45 HCRO, 31M67 PV1, 21M71 PV2, 30M77 PV2, 47M81 PV3, 4M69 PV1, Milford on Sea Vestry minute, 2 December, Alton Saint Lawrence Vestry minute, 24 December, Bishop's Waltham Vestry minute, 31 December, Odiham Vestry minutes, 31 December 1830 and 14 January, Eling Vestry minutes, 6 and 14 January 1831.

46 Burchardt, *The Allotment Movement*, pp. 36–40.

47 *HC*, 3 May and 14 June; HCRO, 30M77 PV2, Bishop's Waltham Vestry minute, 31 December 1830.

48 TNA, HO 52/10, fos 422–3 and 428, Sir Godfrey Webster, Battle to Peel, 20 November, enclosing examination of Joseph Bryant, labourer, 19 November; HCRO, 92M95/F2 8/3, Rev. D. Cockerton, Stoke Charity to Sir Thomas Baring, 2 December 1830.

49 TNA, HO 52/10, fos 388–9 and 52/8, fos 160–70, Godfrey Webster, Battle, 9 November, Messrs Collingwood and Young, Hawkhurst, 11 November 1830, both to Peel.

50 TNA, HO 52/8 fos 166–70 and 52/10 fos 305–6, Collingwood and Young, Hawkhurst, 11 November, W. Collingwood, Brighton to Phillips, 22 November; TNA, TS 11/943, Prosecution Briefs prepared by the Treasury Solicitor in the case of *The King* v. *George Barrow, John Ballard, John Tuckner, William Chrisford and John Beale*, Kent Winter Assizes 1830. Cooperation between labourers and farmers went one step further at Woodchurch in Kentish Low Weald. An initial meeting between a reported 500 labourers from local parishes and the farmers agreed to an increase in wages, the labourers promising that they would help to secure a reduction in tithes and rents and by 'refusing to pay taxes'. They were then to meet again to jointly

petition Parliament for electoral reform, a reduction in taxes and a 'revisitation' of the tithe laws: *Cobbett's Weekly Political Register*, 15 November 1830.

51 *RG*, 16 November 1830.

52 The meeting at Whitchurch occurred two days later, wherein wages and child allowances were raised. I could not find a record of a meeting at Freefolk: *HC*, 22 and 29 November 1830.

53 ESCRO, AMS5995 3/15 and 14, Resolutions of a meeting of the Etchingham occupiers, 10 November, forwarded to H.B. Curteis, same day, Anne Mascall, to H.B. Curteis, 10 November; TNA, HO 52/10, fos 394–5, Battle Bench to Peel, 12 November 1830.

54 *PHer*, 28 November 1830.

55 *SM*, 27 November; *HC*, 29 November and 6 December 1830.

56 TNA, HO 52/13, fos 111–12, Wellington, Strathfieldsaye to Melbourne, 24 November; HCRO, 21M71 PV2, Alton St Lawrence Vestry Minute, 26 November 1830.

57 TNA, HO 52/6, fos 37–8, Rector of Ashmansworth, East Woodhay, to C. Hodgson, Westminster, 23 November 1830.

58 *HA*, 4 December 1830.

59 *Sherborne Journal*, 9 and 16 December 1830.

60 *HA*, 27 November; *PHer*, 28 November 1830.

61 SM, 27 November 1830.

62 *HT*, 22 November; *PHer*, 28 November 1830.

63 *HC*, 22 November 1830.

64 University of Southampton Special Collections, WP4/2/2/20, Copy of the resolutions of the Hampshire magistrates assembled at Winchester, 25 November; *HC*, 29 November 1830.

65 HCRO, 44M69 J9/77 I and F, 86M82 PV1, Herriard Vestry Minutes, 29 November, 2 and 6 December 1830.

66 CKS, U951 C14/12, Knatchbull to Camden, 30 October 1830.

67 TNA, HO 52/10, fos 386–7, 383–5 and 388–9, J.C. Sharpe, Dormons, Northiam, 9 November, Godfrey Webster, Battle Abbey, 8 and 9 November, to Peel; ESCRO, AMS 5995/3/13, E.J. Curteis to H.B. Curteis, Windmill Hill, Battle, 9 November; *TT*, 11 November; *RG*, 16 November 1830.

68 TNA, HO 52/10, fos 420–1 and 426–7, Petitions from Dallington, n.d. (but *c.*17 November), and George Courthope Esq., Battle to Peel, 19 November; TNA, HO 41/8, p. 64, Phillips to Courthope, 18 November 1830.

69 Sussex was divided into six rapes, a pre-Norman administrative division unique to the county that continued to underpin some forms of judicial organisation.

70 *TT*, 19 November; *HT*, 22 November 1830.

71 TNA, HO 52/10, fos 555–6, Walter Burrell, West Grinstead Park, to Peel, 21 November 1830.

72 *Sussex Advertiser*, 22 November; *Morning Post*, 23 November; *BG*, 25 November; TNA, HO 41/8, pp. 63–4: Phillips to W. Holmes, Arundel, 18 November; TNA, HO 52/10, fos 287–8 and 290–1, William Holmes, Arundel to Peel, 17 and 19 November 1830.

73 *Morning Post*, 25 November 1830; BPP. Commons, 'Report from His Majesty's Commissioners for Inquiring into the Administration and Practical Operation of the Poor Laws' (1834), vol. xliv (hereafter 'Operation of the Poor Laws'), report of Charles Hope Maclean Esq., appendix a, p. 547a.

74 TNA, HO 52/7, fos 191–3, Rev. D. Newbolt, Winchester to Melbourne, 10 December; TNA, HO 41/8, pp. 471–3, Phillips to Newbolt, 11 December 1830.

75 TNA, HO 52/7, fo. 72, R. Parsons, Petersfield Post Office Deputy, to Freeling, 22 November 1830.

76 TNA, HO 52/7, fos 44–5, 48–9, 105–7, and 116–17, Alton Bench, Alresford to Peel, 19 November, Andover Bench to Peel, 21 November, and to Melbourne, 24 November (enclosing a poster detailing the resolutions of the Andover meeting), C.W. Foster, Andover to Melbourne, 26 November 1830.

77 HCRO, 43M67/PV2, Amport Vestry minute, 22 November 1830; BPP. (1834) 'Operation of the Poor Laws', Report of Captain Pringle, appendix a, p. 300a.

78 WSCRO, QR/W/758 fos 280, 269, 270, 271 and 272, Informations of Timothy Town, 18 December, William Mates, 6 December, Examinations of John Pennicott, William Searle and Robert Braby, all 27 December 1830.

79 TNA, HO 40/27/5 fos 440–1, Lieut Col Mair, Winchester to Melbourne, 14 December 1830.

Something after Swing?[1]

The way Swing ended remains a source of ambiguity. The received understanding is as follows. The 'draconian punishments distributed ... [and] the deportation of hapless men and boys to antipodean semi-slavery' helped to thoroughly demoralise rural workers.[2] In those counties in which activists were not tried at government-sponsored special commissions but instead at the regular provincial courts of Quarter Sessions and Assize, Swing is supposed to have 'died a natural death', little affected by the 'active intervention of the government or magistrates'. Swing, so such an analysis goes, was either stopped in its tracks or, instead, achieved its multifarious aims and therefore faded.[3]

All such theories are necessarily predicated on the understanding that Swing did end at some point in the winter of 1830. Such an interpretation would be understandable if the 'bitter vindictiveness' of the special commissions snuffed out what will there was left to protest. But even Hobsbawm and Rudé, echoed by more recent historians of Swing, stated that the response to the brutal judicial repression was a renewed resort to incendiarism.[4] Between Christmas 1830 and the end of 1831, in the south-east there were, they claimed, 12 further incendiary fires, 2 'Swing' letters received, 5 further 'riots' and 6 machines destroyed. These were carried out by 'the wild, independent, savage marginal men ... and the youths'.[5] While Roger Wells has suggested that Hobsbawm and Rudé's protest tabulations for 1831 are 'hopelessly defective', the suggestion that the 'repression' of late 1830 might not have been as successful in stemming protest has not been systematically explored.[6] Besides, as Chapter 10 shows, the interplay between protest and judicial response varied significantly in different parts of the south-east.

What follows examines the resort to protest beyond Swing's

'repression'. If the trials did represent the end of Swing, then the protests that followed were something post-Swing. But, as Hobsbawm and Rudé tabulated, Swing-like incidents occurred both during the immediate aftermath of the trials and in the summers of 1831 and 1832. Were such incidents post-Swing? Did they represent attempts to revive Swing? Or were they instead evidence that Swing had never actually died? Beyond 1833, the early implementation of the principles of the New Poor Law by vestries acting under the impression of roving Assistant Poor Law Commissioners and, from early 1835, the actual imposition of the new union-focused system provoked a quite different wave of protests. This chapter starts by examining the response to repression and goes on to ask whether protests in the post-trial period represented an attempt to address 'unfinished business', and how the protest discourses of Swing were mobilised between 1831 and 1833 respectively. It ends with a consideration of whether the protests in this period represented something genuinely different from the events of late 1830.

The response to repression

On the morning of Sunday 14 November 1830, Mr Franks's Albury mill was set on fire. Several gunshots were also fired through his bedroom window, Franks having become 'odious to the people' in his capacity as the Albury overseer.[7] Five days later, James Warner, a 30-year-old labourer, was committed to stand trial at the Surrey Assizes as the alleged culprit. Warner was subsequently found guilty and sentenced to be hanged. News of the conviction immediately provoked 'a strong sensation' in the locality.[8] On the night of 6 January 1831, shots were fired through the bedroom windows of the Master of Albury workhouse and a threatening letter was fixed to a post near Albury Park, the residence of committing magistrate Drummond. Reports of the exact wording of the letter vary, but the sentiments were clear. 'We fired the mill; starving and firing shall go together' reported the *Kentish Gazette*. The *County Chronicle*, four days later, claimed it read 'It was *me* who fired the Mill – starve and fire go together'. Another threatening letter, found near the Guildford workhouse, went further: 'If Wrner is mured Franks Dromans [Drummond] an Smallpiece [a "witness"] shal dye i culd clear im … you fals swaring villing.'[9] Notwithstanding the threats, Warner was the sole Surrey resident to be executed or transported to New South

Wales or Van Diemen's Land. While the judicial toll taken by the other south-eastern courts was, cumulatively, more severe,[10] crude numbers do little justice to the sense of loss engendered in the communities from which these individuals were removed. Nor do numbers help us understand the popular reaction to executions and transportations.

The intention of the Winchester Special Commission, according to a briefing sent to the Hampshire magistrates by the Attorney General, was to demonstrate that 'the ends of public justice' had been 'sufficiently answered' by convicting and punishing 'a certain number' of the offenders 'in the different mobs'. However, according to Rev. Dallas of Wonston in the Dever Valley, this policy had been carried out too dogmatically. Having 'bared the sword of justice with manly firmness, and ... a solemn Christian spirit', the Commission had initially evoked 'in a most wholesome manner' the 'desired effect' among his parishioners, many of whom had been active in local Swing groups. Having 'learnt to fear for the consequences', they eagerly waited and speculated upon the outcome of the trials thus helping to deepen the impression of fear and 'prolong[ing] the conviction of error'. However, the penalty of death had not been seriously discussed. Thus, when the sentences were announced, the effect was dramatic. That six men were to be condemned altered the mood from the 'wholesome conviction' of error to 'bitterness'.[11] The people of Sutton Scotney now 'easy dupes of the vile agitators' and 'likely' to resist the 'execution of the law'. Executing the six men who were not found guilty of arson or 'acts of malicious personal violence' – for which death was a fitting penalty – would tend to produce 'a rankling resentment which ... will be widely felt'.[12] As Robert Mason, writing to Rev. Joliffe, his prosecutor at the Special Commission, from his prison cell in Winchester Gaol whilst awaiting transportation to Australia, exclaimed: 'I did not know that what I did was a "fault" much less a "FELONY".'[13]

And yet, with the exception of events at Albury, the combination of the conviction of such men for seemingly minor acts and the judicial murder of incendiarists did not prompt a resort to protest. This may have been due to the terror effected by the law. It may also have been a function of the fact that many towns in the south-east still hosted garrisons of troops dispatched to keep order during late 1830. For instance, the environs of Sittingbourne, the area in which Swing was first manifest in its overt form beyond its initial East Kent centres, remained entirely protest free in the early months of 1831. Magistrate

Rev. Poore wrote to Melbourne on 21 March to proclaim that all was now 'quiet' and that the troops were no longer required.[14]

Instead, initial recriminations appear to have taken a more ruminative form. For instance, a relative of Sussex incendiarist Bushby was heard to leave the scene of his execution making 'threats of vengeance'.[15] What evidence of vengeance there is tends towards suggestion rather than offering any explicit connection. Farmer Hayward at Whitstable received three threatening letters in early January warning that unless he brought his threshing machine 'forward' his premises would be fired. On 17 January the threats were made good.[16] Hayward's farm was located only four miles from Wraight's Denstroud farm for which incendiary fire the brothers Packman hanged. Whether there was a direct link is unclear, but it seems likely that the execution of the brothers would have further inflamed already perilous social relations in the area.

We must not forget that judicial repression, both in the issuing of punitive sentences and the considerable pressure placed on fellow workers to inform against their comrades and neighbours, took a heavy toll on plebeian community cohesion. The following case is instructive. Labourer Bartholomew was subjected to a bitter verbal tirade and an even more violent assault at the William IV pub at Bridge, in the Elham Valley, being accused of having 'split against the Party'. His actions were seemingly responsible for Henry Hulkes having been sentenced to seven years' transportation for breaking farmer Friday's threshing machine at neighbouring Bekesbourne. Those guilty of the assault even offered a gallon of beer to anyone who would lynch Bartholomew.[17]

There was, however, a definite link between the targets of these post-repression months and the targets of the winter of 1830. An incendiary letter sent to the Greenwich overseer threatened that three men were coming from 'Barkshire' to destroy his machines, set fire to his straw and poison all his horses.[18] At Amberley, near Arundel, a special constable, presumably sworn in at the height of Swing, was attacked on Boxing Day.[19] Elsewhere, the flurry of incendiary fires and threatening letters were disproportionately targeted at poor law officials. This was not in itself unusual but novel in its intensity.[20] The recurring motif of the hatred of machinery and the use of the monosyllable 'Swing' was also novel in relation to previous winters. Farmer Humphrey of Donnington, near Chichester, received a 'Swing' letter threatening to burn his premises if he used his threshing machine. Farmer Godwin at Fareham was less fortunate. The incendiary threats detailed in a series of 'Swing' letters were acted upon at 4 a.m. on 3 February, even though he had long since stopped using his threshing machine.[21]

There is a sense in which the tenor of such attacks represented something defiantly post-repression. Both Donnington and Fareham were in areas where threshing machine-breaking the previous November had led to successful prosecutions at the Sussex Winter Assizes.[22] If the continued existence, if not necessarily use, of threshing machines remained a source of local contention, then the resort to covert rather than overt protests suggests either an inability to raise machine-breaking groups or a general fear that to openly protest would lead to severe sanctions. This sense is reinforced by a petition drafted and signed by the working population of Bilsington, on the fringes of Romney Marsh, calling for threshing machines to be banned.[23] Again, only the previous winter, Bilsington had witnessed an unusually violent contretemps between a mobile Swing gang and a force of special constables that led to the successful prosecutions of five men for riotous assembly.[24]

Similarly, the tone of an incident in East Kent was suggestive of a new defiantly post-repression modus operandi. On New Year's Day, a group of between '14 and 18 Herne paupers' marched to Canterbury to lodge a complaint with the Magistrates against Mr Thorpe, the assistant overseer. The magistrates listened to their complaints and duly ordered the parish officers to increase the men's pay to 13/6 a week. Initially, the officers refused to assent to the order, for, so they claimed, the parish could not afford such a sum. The Bench retorted that whether the parish could afford the payment was not important, it was the responsibility of the Vestry to find the money.[25] Magistrates, so this public performance of paternalism was intended to infer, were the labourers' friends. If called on to right injustice, they would set right all wrongs. But the complicity of many magistrates in the government's schema of bloody repression engendered a deep-seated mistrust among many rural workers, something evidenced in protests directed at individual magistrates in January 1831.[26]

The popular response to wage cuts in the early months of 1831 also represented a post-repression phenomena. Swing's many successes were hard won, something felt particularly in areas where the various trials had taken individuals from their families and friends. Any attempts by farmers and vestrymen to renege on earlier commitments were therefore a tacit admission that the deal forged during the autumn and winter of 1830 had, at least partially, collapsed. The potential danger in lowering wages was well understood by Wealden magistrate Sir Charles Blunt. He reported in disapproving tones to the 1831 East Sussex Epiphany Quarter Sessions that several parishes were again lowering wages. At Billingshurst, so the *Kentish Gazette* reported, the farmers, in concert, had reduced the wages of married men to 10 shillings a week and those of single men to 6 shillings.[27]

The response of labourers to wage cuts was twofold: covert terrorism and open agitation. The former is necessarily harder to read for the simple fact that the specific motivations of incendiaries and maimers were infrequently recorded. A threatening letter sent to a Morden farmer offered explicit analysis: 'Sir I will burn your place down to the G[r]ound if you don't rise the men money and let the men keep a pig and do away with your hay devil.' The writer, labourer John Longhurst, was subsequently found guilty of the act and sentenced to seven years' transportation at the Surrey Lent Assizes.[28] At Ockley, two incendiary fires on 21 April were considered evidence that a 'plan of operations' regarding a 'disposition' to strike had begun, thus combining open and covert protests in the classic Swing modus operandi. Fears of a renewal of 1830 were quite understandable, for plans were afoot in Horsham and Dorking to 'create tumult like on 10 Nov last year'. Handbills were posted in the towns and the surrounding countryside calling for a mass assemblage on 13 April to harass the magistrates during their examination of the overseers' accounts. Such was the panic generated, that the Bench informed the Home Office that they were unable to rely on special constables to put down affrays.[29]

The Horsham events were not unique. In late January, labourers in the vicinity of Wonston struck their work for higher wages, thereby suggesting that Rev. Dallas's analysis of judicial policy was unerringly accurate.[30] Similarly, at the East Sussex Swing centre of Battle, a plan was afoot in late March to effect a rise in wages. 'Many parishes in this part', so local grandee Sir Godfrey Webster informed the Home Office, 'are afflicted and communicate with each other by means of Delegates, and are determined upon a compulsory increase of wage[s]'.[31]

Unfinished business?

The response to wage cuts can also be interpreted not as the start of something defiantly post-Swing, the massive promise of Swing quickly giving way to a battle of attrition between labourers and farmers, but instead as an attempt to reinforce Swing's gains.[32] If the events around Horsham and Battle were suggestive of a desire among labourers to protect living wages, events in the late spring and summer of 1831 were proof positive. Initially, this resistance to the 'lowness of wages' took the form of 'open' complaints in the country parishes in the vicinity of Rochester and open threats in the parishes between Sittingbourne and Faversham that 'burnings and nocturnal depredations' would be revived. Both were, importantly, areas central to the early diffusion of Swing beyond its initial local centres.

Meanwhile at Aldington, within the area where the Elham machine-breakers operated, labourers were reported to be holding secretive nightly meetings – a move uncannily reminiscent of the start of Swing in East Sussex at Brede.[33] The first evidence that threats and plans were put into operation came not from Kent though but from the parishes to the south and east of Chichester, a major centre of ferment the previous November. In the final week of July, prompted by an influx of migrant 'West Countrymen' seeking employ in the early harvest, 'great numbers' of men combined at Oving and Aldingbourne to 'fix' the price of harvest labour with the farmers. At nearby Siddlesham, fifty labourers met on Sunday 24 July for the same purpose. On attempting to carry their plan into operation at neighbouring Selsey, they were resisted by the local labourers who refused to join them. The next day, at nearby West Wittering, a group of 'strangers' seeking harvest work were also 'roughly handled'.[34]

This model of localised, but intensive, open protest was also adopted in other centres of Swing activity. The earlier threats in the Swale parishes were made good on 2 August. Three individual, but interconnected, groups traversed an area between Newington-next-Sittingbourne and the Isle of Grain in a concerted attempt to 'compel an increase of farming mens wages' and prevent the farmers from employing migrant harvest labourers. Three members of the Isle of Grain group were apprehended and later committed to trial by the Chatham Bench. On 4 August another 'rising' occurred, this time in the vicinity of Sittingbourne. Again, the magistrates were quick to act, lodging 'several' members of the group in Canterbury gaol. Although

Rev. Poore wrote to Melbourne the following day expressing his satisfaction that the 'mobbings' had been 'suppressed', a detachment of Dragoons was sent to Sittingbourne.[35] Evidently, this planned – and intensive – resort to open protest was too uncannily similar to the events of the previous winter for the government not to take action.

The other major centre of protest that summer was the area between Canterbury, Dover and Sandwich, broadly contiguous with part of the area operated by the Elham and Ash machine-breaking gangs of 1830. Evidence precludes any accurate assessment of the actual individuals involved, or even whether the same individuals were responsible for the several acts of protest committed. However, it was clear that a spirit of open plebeian resistance permeated large parts of the area that had been responsible for the start of Swing the previous summer. The first incident occurred at Barham on 30 July when a small group of men destroyed Mr Harvey's threshing machine. Harvey, instructively, had also been targeted by machine-breakers on 23 October 1830. This was not so much unfinished business as a return to the previous winter's agenda.[36] Five days later another machine was destroyed at Ripple near Deal. According to the Deal bench:

> The Peasantry openly state that it has arisen from the conviction of Government that they cannot punish Machine breaking by law and that consequently orders are sent out to New South Wales to release and send home those who have been transported for that offence.

There was also supposed to be 'a bad spirit abroad', something allegedly exacerbated by the popularity of Cobbett's papers in local pubs.

Further evidence of this tendency to resist was provided by reports that the mown – as opposed to the more labour intensive sickle-cut – wheat of a farmer in a neighbouring parish to Ripple had been scattered over a field, littered across the road and thrown into a pond. A wheat stack in a village close to Canterbury was also set on fire the same evening. On 9 August the Deal Bench, a little prematurely, again wrote to Melbourne. A blacksmith, a farm servant and six day labourers had been taken up for the offence. This was likely, so thought the Bench, to 'check' the bad spirit.[37] It might have had some effect at Ripple but it did nothing to stop the mass destruction of scythes by a 'large party of fellows', comprised of 'many bricklayers' but few field labourers, at Maxton, near Dover. Farmer Rutley, it was widely known, was planning to mow his wheat.

The same complaint, combined with the now seasonal vehement opposition to the employment of Irish labourers, also provoked a 'turn out' of the labourers at Bridge. Here, the striking labourers went to farmer Brice's harvest fields, seized the scythes and destroyed them, prompting Brice to 'come to terms' with the local men. The provincial press probably woefully underreported such tensions. The *Kentish Gazette* rather obtusely admitted in the aftermath of the Bridge strike – which they did not report – that they had received 'reports' of disputes between the indigent labour force and migrant Irish workers. The latter group were apparently willing to work 'for whatever wages they received' and were happy to use scythes as opposed to the natives' traditional sickle. Further attacks occurred at Wingham and also at Hougham where Irish workers were assaulted, stripped, robbed and then dragged through a horsepond and had their sickles broken.[38]

The protests at the latter place took a more Swing-like form. A 'considerable' number of the 'peasantry' assembled pressing others to join them as they paraded the district complaining that the farmers had mown their wheat. They also expressed their 'determination' not to allow threshing machines to be used again.[39] Plebeian solidarity was also central to what were probably the last dramatic acts of protest to occur in the area. The arrest of Bridge labourer John Graves in late August on suspicion of destroying Harvey's threshing machine at Barham, provoked prolonged recriminations. Farmer Harvey of Barham was again targeted, his situation made yet worse by his hiring of labourers, presumably migrants, to mow his wheat, and by the involvement of his landlord, local magistrate General Mulcaster, in Graves's committal. On the night of 31 August, a 'very large' stack of Harvey's wheat was set on fire, the local labourers standing by refusing to assist in extinguishing the flames. Open protest begat covert protest which, in turn, begat further open protest. According to the correspondent of *The Times*: a 'continued state of warfare [exists] between employers and labourers'.[40] But here, with the exception of a case of incendiarism against farmer Every at Singledge, and a case of animal maiming against another farmer in the vicinity of Singledge, this intensive wave of protest ended.[41]

The only other locale in the south-east to experience systematic open protests was the edge of Romney Marsh, where labourers had already petitioned against the use of threshing machines (Bilsington) and had been holding secret nightly meetings (Aldington). It was perhaps not too surprising, therefore, that the use of threshing machines on the Marsh would provoke considerable anger. On the night of 15 August, despite the fact that a party of Dragoons had been stationed at Romney 'for some days' in anticipation of an attack, two threshing machines were destroyed: one at Bonnington and one at Burmarsh. A party of 25–30 individuals, many of whom were 'boys', came down 'from the Hills' and entered the Marsh over the bridges. According to magistrate Stringer, the Marsh was free from Swing in 1830 because he and his fellow magistrates had been quick to swear in special constables. One assumes that the continued existence of threshing machines especially rankled with those neighbouring communities who had paid a heavy price for their involvement in the autumn and winter of 1830. Thus, they descended the hills and sought to right a local anomaly. Their actions were given further popular legitimacy by the widespread belief, as at Ripple, that it was no offence to break threshing machines.[42] These were necessarily self-contained protests, acts of unfinished business.

Here acts of organised protest, with some notable exceptions, ended. The march by 100 labourers to the vestry at Billingshurst on 7 November demanding wages of 2 shillings a day for married men and child allowances of 2 shillings a week for every child beyond the second in the family, harked back to the (temporary) success of such strategies a year previously. That Swing's gains had been short-lived was clearly the motivation, for, so it was reported, many of the ninety-nine men out of work and employed by Billingshurst parish existed solely on a diet of potatoes and lodged in outhouses. The other notable exception occurred two days later at the perennially disturbed Rye – the scene of a 'fracas' that April – where the millers, farmers and merchants were summoned to the 'annual meeting' of the labourers. The meeting had been advertised in the adjacent parishes by a series of 'bills'. Fifty soldiers were duly despatched, while the local farmers tried to dissuade their labourers from attending. By noon, several men were seen lurking about the site of the proposed meeting carrying short bludgeons and sticks. Here reports differ. The Kent press stated that a 'serious riot' had taken place, while Mayor Lamb, a normally diligent Home Office correspondent, made no such report.[43]

While the swift repression of these intensive, if localised, protests eliminated any fear that the rural poor would again rise en masse, the high level of covert protest did raise concerns regarding the social stability of the countryside. In the face of hostility from the authorities and the abiding presence of military detachments in several areas, those seeking redress and psychological release through protest turned to incendiarism. Indeed, fire raising in the final three months of 1831 assumed an 1830-like level of intensity that some feared would inevitably lead to renewed overt protests. As Sir James Grey, informing Melbourne of an incendiary fire at Eastry, exclaimed, 'the Horrid scenes of last year have returned'.[44] While the fires assumed a Swing-like intensity, they did not represent unfinished business, instead embodying, as Archer has put it, 'a deep-seated anger'.[45] Indeed, it is particularly telling that the Eastry fire followed, so it later transpired, a strike of local labourers who 'debated whether a fire was not likely to frighten the farmers into an advance of wages'.[46]

The trial, and subsequent execution, of young labourers for incendiarism at Guestling (Thomas Bufford, executed at Horsham on New Year's Eve 1831), Eastry (Richard Dixon, executed on Penenden Heath on 22 December 1831), Barton Stacey (Thomas Berriman, whose father was transported by the Hampshire Special Commission, and Henry Hunt, both executed at Winchester in March 1832) tended to worsen already severely strained rural social relations.[47] Indeed, the use of the full powers of the state without going as far as mustering troops in all towns and major villages – a move that would have indicated civil war – did not terrorise everyone. An incendiary fire occurred only a few miles away from Penenden Heath within hours of Dixon's execution, the strongest possible statement that the poor would not be cowed into passive quiescence.[48]

There was a noticeable lack of remorse in these later gallows speeches in comparison to earlier Swing execution exultations to fear God and avoid beer shops. The most forceful demonstration of this came in an extraordinarily defiant and articulate speech made by nineteen-year-old George Wren on the Horsham scaffold in December 1832. Wren, along with his brother, had been accused of firing Uckfield vestryman Kenward's barn in June 1832. Nothing initially transpired, presumably owing to a lack of non-circumstantial evidence, but on 8 November George Wren was again apprehended. Wren, 'whose conduct and levity were notorious', was subsequently indicted and found guilty at the Sussex Assizes for a crime he vehemently denied. He launched into his riposte on the scaffold:

> I am brought to this fatal scaffold to be murdered ... I am brought to this like a bullock to the slaughter ... what must those poor people feel, at the last moment, who brought me to this ignominious end ... I was

condemned by the people of Uckfield, but God forbid I should accuse all the people of that parish.

He ended his speech by naming those who were instrumental in his demise.[49]

This anger and bitterness was not reflected through a widespread resort to machine-breaking in 1832 and 1833, other than the attack at Hougham near Dover on 18 August 1833.[50] Nor was it expressed through a mass striking or lobbying of rural vestries. The record, as Wells has suggested, probably tends to underrepresent such acts because of the magisterial belief that resorting to the full course of their powers would tend to 'regalvinise Swing'.[51] Notwithstanding evidential concerns, it would appear that such protests in 1832 and 1833 occurred only sporadically and without any tendency to cluster in time or space. Instead, the level of incendiarism following a decline in the early months of 1832 – mirroring the experience of 1831 – again increased dramatically in the post-harvest period. The experience of 1833, while less marked than in 1831 and 1832, followed a similar pattern.

Swing as public discourse

The resort to protest in the aftermath of the Swing trials of 1830 was undeniably multifaceted. It also displayed a strikingly concentrated geography, at least in relation to organised protest. Wider public, governmental and media discourses were more straightforward. This was in no small part due to the continued, if occasional, use of the threatening monosyllable 'Swing'. While the archive is probably defective in recording such usages – it was, after all, a pseudonym – several instances received widespread publicity in the provincial press. On 20 January 1831 farmer Humphrey at Donnington, near Chichester, received a 'Swing' letter threatening to burn his premises if he employed his threshing machine. The letter was, presumably intended to reinforce the perceived threat, wrapped up in a handbill entitled the 'Starvation of the Poor'. Similarly, in February 1831, it was reported that prior to an incendiary fire, farmer Godwin at Fareham had received 'some' 'Swing' letters. 'Swing' graffiti also appeared on 'most' walls and buildings in the vicinity of Dover following the reduction of labourers' wages in the surrounding villages in late May 1831. This was both the location and the style in which the pseudonym was first used in 1830.[52] And thereafter 'Swing', the protestors' pseudonym, fell into abeyance in the south-east. The sole exceptions were a 'Swing' letter sent to an individual at Milton Chapel near Canterbury in obscure circumstances, and its later use, as detailed in the next section, at Hambledon (Hampshire) in late 1831.[53]

'Swing' lived on in the public mind, both literally as the mythic leader of a quasi-insurrectionary movement of the poor and in a more diffuse way as the totem for the manifestation of broader tensions. This dynamic was partly a function of the several 'instant' histories of Swing, written in the early months of 1831, which served to keep the movement firmly in people's minds. It was also partly a function of the ability of even isolated acts of protest to reinvigorate Swing in the public mind. For instance, a letter to the *Hampshire Advertiser* in November 1831 labelled the recent spate of covert protests in Wiltshire as 'Swing' fires. Furthermore, as a *Times* report of an incendiary fire, which targeted a tenant of Kentish grandee Lord Sondes at Throwley (Kent), on 30 December 1831 exclaimed:

> 'Swing' is no respecter of persons, or & noblemen so truly benevolent as Lord Sondes ... might indeed, expect some consideration.[54]

Because of the heightened sense of alarm generated by the events of 1830, commentators, and some newspaper editors, were quick to seize on both incendiary fires and 'riotous' assemblies as evidence that Swing had been restoked, resurrected, or had morphed into some new, terrifying form. A fire in November 1832 at Riverhill, near Petworth, the location of the fire that announced Swing's arrival in West Sussex, was reported in the *Brighton Herald* under the banner 'Swing Again'. A fire at Rainham in June 1831, combined with the open threats of incendiarism in the Swale area, prompted the normally temperate Earl of Camden to express that there were now 'alarming symptoms of an evil aspect' in East Kent.[55] The Earl of Winchelsea was three times the victim of incendiarism, supposedly, so reckoned the *Kentish Gazette*, in protest at the Earl's position as Colonel of the East Kent Yeomanry.[56]

The word 'Swing' was also deployed by Horsham radicals attempting to generate support for a 'very violent' Political Union. Here the strong anti-clerical spirit generated in November 1830 was used to build popular support to resist property being distrained for the non-payment of church rates. Although the distrainment did occur, when the property was put up for auction not a single bid was made. The Political Union seized on this failure and organised a march through the streets of Horsham, whereupon some of the reclaimed property was triumphantly paraded. Even more suggestively, they also printed a 'one penny paper' that was hawked about the streets of the town entitled 'Swing Redivious [*sic*]'. Thus, the spirit of Swing was subtly reworked to launch a sustained attack on both the established Church and the local authorities.[57]

Popular politicking: something after Swing?

Horsham was by no means the only hotbed of radical political agitation in the autumn and winter of 1830, as Chapter 7 shows. What occurred beyond the 'repression' of 1830, though, was rather different. While meetings calling for a moderate reform of the electoral system were a major feature of civic life in southern England throughout 1831 and 1832,[58] more radically charged meetings were far from obscure. Analysing the foundation of such radical societies is complicated by the tendency of the press and Home Office correspondents to conflate judicially-tolerated reform unions with judicially-prohibited political unions. For instance, the *Kent Herald*, a paper in favour of moderate reform, referred to a group of pro-active reform campaigners at Canterbury as the Canterbury Reform Union. However, the activities of this 'union' were uncannily similar to those of political unions elsewhere, not least in relation to their adopted practice of sending 'delegations' to nearby places to stimulate campaigning.[59]

Many other unions did not hide behind the cloak of ambiguity but instead proudly – and publicly – proclaimed their beliefs and objectives. At Rochester, a well-established centre of radical and popular politics as far back as the 1790s, the Political Union established in late 1831 openly made calls for universal male suffrage and voting by ballot. At Faversham, a group of 'radicals' headed by their 'recruiting sergeant', 'a republican Frenchman in exile', marched to Sittingbourne on 27 October 1831 to help frame a petition to the King expressing their disappointment at the rejection of the second Reform Bill. This public militancy was in many ways novel, eclipsing the far more circumspect calls for radical reform in the Medway towns in the 1790s and early 1800s.[60] Moreover, this burgeoning campaign was more explicit in its denunciation of the existing parliamentary system than the relatively obtuse 'rights' rhetoric that had infused many of the 1830 protests. Even in locales without active political unions, individuals took their arguments to the people. For instance, at Eastbourne in November 1831, 'a stranger' was bold enough to launch his tirade against 'the Peers, Bishops, &c' in the churchyard on a Sunday morning.[61]

This growing clamour, combative in both organisation and in terms of its overt profile, was in large part a function of the floundering of the second Reform Bill in October 1831. The unsuccessful vote was, as Wells has suggested, evidence that the calls of moderate reformers had not been heeded but that a more strident approach might reap dividends.[62] Thus, a 'very peaceable' meeting of the Winchester operatives at Oram's Arbour in early November 1831 demanded 'Universal Suffrage – Vote by Ballot – and no property qualifications'. Nine months later political unions in the vicinity of Winchester (see below) were actively politicking in the 1832 General Election to get Henry Hunt's son elected in place of popularly despised local grandee Bingham Baring.[63]

The growing strength of political unions stoked a deep-seated fear among many employers and the magistracy that they could utilise their platform for a far wider Swing-like tumult. In part, this stemmed from the hierarchical, national organisational frame deployed by the political unions: 'Parent' unions were affiliated to, initially, the London Union and later on the 'Birmingham and National Union' and in turn were charged with founding local satellite unions.[64] Even the government's 22 November 1831 proclamation, issued under the auspices of the 1799 Corresponding Societies Act, that political unions were 'unconstitutional and illegal' did little to quell the ardour of south-eastern unions.

The other reason for such deep-seated fears was the apparent ease with which satellite unions were founded in even very small rural communities. Nancy Lopatin's now standard work on political unions details the existence of south-eastern unions at Brighton, Ramsgate and Thanet, Sittingbourne, Winchester, but not the multitude of small rural unions. She claims, though, 'there is no indication that Political Unions included agricultural labourers' and that 'urban and commercial interests' were dominant among political union membership.[65] But south-eastern unions were far more extensive than Lopatin suggests, penetrating even small country parishes. These unions also developed in a very different local political context to the better known unions in the urban Midlands, their existence highlighting the readiness for even field workers and rural artisans to embrace constitutional politicking as a protest strategy.

The union at Brighton was initially founded on 29 August 1831 by a group of local operatives as a branch of the London Union. The Brighton 'delegates', in turn, were instantly active in spreading their message to the nearby towns and villages. As the *Brighton Gazette* harrumphed: 'The delegates doubtless find riding about the county and making speeches more agreeable and more profitable than work'.[66] The attempt to revive the union in the summer of 1832 was also founded upon 'missionary' work, five 'branches' existing besides the 'parent society' based at the Bricklayer's Arms. While this initial effervescence was short-lived, retreat swiftly following revival, a visit by *Poor Man's Guardian* publisher Henry Hetherington in October 1832 led to a renewed enthusiasm for campaigning.[67] In conjunction with a satellite union at Uckfield, which presumably dated from the summer campaign, the Brighton Union helped found a union 'on political subjects' at Horsted Keynes in November 1832. Despite attempts to suppress the Horsted Keynes Union by, rather bluntly, using the Riot Act, similar meetings continued well into 1833. At nearby West Chiltington, a union was founded which was linked 'to the one in Billingshurst, which is a branch of a very violent one in Horsham'. It met every Wednesday at 'the house of a publican whose principles of both politics and religion are notorious', the pub having been the scene of 'a violent riot ... in November 1830'.[68]

The Winchester Union too was active in founding satellite unions in surrounding villages. The Dever Valley was, again, well represented. Perhaps in part inspired by Cobbett's 'Chopsticks Festival' – held symbolically at Sutton Scotney in July 1832 to 'celebrate the fall of the villainous boroughmongers'[69] – the villages of Wonston and Sutton Scotney, Bullington and Barton Stacey were all covered by a union. Further north of Winchester, several villages, including Chilbolton and Wherwell, also hosted unions. Newport hosted the Isle of Wight Political Union as early as the autumn of 1831, and was soon active in helping found an affiliated union at nearby Ryde. Even tiny Itchen Abbas, home of the Duke of Buckingham and Chandos who had earlier spoken out in the Lords against the Birmingham Union, was home to a political union.[70] According to rural informers of Hampshire Lord Lieutenant, the Duke of Wellington, as many as half of all Hampshire labourers were thought to be involved 'in the clubs'. In light of the events of 1830, this perception made the farmers 'a good deal alarmed' by the potential of large assemblages of labourers. Thus at Chilbolton on 28 October 1832, thirteen labouring members of the political union were discharged by their employers and on applying to the overseer – 'one of the tyrant-slaves' – were refused relief.[71] This was not, according to Colonel William Iremonger JP, 'only a matter of wages', for the labourers were 'ready to follow anyone, who will lead them into mischief – indeed "mischief" is their motto'.[72]

The perennially disturbed east Hampshire parish of Hambledon was another centre of political union activity. It is unclear whether the 'Hambledon Independent Union Society' was truly independent or was connected to other larger unions elsewhere. Either way, it is clear that it was a vibrant, well-organised and politically astute group. One of two placards placed in the 'town' (one in November 1831 and another on 5 January 1832), warned that if any member of the union was prosecuted 'the hand of Burke or Swing will be put in force against the prosecutor'. The purpose of the union, so claimed the placards, was to 'eradicate Tyranny oppression and petty interferences' and to apply 'the rules of common sense'. The combining of Swing with radical politics was made even more explicit after an incendiary fire on 3 January: if a prosecution took place 'for the fire', there would be 'a worst disaster'. The notice was signed 'The true Hambledon Union or *Swing*' (original emphasis). Lord Melbourne duly responded to local demands for help with the offer of a £500 reward, the same amount offered in King William's Swing proclamation.[73]

Although the record suggests that urban political unions remained active until the summer of 1834,[74] it would appear that rural unions fell into abeyance in the second half of 1833. While further microstudies are required to find out whether the same individuals and families were involved, it is surely telling that many of the rural areas which witnessed anti-New Poor Law protests had also been hotbeds of Swing activity and had subsequently hosted political unions. Thus in the south-east, the Swale and Medway area, the area between Battle, Rye and Hythe, the area between Brighton and Horsham, and the Dever Valley, all witnessed the most trenchant and bitter protests.[75] Indeed, demonstrations of collective force continued in the latter place between the collapse of the political unions and the onset of anti-New Poor Law protests. On 3 June 1834, about 200 people gathered at Micheldever to listen to speeches given by two local labourers. The exact purpose of the gathering is unclear, but the tenor of extant reports suggests popular politicking. Not only was the size of the audience extraordinary, so too was the fact that despite the intervention of the Micheldever 'policeman' Thomas Ellery, the crowd refused to disperse. As one of the speakers, John Rhide, proclaimed '[I do] not care much for magistrates, prisons, police or constables: [I have] been in prison once but would not go again'.[76]

It is also possible that the Micheldever meeting represented a spilling over of political union activity into nascent trade union activity. As – famously – was the case at Tolpuddle in neighbouring Dorset, activists in the Dever Valley might have also made contact with delegates from the Grand National Consolidated Trades Union (GNCTU).[77] On its foundation the GNCTU made a deliberate policy of 'try[ing] to get up a Union among the agricultural labourers' and, elsewhere in the south-east, had some success at getting field worker recruits to urban branches. For instance, in the spring of 1834 labourers reportedly 'flocked' to join the GNCTU at Brighton.[78] There is plenty of evidence to show that in rural Hampshire the line between political unions and trade unions was infinitesimally thin. When farmer Allec of Somborne had attempted to reduce his workers' wages from ten to nine shillings a week, he was met by the claim that his labourers had received directions from 'The Union' not to accept less than ten shillings and that the Union would 'support' them. Indeed, according to Colonel Iremonger, labourers who joined the political unions thought that their subscription of a penny a week supported one of two causes: either 'to purchase ammunition, others, to overawe the government in compelling them to come into their views', or, 'the general impression', 'to keep up a certain rate of wages'.[79]

Afterwords

The post-repression response was far more complex than Hobsbawm and Rudé suggested. It was not simply manifest through physical protests. Instead, it assumed a far greater complexity in the ways in which residual memories of 1830 were continually remapped in response to physical protests. In this sense, Swing was not a static threat but something that was constantly morphing and coming into being. There can be little doubt that the real, as much as the perceived, threat of Swing's talismanic forms of machine-breaking and incendiarism declined post-repression – markedly so during 1833. Moreover, the response to both repression and the reneging of agreements forged in the heat of late 1830 represented a genuine evolution. This was made evident not only in the ways in which the internal balance of rural workers' repertoires of resistance altered, but also in the arguably more dramatic shift in tone. As Sir Francis Head perceived, not only had the tone of labourers' protests evolved but so had their everyday demeanour. What developed, albeit unevenly, between 1831 and 1833 was a new agrarian equipoise built on mutual fear: the Lucifer and Swing's spectre counterbalanced by the gallows and the hulks. On a day-to-day level, the field workers' displayed what Keith Snell has labelled a 'deferential bitterness', something evident before Swing but defiant post-1830.[80]

Yet this model is too simplistic. The geography of protest in the post-repression period suggests something more complex. In some locales, Swing lived on long after the Assizes and Special Commissions had terminated their bloody business on the scaffold. This was, as noted, partly a response to the severity of the judicial repression that impacted disproportionately on some locales. But it was also a response to the localised cutting of wages and the use of threshing machines. This pattern was further complicated by the fact that, even in some areas where protests persisted, they took on a different form from that adopted during the autumn and winter of 1830. Thus, in the area operated by the Elham gang in 1830, the destruction of threshing machines backed up with the resort to incendiarism against those who sought to prosecute machine-breakers continued as the main constituents of the plebeian armoury of protest tools. In the area around Chichester, protests shifted from the destruction of threshing machines to open wages agitations and incendiary attacks on the users of machinery. Moreover, in those areas where protest was either clearly snuffed out or had run its course in 1830, the protests that occurred between 1831 and 1833 did not necessarily fit any neat model. In some locales, these protests clearly were adopted in a framework that, for all intents and purposes, suggested Swing redivivus. In other areas, protests were palpably different in tone and more divisive than the consensus that Swing sought to generate. No one model can be applied to south-eastern England. Swing lived on in some locations and figuratively in most places. In some locales, Swing – or something like Swing – revived. In other, protests assumed a defiantly post-Swing hue.

What is beyond reasonable doubt is that the repression of the protests of 1830 did not, as Hobsbawm and Rudé claimed, '[destroy] what remained of the labourers' will to resist'. Nor was, as the Hammonds claimed, 'the movement crushed'.[81] Indeed, it is clear that the will to resist was just as strong between 1831 and 1833 as it had been in late 1830. That many labourers were willing to dispute their wages, openly question the nature of authority, and even join forbidden political unions, is testimony to a collective will that refused to be beaten into submission by the combined might of capitalist 'logic' and state terror.

Notes

1 An earlier version of this chapter first appeared as C. Griffin, 'Swing, Swing redivivus, or something after Swing? On the death throes of a protest movement, December 1830 – December 1833', *International Review of Social History*, 54:3 (2009), 459–97.

2 E. Hobsbawm and G. Rudé, *Captain Swing* (London: Lawrence & Wishart, 1969), p. 281.

3 *Ibid.*, p. 233.

4 *Ibid.*, ch. 15; R. Wells, 'The moral economy of the English countryside', in A. Randall and A. Charlesworth (eds), *Moral Economy and Popular Protest: Crowds, Conflict and Authority* (Basingstoke: Macmillan, 2000), pp. 246–7; A. Randall and E. Newman, 'Protest, proletarians and paternalists: social conflict in rural Wiltshire 1830–1850', *Rural History*, 6:2 (1995), 205–27.

5 These figures are derived from the extensive tabulations contained in *Captain Swing*, Appendix III, pp. 312–58. The figure of twelve incendiary fires includes a sum of two fires for the 'several fires' reported to have occurred in Kent in June 1831: p. 357. The quote is from page 287.

6 R. Wells, 'Social protest, class, conflict and consciousness, in the English countryside', in M. Reed and R. Wells (eds), *Class, Conflict and Protest in the English Countryside, 1700–1880* (London: Frank Cass, 1990), p. 168.

7 *The Times* (hereafter *TT*), 16 November; TNA, HO 52/10, fos 194–6, Attorney General, Court of King's Bench to Peel, 15 November, enclosing a letter from his son, 14 November 1830.

8 TNA, Assi 94/2070, Indictment of James Warner, Surrey Winter Assizes; *Morning Chronicle*, 3 January; TNA, HO 52/12, fos 367–9, G. Holme-Summers, Hatchlands, Guildford to Melbourne, 4 January 1831, enclosing letter from G.W. Onslow, Guildford, n.d. (late December 1830 or early January 1831).

9 TNA, HO 52/12, fos 363–4, George Walton Onslow, Chairman of the Guildford Bench to Melbourne, 8 January; *Kentish Gazette* (hereafter *KG*), 14 January; *County Chronicle*, 18 January; The *Kentish Gazette* (14 January 1831) gave a slightly different version: 'Warren is murdered; Franks, Drummond and Smallpiece shall die; I could clear him at the place, you false swearing villains!'

10 In addition to those executed, in Sussex, 17 men were transported, in Kent 25 individuals, including one woman for incendiarism, were transported, while in Hampshire 117 men were transported: Hobsbawm and Rudé, *Captain Swing*, pp. 308–9.

11 John Gilmore (Andover), Robert Holdaway (Headley), Henry Eldridge

(Fordingbridge) and James Annals (Barton Stacey) were all reprieved in mid-January 1831.

12 TNA, HO 52/13, fos 113–15, Rev. A.R.C. Dallas, Wonston Rectory to Melbourne, 8 January 1831.
13 Hampshire County Record Office (hereafter HCRO), 92M95/F2/8/5, Letter from Robert Mason, County Gaol to Rev. J. Joliffe, Barton Stacey, 27 January 1831.
14 TNA, HO 52/13, fo.17, Rev. Poore, Murston to Melbourne, 21 March 1831.
15 *Sussex Advertiser* (hereafter *SA*), 31 January 1831.
16 Four men lost their lives while extinguishing the flames, prompting the offer of a huge £1,000 reward for information leading to the conviction of the arsonist. *TT*, 19 January 1831.
17 *TT*, 29 November; CKS, Q/SBe/122, Depositions of labourer Bartholomew and innkeeper Moors, 10 December 1830.
18 *Kent Herald* (hereafter *KH*), 13 January; *Rochester Gazette* (hereafter *RG*), 18 January 1831.
19 West Sussex County Record Office (hereafter WSCRO), QR/W/758, fos 269–72, Examinations of John Pennicott, tailor, William Serle, labourer, and Robert Braby, cordwainer, all 27 December 1830.
20 *KH*, 13 January (Greenwich); *SA*, 22 January (East Grinstead); TNA, HO 52/13, fos 13–14, J. Moneypenny, Hadlow to Melbourne, 5 February (Hadlow: assistant overseer); *Reading Mercury*, 7 February 1831 (Burghclere).
21 *SA*, 31 January; *RG*, 1 February; *Hampshire Telegraph* (hereafter *HT*), 7 February; *Berkshire Chronicle*, 12 February 1831.
22 *HT*, 27 December 1830.
23 *KG*, 1 March 1831.
24 See chapter 4, p. 102.
25 *Kent and Essex Mercury*, 4 January 1831.
26 *County Chronicle*, 18 January (Albury & Shere); *KH*, 20 January (Dover) *KG*, 21 January (Northfleet); *SA*, 31 January 1831 (East Grinstead).
27 *Maidstone Journal* (hereafter *MJ*), 18 January; *KG*, 1 February 1831.
28 TNA, Assi 94/2100, Indictment of John Longhurst, labourer, and Calendar, Surrey Lent Assizes 1831. Longhurst was found guilty and sentenced to seven years' transportation.
29 TNA, HO 52/15, fos 6–8, D. Stedman, Horsham to Melbourne, 8 April; ESCRO, HIC 980, Anon., no location, to 'My Dear John', 21 April 1831.
30 *HT*, 31 March 1831.
31 TNA, HO 52/15, fo. 15, Sir Godfrey Webster, Battle Abbey to Melbourne, 28 March 1831.
32 J. Archer, *By a Flash and a Scare: Incendiarism, Animal Maiming, and Poaching in East Anglia 1815–1870* (Oxford: Oxford University Press, 1990), pp. 250–7.
33 *RG*, 21 June; *MJ*, 21 June; *KH*, 7 July 1831.
34 *Brighton Gazette* (hereafter *BG*), 28 July 1831.
35 TNA, HO 52/13, fos 87–8, 72–4a and 70–1, Rev. Poore, Murston, 5 and 6 August, J. Bradley, Sittingbourne, 6 August 1831, both to Melbourne.
36 *KH*, 4 August and 22 September; *KG*, 2 September 1831.
37 TNA, HO 52/13, fos 75–6, Deal Bench to Melbourne, 5 and 9 August 1831.

38 *KG*, 9 and 12 August; *Kent and Essex Mercury*, 9 August; *MJ*, 16 August; *KH*, 18 August 1831.

39 *MJ*, 30 August; *KH*, 1 September 1831.

40 TNA, HO 52/13, fos 301–2, Earl of Camden, Arlington Street to Melbourne, 7 September, enclosing letter from William Deedes, Sandling to Camden, 4 September; *KG*, 2 September; *TT*, 10 September 1831.

41 *KG*, 20 September 1831.

42 TNA, HO 52/13, fos 89–90, 91–2, 93–103, 79–80 and 66–9, W. Stringer, New Romney/Newhall, Dymchurch, 16, 17, 18 and 20 August, Camden, The Wilderness, to Melbourne, 28 August, enclosing a letter Deedes, Sandling to Camden, n.d.; *KG*, 23 August 1831.

43 *KH*, 6 May, 10 and 24 November; TNA, HO 52/15, fos 22–3 and 39–40, Mayor Lamb, Rye to Melbourne, 7 and 9 November 1831.

44 Sir James Grey, Ramsgate to Melbourne, 17 November 1831, TNA, HO 52/13, fos 32–8.

45 J. Archer, *Social Unrest and Popular Protest in England 1780–1840* (Cambridge: Cambridge University Press, 2000), p. 21.

46 *TT*, 24 December 1831.

47 Guestling: *BG*, 25 August; *SA*, 19 December 1831 and 2 January 1832; TNA, Assi 94/2104, Indictment of Thomas Bufford, Sussex Winter Assizes 1831. Eastry: TNA, HO 64/2, pp. 421–2 and Assi 94/2098, W. Hughes D'Aeath, Knowlton Court, nr Wingham to Melbourne, 16 November, and Indictment of John Dixon, Kent Winter Assizes 1831; *TT*, 17 November and 24 December 1831. Barton Stacey: *TT*, 5 March; *Hampshire Chronicle*, 19 March 1832.

48 *KG*, 27 December 1831 and 6 January 1832.

49 *SA*, 11 June; *Brighton Herald* (hereafter *BH*) 16 June, and 22 December; TNA, Assi 94/2137, Indictment of George Wren, 19, Sussex Winter Assizes, 1832.

50 *Kentish Observer*, 22 August. Three days later an incendiary fire occurred at nearby East Langdon following much 'murmuring' and 'threatening insinuations' regarding some farmers mowing their wheat: *KH*, 22 August 1833.

51 Wells, 'Social protest', p. 167.

52 *SA*, 31 January; *RG*, 1 February; *HT*, 7 February; *Reading Mercury*, 14 February; *KH*, 26 May; *MJ*, 31 May 1831. For the initial use of 'Swing' in 1830 see C. Griffin, 'The violent Captain Swing?', *Past & Present*, 209 (2010), 161–3.

53 *KH*, 4 October 1832.

54 *Hampshire Advertiser* (hereafter *HA*), 26 November 1831; *TT*, 3 January; *KG*, 3 January 1832.

55 *BH*, 24 November 1832; TNA, HO 52/13, fos 54–6, Camden, Willington Street to Melbourne, 15 June 1831.

56 *KH*, 6 September; *KG*, 7 September; *MJ*, 11 September 1832.

57 TNA, HO 52/30 fos 2–3, 7–9 and 52/23 fos 12–13, Thomas Sanctuary, Nunnery, nr Horsham to Melbourne, 21 October, Stedman, Horsham to Phillips, 18 November 1832, Rev. W. Barlee, West Chiltington to Melbourne, 4 May 1833.

58 The Kentish villages of Aylesford, Charing, Stone, Chart, Leeds, Thurnham, Detling, and Sutton Valence, all near Maidstone and affected by Swing in

October and November 1830, sent petitions in support of reform to Parliament in February 1831: *Maidstone Gazette*, 1 March 1831.

59 *KH*, 17 May 1832.

60 *KG*, 1 November 1831; J. Gale Jones, *A Political Tour Through Rochester, Chatham, Maidstone, Gravesend &c.* (Rochester: Baggins, 1796/1997).

61 *HA*, 29 October and 5 November 1831. *Poor Man's Guardian*, 18 August 1832.

62 Wells, 'Social protest', pp. 188–9.

63 *HA*, 12 November 1831; 11 August 1832. For an analysis of Hampshire (high) politics in this period see: R. Foster, *The Politics of County Power: Wellington and the Hampshire Gentlemen 1820–1852* (Hemel Hempstead: Harvester Wheatsheaf, 1990). Ironically, Oram's Arbour, a long-favoured spot for plebeian political meetings, was subsequently the site on which the popularly loathed Winchester New Poor Law Union was built.

64 At a meeting of the revived Brighton Political Union in June 1832, earlier incarnations having floundered in the face of internal fissures, one man was reported to have read out the 'Birmingham Declaration': *HA*, 3 September 1831; *BG*, 21 June 1832.

65 N. Lopatin, *Political Unions, Popular Politics, and the Great Reform Act of 1832* (London: Macmillan, 1999), p. 168.

66 *BG*, 1 September; *HA*, 3 September 1831.

67 *BG*, 21 June, and 26 July; *BH*, 13 October and 10 November 1832.

68 *Poor Man's Guardian*, 20 October; *BH*, 24 November; *SA*, 26 November and 3 December; TNA, HO 52/20, fos 11–12, and 52/23, fos 12–13, W. Mabbott, Uckfield to Melbourne, 20 November 1832; Rev. W. Barlee, West Chiltington to Melbourne, 4 May 1833.

69 Cobbett's visit, though symbolic, was part of a wider tour of market towns. His purpose was to remind people that the Bill would be 'a bundle of waste paper' unless the newly enfranchised campaigned for further change. His purpose was therefore to campaign for 'a *common understanding* amongst the people, with regard to *what measures ought to be adopted by the reformed Parliament*': *Cobbett's Weekly Political Register*, 30 June; *BG*, 26 July; *SA*, 6 August 1832. According to Ian Dyck, Melbourne thought the Chopsticks' Festival to be 'a seditious affair', but as no report of the Festival was made no prosecution could be brought: *William Cobbett and Rural Popular Culture* (Cambridge: Cambridge University Press, 1992), pp. 198–9.

70 *TT*, 6 October; *HT*, 24 October 1831; Wells, 'Social protest', pp. 189–90.

71 Dyck, *William Cobbett*, p. 198; *Poor Man's Guardian*, 1 December 1832. In May 1832 when an attempt was made to found a Political Union at Salisbury (Wiltshire), the 'Masters' resolved not to employ any members: *HA*, 19 May 1832.

72 University of Southampton Special Collections, WP4/4/3/34, Sir J.W. Pollen, Redenham House, Andover to the Duke of Wellington, enclosing Colonel William Iremonger JP, Wherwell Priory to Pollen, 5 November 1832.

73 TNA, HO 64/3, fos 70–3, T. Butter, Hambledon to Melbourne, 6 January 1832.

74 For instance, the Maidstone Political Union was still petitioning Parliament as late as July 1834: *Cobbett's Weekly Political Register*, 26 July 1834.

75 See R. Wells, 'Resistance to the New Poor Law in the rural south', in J. Rule

and R. Wells, *Crime, Protest and Popular Politics in Southern England 1740–1850* (London: Hambledon, 1997), pp. 92–125.

76 HCRO, 92M95/F2/13/3, Warrant for the arrest of Edward Bishop and John Rhide for leading an illegal gathering in Micheldever on 3 June 1834.

77 J. Marlow, *The Tolpuddle Martyrs* (London: André Deutsch, 1971), pp. 43, 46.

78 R. Wells, 'Tolpuddle in the context of English agrarian labour history, 1780–1850', in J. Rule (ed.) *British Trade Unionism: The Formative Years* (London: Longman, 1988), pp. 121–2.

79 University of Southampton Special Collections, WP4/4/3/34, Sir J.W. Pollen, Redenham House, Andover, to the Duke of Wellington, enclosing Colonel William Iremonger JP, Wherwell Priory to Pollen, 5 November 1832.

80 K.D.M. Snell, 'Deferential bitterness: the social outlook of the rural proletariat in eighteenth and nineteenth century England and Wales', in M. Bush (ed.), *Social Orders and Social Classes in Europe since 1500: Studies in Stratification* (London: Longman, 1992), pp. 158–84.

81 Hobsbawm and Rudé, *Captain Swing*, p. 281; J and B Hammond, *The Village Labourer*, p. 199.

Conclusions

By the end of the 1830s threshing machines were no longer in general use in any part of the south-east, and attempts to reintroduce them frequently provoked incendiary attacks.[1] Indeed, post-1830 there was a heightened hostility to all forms of machinery evidenced by machine-breaking in a paper mill at Hawley near Dartford and repeated attacks against a measure manufactory at Hurst Green (Sussex) which deployed a steam engine and a sawing machine.[2] If this is the sole means by which the success of Swing is judged then it was an unprecedented success. During the autumn and winter months of the ensuing years, the threshing barns in the region were enlivened by the sound of flail upon straw, thousands of man-hours given over to the task.

By the mid-1830s, it was possible to claim that wages were also higher because of the agreements forged in the heat of October and November 1830. Indeed, as Chapter 11 shows, attempts to reduce wages to pre-Swing levels in 1831, 1832 and 1833 were met by strikes and a turn to the tools of rural terror. Comments made before the 1836 Select Committee on Agriculture are particularly telling. According to farmer Boniface of Climping near Littlehampton, 'If it had not been for those riots, wages would have been lower at this time than they are. At that time there was a considerable rise of wages and they never have reduced them in proportion to the fall in the price of wheat.' Lord Radnor suggested, however, that while this had been true it was no longer the case. Notwithstanding 'the universal abandonment of machinery for a time, which was certainly disadvantageous to the pockets of the farmer', wages had now fallen back to the same level as before 'the fires'.[3] Indeed, beyond the winter of 1834, the claim was no longer true. The 'reforming' Parliament, elected in part because of the additional political pressure that Swing created for parliamentary reform, in 1834 passed the Poor Law Amendment Act. Under the satirically known 'Poor Man's Robbery Bill', parishes were forced into workhouse-focused poor law unions. Wage subsidies, child allowances, the payment of rent and the provision of clothes and fuel were to stop, and all relief was to be given, except under exceptional circumstances, institutionally. Although poor law reform had, so it has been suggested, been on the cards since the 1790s,[4] Swing served to highlight what was perceived to be the inherent dangers – even evils – of the current system.

In spite of the the huge cost of poor rates to farmers (and hence to landlords in the form of reduced rents), labourers were still prepared to protest their lot, to forfeit their lives on the gallows. Moreover, so the authors of the 1834 Poor Law Report put the case, the system acted to encourage laziness and inefficiency as labourers were materially supported in the same way whether they worked for the farmers or engaged in some sort of menial make-work scheme. So the well-rehearsed argument goes, the committee of Edwin Chadwick, Nassau Senior and other political economists, twisted the evidence to 'prove' that the current laws were immoral and inefficient – and caused Swing.[5] If Swing had not caused (or created) the New Poor Law, it was the trigger for its passing. And as Wells and others have documented, the effect of the New Poor Law was to depress wages, with labourers being prepared to do anything, to accept any wage, to avoid incarceration in the new bastilles.[6]

So, Swing begat the New Poor Law which begat lower wages. On this basis, in the longer term Swing failed. But what power did rural workers – a group for whom demand was structurally falling, yet whose ranks were increasing thanks to the coming of age of those born in the post-1815 demographic boom – have in the face of the will of the state? Certainly the upturn in crime and incendiarism (again) post 1835 when combined with the uselessness of village and special constables in suppressing Swing, provided a clear narrative which created the condition for the passing of the 1840 Rural Constabulary Act.[7]

While Swing was present at the birth of two of the most defining moments in the creation of the modern British state – the centralised provision of welfare and county police forces – this was not a failure on Swing's own terms. The world which Swing inadvertently helped to create was indeed anathema to Swing's values: centralising agendas and political economy as opposed to local customs and mutual reciprocity manifest through strong social bonds. In Swing's world what could be achieved was achieved. Its subsequent betrayal was not Swing's fault, or even a mark of failure.

Beyond this, what have we learnt? Further credence can be given to some things we already knew. Swing was exceptional, the largest ever episode of machine-breaking, the last non-coordinated national protest of rural workers, indeed the biggest ever rural uprising. Other recent revisions can also be corroborated. Incendiarism was evidently far more important than we once thought. It was more frequently resorted to, was critical to the events of 1831–33, and was in many locations a protest tool deployed in support of 'open' protests. Machine-breaking too was more important in Kent than has hitherto been known, the anti-machine rhetoric of many locales not simply confined to late 1830 but put into practice over a period of at least three successive years. Also, in several locales radical political discourses were not only made audible during Swing but were actually central to the shape and form of mobilisations. If the link between belief and putting belief into action through protesting was often obtuse, some evidence is far more explicit. That Maidstone radicals Robert Price and John Adams led the Swing groups which were responsible for physically diffusing protests from the parishes to the north-east of Maidstone into the Weald proves that radical politics could be central to Swing's form and diffusion. In short, radical politics was fundamental to Swing's evolution for without Price and Adams it is questionable whether Swing would have ever spread beyond mid-Kent.

There are also bigger questions which we can now answer with some degree of certainty, or rather provide feasible answers for, which future studies can seek to support or falsify. One of the most contentious questions in the historiography of Swing relates to the question of whether Swing was a protest movement. On one conceptual level this is easily addressed by examining in turn the different fundamental dynamics that define protest movements: did activists share the same objectives; did events/claims in one location inspire events elsewhere; were the protests organised rather than always random and spontaneous; and did protests diffuse from one locale to another.

In relation to Swing, the same (or similar) claims were made from place to place, whatever the local contexts. For wherever sustained protests occurred in the autumn and winter of 1830 the objectives were always driven by a desire to improve the material condition of rural workers. As regards organisation, there was no leader for the protests of 1830, Captain Swing or otherwise. Locally, though, many Swing risings were coordinated, whether through pre-existing gangs or through groups which coalesced around charismatic strangers or labourers' leaders. Indeed, through the activities of coordinated groups, Swing physically diffused throughout the south-east. It was neither entirely spontaneous nor totally disorganised. Moreover, while there was no pan-regional or national coordination, solidarities extended across large areas and between individuals and groups who had never met, evidenced in the attack on farmer Chapman of Lenham who had made vitriolic remarks about the Elham machine-breakers.[8] It is also clear that in this diffusion, events occurring in one locale – the protests 'in Kent' often held up as inspirational to would-be protestors in Sussex, Surrey and Hampshire – inspired events elsewhere.

And yet, very few protestors actually tried to forge a movement or even wanted to achieve anything beyond better material conditions in their parish. So while Swing meets the definition of a protest movement, in essence there was no attempt to forge a movement. Peter Jones's identification of a meta-movement that tied together local movements offers a useful distinction.[9] Either way, Swing presented poor rural workers with an opportunity to rise, giving them an outlet to both make claims and to collectively release tension. When Richard Hodd, a member of a Swing gang who visited Mayfield, Rotherfield, Buxted and Withyham, exclaimed that 'he was never so happy in his life as he was on that day', he articulated the most important aspect of Swing: the sense of relief and joy that the participants were being heard, that labouring communities were being heard.[10]

Swing was clearly rooted in customary ritual and ceremony, using protest forms that ostensibly had long histories. But custom was not always the wellspring of protest. As Andy Wood has shown for the early modern period, militia-inspired forms of organisation were central to many protests, something learnt through experience rather than community memory and custom.[11] And so it was with Swing. If many of the negotiations in the playing out of parish politics looked much like the 'stately gavotte' that Andrew Charlesworth identified in earlier food 'riots', not least regarding the role of magistrates in negotiating farmers' concessions, and labourers claims were only ever for 'fair' wages, there was a sense of also transcending the 'moral economy'.[12] By operating threshing machines, by manipulating the poor laws to keep the cost of labour down, by watching their premises to ward against labourers firing their ricks, and acting as witnesses and prosecutors at the ensuing Swing trials, large(r) farmers had clearly broken the compact. Such actions gave labourers licence to also act differently. In throwing off work and going about the parish demanding higher wages we see a coming together of ritual and proto trade unionism. This, combined with a readiness to resort to the tools of rural terror, is suggestive of a fracturing of social relations – and the ability of rural workers to innovate in the face of capitalist innovation.

Was Swing therefore evidence of the existence (or the emergence) or a rural working class? As noted, in some locales there is clear evidence that the interests of farmers and labourers were diametrically opposed. The fires of 1831, 1832 and 1833 against Swing's oppressors in many ways offered a perfect definition of class politics, labour in direct opposition to the means of production. In these repeated events there is a sense not of trying to restore old social bonds but instead of an attritional struggle being played out. When collective protests again broke out in 1835 against the implementation of the New Poor Law, the broad-based coalition of labourers, artisans and farmers achieved in some locales during Swing did not coalesce, despite the fact that only the most wealthy farmers welcomed the New Poor Law. This failure to coalesce was a direct result of farmers backtracking in 1831 and 1832 from Swing agreements. As Wells has asserted in relation to the experience of the post-1815 depression, the post-1830 experience was broadly similar throughout the cornland communities of southern England.[13] The patchwork of local contexts cohered to form a spatially coherent labouring ideology which recognised that landowners, magistrates, clergymen and the parish vestry did not usually best serve the interests of rural workers.

Was this 'fracturing' itself evidence of class consciousness? It is certainly evidence of one group struggle against another. But despite the genuine menace of these post-1830 protests the demands of labour were still modest. There were, for instance, no sustained calls by rural workers that landlords and farmers should give up their means of production: the land, their farms. Labourers still wanted to labour (and receive a wage). As such, this 'new' consciousness was manifested in ancient labour processes, and farm labourers in the early 1830s were engaged in same day-to-day tasks as their medieval forebears. They were not to echo Alun Howkins's assertion, a proletariat in the way that Marx had defined, the performance of agricultural labour not changing dramatically until the widespread mechanisation of many tasks from the late 1860s.[14] Herein lays an irony. By attempting to prevent the further mechanisation (and hence capitalisation) of agricultural tasks, Swing activists were also preventing their own transformation into a Marxian working class.

If this was not a rural working class (or even a working class in the making), Swing shows, and its aftermath emphatically shows, that calls to restore old social bonds and thereby cure all social ills were only partially successful. Farmers might have been victorious in securing reduced rents and tithes but many were quick to again reduce wages. If paternalism had been revived it was the briefest of revivals, and then probably only predicated by landlords and farmers desire to save their property from the incendiarists' hand. This is not to say that in all locations the apparent connection between Swing protestors and farmers was based on a paper-thin pretence. In large parts of the Weald, in and around the forests of Hampshire, and in the maze of tracks and green lanes around Elham, the small farmers were socially and culturally closer to the labourers, the introduction of threshing machines placing them at a disadvantage compared to the most highly capitalised farms. But these smaller farmers were already being squeezed out.[15] Swing therefore represented an opportunity to protect both their livelihoods and their way of life.

Such an analysis necessarily posits the question as to whom Swing activists were. While the analysis presented here has not sought to systematically deconstruct the sociological composition of Swing groups – besides, Hobsbawm and Rudé's identification of Swing defendants appears to be comprehensive and accurate[16] – the evidence related in Chapters 4 and 9 shows that Swing groups were far from homogeneous. If most Swing protestors appear to have been young men this was not to the exclusion of older hands, as ringleaders Henry and Edward Read at Elham were, for instance, in their 50s.[17] Other Swing activists were drawn from outside the ranks of those who relied only on farm work to subsist. Many were artisans, some but not all of whom occasionally had to go labouring to support their families, and some were urban workers and small (and occasionally as at Owslebury, Selborne and Headley larger) farmers too. As Chapter 8 shows, though, to simply focus on the activists is to ignore the broader constituency of support for the protests. From wives and children, to publicans and petty dealers, and the many field workers, artisans and small farmers who did not protest but supported the cause, Swing was more than just a rebellion of young labouring men.

Swing was also more than just a brief but dramatic moment in the history of the English countryside. As noted above, it was mobilised as a justification for the passing of the Poor Law Amendment Act and Rural Constabulary Act. It also gave considerable impetus, as Jeremy Burchardt has shown, to the adoption and state support for allotments.[18] The repression of Swing and its subsequent swift betrayal by many farmers and vestries had a more immediate and visceral legacy. Rural workers' defiance in the face of continued repression not only taught them how to organise and innovate in the arts of resistance but also to assume a different set of everyday social relations than those that Swing had sought to restore. As Assistant Poor Law Commissioner Sir Francis Head remarked of the labourers of the vicinity of Dover: 'In no enemy's country that we have seen have we ever encountered the churlish demeanour which these men, as one meets them in the lanes, now assume.'[19]

The protests that followed Swing were fractured in space, time and protest practice. Swing also took on a phantasmagorical quality. For even when an area remained free from Swing-like protests, the fear generated in 1830 converted Captain Swing into a spectral presence that continued to wreak terror on the minds of farmers and the rulers of rural England. Over and above Swing's continuities and revivals, it was as a concept that Swing most meaningfully lived on. Thus in 1852 at a public meeting on the Isle of Wight, one speaker juxtaposed the (relative) rural prosperity of the early 1850s with the time 'a few years ago, when Swing was abroad and incendiary fires and public prosecutions for riot were rife'. Swing was even raised as a fearful spectre during the Revolt of the Field in the 1870s.[20] If the protests that followed were not Swing, they were informed and shaped by Swing's lessons. Protests against the New Poor Law, and support in the countryside for the Grand National Consolidated Trade Union, Chartism and for the Anti-Corn Law League were all made possible by the changes in rural society wrought by Swing.

Notes

1 For instance fires at Emsworth (29 November 1834) and Seaford (16 May 1835) targeted threshing machines: *Brighton Herald*, 6 December 1834; *Brighton Guardian*, 20 May 1835.
2 *Gravesend and Milton Journal*, 2 May 1835; *Kent Herald*, 19 October 1837.

3 BPP. Commons, 'Third Report from the Select Committee appointed to inquire into the state of agriculture' (1836), viii, Evidence of Mr Thomas Boniface, Climping, Sussex, 3 May, and of Lord Radnor, 14 June 1836.

4 For the classic exposition of this point see: A. Mandler, 'The making of the New Poor Law redivivus', *Past & Present*, 117 (1987), 131–57.

5 For the edited report with a useful contextual introduction see: S. Checkland and E. Checkland (eds), *The Poor Law Report of 1834* (Harmondsworth: Penguin, 1974).

6 R. Wells, 'Resistance to the New Poor Law in the rural south', in J. Rule and R. Wells, *Crime, Protest and Popular Politics in Southern England 1740–1850* (London: Hambledon, 1997), pp. 92–125; A. Clark, 'The New Poor Law and the breadwinner wage', *Journal of Social History*, 34:2 (2000), 267.

7 D. Philips and R. Storch, *Policing Provincial England, 1829–1856: The Politics of Reform* (London: Leicester University Press, 1999), pp. 71–2, 170, 173 and 187.

8 *Maidstone Gazette*, 19 October; *Kent Herald*, 21 October 1830.

9 P. Jones, 'Finding Captain Swing: protest, parish relations, and the state of the public mind in 1830', *International Review of Social History*, 54:3 (2009), 434.

10 TNA, TS 11/1007, Prosecution brief prepared by the Treasury Solicitor in the case of the King, for William Endersby Esq., against Richard Hodd, John Wickens for Riot, Lewes Winter Assizes 1830.

11 A. Wood, 'Collective violence, social drama and rituals of rebellion in late medieval and early modern England', in S. Carroll (ed.) *Cultures of Violence: Interpersonal Violence in Historical Perspective* (Basingstoke: Palgrave, 2007), pp. 101–2.

12 A. Charlesworth, 'From the moral economy of Devon to the political economy of Manchester, 1790–1812', *Social History*, 17:2 (1993), 210.

13 R. Wells, 'The moral economy of the English countryside', in A. Randall and A. Charlesworth (eds), *Moral Economy and Popular Protest: Crowds, Conflict and Authority* (Basingstoke: Macmillan, 2000), pp. 209–12.

14 A. Howkins, 'Labour History and the rural poor, 1850–1980', *Rural History*, 1:1 (1991), 114, 117–18.

15 See: J. Sheppard, 'Small farms in a Sussex Weald parish 1800–60', *Agricultural History Review*, 40:2 (1992), 127–41.

16 E. Hobsbawm and G. Rudé, *Captain Swing* (London: Lawrence & Wishart, 1969), pp. 241–7.

17 Centre for Kentish Studies, Q/SBe 120/36, Calendar of prisoners for trial at the 1830 Michaelmas East Kent Quarter Sessions.

18 J. Burchardt, *The Allotment Movement in England, 1793–1873* (Woodbridge: Boydell Press, 2002), ch. 2. A slew of legislation in the early 1830s supported the nascent allotment 'movement'. 1 and 2 William IV C.42 sanctioned overseers and churchwardens to hire up to 50 acres to be let to the poor in allotments. 1 and 2 William IV, c.59, 1831 authorised vestries to enclose up to 50 acres of Crown Lands (with the consent of the Treasury) for 'poor's allotments', while 2. William IV C.42 allowed parishes to let land set out in earlier enclosures in small allotments for 'industrious cottagers of good character'.

19 *Kent Herald*, 7 May 1835.

20 *Hampshire Telegraph*, 17 April 1852; *Jackson's Oxford Journal*, 25 May 1872.

Appendix

Reported protest incidents, 24 August–31 December 1830

Method: this table is compiled of those protest incidents recorded in provincial and national newspaper reports, estate correspondence, letters to and from the Home, Post and War Offices, and judicial records. As the case of a report of fires in the Farningham area in early October attests, the record is not comprehensive and as such this table should not be read as a register of all south-eastern Swing incidents. In relation to the protest activities of mobile gangs, I have simply included *one* entry in the table if their activities extended to that parish on that day. If they returned to the parish on the following day, a further entry is made. Again, limitations in the record, not least for the fast evolving events in Hampshire, mean that it is likely that many such incidents are not detailed.

Italics = reports unclear

Date	Parish	County	Incident
24 Aug	Wingmore (Elham)	Kent	Threshing machine
24 Aug	Brasted	Kent	Arson
28 Aug	Palmstead (Upper Hardres)	Kent	Threshing machine
28 Aug	Stone Street (Lyminge)	Kent	Threshing machines (2)
28 Aug	Sundridge	Kent	Arson
29 Aug	Newington-next-Hythe	Kent	Threshing machine
1–2 Sep	Sundridge	Kent	Arson
1–2 Sep	Sundridge	Kent	Arson
1–2 Sep	Brasted	Kent	Arson
3 Sep– 6 Oct	Sundridge	Kent	Arson (3)
4 Sep	Shirley (Southampton)	Hants	Plant maiming
5 Sep	Hound	Hants	Arson
8 Sep	Albury (Brook)	Surrey	Arson

Date	Parish	County	Incident
8–15 Sep	Shere	Surrey	Animal maiming
9 Sep	Cowden	Kent	Arson
11 Sep	Ryde, IOW	Hants	'Riot'
Mid-Sep	Sundridge	Kent	Threatening letter
Mid-Sep	Ide Hill (Sundridge)	Kent	Threatening letter
Mid-Sep	Westerham	Kent	Threatening letter
Mid-Sep	Sevenoaks	Kent	Threatening letter
16 Sep	Brabourne	Kent	Threshing machine
18 Sep	Stone Street (Lyminge)	Kent	Threshing machine (2)
18 Sep	Upper Hardres	Kent	Threshing machine (2)
20 Sep	Sellindge ('Lees')	Kent	Threshing machine
20 Sep	Barham	Kent	Threshing machine (unclear)
20 Sep	Barham	Kent	Threshing machine
20 Sep	Denne Hill (Womenswold)	Kent	Threshing machine
20 Sep	Womenswold	Kent	Threshing machine
20 Sep	Barham	Kent	Threshing machine
22 Sep	Stanford	Kent	Threshing machine
22 Sep	Brabourne	Kent	Threshing machine
25 Sep	Dover	Kent	Malicious damage
27 Sep	Farthingloe (Hougham)	Kent	Threshing machine
29 Sep	Swan Inn, Sutton Scotney	Hants	Radical meeting/petition
1 Oct	Hougham	Kent	Threshing machine
1–5 Oct	Sturry (area)	Kent	Threatening letters (2)
2 Oct	Sturry	Kent	Threshing machine
2 Oct	Sturry	Kent	Threshing machine
2–6 Oct*	*Farningham area*	*Kent*	*Arson (multiple cases)*
5 Oct	Oxted	Surrey	Arson
5 Oct	Ash-Lyminge (between)	Kent	Rockets fired (in a line)
5 Oct	Lyminge	Kent	Arson
5 Oct	Ash	Kent	Arson
6 Oct	Iford, nr Christchurch	Hants	Arson
6 Oct	Dover – Canterbury	Kent	'Swing' graffiti
6 Oct	Dover	Kent	Threatening letter
6 Oct	Dover	Kent	Threatening letter
6 Oct	Margate	Kent	Threat to destroy threshing machine
7 Oct	Otford	Kent	Arson
7 Oct	Sundridge	Kent	Arson
7 Oct	Otford	Kent	Threatening letter
8 Oct	Wrotham – Farningham	Kent	Arson
c.8 Oct	Kearsney/Ewell	Kent	Threshing machines placed in fields for destruction
8 Oct	Hougham	Kent	Threshing machine
8 Oct	Hougham	Kent	Threatening letter

9 Oct	Exton	Hants	Arson
10 Oct	Dumpton (Ramsgate)	Kent	Arson
11 Oct	Hadlow	Kent	Arson
12 Oct	Lenham	Kent	Implements destroyed
12–13 Oct	Maidstone	Kent	Radical political demo
12–16 Oct	Maidstone (vicinity)	Kent	Threatening letters (2)
12–16 Oct	Wrotham	Kent	Threatening letter
13 Oct	Sevenoaks	Kent	Threatening letters (several)
Before			
14 Oct	Romsey	Hants	Malicious damage
14 Oct	Maidstone	Kent	Radical political demo
15 Oct	Maidstone	Kent	Threatening letter
16 Oct	Battle	Sussex	Radical political demo
17 Oct	Hartfield	Sussex	Arson
18–23 Oct	Isfield Place (Northfleet)	Kent	Threatening letter
18–23 Oct	Maidstone (area)	Kent	Threatening letters (several)
18–25 Oct	Northfleet	Kent	Threatening letter
21 Oct	Newington-next-Sittingbourne	Kent	Arson
21 Oct	Borden	Kent	Arson
22 Oct	Ulcomb	Kent	Assemblage
22 Oct	Ash	Kent	Arson
22 Oct	Hartlip	Kent	Threshing machine
22 Oct	Boxley	Kent	Arson
23 Oct	Shipbourne (Green)	Kent	Arson
23 Oct	Sandwich	Kent	Arson (inc. threshing machine)
23 Oct	Ash	Kent	Arson (foiled)
23 Oct	Barham (nr Patrixbourne)	Kent	Threshing machine
23 Oct	Bekesbourne	Kent	Threshing machine
23 Oct	Patrixbourne	Kent	Threshing machine
23 Oct	Sandwich	Kent	Threshing machine
23 Oct	Hollanden/Leigh (Tonbridge)	Kent	Arson
24 Oct	Cobham	Kent	Arson
24 Oct	Tunbridge	Kent	Political placard
24 Oct	Dover	Kent	Arson
24 Oct	Stockbury	Kent	Arson
24 Oct	Stockbury	Kent	Demonstration
24–26 Oct	Rainham	Kent	Assemblages
25 Oct	Wormshill	Kent	Assemblage
25 Oct	Frinstead	Kent	Assemblage
25 Oct	Goldstone (Ash)	Kent	Threshing machine
25 Oct	Oversland (Ash)	Kent	Threshing machine
25 Oct	Stourmouth	Kent	Threshing machine
25 Oct	Stourmouth	Kent	Threshing machine
25 Oct	Stourmouth	Kent	Threshing machine

Date	Parish	County	Incident
25 Oct	Stourmouth	Kent	Threshing machine
25 Oct	Wingham	Kent	Threshing machine
25 Oct	Wingham	Kent	Threshing machine
25 Oct	Wingham	Kent	Threshing machine
25 Oct	Queenborough	Kent	Riot
25 Oct	Sittingbourne	Kent	Strike
25 Oct	Newington	Kent	Assemblage
25 Oct	Sheffield Park (Fletching)	Sussex	Threatening letter
25–27 Oct	Isle of Sheppey	Kent	Arson (2)
26 Oct	Frinstead	Kent	Assemblage
26 Oct	Wormshill	Kent	Assemblage
26 Oct	Lenham	Kent	Assemblage
26 Oct	Selling	Kent	Arson
26 Oct	Ospringe	Kent	Assemblage
26 Oct	Ash	Kent	Strike
26 Oct	Boughton-under-Blean	Kent	Arson
27 Oct	Stockbury	Kent	Assemblage
27 Oct	Hucking	Kent	Assemblage
27 Oct	Debtling	Kent	Assemblage
27 Oct	Hartlip	Kent	Assemblage
27 Oct	Rainham	Kent	Assemblage
28 Oct	Sandwich	Kent	Threshing machines (number unclear)
28 Oct	Crundale	Kent	Threshing machine
28 Oct	Stone (Greenhithe)	Kent	Arson
28 Oct	Orpington	Kent	Arson
28 Oct	Sandwich	Kent	Arson
28 Oct	Hollingbourne	Kent	Assemblage
28 Oct	Monkton	Kent	Arson
28 Oct	Warren Street (Lenham)	Kent	Arson
28–29 Oct	Stodmarsh (near)	Kent	Arson
29 Oct	Hollingbourne	Kent	Assemblage
29 Oct	East Sutton	Kent	Assemblage
29 Oct	Langley	Kent	Assemblage
29 Oct	Town Sutton (Sutton Valence)	Kent	Assemblage
29 Oct	Sharsted (Doddington)	Kent	Arson
29 Oct	Sandwich	Kent	Threats of destruction
29 Oct	Birchington	Kent	Arson
30 Oct	Hollingbourne	Kent	Assemblage
30 Oct	Sutton Valence	Kent	Assemblage
30 Oct	Linton	Kent	Assemblage
30 Oct	Chart Sutton	Kent	Assemblage
30 Oct	Boughton Monchelsea	Kent	Assemblage
30 Oct	Langley	Kent	Assemblage
30 Oct	Littlebourne	Kent	Attack on soldiers

30 Oct	Greenstreet Green (Meopham)	Kent	Arson
30 Oct	Cooling	Kent	Strike
30 Oct	Battle	Sussex	Threat against the overseer
31 Oct	Minster-in-Thanet	Kent	Arson
31 Oct	Isle of Grain	Kent	Arson
Late Oct	Firle (Place)	Sussex	Threatening letter
1 Nov	Penenden Heath (Maidstone)	Kent	Assemblage/Grand Meeting
1 Nov	Maidstone	Kent	Strike
1 Nov	Wouldham	Kent	Arson
1 Nov	Faversham	Kent	Assemblage
1 Nov	Boughton	Kent	Assemblage
1 Nov	Battle	Sussex	Assemblage re. the arrest of man who threatened the overseer
1–2 Nov	Battle	Sussex	Threatening letter
1–2 Nov	Battle	Sussex	Strike
1–5 Nov	Wrotham	Kent	Arson
1–5 Nov	Kent	Kent	Threatening letters (several)
1–5 Nov	Hawkhurst	Kent	Threatening letter
1–5 Nov	Frittenden	Kent	Threatening letter
1–6 Nov	East Grinstead (area)	Sussex	Threatening letters
1–6 Nov	Blackheath	Kent	Arson
1–6 Nov	Eastbourne	Sussex	Threatening letters (several)
1–6 Nov	Chatham	Kent	Sentry fired at
2 Nov	Whitfield	Kent	Threshing machine
2 Nov	Singledge (Coldred)	Kent	Threshing machine
2 Nov	Old Park (Dover)	Kent	Threshing machine
2–3 Nov	Frittenden	Kent	Assemblage
2–3 Nov	Marden	Kent	Assemblage
2–3 Nov	Staplehurst	Kent	Assemblage
2–8 Nov	Blackheath	Kent	Threatening letter
2–8 Nov	Greenwich (steam mills)	Kent	Threatening letter
3 Nov	Ashford direction (from Canterbury)	Kent	Arson
3 Nov	Battle (near)	Sussex	Arson (suspected cases)
3 Nov	East Malling	Kent	Assemblage
3 Nov	Battle	Sussex	Arson
3 Nov	Chartham	Kent	Arson
4 Nov	Battle	Sussex	Arson
4 Nov	Battle	Sussex	Assemblage
4 Nov	Icklesham	Sussex	Arson
4 Nov	Battle	Sussex	Threats of arson
4 Nov	Battle	Sussex	Arson

Date	Parish	County	Incident
4 Nov	Cranbrook	Kent	Rising
5 Nov	East Malling	Kent	Attempt to break machines
5 Nov	Caterham	Surrey	Arson
5 Nov	Brede	Sussex	Assemblage
5 Nov	Brede	Sussex	Arson
5 Nov	Tunbridge Wells	Kent	Arson
6 Nov	Tunbridge Wells	Kent	Arson
6 Nov	Lewes (direction)	Sussex	Arson
7 Nov	Roberstbridge	Sussex	Arson
7 Nov	Northfleet	Kent	Arson
7 Nov	Burwash	Sussex	Assemblage
c.7 Nov	Ticehurst	Sussex	Assemblage (planned)
7–8 Nov	Battle	Sussex	Threatening poster
8 Nov	Hawkhurst	Kent	Assemblage
8 Nov	Benenden	Kent	Assemblage
8 Nov	Fairlight	Sussex	Assemblage
8 Nov	Hooe	Sussex	Assemblage
8 Nov	Westwell Court	Kent	Destruction of ploughs
8 Nov	East Sussex	Sussex	Arson
8 Nov	Hooe	Sussex	Arson
8 Nov	Hastings	Sussex	Assemblage
8 Nov	Guestling	Sussex	Assemblage
8 Nov	Robertsbridge	Sussex	Assemblage
8 Nov	Seddlescomb	Sussex	Assemblage
8 Nov	Battle	Sussex	Assemblage
8 Nov	Wingham & Preston	Kent	Attack on watch/rockets fired in air
8 Nov	Rye	Sussex	Assemblage
8 Nov	Eastbourne	Sussex	Arson
8–9 Nov	Lewisham	Kent	Threatening letters (2)
8–12 Nov	Horsham (area)	Sussex	Threatening letters (many)
8–12 Nov	Eastry	Kent	Threshing machine
8–12 Nov	Eastry (Court)	Kent	Threshing machine (destroyed by farmer)
8–13 Nov	Lydd	Kent	Assemblage
8–13 Nov	Otham	Kent	Assemblage
9 Nov	Rye	Sussex	Assemblage
9 Nov	Westham	Sussex	Assemblage
9 Nov	Rodmersham	Kent	Arson
9 Nov	Goose Green (Hadlow)	Kent	Assemblage
9 Nov	Waltham	Kent	Threat of arson
9 Nov	Brede	Sussex	Assemblage
9 Nov	Northiam	Sussex	Assemblage

9 Nov	Ewhurst	Sussex	Assemblage
9 Nov	Benenden	Kent	Threshing machine
9 Nov	Holtye Common (Hartfield)	Sussex	Arson
9 Nov	Hawkhurst	Kent	Threshing machine
9 Nov	Etchingham	Sussex	Assemblage
9 Nov	Bodiam	Sussex	Assemblage
9 Nov	Ninfield	Sussex	Assemblage/attack
9 Nov	Goudhurst	Kent	Assemblage
9 Nov	Hawkhurst	Kent	Assemblage/rising
9 Nov	Hurst Green (Salehurst)	Sussex	Assemblage
9 Nov	Benenden	Kent	Assemblage
9 Nov	Newenden	Kent	Assemblage
9 Nov	Rolvenden	Kent	Assemblage
9 Nov	Sandhurst	Kent	Assemblage
9 Nov	Udimore	Sussex	Assemblage
9 Nov	Tenterden	Kent	Assemblage
9 Nov	Peasmarsh	Sussex	Assemblage
9 Nov	Stone Crouch (unclear)	Kent (?)	Arson
9 Nov	Fairlight	Sussex	Assemblage
9 Nov	Burwash	Sussex	Assemblage
9–13 Nov	Sevenoaks	Kent	Assemblage(s)
10 Nov	Newington-next-Hythe	Kent	Arson
10 Nov	Bearsted	Kent	Arson
10 Nov (prob)	Lamberhurst	Kent	Assemblage
10 Nov	Ticehurst	Sussex	Assemblage
10 Nov	Byfleet	Surrey	Arson
10 Nov	Kingston-upon-Thames	Surrey	Arson
10 Nov	Thurnham	Kent	Arson
10 Nov	Etchingham	Sussex	Assemblage
10 Nov	Rock Hill (Maidstone)	Kent	Arson
10 Nov	Playden	Sussex	Assemblage
10 Nov	Rye	Sussex	Assemblage
10 Nov	Wadhurst	Sussex	Assemblage
10 Nov	Horsmonden	Kent	Assemblage
10 Nov	Goudhurst	Kent	Assemblage
10 Nov	Mayfield	Sussex	Assemblage
10 Nov	Cuckfield	Sussex	Threatening letter
10 Nov	Marden	Kent	Arson
10 Nov	Eastbourne	Sussex	Assemblage
10–12 Nov	Oxted	Surrey	Arson
Around 11 Nov	Gosport	Hants	Threatening letters
Around 11 Nov	Brockhurst (Gosport)	Hants	Incendiary letter
11 Nov	Bingham (Gosport)	Hants	Arson
11 Nov	Bingham (Gosport)	Hants	Incendiary letter

Date	Parish	County	Incident
11 Nov	East Peckham	Kent	Assemblage
11 Nov	Cuckfield	Sussex	Threatening letter
11 Nov	Cuckfield	Sussex	Threatening letter
11 Nov	Frant	Sussex	Assemblage
11 Nov	West Peckham	Kent	Assemblage
11 Nov	Yotes Court (Mereworth)	Kent	Assemblage
11 Nov	Hadlow	Kent	Assemblage
11 Nov	Yalding	Kent	Assemblage
11 Nov	Benenden	Kent	Assemblage
11 Nov	Rolvenden	Kent	Assemblage
11 Nov	Nettlestead	Kent	Assemblage
11 Nov	Cranbrook	Kent	Assemblage
11 Nov	Hawkhurst	Kent	Assemblage
11 Nov	Rock Hill (Maidstone)	Kent	Arson
11 Nov	Wadhurst	Sussex	Assemblage
11 Nov	Dallington	Sussex	Assemblage
11 Nov	Ditton	Surrey	Arson
11 Nov	Cobham	Surrey	Arson
11 Nov	Cheam	Surrey	Arson
11–12 Nov	Merstham	Surrey	Arson
11–12 Nov	Kingston (area)	Surrey	Arson
12 Nov	Boxley	Kent	Farmers refused to pay tithes
12 Nov	Headcorn	Kent	Assemblage
12 Nov	Tonbridge	Kent	Assemblage
12 Nov	Otham	Kent	Arson
12 Nov	Beckley	Sussex	Assemblage
12 Nov	Frant	Sussex	Assemblage
12 Nov	Mayfield	Sussex	Assemblage
12 Nov	Mountfield	Sussex	Assemblage
12 Nov	Rotherfield	Sussex	Assemblage
12 Nov	Wadhurst	Sussex	Assemblage
12 Nov	Walberton (East)	Sussex	Assemblage
12 Nov	Coldwaltham	Sussex	Arson
12 Nov	Petworth	Sussex	Threatening letter
12 Nov	Englefield Green (Egham)	Surrey	Arson
12 Nov	Epsom	Surrey	Threatening letter
12–13 Nov	Hurstpierpoint	Sussex	Assemblage(s)
12–16 Nov	East Grinstead (churchyard)	Sussex	Assemblage
c.13 Nov	Arundel	Sussex	Threatening letter
13 Nov	Longparish	Hants	Arson
13 Nov	Swan Inn (Sutton Scotney)	Hants	Radical meeting/petition
13 Nov	Cuckfield	Sussex	Threatening letter
13 Nov	Boughton-under-Blean	Kent	Arson
13 Nov	Guildford	Surrey	Arson

13 Nov	Bridge	Kent	Assemblages
13 Nov	Mayfield	Sussex	Assemblage
13 Nov	Benenden	Kent	Assemblage
13 Nov	Bexhill	Sussex	Arson
13 Nov	Groombridge (Speldhurst)	Kent	Assemblage
13 Nov	Bignor – Petworth area	Sussex	Turbulent spirit
13 Nov	Maresfield	Sussex	Attempt to excite a mob
13 Nov	Kirdford	Sussex	Assemblage
13 Nov	Withyham	Sussex	Assemblage
13 Nov	Cuckfield	Sussex	Threatening letter
13 Nov	Frant	Sussex	Assemblage
13 Nov	Peasmarsh	Sussex	Assemblage
13 Nov	Rotherfield	Sussex	Assemblage
13 Nov	Cuckfield	Sussex	Threatening letter
13 Nov	Bodiam	Sussex	Arson
13 Nov	Dallington	Sussex	Arson
13 Nov	Fletching & Newick – Maresfield	Sussex	Threatening letter
13 Nov	Wisborough Green	Sussex	Regulation of wages
13–14 Nov	nr. Guildford	Surrey	Arson
13–14 Nov	Cobham	Surrey	Arson
14 Nov	Eastchurch	Kent	Destruction of 3 ploughs
14 Nov	Hernhill	Kent	Arson
14 Nov	Petworth	Sussex	Small assemblage
14 Nov (prob)	Tenterden	Kent	Assemblage
14 Nov	Burwash	Sussex	Assemblage
14 Nov	Ringmer	Sussex	Assemblage/rising
14 Nov	Canterbury	Kent	Riot
14 Nov	Albury	Surrey	Arson
14–20 Nov	East Grinstead	Sussex	Arson (multiple cases)
14–20 Nov	East Grinstead	Sussex	Threshing machines
Mid-Nov	Chiddingfold	Surrey	Threats to farmers not to pay tithes
Mid-Nov	Catsfield	Sussex	Assemblage
15 Nov	Strathfieldsaye	Hants	Arson (unclear)
15 Nov	Easton	Hants	Incendiary letter
15 Nov	Cowes, IOW	Hants	Malicious damage
15 Nov	Thakeham	Sussex	Assemblage
15 Nov	Ringmer	Sussex	Assemblage
15 Nov	Ham Street	Kent	Assemblage
15 Nov	Ham Street (unclear)	Kent	Threshing machines (2)
15 Nov	Yapton	Sussex	Assemblage
15 Nov	Crowborough	Sussex	Assemblage
15 Nov	Felpham	Sussex	Assemblage
15 Nov	Littlehampton	Sussex	Assemblage
15 Nov	Bognor	Sussex	Assemblage

Date	Parish	County	Incident
15 Nov	Aldingbourne	Sussex	Assemblage
15 Nov	Withyham	Sussex	Assemblage
15 Nov	Sullington	Sussex	Assemblage
15 Nov	Uckfield (area)	Sussex	Assemblage
15 Nov	Crowborough	Sussex	Threshing machine and other farm machinery
15 Nov	Rotherfield	Sussex	Assemblage
15 Nov	West Chiltington	Sussex	Assemblage
15 Nov	Worthing (and area)	Sussex	Assemblage
15 Nov	Arundel/Bognor	Sussex	Assemblage
15 Nov	Deal (neighbourhood)	Kent	Wage tumult
15 Nov	Canterbury	Kent	Riot
15 Nov	Warminghurst	Sussex	Assemblage
15 Nov	Broadwater	Sussex	Assemblage
15 Nov	Alland Grange (Thanet)	Kent	Arson
15 Nov	Goudhurst	Kent	Assemblage
15 Nov	Biddenden	Kent	Assemblages
15 Nov	Woodchurch	Kent	Assemblages
15 Nov	High Halden	Kent	Assemblages
15 Nov	Gardner Street (Herstmonceaux)	Sussex	Rising/assemblage
15 Nov	Shoreham	Sussex	Assemblage
15 Nov	Walberton	Sussex	Arson
15 Nov	Ashington	Sussex	Arson
15 Nov	Sturry + Fordwich	Kent	Incitement
15 Nov	Lewes (+ area)	Sussex	Assemblage
15 Nov	Bersted	Sussex	Assemblage
15 Nov	Felpham, Bognor, Bersted & Yapton	Sussex	Threshing machines (several)
15 Nov	Ockley	Surrey	Arson
15 Nov	Buxted	Sussex	Assemblage
15–17 Nov	Billingshurst	Sussex	Assemblage
15–18 Nov	Petworth (area)	Sussex	Threshing machines
15–18 Nov	Romney Marsh	Kent	Threatening letters (several)
15–19 Nov	Castle (Arundel)	Sussex	Crowds lurking around
15–19 Nov	Donnington (& area)	Sussex	Threshing machines (destroyed by farmers)
15–19 Nov	Herne	Kent	Threatening letter
15–19 Nov	Barcombe	Sussex	Assemblage
15–19 Nov	Cooksbridge (Hamsey)	Sussex	Assemblage
15–19 Nov	Petworth	Sussex	Threatening letter
15–20 Nov	Rye	Sussex	Threatening letters
15–21 Nov	Hickstead	Sussex	Animal maiming
15–21 Nov	Tunbridge Wells	Kent	Threatening letters (several)

15–22 Nov	Canterbury (all nearby villages)	Kent	Threatening letters
16 Nov	Wallington (Fareham)	Hants	Arson
16 Nov	Chichester	Sussex	Assemblage
16 Nov	Hailsham	Sussex	Assemblage
16 Nov	Stodmarsh	Kent	Arson
16 Nov	Hamstreet	Kent	Assemblage
16 Nov	Kingsfold (Warnham)	Sussex	Arson
16 Nov	Egham (direction)	Surrey	Arson
16 Nov	Hythe	Kent	Expected riot
16 Nov	Cranbrook	Kent	Tumult
16 Nov	Bilsington	Kent	Assemblage
16 Nov	East Molesey	Surrey	Arson
16 Nov	Thakeham	Sussex	Threshing machine (destroyed by farmer)
16 Nov	Felpham	Sussex	Strike
16 Nov	Nutbourne (Pulborough)	Sussex	Assemblage
16 Nov	Fulking	Sussex	Threatening letter
16 Nov	Chart (Great Chart?)	Kent	Assemblage
16 Nov	Ruckinge	Kent	Assemblage
16 Nov	West Hoathly	Sussex	Arson
16 Nov	Augmering	Sussex	Arson
16 Nov	Cuckfield	Sussex	Riot
16 Nov	Withyham	Sussex	Assemblage
16 Nov	Frant	Sussex	Assemblage
16 Nov	Rusper	Sussex	Arson
16 Nov	Rotherfield	Sussex	Assemblage
16 Nov	Chichester (neighbourhood)	Sussex	Levying money
16 Nov	Hawkhurst	Kent	Assemblage
16 Nov	Wisborough Green	Sussex	Assemblage
16 Nov	Pulborough	Sussex	Assemblage
16–19 Nov	Augmering	Sussex	Arson
17 Nov	Hamble	Hants	Arson
17 Nov	Droxford	Hants	Arson
17 Nov	Portsdown Hill	Hants	Arson
17 Nov	Whitchuch	Hants	Assemblage
17 Nov	Laverstoke	Hants	Assemblage
17 Nov	Freefolk	Hants	Assemblage
17 Nov	Ham Street	Kent	Assemblage
17 Nov	Chichester	Sussex	Assemblage
17 Nov	Horsham	Sussex	Assemblage
17 Nov	Harting	Sussex	Assemblage
17 Nov	Preston	Kent	Arson
17 Nov	Laughton	Sussex	Assemblage
17 Nov	Goodwood	Sussex	Assemblage
17 Nov	Horsham (nr.)	Sussex	Threatening letter
17 Nov	Pagham	Sussex	Assemblage
17 Nov	Chart + Ruckinge	Kent	Assemblage

Date	Parish	County	Incident
17–18 Nov (night)	nr. Bosham	Sussex	Threshing machines (3)
	Bosham		Threshing machines (2)
	(Salt Hill) Fishbourne		Threshing machine (at least 1)
17 Nov	Westbourne	Sussex	Threshing machine
17 Nov	Prinsted (Westbourne)	Sussex	Attempted threshing machine-breaking
17 Nov	Aldingbourne	Sussex	Assemblage
17 Nov	Ringmer	Sussex	Assemblage
17 Nov	Ham Street/Ashford area	Kent	Destruction of property
17 Nov	Rogate	Sussex	Assemblage
17 Nov	Arundel	Sussex	Assemblage
17 Nov	Eartham	Sussex	Assemblage
17 Nov	East Hampnett (Halnaker)	Sussex	Assemblage
17 Nov	Eastergate	Sussex	Money with menaces
17–18 Nov	Hamble area	Hants	Threatening letters
17–23 Nov	Nutbourne	Sussex	Threatening letter
18 Nov	Barton Stacey	Hants	Assemblage
18 Nov	Bullington	Hants	Assemblage
18 Nov	Sutton Scotney (Wonston)	Hants	Assemblage
18 Nov	Wonston	Hants	Assemblage
18 Nov	Mitcheldever	Hants	Assemblage & extortion & assault
18 Nov	Overton (& neighbourhood)	Hants	Assemblage
18 Nov	Steventon	Hants	Assemblage
18 Nov	Deane	Hants	Assemblage
18 Nov	North Waltham	Hants	Assemblage
18 Nov (am)	Emsworth	Hants	Threshing machines (2)
	Warblington		Threshing machines (3?)
	Havant		Threshing machine (1)
	Leigh		Threshing machine (1)
18 Nov (pm)	east of Havant	Hants/ Sussex	Threshing machines (upwards of 9)
18 Nov	Compton	Sussex	Assemblage
18 Nov	Crowhurst	Sussex	Assemblage
18 Nov	Horsebridge (Hellingly)	Sussex	Assemblage
18 Nov	Selsey	Sussex	Assemblage
18 Nov	West Marden	Sussex	Assemblage
18 Nov	Dallington	Sussex	Petition (against taxes, tithes)
18 Nov	Hollington	Sussex	Assemblage
18 Nov	Houghton	Sussex	Threshing machine (destroyed by farmer)
18 Nov	East Dean	Sussex	Arson
18 Nov	West Dean	Sussex	Arson

18 Nov	Barracks (Brighton)	Sussex	Attempt to break open powder magazine
18 Nov	Worthing	Sussex	Sale of inflammatory placards
18 Nov	Folkestone	Kent	Robbery / attack
18 Nov	Hellingly	Sussex	Assemblage
18 Nov	parishes west of Chichester	Sussex	Assemblages
18 Nov	Herne	Kent	Assemblage
18 Nov	Boxgrove (Halnaker)	Sussex	Assemblage
18 Nov	Beeding	Sussex	Assemblage
18 Nov	Horsham	Sussex	Assemblage
18 Nov	Southover	Sussex	Arson
18 Nov	Birstall Hall (Minster in Sheppey)	Kent	Threatening Letter
18 Nov	Boxgrove	Sussex	Assemblage
18 Nov	Manhood (between Chichester and the sea)	Sussex	Assemblage
18 Nov	Arundel	Sussex	Assemblage
18 Nov	Leysdown (Eastchurch)	Kent	Arson
18 Nov	Bosham + area	Sussex	Assemblage
18 Nov	Westbourne	Sussex	Assemblage
18 Nov	Fishbourne	Sussex	Threshing machine
18 Nov	Ewhurst	Sussex	Assemblage
Before 19 Nov	Newport, IOW	Hants	Assemblage/strike
18/19 Nov	Framfield (direction)	Sussex	Arson
19 Nov	Basingstoke	Hants	Assemblage & extortion
19 Nov	nr Basingstoke	Hants	Assemblage
19 Nov	Warnford	Hants	Assemblage
19 Nov	West Meon	Hants	Assemblage
19 Nov	Overton	Hants	Assemblage
19 Nov	Nether Wallop ('Wallop')	Hants	Assemblage
19 Nov	Mitcheldever	Hants	Assemblage & threshing machines (4 – at least) & assaults & extortions
19 Nov	Northington	Hants	Assemblage & threshing machines (2)
19 Nov	nr Winchester	Hants	Assemblage & threshing machine
19 Nov	Sutton Scotney	Hants	Assemblages & threshing machine
19 Nov	Cliddesden	Hants	Assemblage
19 Nov	East Stratton	Hants	Assemblage & threshing & grass sowing & chaff cutting machines & assault & extortion
19 Nov	Wonston	Hants	Assemblage

Date	Parish	County	Incident
19 Nov	Hunston	Hants	Assemblage
19 Nov	Barton Stacey	Hants	Assemblage
19 Nov	St. Mary Bourne (inferred)	Hants	Assemblage
19 Nov	Chilbolton	Hants	Assemblage
19 Nov	Longparish	Hants	Assemblage
19 Nov	Stoke Charity	Hants	Assemblage
19 Nov	Bullington	Hants	Assemblage
19 Nov	New & Old Alresford	Hants	Assemblage
19 Nov	Andover	Hants	Assemblage & threshing machines (2 – perhaps 3)/release of prisoners
19 Nov	Barton Stacey	Hants	Arson
19 Nov	Wadwick (St Mary Bourne)	Hants	Arson
19 Nov	Whitchurch	Hants	Arson
19 Nov	Southsea	Hants	Arson
19 Nov	Abinger	Surrey	Assemblage
19 Nov	Lenham	Kent	Assemblage
19 Nov	Ockley	Surrey	Assemblage
19 Nov	Wootton	Surrey	Assemblage
19 Nov	Itchingfield	Sussex	Assemblage
19 Nov	Arundel (+ vicinity)	Sussex	Assemblage
19 Nov	Rusper	Sussex	Assemblage
19 Nov	Ore	Sussex	Assemblage
19 Nov	Lewes (vicinity)	Sussex	Circulation of seditious handbills
19 Nov	Woking	Surrey	Assemblage
19 Nov	Horsham	Sussex	Assemblage
19 Nov	Reigate	Surrey	Arson
19 Nov	Wyke (Farnham/Ash)	Surrey	Arson
19 Nov	Prinsted (Westbourne)	Sussex	Threshing machine
19 Nov	Funtington	Sussex	Threshing machines (2)
19 Nov	Woodmancot, Funtingdon, Prinsted & Nutbourne	Sussex	Threshing machines (unknown number)
19 Nov	Rotherfield	Sussex	Assemblage
19 Nov	Hambrook (Westbourne)	Sussex	Arson
before 20 Nov	East end of IOW	Hants	Swing letter
before	nr Winchester	Hants	Threatening letters
before 20 Nov	Eastrop	Hants	Incendiary letter
20 Nov	Selborne	Hants	Declared intention of wages assemblage/shots fired into workhouse
20 Nov	Micheldever	Hants	Assemblage
20 Nov	Barton Stacey	Hants	Assemblage & assault

20 Nov	Bullington	Hants	Assemblage
20 Nov	Newton Stacey (Barton Stacey)	Hants	Assemblage
20 Nov	Longparish	Hants	Assemblage
20 Nov	Andover	Hants	Assemblage
20 Nov	Upper Clatford	Hants	Assemblage & destruction of foundry
20 Nov	South Park Farm, Andover	Hants	Arson
20 Nov	Lower Wallop (Nether Wallop)	Hants	Assemblage
20 Nov	Stockbridge	Hants	Assemblage
20 Nov	Houghton, Compton, Broughton, Mottisfont Michelmersh, Lockerley, Tytherley, Ashley / Kings Somborne, Rookley (Little Somborne), Crawley, Upper Somborne (Kings Somborne), Littleton	Hants	Assemblage
20 Nov	Martyr Worthy	Hants	Assemblage, assault & threshing machine
20 Nov	Headbourne Worthy	Hants	Assemblage
20 Nov	Avington	Hants	Assemblage
20 Nov	Easton	Hants	Assemblage
20 Nov	New Inn (2 miles from Martyr Worthy)	Hants	Assemblage
20 Nov	Southampton	Hants	Threatening letters
20 Nov	Herne	Kent	Shots fired at watch
20 Nov	Steyning	Sussex	Assemblage
20 Nov	Petworth	Sussex	Arson
20 Nov	Riverhead (Sevenoaks)	Kent	Arson
20 Nov	Hamsey	Sussex	Meeting of farmers
20 Nov	Dargate (Hern Hill)	Kent	Arson
20 Nov	Norwood	Surrey	Arson
20 Nov	Beeding	Sussex	Assemblage
20 Nov	Margate	Kent	Threshing machine
21 Nov	Vernham Dean	Hants	Assemblage, assault & winnowing machine
21 Nov	Kimpton	Hants	Assemblage & threshing machine
21 Nov	Shoddesden (Kimpton)	Hants	Arson
21 Nov	Fyfield	Hants	Assemblage
21 Nov	Weyhill	Hants	Assemblage
21 Nov	Southampton	Hants	Incendiary letter
21 Nov	Bossington House (Houghton)	Hants	Assemblage & burglary
21 Nov	Compton	Hants	Assemblage
21 Nov	Titherly	Hants	Assemblage
21 Nov	Awbridge	Hants	Assemblage

Date	Parish	County	Incident
21 Nov	Littleton	Hants	Assemblage
21 Nov	Sparsholt	Hants	Assemblage
21 Nov	Stockbridge	Hants	Assemblage
21 Nov	Kings Somborne	Hants	Assemblage & threshing machine
21 Nov	Little Somborne	Hants	Assemblage & threshing machine
21 Nov	Crawley	Hants	Assemblage
21 Nov	Church Levine (?)	Hants	Assemblage & threshing machines (several)
21 Nov	Gosport (Alverstoke)	Hants	Threatening letter
21 Nov	Barton Stacey	Hants	Arson
21 Nov	Blean	Kent	Arson
21 Nov	Castle (Arundel)	Sussex	Arson
21 Nov	Boughton Aluph	Kent	Arson
21 Nov	Sullington	Sussex	Arson stopped
21 Nov	Crowhurst	Sussex	Arson
21 Nov	Seal	Kent	Arson
21 Nov	Findon	Sussex	Arson
21–22 Nov (night)	nr Andover	Hants	Arson (x4 – 1 probably Weyhill fire)
21–22 Nov	Broughton	Hants	Threshing machines
Before 22 Nov	Southwick	Hants	Incendiary letter
22 Nov	East Woodhay	Hants	Assemblage
22 Nov	Vernham's Dean	Hants	Assemblage
22 Nov	Bullington	Hants	Assemblage
22 Nov	Ashmansworth	Hants	Assemblage
22 Nov	Hurstborne Tarrant	Hants	Assemblage
22 Nov	Saint Lawrence Wootton (inc. Many Down & Tangier Park)	Hants	Assemblage & winnowing machine
22 Nov	Church Oakley	Hants	Assemblage
22 Nov	Andover	Hants	Assemblage
22 Nov	Selborne	Hants	Assemblage
22 Nov	Liphook (Bramshott)	Hants	Assemblage
22 Nov	Farringdon	Hants	Assemblage
22 Nov	Steep	Hants	Assemblage
22 Nov	Petersfield	Hants	Assemblage
22 Nov	Buriton	Hants	Assemblage
22 Nov	Thruxton	Hants	Assemblage & threshing machine
22 Nov	Weyhill	Hants	Assemblage
22 Nov	Penton Grafton	Hants	Assemblage & threshing machine & chaff-cutting machine

22 Nov	Basingstoke	Hants	Assemblage
22 Nov	St Mary Bourne	Hants	Assemblage & threshing machine
22 Nov	Worting	Hants	Assemblage
22 Nov	Crux Easton	Hants	Assemblage
22 Nov	Bucket Down (Woodcott)	Hants	Assemblage
22 Nov	Weyhill	Hants	Arson
22 Nov	Crawley	Hants	Assemblage
22 Nov	Carisbrooke, IOW	Hants	Assemblage – malicious damage
22 Nov	Newton (Youngswood), IOW	Hants	Assemblage
22 Nov	Romsey Extra (Luzborough; Woodley; Jermyns)	Hants	Assemblage & machine-breaking
22 Nov	North Baddesley	Hants	Assemblage & threshing machine
22 Nov	Michelmersh	Hants	Assemblage & threshing machines (2)
22 Nov	Timsbury	Hants	Assemblage
22 Nov	Mottisfont	Hants	Assemblage
22 Nov	Martyr Worthy	Hants	Assemblage
22 Nov	Itchen Abbas	Hants	Assemblage & threshing machine
22 Nov	Avington	Hants	Assemblage
22 Nov	Alresford	Hants	Threshing machine
22 Nov	Bighton	Hants	Assemblage
22 Nov	East Tytherley	Hants	Assemblage & destruction of turnpike gate
22 Nov	Broughton	Hants	Assemblage & threshing machines (2)
22 Nov	Bossington	Hants	Threshing machine
22 Nov	Lockerly	Hants	Assemblage
22 Nov	Kimbridge (Michelmersh)	Hants	Assemblage
22 Nov	Kings Somborne Little Somborne Ashley Houghton	Hants	Assemblages
22 Nov	Corhampton	Hants	Assemblage
22 Nov	Dursley	Hants	Assemblage & threshing machines (2)
22 Nov	Bishops Waltham	Hants	Assemblage
22 Nov	Upham	Hants	Assemblage & threshing machine
22 Nov	Preshaw (Exton)	Hants	Hay-making machine
22 Nov	Exton	Hants	Assemblage
22 Nov	Swanmore	Hants	Assemblage

Date	Parish	County	Incident
22 Nov	Soberton	Hants	Assemblage
22 Nov	Parhurst Forest (Newport), IOW	Hants	Assemblage
22 Nov	Longstock	Hants	Assemblage
22 Nov	Leckford	Hants	Assemblage
22 Nov	Tichfont (? – nr Longstock)	Hants	Assemblage
22 Nov	Stockbridge	Hants	Assemblage
22 Nov	Hursley	Hants	Assemblage
22 Nov	Steyning	Sussex	Assemblage
22 Nov	Cowfold	Sussex	Assemblage
22 Nov	Dorking	Surrey	Assemblage
22 Nov	Hicksted (Twineham)	Sussex	Assemblage
22 Nov	Woodnesborough	Kent	Arson
22 Nov	Falworth (Sullington?)	Sussex	Arson
22 Nov	Horley	Surrey	Assemblage
22 Nov	Battle	Sussex	Seditious lecture
22 Nov	Charlwood	Surrey	Assemblage
22 Nov	Chilham	Kent	Refusal of farmers to pay tithes at audit
22 Nov	Poynings	Sussex	Assemblage
22 Nov	Alland Grange (Minster in Thanet)	Kent	Threshing machines (2)
22 Nov	Newdigate	Surrey	Assemblage
22 Nov	Blean	Kent	Arson
22 Nov	Nuthurst	Surrey	Assemblage
22 Nov	Leigh	Surrey	Assemblage
22 Nov	Worthing	Sussex	Assemblage
22 Nov	Lancing	Sussex	Assemblage
22–25 Nov	Berwick	Sussex	Threatening letters (2)
22–27 Nov	Romsey area	Hants	Incendiary letters
22–27 Nov	Botley	Hants	Threatening letter
22–26 Nov	Rowner (Gosport area)	Hants	Swing letters
22–26 Nov	Isle of Wight	Hants	Incendiary letters
22–27 Nov	Portsmouth	Hants	Swing letters
22–27 Nov	Eling	Hants	Threatening letter
22–27 Nov	Millbroook	Hants	Threatening letter
22–27 Nov	Chatham	Kent	Threatening letters (several)
22–28 Nov	Putney (area)	Surrey	Threat
23 Nov	Steep	Hants	Assemblage
23 Nov	Greatham	Hants	Assemblage
23 Nov	Liss	Hants	Assemblage
23 Nov	Selborne	Hants	Assemblage
23 Nov	Headley	Hants	Destruction of poor house & theft of bread, cheese + beer

22 Nov	Kingsley	Hants	Assemblage & threshing machine
23 Nov	Tadley	Hants	Assemblage
23 Nov	Baughurst	Hants	Assemblage
23 Nov	Woolverton	Hants	Assemblage
23 Nov	Highclere	Hants	Assemblage/threshing machines/hay making machines (2)
23 Nov	Burghclere	Hants	Assemblage & threshing machines (3)
23 Nov	Sydmonton	Hants	Assemblage & extortion & threshing machine
23 Nov	Newtown	Hants	Assemblage
23 Nov	Ashmansworth	Hants	Assemblage
23 Nov	East Woodhay	Hants	Assemblage & threshing machine
23 Nov	Quarley	Hants	Assemblage & threshing machines (2) & chaff cutting machine
23 Nov	Romsey Extra	Hants	Assemblage & winnowing machine
23 Nov	nr Romsey	Hants	Assemblage & threshing machines (2)
23 Nov	Sherfield English	Hants	Assemblage
23 Nov	Breamore	Hants	Assemblage
23 Nov	Stuckton & East Mill (Fordingbridge)	Hants	Machine-breaking & 'certain' threshing machines/flax machinery
23 Nov	Rockbourne (& Aldersholt)	Hants	Assemblage
23 Nov	Damerham	Wilts/Hants	Assemblage
23 Nov	Whitsbury	Hants	Assemblage
23 Nov	West Park, Rockbourne	Hants	Assemblage
23 Nov	Lymington (from Boldre)	Hants	Assemblage
23 Nov	Southampton	Hants	Arson
23 Nov	Durley	Hants	Assemblage
23 Nov	Horton Heath (Bishopstoke)	Hants	Assemblage & threshing machine (Owton)
23 Nov	Fair Oak (Bishopstoke)	Hants	
23 Nov	Moor Green (South Stoneham)	Hants	Assemblage & assault & threshing machines (Hallett and Gosling)
23 Nov	West End (South Stoneham)	Hants	
23 Nov	Swaythling (North Stoneham)/ Portswood (South Stoneham)	Hants	Assemblage & threshing machine (Gubbin)
23 Nov	Stoneham Park (South Stoneham)	Hants	Assemblage

Date	Parish	County	Incident
23 Nov	Owslebury	Hants	Assemblage & assault & winnowing machine & threshing machine
23 Nov	Shedfield (Droxford)	Hants	Assemblage & threshing machines ('some' – only one detailed)
23 Nov	Wickham	Hants	Assemblage & machine-breaking
23 Nov	Botley	Hants	Assemblage
23 Nov	Bishops Waltham	Hants	Assemblage
23 Nov	Droxford	Hants	Assemblage
23 Nov	Soberton	Hants	Assemblage
23 Nov	Eyton (Exton?)	Hants	Threshing machine
23 Nov	Stoney Heath (Baughurst)	Hants	Assemblage
23 Nov	Monk Sherborne	Hants	Assemblage
23 Nov	Sherborne St. John	Hants	Assemblage
23 Nov	Pamber	Hants	Assemblage/extortion/threshing machine & winnowing machine
23 Nov	West Heath (Wootton St Lawerence)	Hants	Assemblage
23 Nov	Ewhurst (Baughurst)	Hants	Assemblage
23 Nov	East Dean	Hants	Assemblage & arson
23 Nov	Tytherley	Hants	Assemblage & arson
23 Nov	Lymington	Hants	Swing letters
23 Nov	7 miles from Winchester	Hants	Arson
23 Nov	Clayton	Sussex	Assemblage (planned)
23 Nov	Broadwater	Sussex	Threatening letter
23 Nov	Twineham	Sussex	Arson
23 Nov	Rusthall (Speldhurst)	Kent	Arson
23 Nov	Bexhill	Sussex	Arson
24 Nov	Grange (Northington)	Hants	Assemblage (planned & expected)
24 Nov	Preston Candover	Hants	Assemblage
24 Nov	Wield	Hants	Assemblage
24 Nov	Bentworth	Hants	Assemblage
24 Nov	East Woodhay	Hants	Assemblage
24 Nov (midnight)	Whitway (Burghclere)	Hants	Assemblage
24 Nov	Litchfield	Hants	Assemblage & threshing machines
24 Nov	St. Mary Bourne	Hants	Assemblage & threshing machines
24 Nov	Woodcott	Hants	Assemblage & threshing machines
24 Nov	Crux Easton	Hants	Assemblage & threshing machines

24 Nov	Alton	Hants	Assemblage
24 Nov	Binstead (Week)	Hants	Threshing machine
24 Nov	Headley	Hants	Assemblage
24 Nov	Highclere	Hants	Assemblage
24 Nov	Hurstborne Tarrant	Hants	Assemblage
24 Nov	Vernham's Dean	Hants	Assemblage
24 Nov	nr Ringwood	Hants	Assemblage(s)
24 Nov	East Wellow	Hants	Assemblage & machine-breaking
24 Nov	*Wallop (not clear if they arrived)*	*Hants*	*Assemblage*
24 Nov	Soberton	Hants	Assemblage
24 Nov	Droxford	Hants	Assemblage & threshing machine
24 Nov	Swanmore	Hants	Assemblage
24 Nov	Redbridge (Millbrook)	Hants	Assemblage
24 Nov	Shirley (Millbrook/Southampton)	Hants	Assemblage
24 Nov	Dockenfield (Frensham)	Hants	Assemblage
24 Nov	Newick	Sussex	Assemblage
24 Nov	Henfield	Sussex	Assemblage
24 Nov	Hastings	Sussex	Assault on nightly watch
24 Nov	Framfield	Sussex	Assemblage
24 Nov	Margate (area)	Kent	Threshing machines (6)
24 Nov	Woodmancote	Sussex (East)	Assemblage
24 Nov	Wrotham	Kent	Assemblage
24 Nov	Treyford	Sussex	Assemblage
24 Nov	Shermanbury	Sussex	Assemblage
25 Nov	Durley	Hants	Threatening letters (2)
25 Nov	Fawley	Hants	Assemblage
25 Nov	Liss	Hants	Assemblage & destruction of a large house
25 Nov	Berwick	Sussex	Arson
25 Nov	Petworth	Sussex	Assemblage
25 Nov	Kirdford	Sussex	Assemblage
25 Nov	Hastingleigh	Kent	Arson
25 Nov	Oxted	Surrey	Assemblage
25 Nov	Limpsfield	Surrey	Assemblage
25 Nov	Slinfold	Sussex	Assemblage
25 Nov	Egham	Surrey	Arson
25–27 Nov	Hythe, Dibden	Hants	Assemblage
c.25 Nov	Lymington ('almost every village about here')	Hants	Assemblages
c.25 Nov	nr Ringwood	Hants	Assemblage
c.25 Nov	Romsey	Hants	Extortion from houses; coaches stopped

Date	Parish	County	Incident
25–28 Nov Before	Sevenoaks	Kent	Assemblage
26 Nov	Yapton	Sussex	Threatening letter
26 Nov	Eldon (King's Somborne)	Hants	Assemblage
26 Nov	Fawley	Hants	Assemblage
26 Nov	Exbury & Lepe	Hants	Assemblage & assault
26 Nov	Battle	Sussex	Arson
26 Nov	Barcombe	Sussex	Assemblage
26 Nov	Brighton	Sussex	Att. to break into office of guardians of the poor
26 Nov	Hellingly	Sussex	Arson
26 Nov	Margate (area)	Kent	Planned attack
26–28 Nov	Southampton	Hants	Malicious damage
26–30 Nov	Battle	Sussex	Letter instigating arson
27 Nov	Fareham	Hants	Assemblage (thwarted)
27 Nov	Andover	Hants	Meeting of farmers to 'agitate' over rents & tithes
27 Nov?	*Holybourne*	*Hants*	*Assemblage*
27 Nov	Newport, IOW	Hants	Arson
27 Nov	Margate	Kent	Assemblage
27 Nov	Danehill (Fletching)	Sussex	Arson
27–28 Nov	Carisbrook, IOW	Hants	Threat to burn houses & threshing machines
28 Nov	Bishop's Waltham	Hants	Threat to set fire to house & injure William Gunner
28 Nov	Selborne	Hants	Arson
28 Nov	Rookley, IOW	Hants	Arson
28 Nov	Ryde, IOW	Hants	Arson
28 Nov	Freshwater, IOW	Hants	Arson
28 Nov	Epsom (nr. Nork)	Surrey	Arson
28 Nov	Merton (or Wandsworth)	Surrey	Arson
28 Nov	South Heighton	Sussex	Arson
28 Nov	Denton	Sussex	Arson
28 Nov	Banstead	Surrey	Arson
28 Nov	Kingston	Sussex (West)	Arson
28 Nov	Banstead	Surrey	Arson
29 Nov	Freshwater, IOW	Hants	Threatening letter
29 Nov	Petersfield	Hants	Arson
29 Nov	West Hoathly	Sussex	Assemblage
29 Nov	Alfriston	Sussex	Assault
29 Nov	Bredhurst – Rainham	Kent	Assemblage
29 Nov	Seaford (neighbourhood)	Sussex	Threatening letters (4)

29 Nov	Cobham	Kent	Assemblage
29 Nov	Meopham	Kent	Assemblage
30 Nov	Newchurch, IOW	Hants	Incitement to destroy threshing machines & destroy property
30 Nov	Hurstpierpoint (unclear)	Sussex	Animal maiming
30 Nov	Wisborough Green	Sussex	Assemblage + assault
30 Nov	Kirdford	Sussex	Assemblage
Late Nov	Banstead (neighbourhood)	Surrey	Threatening letters (several)
Late Nov	Thanet	Kent	Threatening letters (several)
Early Dec	Exton	Hants	Arson
Early Dec	Burnt Stub (Godstone)	Surrey	Threatening letter
Early Dec	Chessington	Surrey	Threatening letter
Early Dec	Godstone	Surrey	Threatening letter
c.4 Dec	*Fullerton (Wherwell)*	*Hants*	*Incendiary letter*
1 Dec	Battle	Sussex	Arson
1–4 Dec	Deptford	Kent	Threatening letters (several)
1–4 Dec	Greenwich	Kent	Threatening letters (several)
1–6 Dec	Lewes (area)	Sussex	Threatening letters (several)
2 Dec	Broadwater	Sussex	Threatening letter
2 Dec	Battle	Sussex	Arson
2 Dec	Worthing	Sussex	Threatening letter
2–3 Dec	Hailsham	Sussex	Threatening poster
3 Dec	Aylesford	Kent	Threatening letters (many)
3 Dec	Battle	Sussex	Arson
3–4 Dec	Dartford	Kent	Assemblage
4 Dec	West Chiltington- Petworth	Sussex	Assemblage
4 Dec	Aylesford	Kent	Arson
5 Dec	Augmering	Sussex	Attack
5 Dec	West Chiltington	Sussex	Confrontation with parish surveyor
6 Dec	Oxshott	Surrey	Arson
6 Dec	Salehurst	Sussex	Threat to farmers not to pay more than 50% of tithe
6–8 Dec	Chatham (neighbourhood)	Kent	Assemblage
7 Dec	Cliffe	Kent	Arson
7 Dec	Bredhurst (unclear)	Kent	Assemblage
8 Dec	Hernhill	Kent	Arson
8–9 Dec	Brighton	Sussex	Assemblage
9 Dec	Worthing	Sussex	Threatening letter
10 Dec	North Frith (Hadlow)	Kent	Arson

Date	Parish	County	Incident
11 Dec	Ospringe	Kent	Arson
12 Dec	Carshalton	Surrey	Arson
13 Dec	Twyford	Hants	Strike
13 Dec	Ockley	Surrey	Arson
13 Dec	Bolney/Cuckfield	Sussex	Arson
14 Dec	Fullerton (Wherwell)	Hants	Arson
14 Dec	Hassocks (Clayton)	Sussex	Assemblage
14 Dec	Wingham	Kent	Arson
15 Dec	Guildford	Surrey	Arson
15 Dec	Chichester	Sussex	Meeting to petition parliament
16 Dec	Strathfieldsaye	Hants	Arson
18 Dec	Oxted	Surrey	Arson
18 Dec	Chiddingly	Sussex	Arson
19 Dec	Charlesson (Basingstoke)	Hants	Arson
19 Dec	Woldingham (Warlingham?)	Surrey	Arson
19 Dec	Cuckfield area	Sussex	Arson (2)
20 Dec	Charing	Kent	Arson
20 Dec	Chiddingly	Sussex	Arson
21 Dec	Eversley	Hants	Arson
21 Dec	Pulborough (area)	Sussex	Arson
22–28 Dec	Dorking (neighbourhood)	Surrey	Radical handbills
25 Dec	Newport, IOW	Hants	Arson
26 Dec	Amberly	Sussex	Assault
27 Dec	Funtington	Sussex	Arson
27 Dec	Cootham (Parham)	Sussex	Arson
28 Dec	Adbury (Burghclere)	Hants	Arson
Late Dec	Bromley	Kent	Radical lectures

* This report might relate to fires recorded (but not dated) in farmer Andrus of Southfleet's diary on the farms of Mr Haysell at Enysford and Mr Rayshleigh at Horton Kirby: F.S. Andrus, 'Extracts from the miscellany and farm accounts of Francis Andrus of Scadbury in the parish of Southfleet', *Archaeologia Cantiana*, 100 (1984), 376.

Index

Note: 'n.' after a page number indicates the number of a note on that page